TRUTH
TRIUMPHANT

THE CHURCH
IN THE WILDERNESS

by

BENJAMIN GEORGE WILKINSON, PH. D.

Our Authorized Bible Vindicated

Alex,
  May you be like Joseph, Daniel
& the other nearly young heroes in
these chapters as you "stand firm
in your faith" Ps 1:9; may your
impact on the world around you
be as decisive, bold & lasting
for God as theirs; may your
hold on His love & truth never
waiver. Much love & many
prayers,

TEACH Services, Inc.

New York   The Penps

2005 06 07 08 09 10 11 12 · 5 4 3 2 1

Copyright © 1994, 2005 TEACH Services, Inc.
ISBN-13: 978-1-57258-329-0
ISBN-10: 1-57258-329-0
Library of Congress Control Number: 95-61346

Published by
TEACH Services, Inc.
www.TEACHServices.com

Preface

THE author sends forth this book with the hope that it may open a new world to its readers. The prominence given to the Church in the Wilderness in the Scriptures establishes without argumentation the existence of such an organization, and emphasizes its importance.

Appealing for attention to this thrilling theme, the writer has sought to bring together in a comprehensive view the forceful, even if at times apparently disjointed, narrative of the Church in the Wilderness in different countries. The cumulative character of the historical proof will be clear to the seeker after truth. Supported by the many converging lines of evidence, the author believes that he has opened new doors into the realm of history in which the providence of God has a most prominent place.

While the author has used a great number of original sources, he has also entered into the labors of many scholars and writers who have gone before him. From both these original and secondary sources he has sought to fashion this study. It is his aim that this information will be of value in pointing out present-day deceptions and in revealing the way to meet many insidious teachings. He attempts to make clear man's present duty in terms of world history.

Confident that this book will reveal a new story and throw strong light on the history of God's people, the author presents this volume. He fervently prays that the promised latter rain of the Holy Spirit will use these pages to enlighten others so that they may share the blessing promised to those who live victoriously in the closing scenes of earth's history.

THE AUTHOR.

Contents

Introduction

A much-neglected field of study has been opened by the research of the author into the history of the Christian church from its apostolic origins to the close of the eighteenth century. Taking as his thesis the prominence given to the Church in the Wilderness in Bible prophecy, and the fact that " 'the Church in the Wilderness,' and not the proud hierarchy enthroned in the world's great capital, was the true church of Christ," he has spent years developing this subject. In its present form, *Truth Triumphant* represents much arduous research in the libraries of Europe as well as in America. Excellent ancient sources are most difficult to obtain, but the author has been successful in gaining access to many of them. To crystallize the subject matter and make the historical facts live in modern times, the author also made extensive travels through Europe and Asia.

The doctrines of the primitive Christian church spread to Ireland, Scotland, and Wales. As grains of mustard seed they lodged in the hearts of many godly souls in southern France and northern Italy— people known as the Albigenses and the Waldenses. The faith of Jesus was valiantly upheld by the Church of the East. This term, as used by the author, not only includes the Syrian and Assyrian Churches, but is also the term applied to the development of apostolic Christianity throughout the lands of the East.

The spirit of Christ, burning in the hearts of loyal men who would not compromise with paganism, sent them forth as missionaries to lands afar. Patrick, Columbanus, Marcos, and a host of others were missionaries to distant lands. They braved the ignorance of the barbarian, the intolerance of the apostate church leaders, and the persecution of the state in order that they might win souls to God.

To unfold the dangers that were ever present in the conflict of the true church against error, to reveal the sinister working of evil and the divine strength by which men of God made truth triumphant, to challenge the Remnant Church today in its final controversy against the powers of evil, and to show the holy, unchanging message of the Bible as it has been preserved for those who will "fear God, and keep His commandments"—these are the sincere aims of the author as he presents this book to those who know the truth.

MERLIN L. NEFF.

CHAPTER I

What Is the Church in the Wilderness?

*And to the woman were given two wings of a great eagle,
that she might fly into the wilderness, into her place, where
she is nourished for a time, and times, and half a time, from
the face of the serpent.*

*And the woman fled into the wilderness, where she hath a
place prepared of God, that they should feed her there a
thousand two hundred and threescore days.* [1]

THE Church in the Wilderness is the connecting link between
apostolic Christianity and God's people today. The purpose of
this volume is to show that there were Christian people in every
country during this long period of history who possessed churches,
colleges, mission stations, and theological schools; who followed
closely and adhered steadfastly to the beliefs and practices delivered
by the apostles to the saints; and who possessed and preserved the
original Scriptures given to the church in the first century. These
people constitute the Church in the Wilderness. This is a conception
which is not generally held. The title, Church in the Wilderness, is
taken from the Bible prophecy of Revelation 12 describing the woman
who fled into the wilderness. The woman is the church. [2] The title
clearly shows that it was not the popular or predominant church.
These faithful believers held high the banner of truth, and withstood
the encroachments of apostasy. Their fortunes varied, for at times
they possessed many churches, famous schools, and distant mission
stations, while in other ages they suffered from poverty and dire
persecution.

The great missionary work of this church is little known, its
sufferings have been overlooked, and its heroes unsung. In the following pages is presented the precious heritage which it has bequeathed
to modern times. By restoring the true church to its rightful place,
the key is recovered which unlocks the meaning of great issues con-
fronting this present generation.

---

[1] Revelation 12:14, 6.
[2] Clarke, *Commentary*, on Revelation 12; also Jeremiah 3:14; Hosea 2:19; Ephe-
sians 5:23-32; Revelation 17.

Some will ask, Should not we look to the church which for ages has been the favored of kings and nations to find the true church instead of looking to a people who for centuries were never the dominant church, and who many times were obscure? Let the prophet John answer this question: "The woman [church] fled into the wilderness."[3] In order to recognize the true church, it is imperative that we fix our eyes upon those Christian bodies which have largely been forgotten in the works of history.

Divine revelation teaches that the light which was to shine upon the last generation of men would be a continuation and an enlargement of the light which shone upon the Church in the Wilderness throughout almost thirteen centuries; namely, the 1260-year period. While it is generally recognized that the 1260-year period of the Church in the Wilderness did not begin in apostolic times, it is nevertheless necessary to introduce this prophetic period with a proper background. The beginning and ending of the 1260-year period is established in later chapters. No particular effort is made, however, to differentiate in nomenclature between the Church in the Wilderness and its apostolic origins.

It should be understood at the outset that in giving the surprising record of this remarkable church, the old beaten paths used by almost all the writers of church history cannot be followed. The light of Bible prophecy has pointed the way for this investigation and the method in which this theme should be treated. This subject has rarely, if ever, been presented in such a way as to reveal the amazingly interesting interrelationships which existed between and among the various groups of faithful believers in widely separated areas.

Certain modern authors have assiduously labored to belittle the American founders of religious liberty and democracy, such as Washington, Jefferson, and others. This same class of writers has invaded the realm of church history, and that which was obscure before, is growing darker. These men seek to give the glory of the Church in the Wilderness to another. Sad to relate, many sincere persons are being deceived by the astounding propaganda in books and articles founded on misleading historical bases. It is time to bring to light the many heroic struggles of the men whom God used to preserve the

---

[3] Revelation 12:6.

divine doctrines and the Holy Scriptures. The statements here made concerning the Church in the Wilderness and its history will be clarified, enlarged upon, and further explained and supported by references from dependable sources.

The Church in the Wilderness did not arrive at the truth by opposition to prevailing dogmas and heresies. Its faith was not a faith newly received. The religious beliefs of its members were an inheritance from the days of the apostles. To them men owe the preservation of the Bible. Contrary to almost universal belief, the Church in the Wilderness embraced the true missionary churches during the long night of the Dark Ages. It held aloft the torch of education while the rest of the world about it was falling into the darkness of ignorance and superstition. Its territory was not circumscribed. On the contrary, its influence penetrated into all parts of the known world.

From the Days of the Apostles

The history of nominal Christianity is the record of bitter theological controversies, and, at times, even of bloody encounters to achieve its aims; it is a record of incredible activity to secure political power. The history of the Church in the Wilderness is a stirring revelation of consecrated, evangelical labor in continent-wide leadership for the salvation of the hopeless and benighted. It did not, as its rivals did, claim intellectual logic in doctrine; it did not attempt to enforce its views by political cruelty. It severed all territorial and family ties which might have held it to the world and to the rapacious churches of empires, thus successfully preserving its scriptural doctrines and its apostolic organization.

The present can never be properly understood without correct information concerning the past. Those who have been taught falsified history or who have had their minds filled with twisted interpretations of events gone by, stagger like the blind with a darkened mind. Everyone today wants to be modern. But those who neglect the lessons of the past do not achieve modernity. They achieve only contemporaneity. Minds indoctrinated by histories and encyclopedias which glorify a union of church and state will pass a discontented present in a democracy which completely separates the state and the church, for they will long for, and labor to make, a different

order of things. The ideas that one has concerning vanished generations has a great deal to do with one's relation to the present.

It is equally true that a person who has distorted views of the
present cannot build for a better future. Those who look upon the
medieval years of European history with its serfdom and theocracy
as the ideal will be in revolt against modern society and will seek
ways to re-establish those systems. Those who do not believe in
Jesus Christ, the divine Creator, who unselfishly died upon a cross,
will find no joy in self-sacrifice and loving service, but will reach out
to seize all they can for themselves. Those who are convinced that
there was a rebellion in heaven and that humanity today is surrounded by principalities and powers of darkness will be more willing to seek the help of the Holy Spirit than if they reject the teaching
of the Scripture concerning Satan and evil angels. In other words,
man visualizes a future which should logically follow his estimate
of present potentialities, be his estimate right or wrong.

All have not been made aware of the decisive struggles which
occurred behind the scenes over the Church in the Wilderness. Many
have failed to note the true centers of Christian activity in the past.
They realize altogether too little the meaning of the momentous events
taking place today because they are ignorant of this historical background. The correct perspective of past history is as necessary to
effective leadership as the appreciation of present values. Many have
but slight knowledge of the messages of God for this generation,
because they have been taught to gaze not upon the underlying, but
upon the superficial, origins of the past. The past which gave us
democracy and religious liberty is the history which should be known
and studied. We need the Sacred Book to point the way to the true
history.

The Church in the Wilderness, surrounded by savage tribes and
battling against barbaric darkness, has been painted by its enemies
without its victories. Driven often by opposition to mountain retreats,
it was saved from the corrupting influences of ecclesiastical and
political power. In many parts of the world, all the way from Ireland in the west to China in the east, there were centers of truth. The
leaders in these centers were united in their desire to remain in the
faith, and to perpetuate from generation to generation the pure truths
of the gospel handed down from the days of the apostles. Their

records have been systematically destroyed.[4] Remoteness and obscurity, however, could not entirely conceal these heroes, because the fires of their persecution have continued to light up the scenes of their sacrificing labors.

The ungarbled history of the true church will lead to the realization that God's church of today is the successor of the Church in the Wilderness. The true church today unites the present to eternity, even as the Church in the Wilderness united the apostolic past to the present. As one follows the history of the Church in the Wilderness, the marks of identification will be given by which the final remnant church may be recognized. Such a presentation will, moreover, unmask the false, preposterous, and misleading history widely used today to discredit true history.

---

[4] Gilly, *Waldensian Researches,* page 78.

CHAPTER II

The Church in the Wilderness in Prophecy

We have also a more sure word of prophecy; whereunto ye do well that ye take heed, as unto a light that shineth in a dark place.[1]

Now all these things happened unto them for ensamples: and they are written for our admonition, upon whom the ends of the world are come.[2]

THE Biblical picture of the Church in the Wilderness and the emphasis of inspiration on its importance, especially as found in the writings of Daniel the prophet and of John the apostle, are now considered. These two prophetic studies shine with unusual brilliance amid the sixty-six books which make up the Holy Scriptures. Isaiah, Jeremiah, Ezekiel, and the other prophets spoke particularly of the things already established in Israel; Daniel and the revelator on the other hand presented the prophetic blueprints of world history. Daniel spoke from his high pedestal as prime minister of Babylon, the first of the world's four universal monarchies. John, the last living star in the crown of the twelve apostles, was banished by the emperor of Rome, a ruler of the last of the four universal monarchies.

The Saviour in His teachings referred to many passages in the books of the Old Testament; but none did He single out and command to be studied with more directness than the book of the prophet Daniel.[3] To the beloved apostle, in exile on the Isle of Patmos, Christ presented glories for which the Roman emperor would have exchanged all he had. These two books are not the concealing, but the revealing, of the will of God. In both these writings God unfolded the supremely thrilling story of the beginnings, the growth, the struggles, and the final triumph of His church. He also exposed the daring impiety, the alliances with the kings of the earth, the long cruelty, and the final overthrow of the "mystery of iniquity," the religious rival of His church.

---

[1] 2 Peter 1:19.   [2] 1 Corinthians 10:11.   [3] Matthew 24:15.

(14)

With far-reaching vision, these two prophets, Daniel and John, foresaw the conflicts of the Christian Era and the final crisis. Using the well-known Biblical figure of a woman to symbolize a church, John the revelator said, "And the woman fled into the wilderness, where she hath a place prepared of God, that they should feed her there a thousand two hundred and threescore days."[4] In the same chapter, in order to make the prediction prominent, the apostle John again said, "And to the woman were given two wings of a great eagle, that she might fly into the wilderness, into her place, where she is nourished for a time, and times, and half a time, from the face of the serpent."[5]

When one accepts the Bible rule that a day in prophecy stands for a literal year of 360 days, he can explain scriptural prophetic time periods. It is the rule laid down by God Himself.[6] Furthermore, a "time" is a prophetic year, or 360 literal years. By these two direct statements of the prophetic period we know that the church was to be in the wilderness for 1260 years.

The vision continues further to show that the remnant, or the last church, would be a successor to the wilderness church. The prophetic use of the word "remnant" is significant. Even as a remnant of cloth will identify the bolt from which it is taken, so the last church is a continuation of the Church in the Wilderness, and identifies it. In his vision John turns immediately from the scenes of the Church in the Wilderness to the outstanding work of the *remnant* church in the following words: "And the dragon was wroth with the woman, and went to make war with the *remnant* of her seed, which keep the commandments of God, and have the testimony of Jesus Christ."[7] These scriptures plainly present inspiration's insistent call upon the children of men to know and recognize God's true church in all ages.

Mankind should ponder the fact that the history of the Church in the Wilderness is linked with a definite period of 1260 years. Not only are these 1260 years specifically presented seven times in the Bible, but this period is treated many other times in Holy Writ without using the definite number of years.[8] Was the history of

---

[4] Revelation 12:6.   [6] Numbers 14:34; Ezekiel 4:6.
[5] Revelation 12:14.   [7] Revelation 12:17.
[8] See Daniel 11:32-35; Matthew 24:21-29; 2 Thessalonians 2:1-7.

this church during these long centuries a blank, as church historians usually treat it? Why have they ignored its vast achievements? Have the Holy Scriptures prophesied in vain concerning it? Is the allotment by divine revelation of 1260 years of history to this organization nothing in the judgment of historical researchers?

Any organization or connected movement among men which could hold the center of the stage for 1260 years ought to be a subject of vast importance. What other political kingdom or empire of prominence had so lengthy a history? Longer than the days of Great Britain, enduring more years than imperial Rome, even rivaling the centuries wherein the Jews were the chosen people, is the record of the Church in the Wilderness. No study of the nineteen centuries of the Christian Era can be harmonized with God's revealed purpose unless it recognizes the dominant place of the Church in the Wilderness.

How Her Rivals in Religion Counterfeited the Prophecies

Apostolic Christianity, as a religion supremely superior to paganism, caused widespread upheavals in the world. So strong were her prospects of success that Jesus and His apostles were fearful of the great deceptions that would come because of imitations and counterfeits. To make a clear-cut distinction between these counterfeits and genuine Christianity, new light from heaven was needed. Such revelations were provided in the last books of the New Testament. All the truths needed to chart the future course of gospel believers were to be found in the messages from the apostles.

There is little point in claiming that a certain church or doctrine came down from the days of the apostles. Sin came down from the days of the apostles, and the devil also was active at that time and before. It is not so much what came down from the *days* of the apostles, as what came down from the apostles themselves. Even in his day the apostle Paul wrote: "The mystery of iniquity doth already work." The growth and final form of the mystery of iniquity which was already operating before Paul's death is seen more clearly in the story of the Church in the Wilderness.

Approximately thirty-six years stand between the writing of the first three Gospels—Matthew, Mark, and Luke—and the writing of the last—John. This gave that many years for the mystery of iniquity, already at work in Paul's day, to develop more powerfully.

The outstanding difference between the character of the Gospel by John and the first three gospels has long been recognized.[9] It was the task of the beloved apostle to emphasize those events and teachings in the life of the divine Son of God which would enable His followers to meet the devastating growth of the organized "mystery of iniquity." This power was pointed out in the symbols of the book of Revelation, and it had already advanced in a threatening manner in the days of the last Gospel writer.[10] In order to understand properly this significant background it is necessary to take a short retrospect of the movements which swept over the nations in the centuries immediately preceding the birth of Christ. This will explain why powerful bodies, Christian in name, but antagonistic in spirit to Bible believers, sprang into existence soon after the appearance of the gospel.

When Christianity boldly set forth, it faced a rising tide of Bible-counterfeiting religions. To grapple with all these, God imbued the Sacred Writings with latent power. The Holy Spirit and the Bible agree. Without the Spirit, the Bible is dead; and without the Bible, the Holy Spirit is dumb. The Holy Spirit had occupied the ground of truth in advance. Yet the revelations of the Old Testament which were designed by the divine Author to warn against these forces of darkness were employed by the enemies of truth as weapons for their own use. In the visions of the prophets, warnings as well as descriptions had been given beforehand—especially by Daniel—concerning apostate religions that would arise, counterfeiting the truth, and seeking supremacy over the nations. It is an astonishing and significant fact that within one hundred years after the death of the prophet Daniel, Zoroastrianism flourished in Persia, Buddhism arose in India, Confucianism arose in China, and a little later, Socrates, famous Grecian philosopher, became a renowned thinker.

This was at the moment when the visions of Daniel were sowing the world with electrifying conceptions. There is evidence which leads one to conclude that Daniel's visions were an influence upon the state religion of Persia.[11]

---

[9] Goddard, *Was Jesus Influenced by Buddha?* page 9.

[10] Horne, *Introduction to the Critical Study and Knowledge of the Holy Scriptures,* vol. 2, pt. 6, ch. 2, p. 316.

[11] See the author's discussion in the chapters, "Papas, First Head of the Church in Asia" and "Adam and the Church in China."

Great Prophetic Time Periods

The fulfillment of such predictions as the doom of Tyre and the overthrow of the Jews has attracted universal attention. In events still more thrilling did the prophecies of the Church in the Wilderness, as given in the books of Daniel and the Revelation, meet their realization.

What value does the Bible place on prophetic time periods in general, and upon the 1260-year era in particular? For man to foretell in general terms with noteworthy accuracy some future situation, is a rare occurrence. To do this, is not prophecy, but human calculations. Bible predictions of future situations, however, are given milleniums in advance; they tell of peoples yet to arise and of events to come of which at the moment of the prophecy there was nothing in contemporaneous events to inspire the prediction. Only divine foreknowledge could do this.

Time-period prophecies are found in the books of Daniel and the Revelation. The most important of these in Daniel are the following: the 1260-year prophecy of Daniel 7; the 2300-year prophecy of Daniel 8; the 490-year period, embracing the 483-year and the 486½-year subdivision, of Daniel 9; the many smaller time periods of Daniel 11; and the 1290-year and 1335-year periods of Daniel 12. There are many similar time prophecies in the book of Revelation. The devout mind which has already discovered the eternal value of Biblical truth believes confidently that these divine scriptural predictions will meet their fulfillment.

Jesus Himself constructed His teaching in harmony with the time predictions of the Old Testament, principally those in the book of Daniel. When the Redeemer was covering in prophetic language the whole of the Christian Era, three times He referred to "those days" of Daniel 7[12] which were the 1260 years—a major part of the time intervening between His days and now. Also Peter, speaking of the Old Testament prophets, said that they searched "what manner of time the spirit of Christ which was in them did signify, when it testified beforehand the sufferings of Christ" (that is, His first coming) "and the glory that should follow" (that is, His second coming).[13] Paul warned the Thessalonian church against looking for the second

---

12 Matthew 24:22, 29.   13 1 Peter 1:11.

coming of Christ until Daniel's prophecy of the long reign of the "man of sin" had been accomplished.[14] In truth, the prophetic time periods constitute the skeleton around which the New Testament writers built.

Christ came as the fulfillment of four thousand years of prophecy. Old Testament prophecy was substantiated by its fulfillment in the New Testament. With as great certainty and with no less volume, the prime movements and events which would concern Christ's church to the end of time were also divinely predicted. Provision was made to forewarn His people, to discover for them beforehand the real meaning of movements—political, economic, and religious—in order to inspire their confidence and to send them forth determined to brave anything, even death, that this great salvation might be proclaimed to the ends of the earth.

The 1260-Year Time Period

Second to none among these chains of prophecy was the 1260-year time period concerning the Church in the Wilderness. Seven times it was given.[15] God did not announce it once and leave it. He did not utter it twice and drop the subject. Seven times He pressed it home to the attention of men. What excuse can be made by mortal man for not having carefully read the message of his heavenly Father on this subject?

The importance of this subject will be seen by giving briefly the work of the church during this 1260-year period in Great Britain, France, Italy, Syria, Assyria, Persia, India, Turkestan, China, the Philippines, and Japan. Many books could be written upon it. Yet in all the thousands of published volumes treating of history during this period, how little is said concerning this topic so prominent in God's book!

There remains, however, a still more important phase of this subject. For what purpose did Jesus permit the Church in the Wilderness to suffer during the 1260 years? Surely there is a reason. Was it not to seal with the testimony of martyr's blood the permanent values in the Christian religion? Did not these centuries of severe testing help to substantiate what books constituted the genuine

---

[14] 2 Thessalonians 2:3.
[15] Daniel 7:25; 12:7; Revelation 11:2,3; 12:6,14; 13:5.

collection of the Bible, and to disclose the counterfeit writings? In fulfilling its remarkable destiny as the guardian of the treasures of truth, the noble children of this church fought and bled and marched, and turned and fought and bled again during 1260 years.[16]

It is in a very significant setting that this matter is presented. The twelfth chapter of the Revelation reveals the complete history of the true church under three phases. Employing the well-known figure of a woman to represent His church, God sets forth three distinct phases of her experience to indicate the three periods of His church upon earth from the first to the second coming of Christ. Depicting the apostolic church, the woman wears upon her head a crown of twelve stars. In time of tribulation she fled into the wilderness. The final portrayal in Revelation 12 reveals the remnant church. As a woman is neither imaginary nor abstract it may be said that this woman represents, not an invisible church, but one duly organized, visible, and tangible. It has an organization; it is visible and tangible. By the wilderness condition, God indicated that the true church, though under a long period of strong opposition and persecution, would continue to carry the gospel to the world.

The Church in the Wilderness was to do her great work in quietness. Surrendering to her hierarchical opponents the pompous show, and demonstrating fertility in a comparatively diminished condition, she was to mold the human race. Contrariwise, her rival, clothed in scarlet and living pompously with princes and kings,[17] would, during the same 1260 years, feed her members with those weak and beggarly elements of the world from which the gospel was designed to free them.

Where can one better find that sense of perspective touching the past, so necessary to the sense of correct value of the present and to definiteness of action, except in the divine prophetic time periods of the Scriptures?

---

[16] How much we owe to these heroes, the world will never know. The Reformation was an outgrowth of the Church in the Wilderness. We owe indirectly, at least, the Constitution of the United States to this noble army. The light, liberty, education, and civilization we possess today came because of the firm foundations laid in the convictions and courage of the heroes of the wilderness church.

[17] Revelation 17:2-4.

CHAPTER III

The Apostolic Origins of the Church in the Wilderness

The rise of Christianity and the spread of the Church in Syria was startling in its rapidity.[1]

IN CONTRAST with the four hundred years of silence between Malachi and Matthew, the coming of the great Redeemer brought to the world a powerful, stimulating message and introduced a marvelous new era. None of the prophets before Him had been permitted to change the bases of the dispensation introduced by Moses. Jesus Christ, however, was that Prophet predicted by Moses who was to usher in a new dispensation. He gave to man a new revelation from Jehovah. The twelve apostles, going forth to promulgate the teachings of Jesus, formed the charter membership of the apostolic church which flourished for about five hundred years. Then gradually the combined heretical sects seized the power of the nations and drove the true church into the wilderness. These apostolic origins will be the theme of this chapter.

Previous to the destruction of Jerusalem in A. D. 70 by the Roman army, at which time the apostles were dispersed, the gospel had gone to Samaria, Ethiopia, Syria, Asia Minor, Greece, Italy, and India. The religion of Christ was enriched in all utterance. As a bright and shining light, it evangelized Zoroastrians, Buddhists, Greek philosophers, and Confucianists, laying strong foundations for the future.

As the apostolic church advanced, the gospel was planted not only in diverse nations, but in different languages. Often the same language was used by several nations. Therefore, in this volume Syrian or Syriac Christianity will refer to all churches which are indebted to Syrian origins; that is, to Syrian missionaries and authors to whom later churches looked as pioneers of the Syriac language in their services; as, for example, in Syria, Assyria, Persia, India, and China. Similarly, the term Celtic Christianity will apply to all churches and nations which used the Celtic language in their divine worship, such

---

[1] Burgon and Miller, *The Traditional Text of the Holy Gospels,* page 123.

as Galatia and France, as well as Ireland, Scotland, and England before England was overrun by the pagan Anglo-Saxons. Greek Christianity will refer to the churches throughout the world where the Greek language was used in their literature and worship. Latin Christianity refers particularly to the homeland of the Romans, Italy, and to certain other nations. No hard and fast rule of designation can be laid down for the overspread of these different designations and terms. All that can be given is a general guiding description.

Christianity Among the Jews

The gospel first went to the Jews. It is easy to forget that almost every hero of the Bible was a Jew and that every book of the Sacred Scriptures was written by a Hebrew. Jesus Christ Himself was an Israelite.

It was to those having the blood of Abraham in their veins that the Redeemer first directed His message. His apostles were sent "to the lost sheep of the house of Israel." Tens of thousands received the word gladly, and among them were many priests. Even unto the uttermost parts of the earth, where the Jews had been scattered and their descendants were counted by the millions, did the message penetrate. For a long time, as will be shown in later chapters, the bulk of early church members had been won from among the descendants of Israel.

The first people other than the Jews to accept the gospel were the Samaritans. Christ had predicted that His disciples should witness for Him in Judea, Samaria, and in the uttermost parts of the earth. Philip, the newly elected deacon, was the one who determined to tell the good news to the Samaritans.[2]

Samaria was the only place on earth where they dared to build a temple to rival the one at Jerusalem. It was claimed that it was the successor to Solomon's temple. Here only could be found another Pentateuch.[3] The small group of Samaritans still existing look upon these first five books of Moses, written in the old Hebrew letters, as their greatest treasure.[4]

---

[2] Acts 8:5.
[3] Edersheim, *The Life and Times of Jesus the Messiah,* vol. 1, p. 396.
[4] The writer, in examining this Samaritan manuscript when he visited Samaria, was surprised to find it in so good a condition, considering its great age.

Ethiopia is the second foreign country evangelized by the church at Jerusalem. The story, as told in the book of Acts, represents Philip the evangelist as being conducted southward by the Holy Spirit after his victories in Samaria. There he met the royal treasurer of the queen of Ethiopia returning to his country from Jerusalem where he had been to worship. The treasurer was reading the prophecy of Isaiah, who wrote about eight hundred years before Christ. Philip explained to this searcher for truth the fulfillment of the prophecy. This prophecy and its accurate fulfillment gave Philip a powerful message which caused the eunuch to accept Christ and be baptized. Thus began the evangelization of Ethiopia.[5]

The Beginnings of Syrian Christianity

Christianity was to enter a new field through the leadership of Paul, strong herald of the cross. In Antioch, the capital of the Roman province of Syria, was to be found a new center for the gospel. When Jerusalem, the original headquarters, was destroyed, the leadership passed to Antioch, where it remained for some time.

When the gospel moved into Syria, the whole church was astir. Cornelius, a Roman centurion at Caesarea, had experienced a remarkable conversion. Church members were fired with new zeal, and they entered Antioch "preaching the word to none but unto the Jews only." Syria at that time included Palestine, parts of Arabia, and extended to the Euphrates River. Then began what may be justly described as "the golden age of Syria."[6] In Antioch, its capital, an opulent center, were located the administration building of the Roman officials of the East. Many Jews were there, and so numerous and influential were they that their rights and privileges were recorded on tables of brass.[7]

As a result of the ministry of Barnabas and Paul at Antioch, the name of "Christian" was there first given to the followers of Jesus. The providence of God was looking to the future of the gospel. Soon Jerusalem would be destroyed, and tens of thousands of Christian Jews would be driven northward, rejected by the rabbinical Jews. It would now be greatly to their advantage as followers of Jesus to

---

[5] Geddes, *The Church History of Ethiopia,* page 9.
[6] O'Leary, *The Syriac Church and Fathers,* page 21.
[7] Edersheim, *The Life and Times of Jesus the Messiah,* vol. 1, p. 74. Also Schurer, *A History of the Jewish People in the Time of Christ,* 2d div., vol. 2, p. 271.

be called Christians. They would no longer be classed with the Jews, and the new name would help them to escape the wrath of the Gentile world against the Hebrew race. As will be shown later, these exiles were to populate with beautiful cities, and with institutions of unsurpassed scholarship, a section of country northward beyond the bounds of Canaan.[8] They would furnish an evangelical grasp of Christianity's greatest doctrines which their background of Jewish history enabled them to appreciate more profoundly than could Gentile converts.

 It was from Antioch that Paul and Barnabas, set apart by the Holy Ghost, went forth as the first foreign missionaries. The results were a revelation. Little did the apostles foresee the manner in which the Gentiles would desert the heathen temples for the churches, as they had seen the Jews come into the church from the synagogues. Leaving the island of Cyprus, where the Gentiles had heard with astonishment the doctrines of the Lord, Paul and Barnabas went into Asia Minor. Here, as in Syria, the cities were full of Jews. Paul was proud that he was a son of Israel, because he knew that fifteen hundred years of sacred teaching on each recurring Sabbath had enriched the Hebrews with a mentality in things divine which enabled them to grasp readily such truths as God, sin, morality, and the need of a Redeemer. He entered therefore into the synagogues on the Sabbath day. The synagogues had long been established in the regions which were new to Paul and his helpers, and through the Jews they were able to secure an introduction to the Gentiles. A new vision came to the churches in Syria and Judea when the two men who launched Christianity's foreign mission program returned with the reports of their successes. Even before Paul had finished his labors, or before Jerusalem was in ruins, the apostle Thomas had left for Persia and India.

Eastward into those fertile lands between and around the Tigris and Euphrates Rivers were laid the beginnings of Christianity at the second Syrian center, Edessa. Edessa, now Urfu, in Asia Minor, was at that time the capital of the small kingdom of Osrhoene. This city was about two hundred miles northeast of Antioch. From it Christianity emanated to Persia, India, Parthia, and China, and from

---

[8] See the author's discussion in Chapter IV, entitled, "The Silent Cities of Syria."

it and other near-by cities, came the continued support of the work in those distant Eastern countries. Concerning Edessa, a well-known Orientalist writes as follows: "Edessa had also a celebrated School of Medical Research which was removed to Nisibis. Many famous physicians were numbered in the Nestorian ranks who graduated there."[9] At Edessa, the purest Syriac (Aramaean) was spoken.

Tertullian, who wrote about seventy-five years after the death of the apostle John, speaks of the spread of Christianity in the following language:

> For upon whom else have the universal nations believed, but upon the Christ who has already come? For whom have the nations believed,— Parthians, Medes, Elamites, and they who inhabit Mesopotamia, Armenia, Phrygia, Cappadocia, and they who dwell in Pontus, and Asia, and Pamphylia, tarriers in Egypt, and inhabiters of the region of Africa which is beyond Cyrene, Romans and sojourners, yes, and in Jerusalem Jews, and all other nations; as, for instance, . . . varied races of the Gaetulians, and manifold confines of the Moors, all the limits of the Spains, and the diverse nations of the Gauls, and the haunts of the Britains (inaccessible to the Romans, but subjugated to Christ). . . . In all which places the name of the Christ who is already come reigns.[10]

By whom was the knowledge of Christ brought to all these places? By those Christians who had the spirit of the genuine Syrian theology. However, there were others who taught false doctrines. Gnosticism, a product of Alexandria, Egypt, Antioch's rival, was a union of pagan philosophy and gospel truths. While it was founding churches and building colleges, it rejected the Old Testament, denied creation, and held in contempt all Jews, even Christian Jews. In these words, the historian Newman aptly describes the difference between the theology of Antioch and that of Alexandria. "In the great christological controversies of the fourth and following centuries Alexandria and Antioch were always antagonists, Alexandria representing a mystical transcendentalism and promoting the allegorical interpretation of the Scriptures; Antioch insisting on the grammatico-historical interpretation of the Scriptures, and having no sympathy with mystical modes of thought."[11]

[9] Gordon, *"World Healers,"* p. 450, note 2.
[10] Tertullian, *An Answer to the Jews*, ch. 7, found in *Ante-Nicene Fathers*, vol. 3, pp. 157, 158.
[11] Newman, *A Manual of Church History*, vol. 1, p. 297.

Whence came that marvelous missionary activity of the church of the East for a thousand years? It originated in the regions of Antioch and Edessa. How great was the difference between apostolic Christianity and its perversion at Alexandria in the early history of the church is shown in the following quotation from Bigg: "The Church of the second century rang with alarm, and the consequence was that all the Christian writers of that period except Justin Martyr and Clement of Alexandria, shrank with horror from the name of philosophy."[12]

Shortly after the death of the apostles, the New Testament was translated into Syriac. This noble version, called the Peshitta, meaning "simple," had ·for centuries a wide circulation in the East.[13] It is still the authoritative Bible in large Eastern communions.

The Beginnings of Celtic Christianity

The apostle to the Gentiles, after founding Syrian Christianity, was called to plant the gospel among the Galatians, in the heart of the large Celtic branch of the human family. The Celts of Galatia were of the same family, and spoke the same language as the Irish, Scotch, British, Welsh, and French.[14]

Thus the Holy Spirit set another stream flowing rapidly which was to water the lands of the West. As India and China were to be bound to the West by Syrian Christianity, so Ireland and the western rim of Europe were to touch the East through Celtic Christianity. By one of those strange phenomena of history—may it not well be called providential?—the Galatians, a numerous branch of the Gauls from France, had pushed their way into Asia Minor. With all the fiery nature of the Celtic race, they had invaded and subdued Italy and sacked Rome in the fourth century before Christ.[15] Not satisfied with this success, they broke into Asia Minor, and, settling there, became the founders of the province of Galatia.

Paul prepared to pass them by as he journeyed west, but the Holy Spirit disposed otherwise. A severe affliction compelled him

---

[12] Bigg, *The Origins of Christianity,* pages 143, 144.
[13] Burgon, *The Revision Revised,* page 9; Burkitt, *Early Eastern Christianity,* page 41.
[14] Menzies, *Saint Columba of Iona,* pages xi-xiii, see ch. 11, note 5; Fitzpatrick, *Ireland and the Making of Britain,* page 160.
[15] Ridgeway, *The Early Age of Greece,* vol. 1, p. 356.

to tarry in their midst. He won the love and devotion of these people. and soon there were raised up what he pleased to call "the churches of Galatia."[16] Patrick entered Ireland in the latter half of the fourth century. He found a well-organized and healthy Celtic Christianity there.[17] Evidence goes to show that Celtic Ireland learned the gospel from the believers in Galatia. One writer, who has made special research in Oriental history, says, "The Christianity which first reached France and England (i. e., Gaul and Britain) was of the school of the apostle John, who ruled the churches in Asia Minor, and therefore of a Greek, not Latin, type."[18]

There is abundant evidence of intercommunication between Ireland, France, and Galatia in the three hundred years between Paul and Patrick.[19] That the Celts in France were evangelized by the Celts in Asia Minor is shown by a well-known event in the history of the French church.[20] About seventy years after the death of the apostle John, the churches in southern France suffered a terrible persecution at the hands of the pagans. The distressed believers in 177 sent a pathetic account of their afflictions, not to Italy or to Africa, but to their brethren in Asia Minor.

"In order to understand the situation, political and ecclesiastical, in southern France, we must bear in mind that the Gauls of the West and the Galatae of the East were of the same stock, and that each branch, though several nations intervened, retained unimpaired its racial characteristics."[21]

Thus Ireland received the gospel from Asia Minor, by way of the sea and by way of the Celtic believers in southern France; and they, in turn, obtained the light from the Galatians to whom Paul had ministered.

The facts given by Douglas Hyde show how powerful and how widely spread over Europe was the Celtic race centuries before Christ. Alexander the Great would not embark upon his campaigns into Asia without having first assured himself of the friendship of the Celts.[22]

---

[16] Galatians 1:2.
[17] Fitzpatrick, *Ireland and the Making of Britain,* page 30.
[18] Gordon, *"World Healers,"* page 78.
[19] O'Leary, *The Syriac Church and Fathers,* page 32.
[20] Stokes, *Ireland and the Celtic Church,* page 3.
[21] Warner, *The Albigensian Heresy,* vol. 1, p. 19.
[22] Hyde, *A Literary History of Ireland,* pages 6, 7.

Within the generation following the apostles, if not even before the death of John, the New Testament had been translated into that most beautiful of all Latin texts, the Italic version, often called Itala. For centuries scholars of the Celtic church quoted from the Itala.[23]

The Beginnings of Greek Christianity

After Paul had labored in Galatia he was instructed by the Lord in a vision by night to go into Greece. He might have spent the rest of his days profitably in Asia Minor, but the Holy Spirit purposed otherwise. By his celebrated labors in the Greek centers of Philippi, Thessalonica, Berea, Athens, Corinth, and later in Ephesus, the apostle founded Greek Christianity. At Athens, he entered the world's intellectual center of paganism. Greece was still palpitating with the glorious memories of her victories over Persia's millions, and the nation was reveling in the rich stores of her golden literature. Paul planted the gospel in the midst of the people who spoke the Greek language, that medium through which God was pleased to transmit to the world the most exalted of all literature, the Greek New Testament. The first revelations given to the gospel church were written in Greek.[24]

In later days a deep hatred sprang up between Greek and Latin churches, and Greek and Latin ecclesiastics hurled bitter words at one another. These theological controversies arose because both churches had grown ambitious and had allied themselves with kings and emperors. At length, in 1054, the Greek and Latin churches separated. Long before this the Latin state church feared the effect of the accumulated stores of Greek literature. Latin was made the ecclesiastical language of Western Europe.[25] The Greek language, with its literature, was condemned by Roman ecclesiasticism, its study forbidden, and its writings anathematized. Ireland's Celtic church in the medieval ages remained a center for instruction in Greek long after it had virtually disappeared elsewhere in Western Christendom.[26] The knowledge of Greek was declared in the universities

---

[23] Stokes, *Ireland and the Celtic Church,* pages 27, 28; Gilly, *Vigilantius and His Times,* page 116; Smith and Wace, *A Dictionary of Christian Biography,* art. "Patricius"; Nolan, *The Integrity of the Greek Vulgate,* page xvii; Warner, *The Albigensian Heresy,* vol. 1, p. 12; Betham, *Irish Antiquarian Researches.*

[24] Milman, *History of Latin Christianity,* vol. 1, p. 1, Introduction.

[25] Westcott and Hort, *The New Testament in the Original Greek,* vol. 2, p. 142.

[26] Cubberley, *The History of Education,* page 138.

of the Latin hierarchy to be full of daggers and poison.[27] For more than one thousand years it ceased to exist in the Teutonic kingdoms of Europe, except in the bosom of Greek and Celtic Christianity, and with those evangelical bodies which looked to the Scriptures as their only authority.[28]

The repulse of the Greek church by the Latin hierarchy left the former as a buffer between the astounding activities of Christianity in the East and the victorious sword of the papal kingdoms of Western Europe.

The Beginnings of Latin Christianity

Sometimes the Lord calls, sometimes He impels men to great tasks, not because they are disobedient, but because their interest in near-by labors makes them oblivious to distant opportunities. Paul was directed by a vision to go to Greece, but he went as a prisoner to Rome. Intent on anchoring his great work among the Gentiles to Jewish Christianity, he complied with a dangerous request of the leaders at Jerusalem. The other apostles wished to disarm the prejudices of Jewish authorities against Paul by having him unwisely appear in the temple of Jerusalem in fulfillment of a vow. Paul was willing to risk his life by performing the required ceremonies in the central sanctuary of Israel if only he might avert a rupture between Gentile and Jewish Christianity. He knew that the Gentile believers had received only a meager training in the profound truths of the gospel. Is it for this reason that practically all his epistles are written to the young, inexperienced Gentile churches? Moreover, in vision he foresaw the crushing opposition which would grow into an apostate church and which would pursue the true church for 1260 years, and therefore, he yearned to link the new Gentile churches to an experienced Judaism which had turned to Christ.

In His ministry to the Jews, Jesus was sacrificed at Jerusalem; in his ministry to the Gentiles, Paul was sacrificed at Jerusalem. Only a sacrifice can open the eyes of tardy believers to the greatest spiritual advances. Nothing short of the sacrifice of Jesus could break hard hearts and inspire consecration. Although Paul knew full well the

---

[27] Jones, *The History of the Christian Church*, vol. 2, p. 294.

[28] Westcott and Hort, *The New Testament in the Original Greek*, vol. 2, p. 142.

burning hatred of the rabbis against him, he followed the plan of the other apostles, and entered the temple. He was soon recognized, and fanatical hatred broke out. The temple throngs rushed on him with rage. If the tumult had not reached the ears of the Roman guard, who barely succeeded in snatching him from the hands of his enemies, he would have been torn limb from limb. When he appeared before the Roman tribunal, Paul felt he could not locally obtain justice, therefore he said, "I appeal unto Caesar." The Roman magistrate replied, "Hast thou appealed unto Caesar? unto Caesar shalt thou go."

As a prisoner, Paul was carried to Rome, the capital of the Latin-speaking nations, the mistress of the world. Christianity did not come to Rome first through Paul; he found it there already when he arrived. Whether it preceded Paul by means of merchants, converted soldiers, or humble missionaries, is not known.[29] Nevertheless, the slender beginnings soon grew in strength through the ministry of the great apostle. He at once challenged the higher circles of Judaism and paganism. Having been recognized as a prisoner of no ordinary class, he was allowed the freedom of his own house, and permitted to come and go and to labor in no small public way during the two years before his case came to trial.[30] The epistle known as Second Timothy was written between the acquittal of the apostle at his first hearing and the death sentence at his second hearing.

Greece was the intellectual, but Rome was the military, stronghold of paganism. No one can read scholarly authors such as Auguste Arthur Beugnot, who wrote the history of the destruction of paganism in the West, without realizing how nearly invincible was the resistance of Italian heathenism. Latin Christianity did not so early show the gains which soon adorned the labors of Celtic and Syrian Christianity. Out of the three hundred eighteen bishops who signed the decrees of the great Council of Nicaea in 325—the first general church council—only seven were from the Latin West.[31]

To understand the apostolic origins of the true church, it is necessary to study the triumphs of the other apostles. In the first seven or eight years of gospel history the apostle Peter was a dominant figure. Paul held the center of the stage for the next thirty years.

---

[29] Burgon and Miller, *The Traditional Text of the Holy Gospels,* page 145.
[30] This can be read in the last chapter of Acts and in the second epistle to Timothy.
[31] Michael the Syrian, *Chronique de Michel le Syrien,* vol. 1, pp. 247-253.

Peter's closing years were scenes of wide and significant labors. They ranged from Babylon in the East to Rome in the West. For years he cherished the work at Jerusalem. There is reason to believe that at Rome he followed Paul in martyrdom.[32] What determinative effects came from his labors over widespread areas may be seen by noting carefully the first epistle of Peter.

Peter's Epistle to the Churches

This epistle opens with greetings from the apostle to the believers "scattered throughout Pontus, Galatia, Cappadocia, Asia, and Bithynia," and closes with a salutation from Babylon. All these first five provinces are found in Asia Minor. The significant results of Peter's labors in Bithynia lead the student to glean awhile in that field. Paul was led to evangelize Galatia but was forbidden by the Holy Spirit to go into Bithynia. In Galatia, Paul planted but Peter watered.[33] In Bithynia, Peter both planted and watered. Many learned writers have given valuable time to analyzing the work in Bithynia. In 109, about nine years after the death of the apostle John, the Roman emperor requested the scholarly Pliny, governor of Bithynia, to make investigations concerning Christianity there because of the stories which had come to his ears.

The governor of Bithynia, in rendering his report to the emperor, revealed the irresistible advances of the gospel. Pliny complains that the people are leaving the old gods and their heathen worship to go in throngs to the worship of Christ. He laments because the sale of heathen sacrifices has fallen off. Paying splendid tribute to the virtues of the Christians, he describes how they meet regularly once a week on "a stated day" for worship, which was undoubtedly the seventh-day Sabbath.

While Peter lived, churches sprang up in Chaldea, Assyria, Syria, and Asia Minor. There grew up in this territory noble, heroic, sacrificing leaders of Christianity who for many centuries formed the most learned and stabilizing force in the world to strengthen and to help the true church in the Far East and the West.[34]

According to the writings of Origen (A. D. 185-254), the apostle Andrew was given Scythia as his field of labor, while Thomas was

---

[32] Abul Faraj, *Chronography*, vol. 1, p. 50.
[33] 1 Peter 1:1; Galatians 1:2, 21.   [34] See the next two chapters of this volume.

Thomas and the Other Apostles

assigned to Persia.[35] According to evidence fully discussed in a later chapter, Thomas went farther than Persia. Reliable Syrian history indicates that the gospel was planted at Mosul, in Mesopotamia, in 170.[36] About 150, or fifty years after the death of the apostle John, the gospel had been preached and churches raised up in Persia, Media, Parthia, and Bactria.[37] Rawlinson speaks of Christianity's spreading in the empire of Parthia by 150.[38] Evidently before he was killed in India in 72, the apostle Thomas had raised up many churches.[39]

Pantaeus, one of the founders of the theological school at Alexandria, seventy years after the death of the apostle John, went to a country he called India, it is related, and reported evidences that the apostle Bartholomew had labored there.[40] The gospel must have made great headway among the Syriac- and Latin-speaking peoples within a half century after the death of the apostle John, because by that time the famous Syriac New Testament, called the Peshitta, had appeared.[41] Christianity is indicated as spreading among all ranks throughout Persia, Parthia, Media, and Bactria during the reign of the emperor Marcus Aurelius (A. D. 161-180).[42]

What power drove these early believers to enter the intellectual strongholds of European paganism, to venture within the fanatical pantheons of Asia Minor, to brave the burning heat of Arabia, to spend their lives wandering in Tatary, and, as strangers, to struggle under the blistering sun of India? This power was the word of God, which burned as a fire in their hearts. They cried out with the apostle Paul, "Woe is unto me, if I preach not the gospel!"

---

[35] Eusebius, *Ecclesiastical History,* b. 3, ch. 1, found in *Nicene and Post-Nicene Fathers.*

[36] Adeney, *The Greek and Eastern Churches,* pages 297, 298.

[37] Fisher, *History of the Christian Church,* page 45; Gordon, *"World Healers,"* page 243.

[38] Rawlinson, *The Seven Great Monarchies of the Ancient Eastern World* (Sixth Monarchy), vol. 3, p. 225.

[39] This conclusion has its opponents, but many scholarly and dependable writers have ceased to be in doubt about this and have settled it to their own satisfaction that the apostle Thomas laid the foundation of Christianity in India. See the author's discussion in Chapter XIX, "The St. Thomas Christians of India."

[40] Adeney, *The Greek and Eastern Churches,* page 296.

[41] Burgon, *The Revision Revised,* page 27.

[42] Yohannan, *The Death of a Nation,* page 39.

These early missionaries clung to the Bible as the guidebook which would keep them from being deceived by apostasies, counterfeits, and by wolves in sheep's clothing. Obedience to this Book singled them out for the rage of pagan emperors. They defended the truth against the wiles of Western false christs and of the counterfeit doctrines of the great Eastern religions. Nevertheless, as Paul wrote, "The word of God is quick, and powerful, and sharper than any two-edged sword," [43] and by that word they conquered.

This chapter has traced the origins of Christianity in its various branches (Syrian, Celtic, Greek, Latin) and has revealed how the apostles and their immediate successors delivered its truths to these different peoples. Succeeding chapters will follow up the further history of these origins in different lands and show how and where the primitive New Testament faith with its apostolic origins survived. Then the reader will be better able to see how present-day Christianity compares with primitive Christianity.

---

[43] Hebrews 4:12.

CHAPTER IV

The Silent Cities of Syria

*The ancestry of the Reformers is to be found in the godly
men and women who, even in the darkest days, by their
simple evangelical piety, kept the fire on the altar from
going out altogether.*[1]

IN THE early ages of the Christian Era the flourishing cities of
Syria were the first to occupy a commanding position in the development of the doctrines and missions of the true church. It is an
impressive fact that many of these silent and deserted cities still
remain in a remarkable state of preservation. For many centuries
after the Jewish Christians migrated north when they were driven
out of Jerusalem, they continued to augment the membership of this
already virile Christian region whose chief city was Antioch.[2] Syria
is a district, little known, but full of significance respecting the history
of the true church.

Because of his hatred for the Jews who had rebelled against
Rome and were duly suppressed, the emperor forbade them, in 135,
to enter the city of Jerusalem. This, of course, excluded Christians
of Jewish descent. This act also contributed to the building up of new
Syrian centers of Christianity. Today one finds the splendid remains
of the villas, churches, inscriptions, and public buildings in Syria
which were established in the early Christian centuries.[3] Here church
organizations and mission enterprises took permanent shape under

---

[1] Muir, *The Arrested Reformation,* page 49.

[2] O'Leary, *The Syriac Church and Fathers,* page 29.

[3] After having long contemplated a visit to these silent cities of Syria, the author
several years ago was happily able to personally study their magnificent sites. After
visiting the district on the other side of the Jordan River and in the area about Damascus, the party came to Beyrouth in Syria. Here the author secured the assistance of
Dr. William Lesovsky, a linguist scholar in Arabic, English, French, and German.
Arrangements were made to contact the leading American and Syrian scholars of
Beyrouth. Since Syria was then a French mandate, contact was first made with the
French Director of Antiquities. He was well informed concerning these silent cities,
and from him it was learned that there were about one hundred of them, which
would require much study to investigate thoroughly. We arranged to examine those
most representatively Christian and most important from the standpoint of architecture and sanitation. The director advised that we start with El-Bara, and, although
he gave us good highway directions, we suffered the usual transportation difficulties
experienced by travelers with native automobile drivers. When we reached Oroum-
El-Djoz, the sun was setting; and, as it was the month of February, the weather was

the hands of the apostles and their immediate successors. From this new base, streams of light went out to the ends of the earth.

However, before describing that which research can find in many of these cities, attention is directed to the historical and archaeological background of this early Syrian civilization which formed the earliest base for missionary work, both in the West and in the East.

Historical and Archaeological Background

Jerusalem's fall produced its greatest effect upon the millions of Jews who did not reside in Palestine. Stunned by this event, they listened to the gospel, and untold numbers turned to Christ. These did a great work in establishing the church in all parts of the world.[4] As they had not been under the fanatical legalism of the Jerusalem rabbis, thousands of them were open to the convincing fulfillments of prophecy preached by the leaders of the church.

The victories of the Roman armies aroused the Christian Jews in Palestine to obey the command of Jesus to flee from Judea when the fall of Jerusalem was imminent. The first region to receive beneficial influence from this transfer of population was that portion of Palestine lying to the east of the Jordan, referred to in the Bible as Decapolis,[5] a word meaning "ten cities." Upon these cities the Roman Empire had bestowed special citizen rights and had lavished huge sums of money to beautify and embellish them. It was Rome's purpose to exalt alluring Grecian culture and philosophy in the hope of leading the Jews into pagan art and thought.[6]

---

cold in the Syrian mountains. Here we found the signboard pointing out across the country to El-Bara, but our problem was how to reach it. As it was late, we spent the night with a native, now a Protestant teacher of English, returning about eight o'clock the following morning to the sign pointing into the forest toward El-Bara. After driving through mudholes, out of which we were obliged to push the car, and over rocky roads, we emerged at last into a valley. Upon the hill to our right we could see the Mohammedan mud village, and in the valley lay the remains of the ancient city of El-Bara. We were anxious to inspect the ruins immediately, but prudence advised us to see the *moukdhar* first. As we visited with this chief official of the village a crowd gathered. Finally, we received permission to inspect the ruins of El-Bara.

[4] Foakes-Jackson, *The History of the Christian Church*, page 33.

[5] Matthew 4:25; Mark 5:20; 7:31; Burgon and Miller, *The Traditional Text of the Holy Gospels*, page 123, and note 1.

[6] Schurer, *A History of the Jewish People in the Time of Christ*, 2 div. vol. 1, pp. 29-56. Although he had read much regarding Decapolis, the writer was surprised on visiting these places to behold the grandeur and the magnificence of the remains which still stand. Even now the traveler who goes eastward from the Jordan River is deeply impressed by the magnificent scenery of the area.

In the days of the apostles this trans-Jordan region was a fertile land, enriching its inhabitants by varied and abundant harvests. The Christian Jews fled here to escape the terrors of the Roman war (A. D. 66). The book of Acts would lead one to believe that there were many thousands of them by this time.[7] Possibly from seventy to ninety thousand Christian Jews fled from Palestine eastward. Many Gentile Christians also escaped. According to Eusebius these refugees fled to the city of Pella.[8] The same historian again mentions Pella in connection with the widespread rebellion of the Jews in 135, after which the emperor Hadrian plowed Jerusalem under, changed its name to Aelia, and forbade the Gentile Christians there to have a leader of Jewish descent.[9] Pella, at this time, was one of the famous ten cities. Arriving in such a region of culture, wealth, and liberality of thought, the fleeing Jewish Christians, stirred by having recently seen the fulfillment of one of Christ's major prophecies, could hardly have failed to exercise an irresistible influence upon their new neighbors.

The exiles who settled here multiplied in numbers throughout the following years. Their converts and their descendants formed large and learned Christian communities. The land of these pagan ten cities, or Decapolis, suddenly found itself producing a strong effect upon Christianity.

Another remarkable migration then began from Decapolis to the region about Antioch. Decades had passed since Paul and Barnabas had raised up churches in that part of Syria which lay directly north of Decapolis. There numerous converts to Christ existed among the Gentiles and Jews. The majority of the new believers, however, in the northern Syrian region were from among the sons of Israel. This latter community beckoned to the dwellers in Decapolis. Consequently, descendants of those who originally fled from Jerusalem left Pella and its regions to enrich and multiply Christian centers to the north as far as the Euphrates River.[10]

Syria had early attracted the attention of the cultured as a region in which to erect the magnificent in architecture. It was the richest

---

[7] Acts 21:20.
[8] Eusebius, *Ecclesiastical History*, b. 3, ch. 5, p. 138, found in *Nicene and Post-Nicene Fathers*.
[9] *Ibid.*, b. 4, ch. 6; b. 5, ch. 12.
[10] O'Leary, *The Syriac Church and Fathers*, pages 28, 29.

and most prosperous province of the Roman Empire.[11] It was also famed for culture and learning. In this section are found the grandest temples erected by the Roman emperors for the worship of the sun-god. In the midst of this land stood Antioch, the capital city. Later, when the emperor Justinian wanted, about 530, to build in Constantinople the finest church in the world, he searched diligently throughout Greek and Latin civilizations to secure a gifted builder, but was obliged at last to turn to Syria. Here he found the skill he sought.

> The school of Antioch at that time surpassed almost every other in scientific and literary repute, and its methods dominated all the East. Justinian, in the middle of the sixth century, wished to rebuild the cathedral of Constantinople, and from the school of Antioch he drew both his architects, Anthemus of Tralles and Isidore of Miletus.[12]

Concerning the unrivaled skill and scholarship of Syria, one historian says:

> Now the primary characteristic of Byzantine architecture is its development of the method of roofing with domes. The most perfect specimen of this work is the great church of St. Sophia at Constantinople, which it was the pride of Justinian to have built. Two earlier churches had been burnt—Constantine's church in A. D. 404, at the time of Chrysostom, and its successor in A. D. 532. Strictly speaking, Justinian's St. Sophia—still standing and now used as a mosque—is not typical Byzantine architecture. It is quite unique. Nothing of the kind had preceded it; it was never successfully imitated. Its famous architect, Anthemius, has the proud distinction of having produced a work without peer or parallel in all the ages of building. "St. Sophia," says M. Bayet, "has the double advantage of marking the advent of a new style and reaching at the same time such proportions as have never been surpassed in the East."[13]

In tracing the Celtic Church in Ireland, scholars are much impressed with the influence which these new styles, introduced by the Syrian architects, had on Western architecture. The connection of this style with the West is well established. The new principles of Syrian architecture were adopted in Ireland.

> From Constantinople Byzantine architecture rapidly passed westwards. Greek art was dead. Roman art was dead. In the sixth century, the only

---

[11] O'Leary, *The Syriac Church and Fathers,* page 34.
[12] Stokes, *Ireland and the Celtic Church,* page 242.
[13] Adeney, *The Greek and Eastern Churches,* page 181.

living, powerful, vivifying art was the art and the architecture of Byzantium. I have now to show you two things: first, how Byzantine art and architecture passed over to Gaul; and, then, how from Gaul it passed to Ireland. In the first place, as to the transition of Byzantine architecture from Constantinople to Gaul, the time and place of transit are easily determined.[14]

The splendor of the civilization built up in Syria can still be seen. The glory that remains is described in Howard Crosby Butler's article, "A Land of Deserted Cities":

> Few people appreciate the fact that today, at the dawn of the twentieth century, there are still parts of the old Roman Empire where no traveler of modern times has been; that there are ancient towns which no tourist has seen, temples and towers that no lover of classic architecture has delighted in, inscriptions in ancient Greek that no savant has as yet deciphered, whole regions, in fact, full of antiquities for which no Baedeker has been written, and which are not shown upon the latest maps.
>
> Let the reader for a moment imagine himself withdrawn from the luxuriant landscapes of forest-capped hills and fresh green pastures with which he is familiar, and set down in this wasted land of barren gray hills, beneath a cloudless sky, and let him see before him in the distance a towering mass of broken walls and shattered colonnades, the mighty remnants of a city long deserted by civilized men, silent, sepulchral, with gates wide open and every house within untenanted even by wild beasts. Let him recall that this now lonely city was in existence before the days of Constantine the Great, while Rome was still mistress of the world and the Antonine emperors still sat upon the throne, that its magnificent churches were erected while our ancestors were bowing to Woden and Thor, that its spacious villas and its less pretentious, though still luxurious abodes, were built while the Anglo-Saxon was content with a hut of branches and skins, and then let him reflect that this once wealthy and thriving town has stood uninhabited for thirteen centuries, that no hand has been raised to add a single stone or to brace a tottering wall in all that time, and he will grasp something of the antiquity and something of the desolation of these dead cities.[15]

These silent cities of Syria differ in many respects from the ruins and remains of the archaeological past found elsewhere in the world. The monuments are not the work of some foreign invader, but are indigenous—the work of the inhabitants themselves. Furthermore, the stones were skillfully fitted together without cement or mortar. The construction and arrangements for sanitation were of the highest

---

[14] Stokes, *Ireland and the Celtic Church,* page 243.
[15] *Century Magazine,* vol. 66, N. S. 44, pp. 217, 220.

order and betoken an advanced degree of civilization. Some authors state that the arrangements for health and sanitation would be superior to those found in many places in the Western world today, even in Europe and America.

Tangible remains of their civilization indicate that the people who inhabited the greater number of these smaller towns in northern and southern Syria composed a large, well-to-do middle class. They seem to have had no superiors living near them, for there is only one residence of special magnificence in northern Syria, and one in the south, and these may have been the houses of the local governors.[16]

The apostles foresaw that the future success of the gospel would see many indifferent members coming into the fold. Paul declared that even in his day false brethren had entered in unawares.

In their stand for the pure doctrines of Christianity, the churches of Syria were horrified at the license which many so-called Christian teachers took with the Scriptures, and they rebelled against the doctrines of Gnosticism which arose in the corrupted Christianity of the church in Alexandria. "The school of Antioch led a revolt against the Alexandrian exegesis of Holy Scripture, and founded a more critical method."[17] Lucian, the famous evangelical leader and scholar, was obliged to contend against both Gnosticism and Manichaeism, but more especially against the former, which was the older of the two movements.

As opposition to the allegorizing tendency of the age centered in the theology of the school of Lucian, it later found a home in the Church of the East.[18] Emphasis should be placed upon the fact that the Syrian type of theology had great influence, endured until the Reformation, and kept its apostolic stamp. The inscriptions found on many of the buildings indicate that Syrian Christianity compassed a goodly portion of the territory in which the silent cities are found today.

---

[16] Butler, *Early Churches in Syria*, pt. 1, p. 10.

[17] Hastings, *Encyclopedia of Religion and Ethics*, art. "Alexandrian Theology."

[18] In speaking of Syrian theology, we are following the lead of the majority of the church historians in using the term to designate that communion which we call the Church of the East. We constantly use the term Church of the East to designate that great communion which, for centuries, extended from the Euphrates River to Persia, India, central Asia, and the Orient. Many writers call it the Nestorian Church, which is incorrect and is a misnomer. It is often called the Assyrian Church. To use the term Church of the East to apply to the Greek Orthodox Church is confusing.

It is perhaps interesting to note that the inscriptions from this region (treated by Wm. Kelley Prentice), covering more than three centuries, show, in their phraseology, a primitive Christianity in that they are dedicated to "God and His Christ," sometimes with mention of the Holy Spirit or the Trinity, but without invocation of the saints or even of the Virgin Mary. In this region, as in the Hauran, there are almost no Mohammedan remains, the prosperity of both regions having evidently ended with the Mohammedan conquest.[19]

El-Bara and Other Cities

El-Bara, one of the silent cities on the road between Aleppo and Lattaquia, near Antioch, still contains villas, churches, funeral pyramids, and other edifices giving evidence of the past culture and education. Monograms cut in stone disclose the builder's faith in Christ as the Alpha and Omega.[20]

At Djebel Barisha may be seen many inscriptions and monuments of the second century after Christ. Some prominent inscriptions on these buildings are in Greek, some in Latin, some in Syrian. A few of them as recorded by an American archaeological expedition, read as follows:

If God be for us, who can be against us?

Our Lord Jesus Christ, the Son, the Word of God, dwells here; let no evil enter.

The Lord shall preserve thy going out and thy coming in.

Upon this rock I will build My church, and the gates of hell shall not prevail against it.[21]

Baouda contains the ruins of a large market town. To reach it, the visitor passes over an old Roman road built evidently before the days of Christ. Baouda betrays the marks of having been a strictly commercial, financial, and transportation center. The stone edifices provided for the store below with a dwelling apartment above for the proprietor. A short distance from Baouda is Babiska. Here are two

---

[19] *The Nation,* vol. 95, p. 260.

[20] The author spent some time at El-Bara taking many photographs. From here the party visited Dalozza, where we saw a large ruin of what is said to have been the most beautiful private house in Syria. It seems to have been a commodious villa planned for the use of a single household. Here it was possible to visualize the suburban villas of those first Christian Syrians with their beautiful landscapes and their magnificent views.

[21] Prentice, *Publication of an American Archaeological Expedition to Syria,* part 3. The last inscription is on a church building in Syria.

churches, large and small public baths, with spacious inns near them. The buildings show great care and architectural ability in their construction. The fragment of another large building, probably a temple, dates from 225.[22]

Why Silent and Deserted Cities

To understand why these cities are silent and deserted, one must notice the policy of imperial Christianity during the centuries prior to the time when the scourge of Mohammedanism fell on the Roman Empire in Asia. Immediately after the Council of Nicaea, 325, the inroads of the northern Goths became serious and demanded the attention of the Roman emperors. The victories of these invaders cut off much of the empire in the West and reduced it in Europe to only about one third of its original territory. In order to survive, it was necessary to closely unify that which remained. In addition, imperial Christianity made the punishment of heresy a serious part of its program. Then terrible persecution fell on those who rejected the Church of Rome.

This started a movement among the believers in Syria, long a part of the Roman Empire, which caused them to flee into those Eastern regions already alienated in spirit by imperial exactions. The scourge of heresy hunting had fallen upon the Eastern provinces. Entire Christian populations migrated from the areas of the silent cities and from that part of Assyria near the headwaters of the Euphrates and Tigris Rivers which was included in the Roman Empire. When the emperor Justinian in 532 began his policy of subjecting everything to imperial Christianity, the devout, learned, and industrious portions of the population had already left these parts to find a refuge within the boundaries of the restored Persian Empire.[23]

Imperial Christianity, on the other hand, was wholly unprepared for the Mohammedan hordes which appeared unexpectedly out of Arabia about one hundred years after Justinian. Mohammedanism

---

[22] The author visited and inspected nine of these deserted cities. At El-Bara he found himself in a dangerous situation. For more than an hour he was in the midst of an intertribal war. The fact that these silent cities lie far from the main lines of travel and in the midst of an excitable Mohammedan population undoubtedly accounts for the fact that for centuries they have been practically unvisited and unknown.

[23] See the author's discussion in Chapter x, "How the Church Was Driven Into the Wilderness."

issued from Arabia following 622 with the suddenness and force of a tornado. When Islam had finished its onslaught against Asia Minor and the Eastern provinces, it had wrenched away the Roman Empire's possessions in Asia, north Africa, and Spain. In the first onrush of this new fanatical religion, Palestine was captured. Then followed the overthrow of the Roman emperor and his army on a battlefield in Syria. Followers of Mohammed pursued their work of slaughter, devastation, loot, and deportation. The Christian population that remained in the land of Syria evidently worked its way farther east, leaving behind their cities, silent and deserted.

Further historical recitals involving the Church of the East reveal that those first six and a half centuries of Syrian Christianity were marvelous in establishing the New Testament church, not only in the East, but also in the West. The mingling of the large Gentile and Jewish gospel communities in this region, coupled with the splendid spiritual background of training which the Jews under the Old Testament had in things divine, richly endowed this fruitful soil for the spread of Christianity. Finally, the persecutions carried on by the imperial church, followed by the devastations of the Mohammedans, left the area depopulated and robbed of the gospel church of Syria. The protecting hand of God was over His truth, and the churches far to the west in Europe, and also to the east in Asia, were strong enough to carry forward the light.

A Church Evangelical, Not Papal

The fact that the East was full of Jews, and that the preponderance of converts in the early gospel communities was for a long time from among them,[24] would indicate that the character of the beliefs and observances held by the Church of the East were modeled after the churches of Judea, not after Rome. Early believers for a long time called themselves Nazarenes, a title found in the words of Luke, who reported that the accusers of the apostle Paul said, "For we have found this man a pestilent fellow, and a mover of sedition among all the Jews throughout the world, and a ringleader of the sect of the Nazarenes."[25] They also called themselves Beni-Israel, or Sons of Israel. They usually spoke of our Lord as the Messiah, and

---

[24] *The Catholic Encyclopedia,* art. "Calendar."
[25] Acts 24:5.

therefore were called Messiahans. Many of their rites and ceremonies were performed in such a way as to reveal their connection with the Jews of earlier times.

The majority of writings preserved by the Church of Rome supports the contentions of that ecclesiastical system. Light is thrown on the actual beliefs of the early Christians by studying the fundamental instructions concerning the organization of individual churches as given by the apostle Paul. The great apostle to the Gentiles makes it distinctly clear that the churches which he founded in his missionary labors were modeled after the Christian churches in Judea. Thus he says, "For ye, brethren, became followers of the churches of God which in Judea are in Christ Jesus: for ye also have suffered like things of your own countrymen, even as they have of the Jews." [26] Paul did not pattern the plan of the local church after the heathen temple or after the Gentile models he might have found in his travels. The pattern given him was of God. What was that pattern? It was the first Christian church at Jerusalem and its duplicates in Judea.

It would be difficult to imagine that the apostle Peter, laboring in regions all the way from Babylon to the western borders of Asia Minor, would organize the churches upon any other model. His congregations also were but repetitions of the original Christian communions in the province of Judea, particularly of the churches in Jerusalem. For some time, groups of Christian believers continued to meet in the synagogues on the Sabbath day with the Jews.[27] This fact indicates that the apostolic church, in its primitive organization, did not cast away everything connected with the synagogue. A confirming indication of this is found in the decision of the Apostolic council recorded in the book of Acts, where the assembled delegates voted that they would not pass any ordinances other than the four which they had already sanctioned, because, "Moses of old time hath in every city them that preach him, being read in the synagogues every Sabbath day." [28] The Gnostic theology of Alexandria which was followed by the Church of Rome, was hostile to anything Jewish, even Jewish Christianity. Therefore it is safe to conclude from these historic developments that primitive Syrian Christianity was not

---

[26] 1 Thessalonians 2:14. [28] Acts 15:21.
[27] *The Catholic Encyclopedia,* art. "Calendar."

organized after the pattern of the Church of Rome, but followed an evangelical Judean and Biblical type of church organization.

The thoughtful student cannot but be impressed with the heroic exploits achieved by the missionary churches, offsprings of the Syrian parent communion church, throughout vast domains. Here one finds the spiritual leadership of Lucian of Antioch, of Vigilantius, reputed to be the first supreme head of the Waldenses, and indirectly of Patrick, organizer of Celtic Christianity in Ireland. These leaders are presented fully in succeeding chapters.

CHAPTER V

Lucian and the Church in Syria

*Lucian was really a learned man; his work on the text of
the Old Testament, which he corrected from the original
Hebrew, soon became famous; he was a Hebrew scholar,
and his version was adopted by the greater number of the
churches of Syria and Asia Minor. He occupied himself
also with the New Testament. His exegesis differs widely
from that of Origen. In Antioch allegorical interpretation
was not in fashion.*[1]

CONSIDERATION having been given to the importance of Syria
in conserving the original bases of the true church, attention is
now directed to Lucian (c. A. D. 250-312). Born among the hills of
Syria, this devout scholar was destined to exercise a dominating influence on the thought of men through the ages. He was gifted with an
unusual spirit of discernment, which the Holy Spirit used in enlarging
and strengthening the foundations laid by the apostles. For many
years destructive teachings more deadly to early Christianity than the
poison of serpents had been gaining ground. Lucian was called upon
to face these, and although he did not succeed in completely removing
them, nevertheless he did build for all a safe retreat.

Lucian might be likened to the founders of the American republic.
As authors of the American Declaration of Independence and that
part of the Constitution known as the Bill of Rights, they gave the
nation written documents upon which to build the state. So Lucian,
in an hour when documentary confusion was threatening chaos,
defended, preserved, and passed on to other generations the true
text of the Holy Scriptures. He also left a masterpiece of theology
to evangelical believers. He stimulated and vivified correct church
organization and methods of evangelization. Although his opponents
have seen to it that not much history about him has been preserved,
yet they cannot rob him of his great works.

Lucian was born at Antioch, a center of Greek life and culture.
In his day, Rome ruled supreme. There was no more powerful
metropolis than Antioch. On the outskirts lay the glamorous grove

---

[1] Duchesne, *Early History of the Christian Church*, vol. 1, p. 362.

of Daphne, celebrated above all other groves. In it the pleasure seeker could find many delights, ranging from the most luxurious and sensuous to the highest performances of classical art. Often, in his youth, Lucian looked upon these scenes of worldly folly; but his pious heart turned away from them in complete devotion to his Lord. He could wander eastward a few miles to those beautiful villages and cities, the remains of which have been described in a previous chapter. At that time they were the flourishing home of a learned, devoted Christianity, clinging closely to the early simplicity of the gospel, and refusing to adopt the unscriptural teachings and customs of heathenism which were gaining ground in some professed Christian bodies. The early years of Lucian were years of great contrast. He quickly discerned that there were two movements taking shape in Christendom, one loose in doctrine and affiliating itself with heathenism, the other based on the deep foundations of the Christian faith.

His Boyhood and Youth

In early boyhood an event occurred which opened his eyes to the frailty of empires. The Persians, led by the fanaticism of Mithraism, had made themselves masters of the Near Eastern world, bringing into existence an empire which would be the dreaded antagonist of Rome for five centuries. When Lucian was about ten years of age, Shapur (Sapor) I, the Persian monarch, waged successful warfare to the west, capturing the city of Antioch and taking captive the Roman emperor.[2] Naturally he carried back from the region many captives, among them Syrian Christians who would labor to evangelize Persia. Antioch on the border line between Rome and Persia, the coveted prize of both empires, offered a commanding position from which the work of Lucian could exercise its influence east and west through the coming centuries.

Soon the government of the Roman world passed into the hands of an energetic soldier, the emperor Aurelian, who set about vigorously to repair the damage to the imperial system done by weak predecessors. At this time a certain Paul, born in Samosata, was bishop of Antioch and had brought down upon himself the wrath of the

---

[2] Rawlinson, *The Seven Great Monarchies of the Ancient Eastern World*, vol. 3, ch. 4, p. 283.

Roman and Alexandrian churches because of his teachings. Paul was accused of believing a doctrine concerning the divinity of Christ which in the eyes of the bishops of Rome and Alexandria was considered heresy. Now for the first time Lucian heard the thunders of that struggle concerning the Sonship of our Lord which would go on until and after the first and most famous general council of the church was held at Nicaea in 325.

How difficult and dangerous the situation of Lucian was may quickly be seen. The churches of Rome and Alexandria had entered into an alliance. Alexandria had, for more than two centuries before Christ, been the real capital of the Jews who were compromising with paganism. The church at Alexandria was in this atmosphere. The city of Rome had been for seven hundred years, and was still to be for some time, the world capital of paganism. This environment greatly influenced the church at Rome. Lucian grew up in the churches of Syria and of the Near East, which were modeled after the churches of Judea. Here was the divine pattern for further believers. Lucian founded a college at Antioch which strove to counteract the dangerous ecclesiastical alliance between Rome and Alexandria. How bitter the situation became and how it finally split the West and East will be clarified by the following four facts:

First, the original founders of the ecclesiastical college at Alexandria strove to exalt tradition. Justin Martyr, as early as 150, had stood for this.[3] He was the spiritual father of Tatian, who in turn was a teacher of Clement. Second, Clement, most famous of the Alexandrian college faculty and a teacher of Origen, boasted that he would not teach Christianity unless it were mixed with pagan philosophy.[4] Third, Victor I, bishop of Rome, entered into a compact with Clement, about 190, to carry on research around the Mediterranean basin to secure support to help make Sunday the prominent day of worship in the church.[5] Sunday was already a day exalted among the heathen, being a day on which they worshiped the sun; yet Rome and Alexandria well knew that most of the churches throughout the world sanctified Saturday as the Sabbath of the fourth commandment.[6] Fourth,

---

[3] Schaff, *History of the Christian Church,* vol. 2, p. 720.
[4] See note 20, page 52 of this same chapter for citation.
[5] See pages 121-123 of this book.
[6] See pages 55-57 of this same chapter.

when Victor I, in lordly tones, pronounced excommunication on all the churches of the East who would not with him make Easter always come on Sunday, Alexandria supported this first exhibition of spiritual tyranny by the bishop of Rome. Lucian opposed Alexandria's policies and for this has been bitterly hated and his name kept in the background.

In the church struggle over Paul of Samosata, Lucian held aloof from both parties. When it appeared as if neither side would win, appeal was made to the pagan emperor Aurelian. The party led by the bishops of Rome and Alexandria could well bow its head with shame that the aid of a heathen emperor was invoked to settle a controversy over the divine Son of God. Most astonishing to relate, the emperor declined to judge the case and commanded (A. D. 270) that it should be submitted to the judgment of the bishops of Italy and Rome.[7] In referring this issue to the bishop of the capital city and his associates, it was assumed that they were responsible for the whole Christian church. This came as a recognition from the pagan state to Pope Felix. It could easily be used to support the assumed primacy of Peter.

What must have stirred the mind of Lucian, however, who at this time was about twenty-five years of age, were the philosophical speculations offered to sustain the theological viewpoint held by the bishop of Rome concerning the Godhead. Concerning the Christians after the Council of Nicaea, where the influence of Rome was dominant, the historian Edward Gibbon wrote, "They were more solicitous to explore the nature, than to practice the laws, of their founder."[8]

As no record has been found that Lucian was a participant in this controversy, subsequent historians recognize their inability to accuse him of factionalism or instability. One must read the thorough defense of this holy man by George Bishop Bull to know the errors Lucian opposed and the excellent doctrines he taught.[9] There is no record of any charge of heresy, officially or ecclesiastically, lodged against him by his contemporaries.

In his early youth, Lucian was called to resist the rise and spread of two perverted types of Christianity: Manichaeism and Gnosticism.

[7] Ayer, *A Source Book for Ancient Church History,* page 227.
[8] Gibbon, *Decline and Fall of the Roman Empire,* ch. 47, par. 1.
[9] Bull, *Defence of the Nicene Faith,* vol. 1, pp. 344-351.

Insidious Teachings Met by Lucian

Manichaeism dethroned the first chapter of Genesis by rejecting creation and a miracle-working God, by demanding celibacy of its leaders, and by worshiping the sun as the supreme dwelling place of Deity.[10] Imbued with the ancient Persian hatred of the Old Testament, it ridiculed the Sabbath of the fourth commandment and exalted Sunday.[11] This fanatical darkness, with its own fabricated scriptures, came down upon Syria like a fog. Lucian weakened its attacks by his irresistible defense of the Scriptures and their teachings.

He was next aroused to meet in the primitive church an invasion of subtle hero worship. Gnosticism was eating its way into those sections of the church which were compromising with paganism. The wrath of the papal party was brought down upon him because he refused to participate in a questionable movement to exalt on fraudulent grounds the primacy of the bishop of Rome. For more than a century previously there had appeared considerable deceptive literature giving an exalted place to Peter. In these crafty stories the impetuous apostle was brought to Rome, and with him was brought Simon the magician, whom he had rebuked. Supernatural powers were attributed to Simon. Peter, in these dishonest fables, was reputed to follow Simon, rapidly confuting his heresies and his superhuman feats, and finally destroying this pretended follower of the faith by a mighty miracle. These fabulous exploits of Peter were emblazoned abroad.

> The apocryphal accounts . . . of Peter's deeds at Rome leaped at once beyond all bounds of sober credibility. They may have concealed a modicum of fact beneath the fiction, but the fiction so far exceeded and distorted the fact that it is hopeless now to try to disentangle one from the other. . . . None the less this literature cannot be overlooked by one who aims to comprehend the growth of papal prestige. Conceptions founded upon it and incidents borrowed from it were in time accepted by most of the influential writers of Roman Christendom, even by those who like Eusebius or Jerome fully realized that the literature as a whole was a web of falsehood. In particular, the figure of Simon Magus, once installed at Rome, could never be entirely exorcised, nor could Peter be deprived of the renown of being the first mighty victor over heresy as

---

[10] M'Clintock and Strong, *Cyclopedia;* also *The New International Encyclopedia,* art. "Manichaeism."

[11] Milman, *The History of Christianity,* vol. 2, p. 270. See also M'Clintock and Strong, *Cyclopedia,* and *The New International Encyclopedia,* art. "Manichaeism."

embodied in Simon's person. In fact, it is difficult to name one of the Fathers after the third century who does not sometime allude to that famous story. Ambrose, Jerome, Augustine and others . . . could none of them rid themselves altogether of the impression it made upon them.[12]

Lucian never accepted such doubtful tales. He protested against those who were championing fraudulent claims; but as they became more determined in countenancing these false stories, and so helped to make the bishop of Rome "the vicar of the Son of God," the more hostile they grew toward Lucian.

Lucian's Gift of the Genuine New Testament

The Protestant denominations are built upon that manuscript of the Greek New Testament sometimes called the Textus Receptus, or Received Text. It is that Greek New Testament from which the writings of the apostles in Greek have been translated into English, German, Dutch, and other languages. During the Dark Ages, the Received Text was practically unknown outside the Greek Church. It was restored to Christendom by the labors of that great scholar, Erasmus. It is altogether too little known that the real editor of the Received Text was Lucian. None of Lucian's enemies fails to credit him with this work. Neither Lucian nor Erasmus, but rather the apostles, wrote the Greek New Testament. However, Lucian's day was an age of apostasy when a flood of depravations was systematically attempting to devastate both the Bible manuscripts and Bible theology. Origen, of the Alexandrian college, made his editions and commentaries of the Bible a secure retreat for all errors, and deformed them with philosophical speculations introducing casuistry and lying.[13] Lucian's unrivaled success in verifying, safeguarding, and transmitting those divine writings left a heritage for which all generations should be thankful.

Mutilations of the Sacred Scriptures abounded.[14] There were at least eighty heretical sects all striving for supremacy.[15] Each took unwarranted license in removing or adding pages to Bible manuscripts.[16]

---

12 Shotwell and Loomis, *The See of Peter,* page 122.
13 Mosheim, *Institutes of Ecclesiastical History,* b. 1, cent. 3, pt. 2, ch. 3, pars. 5-10.
14 Gilly, *Vigilantius and His Times,* page 116.
15 Fisher, *History of Christian Doctrines,* page 19.
16 Eusebius, *Ecclesiastical History,* b. 5, ch. 28, found in *Nicene and Post-Nicene Fathers.*

Consider how masterly must have been Lucian's collection of the evidences which identified and protected the writings left to the church by the apostles. From that day to this the Received Text and the New Testaments translated from it are far in the lead of any other Bibles in use.

Rejection of Spurious Old Testament Books

Not only did Lucian certify the genuine New Testament, but he spent years of arduous labor upon the Old Testament.[17] As the Greek language was the prevalent tongue in which leading works were published throughout the civilized world, he translated the Hebrew Scriptures into Greek. He did this work so well that even Jerome, his bitter opponent, admitted that his Greek translation of the Old Testament held sway in the capital city of Constantinople and in most of the Near East.[18]

Jerome also entered the same field and translated the Hebrew Bible, not only into Greek, but also into Latin. When the two translations of the Hebrew Bible appeared, there was a marked difference between the edition of Lucian and that of Jerome. To Jerome's Latin edition were added the seven spurious books called the Apocrypha, which the Protestant world has continuously rejected. The responsibility cannot all be laid upon Jerome, for he did not believe in these seven spurious books. Augustine, whose fame as a father of the papal church outshines Jerome's, favored them.[19] Since, however, Jerome had been employed by the bishop of Rome to publish this translation and had received abundant money from his employer for its accomplishment, the pope took the liberty of adding the seven spurious books in question to the Latin edition of Jerome's Old Testament. Later the papacy pronounced it to be the authoritative Bible of the Roman Catholic Church.

Thus, in many ways Lucian became a blessing to those churches which in later years designated the Church of Rome "a newcomer," and felt themselves compelled to disagree with it, while they persevered in apostolic usages.

---

[17] *The Catholic Encyclopedia,* art. "Lucian."
[18] Nolan, *The Integrity of the Greek Vulgate,* page 72.
[19] Killen, *The Old Catholic Church,* page 153; Jacobus, *Roman Catholic and Protestant Bibles Compared,* page 4.

Exposure of the Allegorizing Theologians

Clement (c. A. D. 194) and Origen (c. A. D. 230) of the metaphysical school of Alexandria, in the days immediately preceding Lucian, welded into an alluring and baffling system the method of allegorizing the Bible. They taught the supremacy of the bishop of Rome and declared that there was no salvation outside the church. Clement played to the applause of the populace by advocating the affinity of Christianity with paganism and of sun worship with the Sun of Righteousness. John Mosheim testifies to this as follows:

> He [Clement], himself expressly tells us in his *Stromata*, that he would not hand down Christian truth pure and unmixed, but "associated with, or rather veiled by, and shrouded under the precepts of philosophy". . . the philosophy of the Greeks.[20]

While Clement, with Pantaeus, mixed Christianity with paganism at Alexandria, Lucian founded at Antioch a school of Syrian theology. The profound difference between his teaching and that of the north African allegorizing theologians, Dr. Williston Walker thus describes:

> With Antioch of this period is to be associated the foundation of a school of theology by Lucian, of whom little is known of biographical detail, save that he was a presbyter, held aloof from the party in Antioch, which opposed and overcame Paul of Samosata, taught there from c. 275 to 303, and died a martyr's death in 312. . . . Like Origen, he busied himself with textual and exegetical labors on the Scriptures, but had little liking for the allegorizing methods of the great Alexandrian. A simpler, more grammatical and historical method of treatment both of text and doctrine characterized his teaching.[21]

It was a critical hour in the history of the church in the days following the efforts of Clement, Origen, and Tertullian—the mystical teachers of north Africa—to substitute new foundations for Christianity. In that time God raised up a tireless champion of truth, Lucian. Speculation within the church was tearing to pieces the faith once delivered to the saints. The very foundation of the gospel itself was at stake. Because of the immense contributions made by Syrian Christianity in the following centuries, later generations are indebted to Lucian. At this time the words of the psalmist were appropriate:

---

[20] Mosheim, *Commentaries,* cent. 2, vol. 1, p. 341.
[21] Walker, *A History of the Christian Church,* page 106.

"If the foundations be destroyed, what can the righteous do?"[22] It was at this time, according to a historian acceptable to the Roman Church, who lived in the same century with Lucian, that the martyr drew up a confession of faith.[23]

Denouncing Tradition Above the Bible

The apostle Paul had prophesied that after his departing men would arise from the ministry, speaking perverse things and entering like grievous wolves among the flock.[24] Paul said it would come; Lucian in his day could say truly that it had come. Within a hundred years after the death of Paul there can be found in the writings of authors who now stand high in the Roman Catholic Church the exaltation of tradition to the level, if not above the level, of the Holy Scriptures. Tertullian (A. D. 150-235), a contemporary of Lucian, after explaining the oblations for the dead, the sign of the cross upon the forehead, and the dipping of candidates in the water three times for baptism, writes:

> If, for these and other such rules, you insist upon having positive Scripture injunction, you will find none. Tradition will be held forth to you as the originator of them, custom as the strengthener, and faith as their observer.[25]

The Church in the Wilderness believed the Bible to be supreme. Its members believed that the Holy Spirit and the word agreed, and they remembered that Jesus met each test Satan put against Him in the hour of temptation with the words, "It is written." To hold the Holy Scriptures as an infallible guide to salvation excludes the admission of any other authority upon as high a level. To exalt tradition and place it on the level with the Bible throws the door open to admit all kinds of writings as bearing the seal of divine authority. Moreover, it places an impossible burden upon believers to verify a wide range of literature.

The Protestant and the Catholic worlds both teach that the Holy Scriptures are of God. There is a difference, however, for the Protestants admit the Bible and the Bible only, while the papacy places

---

[22] Psalm 11:3.
[23] Sozomen, *Ecclesiastical History*, b. 3, ch. 5, found in *Nicene and Post-Nicene Fathers*.
[24] Acts 20:29, 30.
[25] Tertullian, *The Chaplet or De Corona*, chapter 4.

the church traditions on an equality with the Scriptures. The Council of Trent, 1545, whose decisions are supreme authority on doctrine in the Roman Catholic Church, speaks as follows on written and unwritten tradition:

> The sacred and holy, aecumenical and general Synod of Trent, . . . following the examples of the orthodox fathers, receives and venerates with equal affection of piety, and reverence, all the books both of the Old and of the New Testament,—seeing that one God is the author of both, as also the said traditions, as well those appertaining to faith as to morals, as having been dictated, either by Christ's own word of mouth, or by the Holy Ghost, and preserved by a continuous succession in the Catholic Church.[26]

That this principle still prevails in the Roman Catholic Church is shown by the words of the celebrated Cardinal Gibbons of Baltimore, who was long the leading exponent of his church in the United States. Thus he writes:

> A rule of faith, or a competent guide to heaven, must be able to instruct in all the truths necessary for salvation. Now the Scriptures alone do not contain all the truths which a Christian is bound to believe, nor do they explicitly enjoin all the duties which he is obliged to practice. Not to mention other examples, is not every Christian obliged to sanctify Sunday, and to abstain on that day from unnecessary servile work? Is not the observance of this law among the most prominent of our sacred duties? But you may read the Bible from Genesis to Revelation, and you will not find a single line authorizing the sanctification of Sunday. The Scriptures enforce the religious observance of Saturday, a day which we never sanctify.[27]

Lucian was obliged to take his stand against the tide of error that was rising in his day. He was diametrically opposed to the school of theology at Alexandria, whose teachings exalted tradition. Tertullian took the same stand as did other early north African authors directly or indirectly favored by the papacy.[28]

Lucian encountered the contradictory teachings concerning the binding obligation of the Ten Commandments. The same inconsistency is manifest in papal doctrine today, for *The Catholic Encyclo-*

---

[26] Buckley, *Canons and Decrees of the Council of Trent,* pages 17, 18.

[27] Gibbons, *The Faith of Our Fathers,* pp. 111, 112, 63d ed.; p. 86, 76th ed.

[28] Schaff, *History of the Christian Church,* vol. 2, Second Period, par. 196, pp. 822-824.

pedia says: "The Church, on the other hand, after changing the day of rest from the Jewish Sabbath, or seventh day of the week, to the first, made the Third Commandment refer to Sunday as the day to be kept holy as the Lord's Day. The Council of Trent (Sess. VI, can. xix) condemns those who deny that the Ten Commandments are binding on Christians."[29] This directly contradicts the teachings of Thomas Aquinas regarding the fourth commandment.[30] And it is to be remembered that the Roman Church ranks him first as an expositor of papal doctrine.

Standing Against "No-Law" Theory

If any one part of the Ten Commandments is ceremonial, as Thomas Aquinas teaches, then the claim that they all are perfect, immutable, and eternal in their binding power upon all men falls to the ground. The celebrated Reformer, Calvin, indignantly refuted the analysis of Thomas Aquinas.[31] The charge made by Thomas Aquinas that the Sabbath commandment was ceremonial is not sustained by changing Saturday to Sunday, for, if definitely naming one particular day of the week is ceremonial, Sunday would be as ceremonial as is Saturday. Nor would the choice of any other succession of days, as one day in ten, or one day in twenty, escape this condemnation. Since the New Testament teaches that the ceremonial law was nailed to the cross, this attempt to make the fourth commandment partly ceremonial, placing it as a plaything in the hands of the church, clearly taught the abolition of the moral law. Herein can be seen how diametrically the above quotation from *The Catholic Encyclopedia* disagrees with Thomas Aquinas. The first says that the Decalogue is moral; the second claims it to be partially ceremonial. Cardinal Newman praised Alexandria, the seat of Gnosticism, which powerful movement rejected the Old Testament and with it the Ten Commandments. Lucian took his stand against such advocates of the "no-law" theory and taught the binding obligation of the Ten Commandments. Therefore he was called a "Judaizer" by John Henry Cardinal Newman.[32]

---

[29] *The Catholic Encyclopedia*, art. "Commandments of God."
[30] Cox, *The Literature of the Sabbath Question*, vol. 1, pp. 370, 371.
[31] *Ibid.*, vol. 1, pages 128, 129.
[32] Newman, *The Arians of the Fourth Century*, pages 10, 11, 14, 27.

Excessive in his denunciations against Lucian, and master of the use of English, Newman, in founding the Oxford Movement, attempted to de-Protestantize the Western world. All must admit the great debating ability of the Oxford professor who left the Church of England to enter the Roman Catholic priesthood. He set out to defend the Alexandrian theologians.[33] He sought diligently to find and substitute another scapegoat. Newman and the Oxford Movement as antagonists labored to brand the Authorized Version of the Bible as dishonest in doctrine.[34] In order to secure a reason for writing his book entitled *The Arians of the Fourth Century,* which volume is practically atheism wearing a gospel mask, he was. compelled to recognize the outstanding leadership of Lucian. So he said, "Now let us advance to the history of this Lucian, a man of learning, and at length a martyr." He neglected, however, to state that for centuries Lucian's orthodoxy has been defended by such great scholars as Caesar Cardinal Baronius, George Bishop Bull, and Henry Melvill Gwatkin. So Newman resurrected against Lucian the old shibboleth of Judaizing. When a modernist is pressed for a weapon to attack defenders of the Ten Commandments, he brings out again the old bogey of Judaizing. What are the historical facts? Newman recognized that the Jews "became an influential political body in the neighborhood of their ancient home, especially in the Syrian provinces which were at that time the chief residence of the court."[35]

However, Newman failed to add the facts admitted by *The Catholic Encyclopedia,* that "for a long time Jews must have formed the vast majority of the members of the infant Church."[36] Since the majority of believers in the East were for a long time Jewish converts, it can easily be seen that the custom was general in the eastern church of observing Saturday as the Sabbath.[37] It could hardly have been otherwise. The noble Christianity of converted Jews was second to none. Centuries of training under the prophets had endowed Jewish believers in Christ with ability to comprehend and to propagate the truths of the Scriptures. They felt, as the heathen world did not, the force of such terms as God, sin, righteousness, and atonement.

---

[33] Cadmus, *The Three Religious Leaders of Oxford,* pages 479, 481.
[34] Jacobus, *Roman Catholic and Protestant Bibles Compared,* page 280.
[35] Newman, *The Arians of the Fourth Century,* pages 7-11.
[36] *The Catholic Encyclopedia,* art. "Calendar."
[37] Cox, *The Literature of the Sabbath Question,* vol. 1, p. 334.

Lucian, though he was a Gentile, is belittled by Cardinal Newman as a Judaizer. Why? Those who sanctified Saturday by abstaining from labor were stigmatized as Judaizers. Why should Lucian observe Saturday as sacred? It was the general custom. The church historian Socrates writes a century after Lucian: "For although almost all churches throughout the world celebrate the sacred mysteries on the Sabbath of every week, yet the Christians of Alexandria and at Rome, on account of some ancient tradition, have ceased to do this."[38] Here we note the union between the church at Rome and at Alexandria, and their common antagonism to the seventh-day Sabbath.

Sozomen, a contemporary of this Socrates, and also a church historian, writes likewise, "The people of Constantinople, and almost everywhere, assemble together on the Sabbath, as well as on the first day of the week, which custom is never observed at Rome or at Alexandria."[39]

At the Synod of Laodicea (c. A. D. 365) the Roman Catholics passed a decree that "Christians must not Judaize by resting on the Sabbath, but must work on that day. . . . But if any shall be found to be Judaizers, let them be anathema from Christ."[40] Thus this church law not only forbade its followers to sanctify Saturday, but also stigmatized as Judaizers those who did.

A long list of early church writers could be given to show that for centuries the Christian churches generally observed Saturday for the Sabbath and rested from labor on that day. Many churches also celebrated the day of Christ's resurrection by having a religious meeting on Sunday, but they did not recognize that day as the holy day of the fourth commandment.[41]

The churches throughout the world were almost universally patterned after the church of Jerusalem in belief and practice. "It is true that the Antiochene liturgy describes Jerusalem 'as the mother of all churches.' "[42] Paul wrote, "Ye, brethren, became fol-

---

[38] Socrates, *Ecclesiastical History*, b. 5, ch. 22, found in *Nicene and Post-Nicene Fathers*.

[39] Sozomen, *Ecclesiastical History*, b. 7, ch. 19, found in *Nicene and Post-Nicene Fathers*.

[40] Council of Laodicea, Canon 29, Scribner's *Nicene and Post-Nicene Fathers*, 2d Series, vol. 14, p. 148.

[41] See Augustine, Ambrose, Chrysostom, Gregory of Nyssa, Asterius, Gregory of Caesarea, Origen, Cassian, etc.

[42] O'Leary, *The Syriac Church and Fathers*, page 27.

lowers of the churches of God which in Judea are in Christ Jesus."[43]
The apostle Paul, therefore, is the author of the Judean pattern.
How long did this pattern continue? The quotation given above from
The Catholic Encyclopedia, article, "Calendar," reveals that vast
numbers, not a scattered few, of Christians were converts from the
Jews, so that the Judean type of Christianity was almost universal,
and it so continued for a long time.

Syria, the land of Lucian, possessed the Judean type of Christianity. "They [the books DeLacy O'Leary was describing] certainly
do prove the continued and vigorous existence of a Judaistic Christianity within the province of Syria."[44]

Judean Christianity prevailed so widely that it reached far into
Africa, even into Abyssinia. The church in Abyssinia was a great
missionary church. Neither must we forget that the Abyssinian
Church [which is distinctively of Judaic-Christian type] became popular in the fourth century. In the last half of that century St. Ambrose
of Milan stated officially that the Abyssinian bishop, Museus, had
"traveled almost everywhere in the country of the Seres" [China].[45]
For more than seventeen centuries the Abyssinian Church continued
to sanctify Saturday as the holy day of the fourth commandment.

As early as the second century, Judean Christianity in Syria produced scholars famous in Bible manuscripts. "The work of Malchion
is generally regarded as commencing the 'Early School' of Antioch.
. . . The actual leader in the critical work was Lucian who came from
Edessa and was Malchion's pupil. . . . The result was an Antiochene
revised Greek text of both Testaments."[46] Lucian and his school,
like Origen, worked in the field of textual criticism, but he used different manuscripts from those used by Origen. Erasmus rejected
the manuscripts of Origen, as did Lucian.[47]

Lucian prevailed over Origen, especially in the East. "The Bibles
produced by the Syrian scribes presented the Syrian text of the school
of Antioch, and this text became the form which displaced all others
in the Eastern churches and is, indeed, the Textus Receptus (Re-

---

[43] 1 Thessalonians 2:14.
[44] O'Leary, *The Syriac Church and Fathers,* page 28.
[45] Ambrose, De Moribus, *Brachmanorium Opera Omnia,* found in Migne, *Patrologia Latina,* vol. 17, pp. 1131, 1132.
[46] O'Leary, *The Syriac Church and Fathers,* page 44.
[47] Nolan, *The Integrity of the Greek Vulgate,* pages 413-416.

ceived Text) from which our Authorized Version· is translated."[48]

Before his death Lucian was acknowledged throughout all Christendom as orthodox from the standpoint of the Bible, and a fundamentalist. It remained for Cardinal Newman to resurrect the calumny of Judaizing against him fifteen hundred years later.

A brief summary of the theological conditions which prevailed in the days of Lucian, and a review of his work and influence, is now presented.

I
THEOLOGY

The school at Antioch, founded by Lucian, developed a system of theology, so real that though all the power of the papacy was thrown against it, it finally prevailed.

The papacy also developed a great system of theology which was challenged both by the Church in the Wilderness and by the Reformation.

II
QUALITY NOT QUANTITY

The Antioch system of theology which we have been studying was prominent; it extended from England to China and from Turkestan to Ethiopia.

Papal theology was also prominent. It is not necessary to indicate the dominating course it has had throughout the earth. Yet numbers do not constitute the final proof of truth. As an example, more millions of people in the world follow Buddha than follow any other religion.

III
THE GENUINE BIBLE

Lucian and his school produced and edited a definite and complete Bible. It was a collection of the books from Genesis to Revelation. Well-known writers like Jerome, Erasmus, and Luther, and, in the nineteenth century, John William Burgon and Fenton John Anthony Hort, whether friends or opponents, agree that Lucian was the editor who passed on to the world the Received Text—the New Testament text which was adopted at the birth of all the great churches of the Reformation. Not a single church born of the Reformation, such as Lutheran, Calvinistic, Anglican, Baptist, Presbyterian, Methodist, Congregational, or Adventist, adopted any other Bible than that whose New Testament text came down from Lucian.

---

[48] O'Leary, *The Syriac Church and Fathers,* page 49.

The papacy passed on to the world an indefinite and incomplete Bible. While it recognized to a certain extent the books from Genesis to Revelation, it added to them seven other books not considered canonical by the authorities quoted above. In the Latin Vulgate of the papacy it adopted a New Testament text with passages radically different from the same in the Received Text. It also made the decrees of the councils and the bulls of the popes equal to the books of the Bible. In other words, with the Roman Catholic Church, the Scriptures are still in the making. The papacy exalts the church above the Bible. Cardinal Gibbons says, "The Scriptures alone do not contain all the truths which a Christian is bound to believe."[49]

IV
MANUSCRIPTS TRUE AND FALSE

The text which Lucian gave to the world was to all intents pure and correct.[50] Even his opponents declare that there are no Greek New Testaments older than Lucian's, and that with it agree the great mass of Greek manuscripts.[51]

The Roman Catholic text of the regular books from Genesis to Revelation and the seven apocryphal books based upon the manuscripts of Origen —later edited by Jerome—abounded in errors. Thousands of these errors have been noted and presented to the world by eminent Catholic and non-Catholic writers. Catholics admit that Jerome was a polemic theologian and that he allowed his prejudices to warp his translation.[52]

V
RELATION TO THE LAW OF GOD

The theology of Antioch stood for the binding obligation of the Ten Commandments.

The theology of the papacy claims authority to change the Ten Commandments.

VI
CHRIST OUR SUBSTITUTE AND SURETY

The theology of Antioch teaches salvation for sinful man through the substitutionary death of Christ on the cross.

The papacy does not now teach and never has taught salvation for sinful man through the substitutionary death of Christ on the cross. *The Catholic Encyclopedia* states, " 'Vicarious satisfaction,' a term now in

---

[49] Gibbons, *The Faith of Our Fathers,* p. 111, 63d ed; p. 86, 76th ed.
[50] Nolan, *The Integrity of the Greek Vulgate,* pages 125, 126.
[51] *On the Revisers and the Greek Text,* pages 11, 12.
[52] Jacobus, *Roman Catholic and Protestant Bibles Compared,* page 42.

vogue, is not found expressly in the church formularies, and is not an adequate expression of Christ's mediation."[53]

VII
THE SABBATH

The majority of the churches of Syria and of the East continued to observe Saturday, the Sabbath of the fourth commandment from the days of the apostles and throughout the centuries. Hence the attempt to stigmatize them as Judaizers.

The papacy has always endeavored to substitute the observance of Sunday for the sanctification of Saturday, the Sabbath of the fourth commandment. Pope Gregory I, in 603, declared that when antichrist should come, he would keep Saturday as the Sabbath.[54]

VIII
NO UNION OF CHURCH AND STATE

The church organization developed by the apostles and continued largely by Syrian theology was simple and evangelical. Fundamentally, it rejected the union of church and state.

The church organization developed by the papacy is hierarchal. Throughout its history it has believed in the union of church and state.

Lucian died before Constantine had consummated the union of the church with the state. Lucian's teaching, however, lived on to plague imperial Christianity. The heritage he left behind became embosomed in the Church in the Wilderness. As late as the fifteenth century the Catholic clergy displayed a bitter hatred to Greek learning.[55] The knowledge of Greek, however, remained in the bosom of the Church in the Wilderness whether in Syria, northern Italy, among the Celts, or in Oriental lands. And wherever the true faith was held, the New Testament, verified and transmitted by Lucian, was venerated and followed.

Conditions continued thus until the dawn of the Reformation under Luther. The papacy waxed more powerful and more autocratic. The churches remaining true to New Testament Christianity became

---

[53] *The Catholic Encyclopedia,* art. "Mediator." J. E. Canavan, in *The Mystery of the Incarnation,* page 19, says: "The common Catholic theory is that Christ redeemed us, not by standing in our place, not by substituting Himself for us, but by offering to God a work which pleased Him far more than sin displeased Him." See also M'Clintock and Strong, *Cyclopedia,* art. "Christology."

[54] *Epistles* of Gregory I, b. 13, epistle 1, found in *Nicene and Post-Nicene Fathers.*

[55] Fitzpatrick, *Ireland and the Foundations of Europe,* page 161; Draper, *History of the Intellectual Development of Europe,* page 469.

more and more sure of their ground, following the leadership of Lucian. Finally, when the great Reformation began, almost the first thing they did was to reach out, seize, and place at the foundation of the Reformed Church the Greek New Testament of Lucian. On the other hand, the first four decisions of the Council of Trent—the first Catholic world council after the powerful beginnings of the Reformation— condemned Lucian's text and insisted on Jerome's Vulgate. It is true that the Reformation leaders did not part with all the teaching of the papacy subsequently deemed by Protestant bodies as unscriptural, namely: the union of church and state, ceremonialism, hierarchal organization, etc. Protestantism should have gone forward in its reforms until it had returned to the purity of the Church in the Wilderness.

Lucian by his life and by his opposition to Alexandrian errors showed that he would never accept any doctrines of the Trinity which destroyed the moral obligation of the Ten Commandments; that he refused any teaching which exalted the inspiration of the church above the inspiration of the Bible, and that he did not countenance any authority which divided the Decalogue into moral and ceremonial, is proved by his writings.

Lucian is one of those world characters who needs no sculptor to erect a monument to his fame. The transmission of the Received Text with its unparalleled effects down through the centuries is monument enough. Another monument is the influence of Lucian in the great Church of the East, as reproduced in its evangelical thought and life. In its history will be seen the hand of God, building a sure foundation for the divine truths that shall live in the long wilderness period of the church.

CHAPTER VI

Vigilantius, Leader of the Waldenses

*The paganism which so soon began to avenge itself by
creeping into the doctrines and practices of the early church
has never been altogether eradicated, and has always been
ready to become the nucleus of heresy or corruption when
faith declined or ardor cooled.*[1]

THE earliest leader of prominence among the noble Waldenses in
northern Italy and southern France is Vigilantius (A. D. 364-408).
By some he has been accounted the first supreme director of the
Church of the Waldenses.[2] In his time the protests against the introduction of pagan practices into primitive Christianity swelled into
a revolution. Then it was that the throngs who desired to maintain
the faith once delivered to the saints in northern Italy and southwestern France were welded into an organized system. Desiring truth
based on the Bible only, those who refused to follow the superstitious
novelties being brought into the church were greatly influenced by
the clear-cut scriptural teachings of Vigilantius. Undoubtedly Patrick
of Ireland, who was at that same time enlarging the Irish Church, was
profoundly stirred by this great reformer of south central Europe.

Vigilantius was born in southern France near the Pyrenees Mountains.[3] His father was the proprietor of a relay post, a "mansio," one
of those many traveling stations throughout the Roman Empire. The
early home of the reformer was a relay center where change of horses
could be secured for travelers who, perchance, were merchants, ambassadors, illustrious personages, bishops, ordinary tourists, or imperial couriers. The business offered to the growing youth abundant
opportunity to obtain information on all topics from those who tarried
at his father's mountain abode.

---

[1] Muir, *The Arrested Reformation,* p. 13.

[2] Faber, *The Ancient Vallenses and Albigenses,* pages 275-279.

[3] Jerome, *Against Vigilantius,* found in *Nicene and Post-Nicene Fathers,* 2d Series,
vol. 6, p. 418. Jerome here states that Vigilantius was born in Convenae, southern
Gaul. This city bore also the name Lyons, whose pronunciation is like the English
word Leo. Obviously, therefore, he would be called Vigilantius the Leonist. The
Waldenses are often also called Leonists. It has been concluded, therefore, that the
appellation "Leonists" is derived from Vigilantius.

As Vigilantius ranged through the solitudes tending the flocks, pursuing the chase, or guiding travelers through the mountain defiles, he increased in stature and wisdom. Sometime while in contact with Christian travelers he accepted Christ as his Saviour. Near by were the estates of the famous historian Sulpicius Severus. This renowned writer was the idol of the learned class. In his mansion he was at some time host for practically all the distinguished men of his day. He invited Vigilantius to enter his employ, first probably in ordinary service, but later as the collector of rents and the manager of his estates.

While Vigilantius was employed in the services of this historian, a great change came over Sulpicius Severus. He was carried off his feet by the wave of asceticism and monasticism which was sweeping westward. Vigilantius early learned to love his employer. He admired greatly the brilliant intellect of this man who could feed the hungry, clothe the poor, and visit the sick, while engaged in many literary labors.

The Struggle Against Monasticism

Now, not far to the north dwelt Martin, bishop of Tours. Near the banks of the Loire River this prelate had founded the first monastery in France. The extreme austerities of asceticism to which he had subjected himself, coupled with the flaming reports of his so-called miracles, enabled him to set loose in the west the passion for monastic life. Sulpicius Severus, accompanied by Vigilantius, his Celtic financier, set out to visit Martin. That conference produced a profound change in the life of both Sulpicius and Vigilantius, but in opposite directions. The fanaticism of Martin, bishop of Tours, drew Sulpicius and his brilliant talents into the monastic life.

Such were the scenes related to Vigilantius by Sulpicius, if not actually witnessed by him; and he could not remain blind to the fact that his patron was neither happier not better for his visit to the bishop of Tours. After his return home, the image of Martin haunted the sensitive historian: he was pursued by the recollection of the ascetic prelate sleeping on the cold earth, with nothing but ashes strewed beneath him, and covered with sackcloth only; refusing a softer bed, or warmer clothing, even in severe illness; declaring that a Christian ought to die on ashes; feeding on the most unwholesome food, and denying himself every indulgence; praying in the most irksome posture, forcing sleep from his eyes, and exposing himself to the extremes of heat and cold, hunger and thirst. The imagination of

Sulpicius dwelt on what he had seen and heard at Marmoutier, until he believed that heaven would be closed upon him, unless he should practice the same austerities.[4]

The love of the marvelous, the habit of dwelling upon tales of wonders and of practicing ascetic austerities, had seized the employer of Vigilantius. On the other hand, Vigilantius saw in the system a form of religion without the simplicity of the gospel of Christ.

Thus Vigilantius saw on one side vainglorious exaltation, spiritual pride, and pretension to miraculous power; and on the other side, a false humility and prostration of the understanding, both growing out of the same mistaken system of asceticism: a system which undermined the doctrine of Christ's full and sufficient sacrifice, and assigned an undue value to the inflictions and performances of men like Martin of Tours: and which he probably foresaw would in the end elevate them in the minds of weak brethren, to mediatorial thrones, and render them little less than objects of divine worship. Consequently we must attribute to impressions first received in the household of Sulpicius, the efforts, which Vigilantius afterwards made, to expose the errors of asceticism, and to check the progress of hagiolatry.[5]

The gulf between Vigilantius and Sulpicius which was formed by their visit to Martin was widened when Sulpicius employed him as the messenger to Paulinus of Nola, Italy. This excellent man had also gone to a retreat where he could give his time "to those beguiling practices, which afterwards became the characteristics of the Latin Church; and proved so fatal in the end to the simplicity of the gospel. . . . Religious observances, transferred from pagan altars to Christian shrines, were dignified with the name of honors due to the memory of a departed saint: and as the heroes of old were invoked by the ancestors of Paulinus, so did he himself substitute the name of Felix for that of Hercules or Quirinus, and implore the aid of a dead martyr, when no other name in prayer ought to have been upon his lips, than that of the one Mediator between God and man."[6] Furthermore we are told that Pope Gelasius, in the fifth century, introduced into the West the Purification festival, coupled with a Procession of Lights, to supplement the heathen feast Lupercalia.[7]

---

[4] Gilly, *Vigilantius and His Times,* pages 161, 162.
[5] *Ibid.,* pages 163, 164.
[6] *Ibid.,* pages 169, 170.
[7] Gordon, *"World Healers,"* page 469, note 3.

What must have been the effect upon our simple mountaineer when he beheld in Italy gorgeous shrines erected to commemorate a hermit? Through divine grace Vigilantius escaped the infatuation which descends almost irresistibly upon those who yield themselves to practices designed to supplant the simplicity of the gospel.

The age of the apostles faded away into the age of the church fathers. Learning and argument were used to prove the verities of the gospel rather than the words "which the Holy Ghost teacheth."[8] This was especially true of Europe and Africa.

Revolt Against Asceticism and Monasticism

As if the ransom of the Redeemer was not sufficient without their own sufferings, those who practiced asceticism imposed appalling torments upon themselves. They undermined the doctrine of Christ's full and sufficient atonement for sin. Processions were formed, relics displayed, and incense burned before the tomb of some exalted ascetic.

Monasticism followed on the heels of asceticism. Justin Martyr (A. D. 150) was prominent among the early apostates because of his perverted teachings.[9] He was followed by his pupil Tatian, who in turn taught Clement (A. D. 190), a founder of the ecclesiastical school at Alexandria. Clement declared he would hand down the gospel mixed with heathen philosophy. But it remained for Origen, Clement's pupil, who mutilated himself, to start the glorification of celibacy.

Monasticism is not a product of Christianity. It was imported from non-Christian religions. Christianity saw it first introduced into Egypt, evidently coming from Buddhism. There were two classes of monks. The first, the anchorites, sought to live alone in the gloomiest and wildest spots in the wilderness. The second class, monks, evading the solitary life, gathered into communities called monasteries. Refusing obedience to any spiritual superior except the supreme head of the church, they placed at the command of the papacy a vast mobile army of men not responsible to any congregation. Let it be remembered that the Bible training schools of Celtic and Syrian Christianity were not monasteries of this kind, although there are writers who would have it so. The inmates of the monasteries had a different pro-

---

[8] 1 Corinthians 2:13.
[9] Schaff, *History of the Christian Church*, vol. 2, 2d Period, par. 173, pp. 719-723.

gram from the Bible training schools, whose pupils were there, not for life, but for a period of training, as the youth of today leaves home for four years in college.

The monks at certain times had pageantries, prostrations, and genuflexions. All these externals were symptoms of a growing ecclesiastical system, and they helped prepare the way for the union of the papal church with the state. Nevertheless, these and other departures from New Testament Christianity stirred deeply in all lands those who were to become leaders against the new perversions and who would demand a return "to the law and to the testimony."[10]

The Forerunners of Vigilantius

The splendid city of Milan, in northern Italy, was the connecting link between Celtic Christianity in the West and Syrian Christianity in the East.[11] The missionaries from the early churches in Judea and Syria securely stamped upon the region around Milan the simple and apostolic religion. Milan was the rendezvous of numerous councils of clergy from the East, so that the early liturgies of Antioch, Milan, and Gaul were practically identical.[12] It is impossible to find a time throughout the centuries when there was not opposition in northern Italy to the Roman hierarchy, sometimes great, sometimes small, but always evangelical. Dr. Allix states this fact thus:

> To this purpose it will be of use to set forth as well the constitution of the church, as the manner in which the diocese of Milan did continue independent until the midst of the eleventh century, at which time the Waldenses were obliged more openly to testify their aversion for the Church of Rome as an anti-Christian church. It will be easy enough for me to perform what I have proposed to myself, in following the history of the church. Before the Council of Nicaea, we find the diocese of Italy very distinct from that of Rome.[13]

Dr. Faber presents, in the following words, one way in which this gulf between the churches of the Milan district and Rome originated:

> Now this district, on the eastern side of the Cottian Alps, is the precise country of the Vallenses [Waldenses]. *Hither* their ancestors retired,

---

[10] Isaiah 8:20.
[11] Gordon, *"World Healers,"* pages 237, 238.
[12] *Ibid.*, pages 210, 211.
[13] Allix, *The Ancient Churches of Piedmont,* page 109.

during the persecutions of the second and third and fourth centuries: *here,* providentially secluded from the world, they retained the precise doctrines and practices of the primitive church endeared to them by suffering and exile; while the wealthy inhabitants of cities and fertile plains, corrupted by a now opulent and gorgeous and powerful clergy, were daily sinking deeper and deeper into that apostasy which has been so graphically foretold by the great apostle.[14]

Opponents of Pagan Practices

First among those who protested against heathen practices in the church was Helvidius I (A. D. 300-360). It is interesting to note that three of the outstanding opponents of the papal innovations in Latin Christianity were from northern Italy. These were Helvidius, Jovinian, and Vigilantius. As for Helvidius, all that was written by him and for him has been destroyed. Though he lived a century and a half after Justin Martyr and more than a century after Tertullian, Cyprian, Origen, and Clement, their writings have been preserved, while his were destroyed. Helvidius belonged to the church which strove to hand down the doctrines of the Bible in the pure form. He is famous for his exposure of Jerome for using corrupted Greek manuscripts in bringing out the Vulgate, the Latin Bible of the papacy. If the thunders of Jerome had not been turned against Helvidius, we would know less concerning him.

"Helvidius, a so-called heresiarch of the fourth century, a layman who opposed the growing superstitions of the church. . . . He was a pupil of Auxentius, bishop of Milan, and the precursor of Jovinian."[15] Duchesne points out that Auxentius, for twenty years at the head of

---

[14] Faber, *The Ancient Vallenses and Albigenses,* pages 293, 294.

[15] M'Clintock and Strong, *Cyclopedia,* art. "Helvidius." The statement that Helvidius was the pupil of Auxentius opens up wide considerations, when we remember that Ambrose was the successor of Auxentius in the bishopric of Milan. Ambrose sanctified the seventh day as the Sabbath (as he himself says). Ambrose had great influence in Spain, which was also observing the Saturday Sabbath, as we show later. It was Ambrose who recorded with rejoicing the supervising trip of of the illustrious leader of Abyssinia, Bishop Musaen (and Abyssinia observed the Sabbath for seventeen hundred years) who toured the churches of India and China. Since Helvidius and Vigilantius were practically contemporaneous and preachers of the same message, it is safe to conclude that Auxentius, Ambrose, Helvidius, and Vigilantius were Sabbathkeepers. These facts link together Spain, northern Italy, Abyssinia, India, central Asia, and China in Sabbathkeeping. All the foregoing events transpired close to A. D. 400. It is interesting to note that Pope Innocent I, within fifteen years after this date, passed a law which required fasting on Saturday in order to brand its sacredness with austerity instead of joy.

the diocese of Milan, was from Asia Minor and impressed on those regions the Syrian leadership in Christianity. Daring in his scholarship, Helvidius accused Jerome, as Jerome himself admits, of using corrupt Greek manuscripts.[16]

> That part of the ecclesiastical system of the fourth century, which was peculiarly ascetic and rigid, found an impersonation in Jerome, who exhibited its worst and most repulsive traits in the whole tenor of his life and conversation. Sourness, bitterness, envy, intolerance, and dissatisfaction with every manifestation of sanctity which did not come up to his own standard, had become habitual to him, and were betrayed in almost everything that he wrote, said, or did. Censoriousness, and the spirit of invective, were amongst his most strongly marked failings, and the very best men of the age did not escape his censure.[17]

The second renowned reformer in north Italy and forerunner of Vigilantius was Jovinian (A. D. 330-390). He was so superior in scholarship that the united attempts of such learned advocates of the papacy as Jerome, Augustine, and Ambrose failed to overthrow his scriptural and historical arguments.[18] Of him Albert H. Newman says:

> That the protest of Jovinianus awakened great interest and received influential support is evident from the excited polemics of Jerome, and from the public proceedings that were instituted against him in Rome and Milan. . . . The persistence of the influence of Jovinianus is seen in the movement led by Vigilantius. *It is not unlikely that followers of Jovinianus took refuge in the Alpine valleys, and there kept alive the evangelical teaching that was to reappear with vigor in the twelfth century.*[19]

Beuzart relates how a learned French historian speaks of the relentless persecution carried on as late as 1215 by monks against so-called heretics named Jovinianists, Patarines, and Albigenses.[20]

Jovinian drew the wrath of Jerome because he taught that the lives of married people, all other things being equal, are fully as acceptable in the sight of God as those who are not married; that eating with thanksgiving is as commendable with God as abstemiousness; and that all who are faithful to their baptismal vows will be equally rewarded at the day of judgment. Because of this, Jerome

---

[16] Jerome, *Against Helvidius*, found in *Nicene and Post-Nicene Fathers*, 2d Series, vol. 6, p. 338.
[17] Gilly, *Vigilantius and His Times*, page 246.
[18] M'Clintock and Strong, *Cyclopedia*, art. "Jovinian."
[19] Newman, *A Manual of Church History*, vol. 1, p. 376.
[20] Beuzart, *Les Heresies*, page 470.

said that Jovinian had "the hissing of the old serpent," "nauseating trash," and "the devil's poisonous concoction."[21]

Vigilantius was convinced that the new system of austerities, processions, and sacraments did not result in making men pre-eminently happy and holy. Vigilantius witnessed too many of the ecclesiastical riots of the day.

> When Damasus was elected pope, A. D. 366, the dissensions in Rome were so violent that the gates of the basilica, where his rival was consecrated, were broken open, the roof was torn off, the building was set on fire, and one hundred and thirty-seven persons were killed.[22]

Similar ecclesiastical riots were seen at this time in Palestine. Jerome, in one of his epistles, declares that their private quarrels were as furious as were those of the barbarians.

What Caused the Rupture Between Vigilantius and Rome?

When Vigilantius returned to Sulpicius, his employer, he stood at the parting of the ways. On the one hand there was Martin, bishop of Tours, rushing from cave to cell in the excitement of supposed miracles; there was Sulpicius, turning from sound scholarship to fables and visions; and the gentle Paulinus of Nola was groveling before the image of a favorite saint—the victim of delusions. On the other hand, there was Helvidius challenging the corrupt manuscripts in the hands of Jerome, the bishop of Rome, and their followers; there was the great leader Jovinian defending gospel simplicity and a married clergy. The event which decided Vigilantius was his visit to Jerome.

By this time the Goths, Celts, and Franks had forgotten their days of invasion and their religious differences, and were being united by the invisible bonds of community life. They prized their Latin Bible (not the Latin Bible of Jerome), generally called the *Itala,* "because it was read publicly in all the churches of Italy, France, Spain, Africa, and Germany, where Latin was understood; and Vetus, on account of its being more ancient than any of the rest."[23] To supplant this noble version, Jerome, at the request of the pope and with

---

[21] Jerome, *Against Jovinian,* found in *Nicene and Post-Nicene Fathers,* 2d Series, vol. 6, p. 348.

[22] Gilly, *Vigilantius and His Times,* page 99.

[23] *Ibid.,* page 116.

money furnished by him, brought out a new Latin Bible. He was looked up to by the imperial church as the oracle of his age. Vigilantius having inherited his father's wealth and desiring to consult Jerome, determined to visit him in his cell at Bethlehem. He went by way of Italy, paying a second visit to Paulinus. While he was there, processions to the tomb of the saint were made, accompanied by the swinging of incense and the carrying of lighted tapers; but Vigilantius said nothing. The gentle manners of Sulpicius and Paulinus coupled with their meek devotion softened their delusions. When, however, he encountered the fierce polemics of Jerome, the eyes of the Gallic reformer were opened.

> Vigilantius, A. D. 396, was the bearer of a letter from Paulinus to Jerome, and this was the introduction which made him personally acquainted with the most extraordinary man of that age. Jerome was the terror of his contemporaries; the man above all others, who, in a mistaken attempt to do his duty to God, failed most signally in his duty towards men, unmindful of the apostle's words, 'If a man say, I love God, and hateth his brother, he is a liar,' etc. The mortification of the flesh had tended to puff up his spirit, and of all the polemical writers of the fourth century, he was the most bitter and severe.[24]

The first meeting of Vigilantius with Jerome at Bethlehem is described in this language:

> A narrow bypath leading off from the street, at the spot where the tomb of King Archelaus formerly stood, conducted the traveler to the cell of Jerome; here he found the ascetic clad in a vestment so coarse and sordid, that its very vileness bore the stamp of spiritual pride, and seemed to say, 'Stand off, my wearer is holier than thou.' The face of the monk was pale and haggard. He had been slowly recovering from a severe illness, and was wasted to a shadow. Frequent tears had plowed his cheeks with deep furrows; his eyes were sunk in their sockets; all the bones of his face were sharp and projecting. Long fasting, habitual mortification, and the chagrin which perpetual disputation occasions, had given an air of gloominess to his countenance, which accorded but ill with his boast, that his cell to him was like an arbor in the Garden of Eden.[25]

Vigilantius was at first warmly received by Jerome. The scenes at Bethlehem were the same as he had witnessed on the estates of

---

[24] Gilly, *Vigilantius and His Times*, page 231. When the writer visited the reputed cell of Jerome at Bethlehem it was thronged with monks who were devoting their lives to tending that shrine.

[25] *Ibid.*, pages 236, 237.

his friends who had been drawn into the tide of asceticism. The sourness of temper and the fierce invectives of the editor of the Vulgate began to raise doubt in the mind of Vigilantius, however, as to the value of the whole system. The Gallic presbyter was especially incensed at Jerome's criticism of Paulinus; but it was when Jerome turned fiercely upon Rufinus, his former friend, that the break between Vigilantius and Jerome took place.

Vigilantius left Bethlehem to visit Rufinus at Jerusalem. There was nothing in the life and atmosphere of that ancient city to encourage the visitor from southern France. He learned enough from his interview with Rufinus to recoil from Jerome's leadership and to discover the first protest arising in his heart against the new system of asceticism and monasticism. He returned from Jerusalem to Bethlehem fully determined to protest against the unchristian vagaries of the monk whom few dared to oppose. As a result of this encounter, Vigilantius resolved to quit for good the contentious successors of the Alexandrian school, because of their loose theology and because they associated with the swarms of Egyptian monks. He determined to raise his voice in defense of the gospel's primitive simplicity.

Another incident occurred to strengthen his resolution. He revisited Nola, Italy, returning by way of Egypt. One can imagine his indignation when he learned that Jerome was not satisfied with all the humiliations and sufferings Paulinus had undergone to conform to asceticism, but had written a taunting demand that his friend surrender all his wealth immediately.

Then Vigilantius decided to break the silence. How and where and against what, we learn from Jerome's reply to Reparius, a priest of southern France, to whom, about A. D. 404, Jerome wrote the following concerning Vigilantius:

> I have myself before now seen the monster, and have done my best to bind the maniac with texts of Scripture, as Hippocrates binds his patients with chains; but "he went away, he departed, he escaped, he broke out," and taking refuge between the Adriatic and the Alps of King Cotius, declaimed in his turn against me.[26]

In the Cottian Alps, in that region lying between the Alps and the Adriatic Sea, Vigilantius first began public efforts to stop the pagan

---

[26] Jerome, *Select Works and Letters*, Letter 109, found in *Nicene and Post-Nicene Fathers*, 2d Series, vol. 6, p. 213.

ceremonies that were being baptized into the church. Why did he choose that region? Because there he found himself among people who adhered to the teachings of the Scriptures. They had removed to those valleys to escape the armies of Rome. "He was perhaps aware that he would find in the Cottian Alps a race of people, who were opposed to those notions of celibacy and vows of continence, which formed the favorite dogma of Jerome, and were at the bottom of all his ascetic austerities." [27]

How fruitful were the endeavors of Vigilantius, may be seen in the following, taken from another letter of Jerome to Reparius: "Shameful to relate, there are bishops who are said to be associated with him in his wickedness—if at least they are to be called bishops —who ordain no deacons but such as have been previously married." [28] It is not known whether the bishops who were agreeing with Vigilantius in his crusade against the semipagan Christianity of his day were on the Italian or the French side of the Alps. It mattered little as far as Jerome was concerned, since the preaching of Vigilantius on both sides of these mountains produced the thundering denunciations of Jerome, the great champion of the state church, that were heard all the way across the Mediterranean from Bethlehem. Thus the new mission of Vigilantius had created a cleavage between those who elected to walk in the apostolic way and those who gave church "development" as their reason for adding pagan ceremonies to the glamour of state gorgeousness.

The New Organization of Free Churches

The Alpine churches of France and Italy were not swept into the new hysteria. They welcomed Vigilantius with open arms, and his preaching was powerful. "He makes his raid upon the churches of Gaul," cried out Jerome. Those in the south of France who desired the new teachings appealed to Jerome to defend the innovations against the attacks of Vigilantius. Jerome's reply, addressed to Reparius, reveals what doctrines and practices the Gallic reformer was denouncing—church celibacy, worship of relics, lighted tapers, all-night vigils, and prayers to the dead.

---

[27] Gilly, *Vigilantius and His Times,* page 323.
[28] Jerome, *Against Vigilantius,* Introduction, found in *Nicene and Post-Nicene Fathers,* 2d Series, vol. 6, p. 417.

Again and again Jerome begged to have sent to him the book which Vigilantius wrote. The historian Milner has exclaimed, "For a single page of Jovinian or Vigilantius I would gladly give up the whole invectives of Jerome."[29] The new leader of the churches which had not united with the state spent his fortune in collecting manuscripts, circulating the Scriptures, and employing amanuenses to write pamphlets, tracts, and books. Jerome demanded that he be delivered over to the state for banishment or death; and as historians and the decrees of popes point out, the state church, when seeking the life of opponents, turned them over to the secular tribunal for punishment.[30] This was done in order to disguise their crime.[31] "The wretch's tongue should be cut out, or he should be put under treatment for insanity," wrote Jerome. Thus the ecclesiastical leaders, supported by state police power, were abandoning the persuasion of love for the brutal argument of force.

In spite of all this, those in the regions under consideration were determined to follow the Bible only. They were growing in strength, and were coming closer together. Under the impetus of the campaigns of Vigilantius, a new organization was being created, destined to persist through the coming centuries. Vigilantius had prepared himself for this throughout the years by giving days and nights to study and research. It is a regrettable fact that none of his writings have been preserved.

How demoralizing the influence of the monastic hysteria was may be seen in the transformation wrought in Augustine (A. D. 354-430). This renowned writer of the church (probably of all Catholic Fathers, the most adored by the papacy) was forced by the popular pressure into the views of Jerome, and was in correspondence with him. His complete surrender to the policy of persecution is given at length by Limborch.[32] Augustine, from his episcopal throne in north Africa, gave to the papacy a deadly weapon; he invented the monstrous doctrine of "Compel them to come in." Thus he laid the foundation for the Inquisition. Intoxicated with Greek philosophy, he cried out that its spirit filled his soul with incredible fire.[33] He had wandered

---

[29] Milner, *History of the Church of Christ*, vol. 1, p. 456, ed. 1835.
[30] Mansi, *Sacrorum Conciliorum Nova et Amplissima Collectio*, vol. 23, p. 73.
[31] Tillemont, le Nain de, *Memoires*, vol. 10, p. 326.
[32] Limborch, *The History of the Inquisition*, vol. 1, ch. 6, pp. 30-33.
[33] Schaff, *History of the Christian Church*, 2d Period, vol. 2, par. 173, pp. 724, 725.

nine long years in Manichaeism, which taught the union of church and state and exalted the observance of the first day of the week.[34] Augustine found many reasons why the doctrines and practices of the church should be enforced by the sword.[35] The doctrine "Compel them to come in," sent countless millions to death for no greater crime than refusing to believe in the forms of ecclesiastical worship enforced by the state. Such was the atmosphere of the age in which Vigilantius ministered.

In his day another controversy existed which was to rock the Christian world. Milan, center of northern Italy, as well as all the Eastern churches, was sanctifying the seventh-day Sabbath, while Rome was requiring its followers to fast on that day in an effort to discredit it. Interesting pictures of the conflict are given by an eminent scholar and writer, Dr. Peter Heylyn.[36] Ambrose, the celebrated bishop of Milan, and Augustine, the more celebrated bishop of Africa, both contemporaries of Vigilantius, described the interesting situation. Ambrose said that when he was in Milan he observed Saturday, but when in Rome he fasted on Saturday and observed Sunday. This gave rise to the proverb, "When you are in Rome, do as Rome does." Augustine deplored the fact that in two neighboring churches in Africa, one observed the seventh-day Sabbath, another fasted on it.[37]

Vigilantius has been called "the Forerunner of the Reformation," "one of the earliest of our Protestant forefathers."[38] Although the practices against which he inveighed continued for hundreds of years, yet the influence of his preaching and leadership among the Waldenses[39] burned its way across the centuries until it united with the heroic reforms of Luther. As the papacy promoted persecutions from time to time against the Waldenses, it proclaimed the "heresy" of these regions as being the same brand as that of Vigilantius. Two centuries later medieval writers leveled their attacks against Claude, bishop of Milan, and against his followers on the basis that he was infected with

---

[34] Milman, *The History of Christianity*, vol. 2, pp. 270-275.

[35] Ruffini, *Religious Liberty*, pages 26, 27.

[36] Heylyn who, in 1612, wrote *The History of the Sabbath* to expose the Puritans' false claims for Sunday.

[37] Heylyn, *The History of the Sabbath*, in *Historical and Miscellaneous Tracts*, page 416.

[38] Gilly, *Vigilantius and His Times*, page 12.

[39] Faber, *The Ancient Vallenses and Albigenses*, pages 275-279.

the "poison" of Vigilantius.[40] From the days of the Gallic reformer on, multiplied churches of northern Italy and southern France bore an entirely different color from that which rested upon legal ecclesiasticism. Thus, Vigilantius, in southern Europe, like his contemporary, Patrick, of Ireland, can be counted as being one of the early bright stars of the Church in the Wilderness.

---

[40] *Maxima Bibliotheca Veterum Patrum,* vol. 14, pp. 201-216.

CHAPTER VII

Patrick, Organizer of the Church in the Wilderness in Ireland

From all that can be learned of him (Patrick), there never was a nobler Christian missionary. . . . He went to Ireland from love to Christ, and love to the souls of men. . . . Strange that a people who owed Rome nothing in connection with their conversion to Christ, and who long struggled against her pretensions, should be now ranked among her most devoted adherents.[1]

THE heroic figure of Patrick, taken captive as a boy into slavery, stands out as a creator of civilization. He was not only an architect of European society and the father of Irish Christianity, but he raised up a standard against spiritual wolves entering the fold in sheep's clothing. So much legend and fiction has been written about him that one is almost led to believe that there were two individuals — the real Patrick and the fictitious Patrick. The statement may come as a surprise to many, yet it is a fact that the actual Patrick belonged to the Church in the Wilderness. He should not be placed where certain historians seem determined to assign him. The facts presented in the following pages will no doubt be a revelation to many, who, misled by wrong representations, have not realized of what church Patrick was a child and an apostle. As will be shown later, he was of that early church which was brought to Ireland from Syria.[2] He was in no way connected with the type of Christianity which developed in Italy and which was ever at war with the church organized by Patrick.

Patrick belongs to the Celtic race, of which the Britons of England, as well as the Scotch and Irish, are a part. The vivacity of the Celtic temperament is equaled by noble courage under danger and by a deep love for learning. The Celts, like the Germans, possess a profound religious fervor which makes them devoted to the faith of their choice.

---

[1] Maclauchlan, *Early Scottish Church*, pages 97, 98.
[2] Neander, *General History of the Christian Religion and Church*, vol. 1, sec. 1, pp. 85, 86; Moore, *The Culdee Church*, pages 15-20.

This race once extended all the way from Scythia to Ireland.[3] The Celts are descended from Gomer, the grandson of Noah, from whom they obtained through the centuries the name of the Cimmerians. In fact, the Welsh today call themselves Cymry.

Three countries, Britain, Ireland, and France, are claimed by different writers to be the fatherland of Patrick. The weight of evidence plainly indicates that his birthplace was in that kingdom of Strathclyde, inhabited and controlled by the ancient Britons, which lay immediately northwest of England.[4] Rome had divided the island into five provinces, and, in addition, recognized the Strathclyde kingdom. It was then customary to speak of these divisions as "the Britains." To ten of the superior cities in these Britains, the Roman senate had extended the right of citizenship.[5] As his parents resided in one of these ten cities, Patrick in all probability, like Paul, was born a Roman citizen. He was born about A. D. 360.[6]

Fortunately, two of Patrick's writings, his *Confession* and the *Letter* against Coroticus, a near-by British king, survive and may be found readily. In the *Letter* Patrick tells how he surrendered his high privileges to become a slave for Christ. Of his faith and his dedication to God, he says:

> I was a free man according to the flesh. I was born of a father who was a decurion. For I sold my nobility for the good of others, and I do not blush or grieve about it. Finally, I am a servant in Christ delivered to a foreign nation on account of the unspeakable glory of an everlasting life which is in Christ Jesus our Lord.

Of the two writings, namely, the *Confession,* and the *Letter,* Sir William Betham writes:

> In them will be found no arrogant presumption, no spiritual pride, no pretension to superior sanctity, no maledictions of magi, or rivers, because his followers were drowned in them, no veneration for, or adoration of, relics, no consecrated staffs, or donations of his teeth for relics, which occur so frequently in the lives and also in the collections of Tirechan, referring to Palladius, not to Patrick.[7]

---

[3] Ridgeway, *The Early Age of Greece,* vol. 1, page 369.
[4] Neander, *General History of the Christian Religion and Church,* vol. 2, pp. 146-149.
[5] Gibbon, *Decline and Fall of the Roman Empire,* chapter 31.
[6] Smith and Wace, *A Dictionary of Christian Biography,* art. "Patricius."
[7] Betham, *Irish Antiquarian Researches,* vol. 1, p. 270.

At the age of sixteen, Patrick was carried captive to Ireland by freebooters who evidently had sailed up the Clyde River or landed on the near-by coast. Of this he writes in this *Confession*:

> I, Patrick, a sinner, the rudest and least of all the faithful, and most contemptible to great numbers, had Calpurnius for my father, a deacon, son of the late Potitus, the presbyter, who dwelt in the village of Banavan, Tiberniae, for he had a small farm at hand with the place where I was captured. I was then almost sixteen years of age. I did not know the true God; and was taken to Ireland in captivity with many thousand men in accordance with our deserts, because we walked at a distance from God and did not observe His commandments.

It can be noticed in this statement that the grandfather of Patrick was a presbyter, which indicated that he held an office in the church equal to that of bishop in the papal meaning of the term. This is one of the many proofs that celibacy was not an obligation among the early British clergy. Patrick's father was a deacon in the church, a town counselor, a farmer, and a husband. To the glory of God, it came to pass that, during his seven years of slavery in Ireland, Patrick acquired the Irish form of the Celtic language. This was of great value, because the fierce fighting disposition of the pagan Irish, at that time, was a barrier to the Romans' or Britons' attempting missionary work across the channel on a large scale. However, many of those previously carried off into captivity must have been Christians who engaged themselves so earnestly in converting their captors that considerable Christianity was found in Ireland when, after his escape, Patrick dared to return to evangelize the island.

It will be further noted in the quotation above that he was taken into "captivity with many thousand men." The seagoing craft used in those days along the coasts of Ireland, called "coracles," were small vessels made by covering a wicker frame with hide or leather. The problem involved in transporting many thousands of captives by means of such small boats indicates that the raid must have been made on a near-by coast, which is further testimony that his fatherland was "the Britains."

Patrick, like his Master of Galilee, was to learn obedience through suffering. A great task awaited him. The apostolic church had won a comparatively easy victory in her struggle with a pagan world for three centuries. But an almost impossible task awaited her when a compromising Christianity, enforcing its doctrines at the point of the sword, had become the state religion of the Roman Empire. It was an hour when a new line of leaders was needed. As the struggle of free churches to live their lives without the domination of a state clergy began, God was training Patrick.

While considering the early life of this Christian leader, it is most interesting to note what was happening in contemporary history. Vigilantius[8] was doing his work in southern France and in northern Italy, or among the Latin peoples. Shortly before Patrick's time the empire at Constantinople had been under the rule of Constantius II, who recoiled from accepting the extreme views on the Godhead, which had won the vote under his father, Constantine the Great, in the first Council of Nicaea. As will be related later, similar opposition to those extreme views prevailed all over Europe. Patrick's belief was that of the opposition. Dr. Stokes writes: "The British churches of the fourth century took the keenest interest in church controversies. They opposed Arianism, but hesitated, like many others, about the use of the word 'homoousion.' "[9] (This word means "identity of substance.") Thus Celtic Christianity in the years of Patrick refused to accept this test term and the conclusions to which the radical speculations were leading.

It is remarkable that in the time of Patrick, as later testimony from Alphonse Mingana will point out, there were large groups of Christians stretching all the way from the Euphrates to northwestern India. Furthermore, in 411, when Patrick was at the height of his work, the recognized head over the Church of the East at Seleucia, Persia, consecrated a metropolitan administrator for China who must have had many provincial directors under him. This indicates many Christian churches in China in that age. Ambrose reported in 396 that Musaeus, an Abyssinian church leader, had "traveled almost everywhere in the country of the Seres." Seres was the name for the Chinese.[10] Truly, the age in which Patrick labored saw stirring scenes throughout the world.

Both Isaac, supreme director, and Theodore of Mopsuestia, author and theologian, were powerful leaders in the great Church of the East

---

[8] See Chapter VI, entitled, "Vigilantius, Leader of the Waldenses."
[9] Stokes, *Ireland and the Celtic Church*, pages 11, 12.
[10] Gordon, *"World Healers,"* pages 48, 49.

during the period of Patrick's ministry. The influence of the writings of Theodore in molding Oriental Christianity for centuries and his signal work in refuting the doctrines of Mithraism in the East, while Patrick was winning his victories in the West, is of importance.[11]

Christianity in Ireland Before Patrick

Celtic Christianity embraced more than Irish and British Christianity. There was a Gallic (French) Celtic Christianity and a Galatian Celtic Christianity, as well as a British Celtic Christianity. So great were the migrations of peoples in ancient times that not only the Greeks, but also the Assyrians settled in large numbers in the land now called France. Thus for almost a thousand years after Christ there was in southern France a strong Greek and Oriental population. As late as 600, there were people in France who spoke the language of Assyria.[12]

Surely no one could claim that that branch of Celtic Christianity in Asia Minor, whose churches arose as the result of the labors of the apostle Paul, received their gospel from the bishop of Rome. On the other hand, it is evident that Gaul received her knowledge of the gospel from missionaries who traveled from Asia Minor. It was the Celtic, or Galatian type of the New Testament church which evangelized Great Britain.[13] Thus Thomas Yeates writes:

> A large number of this Keltic community (Lyons, A. D. 177)—colonists from Asia Minor — who escaped, migrated to Ireland (Erin) and laid the foundations of the pre-Patrick church.[14]

The Roman Catholic Church throughout the centuries was able to secure a large following in France; but until after the French Revolution she never succeeded in eliminating the spirit of independence in the French hierarchy. This is due largely to the background of the Celtic race. As H. J. Warner writes:

> Such an independence France had constantly shown, and it may be traced not only to the racial antipathy between Gaul and Pelagian, but to the fact that western Gaul had never lost touch with its eastern kin.[15]

---

[11] Bidez and Cumont, *Les Mages Hellenisés,* vol. 1, p. 55. For an amplification of this subject see the writer's discussion in Chapter xviii.

[12] Stokes, *Ireland and the Celtic Church,* page 173.

[13] Moore, *The Culdee Church,* page 21.

[14] Yeates, *East Indian Church History,* page 226 (included in *Asian Cristology and the Mahayana,* by E. A. Gordon).

[15] Warner, *The Albigensian Heresy,* vol. 1, p. 20.

Patrick's Work in Ireland

Two centuries elapsed after Patrick's death before any writer attempted to connect Patrick's work with a papal commission. No pope ever mentioned him, neither is there anything in the ecclesiastical records of Rome concerning him. Nevertheless, by examining the two writings which he left, historical statements are found which locate quite definitely the period in which he labored.

When Patrick speaks of the island from which he was carried captive, he calls it "the Britains." This was the title given the island by the Romans many years before they left it. After the Goths sacked the city of Rome in 410, the imperial legions were recalled from England in order to protect territory nearer home. Upon their departure, savage invaders from the north and from the Continent, sweeping in upon the island, devastated it and erased its diversified features, so that it could no longer be called "the Britains." Following the withdrawal of the Roman legions in 410, the title "the Britains" ceased to be used. Therefore from this evidence it would seem logical to reach the conclusion that Patrick wrote his letters and documents before that date.

This date agrees with the time when Columba, the renowned graduate of Patrick's school who brought Christianity to Scotland, began his ministry. Columba graduated when the schools founded by Patrick had grown to sizable proportions. The time which elapsed between the founding of the schools by Patrick and their growth in the days of Columba would indicate that Patrick began his ministry in Ireland about 390.

What Patrick did between the time of his escape from slavery in Ireland and his return as a missionary to that land is not known. Every effort has been made by propapal writers to place him, in this interval, at Rome. On one such fictitious visit it is said that Patrick with the help of an angel performed the questionable feat of stealing many relics from the pope among which was supposed to have been the bloodstained towel of our Saviour and some hair from the Virgin Mary. One writer exclaims: " 'O wondrous deed! O rare theft of a vast treasure of holy things, committed without sacrilege, the plunder of the most holy place in the world!' "[16]

---

[16] Stokes, *Ireland and the Celtic Church*, page 93.

The words of Patrick himself reveal his unrest of soul after his escape from slavery until he submitted to the call of God to proclaim the news of salvation to the Irish. He had continually heard voices from the woods of Hibernia, begging him, as did the man in the night vision of Paul, "Come over, . . . and help us." Neither the tears of his parents nor the reasonings of his friends could restrain him. He determined, whatever the cost, to turn his back upon the allurements of home and friends and to give his life for the Emerald Isle.

His Authority — The Bible

Patrick preached the Bible. He appealed to it as the sole authority for founding the Irish Church. He gave credit to no other worldly authority; he recited no creed. Several official creeds of the church at Rome had by that time been ratified and commanded, but Patrick mentions none. In his *Confession* he makes a brief statement of his beliefs, but he does not refer to any church council or creed as authority. The training centers he founded, which later grew into colleges and large universities, were all Bible schools. Famous students of these schools — Columba, who brought Scotland to Christ, Aidan, who won pagan England to the gospel, and Columbanus with his successors, who brought Christianity to Germany, France, Switzerland, and Italy — took the Bible as their only authority, and founded renowned Bible training centers for the Christian believers. One authority, describing the handwritten Bibles produced at these schools, says, "In delicacy of handling and minute but faultless execution, the whole range of paleography offers nothing comparable to these early Irish manuscripts."[17]

In the closing words of his *Letter,* Patrick writes: "I testify before God and His angels that it shall be so as He has intimated to my ignorance. These are not my words, but (the words) of God, and of the apostles and prophets, which I have written in Latin, who have never lied."

Patrick, like his example, Jesus, put the words of Scripture above the teachings of men. He differed from the papacy, which puts church tradition above the Bible. In his writings he nowhere appeals to the church at Rome for the authorization of his mission. Whenever he

---

[17] Tymms, *The Art of Illuminating as Practiced in Europe From Earliest Times,* page 15.

speaks in defense of his mission, he refers to God alone, and declares that he received his call direct from heaven. Sir William Betham states that the more recent Latin version of Jerome was not publicly read in Patrick's day. Evidently the earlier Latin version of the Bible, known as the Itala, was publicly used. It is interesting to note that it was approximately nine hundred years before Jerome's Vulgate could make headway in the West against the Itala.[18]

Wherever this Christian leader sowed, he also reaped. Ireland was set on fire for God by the fervor of Patrick's missionary spirit. Leaving England again with a few companions, according to the record in the *Book of Armagh,* he landed at Wicklow Head on the southeastern coast of Ireland. Legendary and fabulous is *The Tripartite Life of Patrick.* It cannot be credited, yet doubtless it was built around certain facts of his life. At least from these records can be traced his steps for a quarter of a century through the isle.

Patrick believed that Christianity should be founded with the home and the family as its strength. Too often the Christian organizations of that age were centered in celibacy. This was not true of the Irish Church and its Celtic daughters in Great Britain, Scotland, and on the Continent. The Celtic Church, as organized and developed under Patrick, permitted its clergy to marry.[19]

The absence of celibacy in the Celtic Church gives added proof to the fact that the believers had no connection with the church at Rome. Thus Dr. J. H. Todd writes: "He [Patrick] says nothing of Rome, or of having been commissioned by Pope Celestine. He attributed his Irish apostleship altogether to an inward call, which he regarded as a divine command."[20]

One of the strongest proofs that Patrick did not belong to papal Christianity is found in the historical fact that for centuries Rome made every effort to destroy the church Patrick had founded. Jules Michelet writes of Boniface, who was the pope's apostle to the Germans about two hundred years after Patrick: "His chief hatred is to the Scots [the name equally given to the Scotch and Irish], and he especially condemns their allowing priests to marry."[21]

[18] Jacobus, *Roman Catholic and Protestant Bibles Compared,* page 4.·
[19] Neander, *General History of the Christian Religion and Church,* vol. 3, p. 53.
[20] Todd, *St. Patrick, Apostle to Ireland,* page 377.
[21] Michelet, *History of France,* vol. 1, p. 74; vol. 1, p. 184, ed. 1844.

Patrick sought two goals in his effort to make truth triumphant. First, he sought the conversion of those among whom he had been a slave, and, secondly, he longed to capture Tara, the central capital of Ireland, for Christ. Therefore he proceeded immediately to County Antrim in the northwest, where he had endured slavery. While he failed to win his former slave master, he was successful in converting the master's household. This threw open a door to further missionary labors not only to this region but also across the adjacent waters into near-by Scotland.

History loves to linger upon the legend of Patrick's attack on Tara, the central capital. The Irish, like other branches of the Celtic race, had local chieftains who were practically independent. They also had, by their own election, an overlord, who might be referred to as a king and who could summon all the people when needed for the defense of the nation. For many years Tara had been the renowned capital of Ireland to which were called the Irish chieftains to conduct the general affairs of the realm. These conventions were given over not only to business, but also to festivals emblazoned with bright scenes and stirring events. As Thomas Moore wrote:

> The harp that once through Tara's halls
>   The soul of music shed,
> Now hangs as mute on Tara's walls,
>   As if that soul were fled.—
> So sleeps the pride of former days,
>   So glory's thrill is o'er;
> And hearts, that once beat high for praise,
>   Now feel that pulse no more.[22]

It was at the time of one of these assemblies, so the story goes, that Patrick personally appeared to proclaim the message of Christ. The event is so surrounded by legends, many of them too fabulous to be considered, that many details cannot be presented as facts. His success did not come up to his expectations, however; but by faithful efforts he placed the banner of Christianity in the political center of the national life.

He did not enter the capital because he felt that God's work needed the help of the state. Patrick rejected the union of church and state. More than one hundred years had passed since the first world council

---

[22]Moore, *Irish Melodies,* page 6.

at Nicaea had united the church with the empire. Patrick rejected this model. He followed the lesson taught in John's Gospel when Christ refused to be made a king. Jesus said, "My kingdom is not of this world."[23] Not only the Irish apostle but his famous successors, Columba in Scotland, and Columbanus on the Continent, ignored the supremacy of the papal pontiff. They never would have agreed to making the pope a king. Although the Roman Empire after the fourth century had favored that supremacy, there was still great discontent throughout Europe against this encroachment of civil power into the church.

While Patrick was laboring in Ireland, the bishop of north Africa in 418 had excommunicated Apiarius, a clergyman, for grave offenses. The offender appealed to the pope, who acquitted him over the heads of his superiors. The bishops retaliated by assembling in council and passing a protest forbidding an appeal of lower clergy against their bishops to an authority beyond the sea. The pope replied with resolutions which he claimed had been passed by the Council of Nicaea. Their illegality was exposed by the African prelates.[24]

Yet it must not be thought, as some writers antagonistic to the Celtic Church claim, that Patrick and his successors lacked church organization. Dr. Benedict Fitzpatrick, a Catholic scholar, resents any such position. He adduces satisfactory proof to show that the Irish founders of Celtic Christianity created a splendid organization.[25]

The Fictitious Patrick

Many miracles have been ascribed to Patrick by the traditional stories which grew up. Two or three will suffice to show the difference between the miraculous hero of the fanatical fiction and the real Patrick. The Celtic Patrick reached Ireland in an ordinary way. The fictitious Patrick, in order to provide passage for a leper when there was no place on the boat, threw his portable stone altar into the sea. The stone did not go to the bottom, nor was it outdistanced by the boat, but it floated around the boat with the leper on it until it reached Ireland.[26]

---

[23] John 18:36.
[24] Foakes-Jackson, *The History of the Christian Church*, page 527.
[25] Fitzpatrick, *Ireland and the Making of Britain*, page 231.
[26] Stokes, *Chronicles and Memorials of Great Britain and Ireland*, vol. 89, pt. 2, pp. 447-449.

In order to connect this great man with the papal see, it was related: "Sleep came over the inhabitants of Rome, so that Patrick brought away as much as he wanted of the relics. Afterward those relics were taken to Armagh by the counsel of God and the counsel of the men of Ireland. What was brought then was three hundred and threescore and five relics, together with the relics of Paul and Peter and Lawrence and Stephen, and many others. And a sheet was there with Christ's blood [thereon] and with the hair of Mary the Virgin."[27] But Dr. Killen refutes this story by declaring:

> He (Patrick) never mentions either Rome or the pope or hints that he was in any way connected with the ecclesiastical capital of Italy. He recognizes no other authority but that of the word of God. . . . When Palladius arrived in the country, it was not to be expected that he would receive a very hearty welcome from the Irish apostle. If he was sent by [Pope] Celestine to the native Christians to be their primate or archbishop, no wonder that stouthearted Patrick refused to bow his neck to any such yoke of bondage.[28]

About two hundred years after Patrick, papal authors began to tell of a certain Palladius, who was sent in 430 by this same Pope Celestine as a bishop to the Irish. They all admit, however, that he stayed only a short time in Ireland and was compelled to withdraw because of the disrespect which was shown him.

One more of the many legendary miracles which sprang from the credulity and tradition of Rome is here repeated. "He went to Rome to have [ecclesiastical] orders given him; and Caelestinus, abbot of Rome, he it is that read orders over him, Germanus and Amatho, king of the Romans, being present with them. . . . And when the orders were a reading out, the three choirs mutually responded, namely, the choir of the household of heaven, and the choir of the Romans, and the choir of the children from the wood of Fochlad. This is what all sang: 'All we Irish beseech thee, holy Patrick, to come and walk among us and to free us.' "[29] It is doubtful whether the choirs in heaven would accept this representation that they were Irish.

---

[27] Stokes, *Chronicles and Memorials of Great Britain and Ireland,* vol. 89, pt. 1, p. 239.

[28] Killen, *Ecclesiastical History of Ireland,* vol. 1, pp. 12-15.

[29] Stokes, *Chronicles and Memorials of Great Britain and Ireland,* vol. 89, pt. 1, pp. 31, 33.

War on the Celtic Church

The growing coldness between the Celtic and the Roman Churches as noted in the foregoing paragraphs did not originate in a hostile attitude of mind in the Celtic clergy. It arose because they considered that the papacy was moving farther and farther away from the apostolic system of the New Testament. No pope ever passed on to the leading bishops of the church the news of the great transformation from heathenism to Christianity wrought by Patrick. This they certainly would have done, as was done in other cases, had he been an agent of the Roman pontiff.

One is struck by the absence of any reference to Patrick in the *Ecclesiastical History of England* written by that fervent follower of the Vatican, the Englishman Bede, who lived about two hundred years after the death of the apostle to Ireland. That history remains today the well from which many draw who would write on Anglo-Saxon England. Bede had access to the archives of Rome. He was well acquainted with the renowned Celtic missionaries who were the products of the schools of Patrick. He also emphasizes the profound differences between the Celtic and Roman Churches which brought about bitter controversies between kings and bishops. Though a great collector of facts, Bede makes no reference whatever to Patrick. The reason apparently is that, when this historian wrote, the papacy had not yet made up its mind to claim Patrick.

When the pope had sent Augustine with his forty monks to convert the heathen Anglo-Saxons, Augustine, with the help of Bertha, the Catholic wife of King Ethelbert of Kent, immediately began war on the Celtic Church in Wales. He demanded submission of the Christian society of nearly three thousand members at Bangor in north Wales.[30] Augustine addressed the president of this society in these words: "Acknowledge the authority of Rome." He promptly received the answer that the pope was not entitled to be called the "Father of fathers" and the only submission that they would render to him would be that which they owed to every Christian. Augustine threatened them with the sword, and, as will be noted later, twelve hundred of these British Christians were slaughtered by a pagan army.[31]

---

[30] d'Aubigné, *History of the Reformation*, vol. 5, pp. 41, 42.
[31] See the author's discussion in Chapter xi, entitled, "Dinooth and the Church in Wales."

As further evidence of the gulf between the Roman and the Celtic Church, another episode occurred in England in 664 when the papacy by state force inflicted a severe wound at the well-known Synod of Whitby in northern England. The king of that region had married a Roman Catholic princess, who, with the help of her priestly confessor, laid the trap for the pastors who were graduates from Patrick's schools. The king, wearied with the strife between the two communions, became a tool to the plan. That conference with its unjust decisions drove the leaders of the Celtic Church out of northern England.[32] About fifty years after this, or in 715, the growing influence of the Roman Catholic Church backed by the papal monarchs of Europe, brought about an attack upon Scotland's center of Celtic Christianity at Iona. Founded by Columba and celebrated in song and story, this was attacked, and the clergy of the Irish Church were expelled from the place.

The Character of Patrick

Patrick, while manifesting all the graces of an apostolic character, also possessed the sterner virtues. Like Moses, he was one of the humblest of men. He revealed that steadfastness of purpose required to accomplish a great task. His splendid ability to organize and execute his Christian enterprises revealed his successful ability to lead. He was frank and honest. He drew men to him, and he was surrounded by a band of men whose hearts God had touched. Such a leader was needed to revive the flickering flames of New Testament faith in the West, to raise up old foundations, and to lay the groundwork for a mighty Christian future.

To guide new converts, Patrick ordained overseers or bishops in charge of the local churches. Wherever he went, new churches sprang up, and to strengthen them he also founded schools. These two organizations were so closely united that some writers have mistakenly called them monasteries. The scholarly and missionary groups created by Patrick were very different from those ascetic and celibate centers which the papacy strove to multiply.[33] According to Sir William Betham, monastic life was considered disgraceful by the

---

[32] See the author's discussion in Chapter XII, entitled, "Aidan and the Church in England."

[33] M'Clintock and Strong, *Cyclopedia*, arts. "Columba" and "Columbanus."

Scots and the Goths during the first four centuries of the Christian Era.[34]

Among the most famous training colleges which Patrick established were Bangor, Clonmacnoise, Clonard, and Armagh. In Armagh, the most renowned center of Ireland, are located today the palaces of both the Church of England primate and the Roman Catholic primate. Two magnificent cathedrals are there which command attention.[35] Each is built upon an eminent hill, a beautiful valley lying between them. One is the cathedral for relics of the Church of Rome, the other for the Church of England. Armagh grew from a small school to a college, then to a university. It is said to have had as many as seven thousand students in attendance at one time. As Ireland became famous for its training centers it acquired the name "Land of saints and scholars."[36] In these schools the Scriptures were diligently read, and ancient books were eagerly collected and studied.

There are historians who see clearly that the Benedictine order of monks was built upon the foundations so wonderfully laid by the Irish system of education. C. W. Bispham raises the question as to why the Benedictine Rule was allowed to supersede the Bangor Rule. His answer is that the Benedictine Rule, a gift of one of the sons of the papacy, was favored by her, and, furthermore, she was jealous of the Celtic Church and crowded out the Bangor Rule.[37] Benedict, the founder of the order, despised learning and took no care for it in his order, and his schools never took it up until they were forced to do so about 900, after Charles the Great had set the pace.[38]

The marvelous educational system of the Celtic Church, revised and better organized by Patrick, spread successfully over Europe until the Benedictine system, favored by the papacy and reinforced by the state, robbed the Celtic Church of its renown and sought to destroy all the records of its educational system.[39]

---

[34] Betham, *Irish Antiquarian Researches,* vol. 1, p. 268.

[35] The writer when visiting Armagh noted the sites traditionally connected with the life of Patrick.

[36] Killen, *The Old Catholic Church,* page 290.

[37] Bispham, *Columban—Saint, Monk, Missionary,* pages 45, 46; Smith and Wace, *A Dictionary of Christian Biography,* art. "Columbanus."

[38] Stillingfleet, *The Antiquities of the British Churches,* vol. 1, p. 304.

[39] Fitzpatrick, *Ireland and the Making of Britain,* pages 47, 185.

The Beliefs and Teachings of Patrick

In the years preceding the birth of Patrick, new and strange doctrines flooded Europe like the billows of the ocean. Gospel truths, stimulating the minds of men, had opened up so many areas of influence that counterfeiting doctrines had been brought in by designing clergy who strove for the crown while shunning the cross. Patrick was obliged to take his stand against these teachings.

The Council of Nicaea, convened in 325 by Emperor Constantine, started the religious controversy which has never ceased. Assembling under the sanction of a united church and state, that famous gathering commanded the submission of believers to new doctrines. During the youth of Patrick and for half a century preceding, forty-five church councils and synods had assembled in various parts of Europe. Of these Samuel Edgar says:

> The boasted unity of Romanism was gloriously displayed, by the diversified councils and confessions of the fourth century. Popery, on that as on every other occasion, eclipsed Protestantism in the manufacture of creeds. Forty-five councils, says Jortin, were held in the fourth century. Of these, thirteen were against Arianism, fifteen for that heresy, and seventeen for Semi-Arianism. The roads were crowded with bishops thronging to synods, and the traveling expenses, which were defrayed by the emperor, exhausted the public funds. These exhibitions became the sneer of the heathen, who were amused to behold men, who, from infancy, had been educated in Christianity, and appointed to instruct others in that religion, hastening, in this manner, to distant places and conventions for the purpose of ascertaining their belief.[40]

The burning question of the decades succeeding the Council of Nicaea was how to state the relations of the Three Persons of the Godhead: Father, Son, and Holy Ghost. The council had decided, and the papacy had appropriated the decision as its own. The personalities of the Trinity were not confounded, and the substance was not divided. The Roman clergy claimed that Christianity had found in the Greek word *homoousios* (in English, "consubstantiality") an appropriate term to express this relationship.[41]

Then the papal party proceeded to call those who would not subscribe to this teaching, Arians, while they took to themselves the title

---

[40] Edgar, *The Variations of Popery*, page 309.
[41] *The Catholic Encyclopedia*, art. "Arianism."

of Trinitarians. An erroneous charge was circulated that all who were called Arians believed that Christ was a created being.[42] This stirred up the indignation of those who were not guilty of the charge.

Patrick was a spectator to many of these conflicting assemblies. It will be interesting, in order to grasp properly his situation, to examine for a moment this word, this term, which has split many a church and has caused many a sincere Christian to be burned at the stake. In English the word is "consubstantial," connoting that more than one person inhabit the same substance without division or separation. The original term in Greek is *homoousios,* from *homos,* meaning "identical," and *ousia,* the word for "being."

However, a great trouble arose, since there are two terms in Greek of historical fame. The first, *homos,* meaning "identical," and the second, *homoios,* meaning "similar" or "like unto," had both of them a stormy history. The spelling of these words is much alike. The difference in meaning, when applied to the Godhead, is bewildering to simplehearted believers. Nevertheless, those who would think in terms of *homoiousian,* or "similar," instead of *homoousian,* or "identical," were promptly labeled as heretics and Arians by the clergy. Yet when the emperor, Constantine, in full assembly of the Council of Nicaea, asked Hosius, the presiding bishop, what the difference was between the two terms, Hosius replied that they were both alike. At this all but a few bishops broke out into laughter and teased the chairman with heresy.[43]

As volumes have been written in centuries past upon this problem, it would be out of place to discuss it here. It had, however, such profound effect upon other doctrines relating to the plan of salvation and upon outward acts of worship that a gulf was created between the papacy and the institutions of the church which Patrick had founded in Ireland.

While Patrick was anything but an Arian, nevertheless he declined to concur in the idea of "sameness" found in that compelling word "consubstantial" or *homoousian.* Usually when violent controversy

---

[42] It is doubtful if many believed Christ to be a created being. Generally, those evangelical bodies who opposed the papacy and who were branded as Arians confessed both the divinity of Christ and that He was begotten, not created, by the Father. They recoiled from other extreme deductions and speculations concerning the Godhead.

[43] Robinson, *Ecclesiastical Researches,* page 183.

rages, there were three parties.   In this instance there were the two extremes, one of which was led by the papacy, the second by the Arians, and the third party was the middle-of-the-road believers whose viewpoint was the same as Patrick's.[44] As Dr. J. H. Todd says of *homoousian,* the test word of the papal hierarchy, when commenting on Patrick's beliefs, "This confession of faith is certainly not *homoousian.*[45] Another fact verifying this opposition of the British churches to the extreme speculations of the Council of Nicaea respecting the Trinity is the story of the Council of Rimini in 359, held approximately at the time of Patrick's birth.   This, it seems, was the last church council to be attended by Celtic delegates from the British Church before the withdrawal of Rome's legions in 410, and it was followed by the overrunning of England by the pagan Anglo-Saxons. This Council of Rimini passed decrees denouncing and rejecting the conclusions of Nicaea respecting the Trinity.   The pope of Rome had recently signed similar decrees in the Council of Sirmium.   No one will blame the evangelicals for recoiling from the papal view of the Trinity, when history shows that their views were strong enough to cause two popes to sign decrees contrary to the policy of the papacy respecting Nicaea.

One of the reasons, no doubt, why the papacy for many years did not mention Patrick's name or his success was the position of the Irish Church respecting the decrees of Nicaea.   Centuries were to pass before the papacy discovered that his merits were too firmly established to be overlooked.   It labored to gather Patrick into its fold by inventing all kinds of history and fables to make him a papal hero.   It surrounded with a halo of glory a certain Palladius, apparently sent by Rome to Ireland in the midst of Patrick's success.   He also has been called Patrick.[46]

Patrick beheld Jesus as his substitute on the cross. He took his stand for the Ten Commandments. He says in his *Confession:* "I was taken to Ireland in captivity with many thousand men, in accordance with our deserts because we walked at a distance from God, and did not observe His commandments."   Those who recoiled from the extreme speculations and conclusions of the so-called Trinitarians

[44] Stokes, *Ireland and the Celtic Church,* page 12.
[45] Todd, *St. Patrick, Apostle to Ireland,* page 390.
[46] Newell, *St. Patrick, His Life and Teaching,* p. 33, note 1.

believed Deuteronomy 29 :29 : "The secret things belong unto the Lord our God: but those things which are revealed belong unto us and to our children forever."

The binding obligation of the Decalogue was a burning issue in Patrick's age. In theory, all the parties in disagreement upon the Trinity recognized the Ten Commandments as the moral law of God, perfect, eternal, and unchangeable. It could easily be seen that in the judgment, the Lord could not have one standard for angels and another for men. There was not one law for the Jews and a different one for the Gentiles. The rebellion of Satan in heaven had initiated the great revolt against the eternal moral law. All the disputants over the Trinity recognized that when God made man in His image it was the equivalent of writing the Ten Commandments in his heart by creating man with a flawless moral nature. All parties went a step further. They confessed and denied not that in all the universe there was found no one, neither angel, cherubim, seraphim, man, nor any other creature, except Christ, whose death could atone for the broken law.

Then the schism came. Those who rejected the intense, exacting definition of three Divine Persons in one body, as laid down by the Council of Nicaea, believed that Calvary had made Christ a divine sacrifice, the sinner's substitute. The papacy repudiated the teaching that Jesus died as man's substitute upon the cross. Consequently it ignored the exalted place given the Decalogue by the crucifixion of Christ. Those who saw the eternal necessity of magnifying the law, and making it honorable, maintained that death claimed the Son of God, but had left untouched the Father and Holy Spirit. This was the teaching of Patrick and his successor.

Thus, the Celtic Church upheld the sacredness of the Ten Commandments. They accepted the prophecy of Isaiah that Christ came to magnify the law and make it honorable. They preached, as Jeremiah and Paul did, that the purpose of the new covenant was to write God's law in the heart. God could be just and justify the sinner who had fled to Christ. No wonder that the Celtic, the Gothic, the Waldensian, the Armenian Churches, and the great Church of the East, as well as other bodies, differed profoundly from the papacy in its metaphysical conceptions of the Trinity and consequently in the importance of the Ten Commandments.

Not overlooking the adoption of images by the Roman Catholic Church — contrary to the second commandment — and other violations of the moral law which the other bodies refused to condone, one of the principal causes of separation was the observance of the Sabbath. As will be presented in other chapters, the Gothic, Waldensian, Armenian, and Syrian Churches, and the Church of the East, as well as the church organization which Patrick founded, largely sanctified Saturday, the seventh day of the week, as the sacred twenty-four-hour period on which God rested after creation. Many also had sacred assemblies on Sunday, even as many churches today have prayer meeting on Wednesday.

Treating of the Celtic Church, the historian A. C. Flick writes, "The Celts used a Latin Bible unlike the Vulgate, and kept Saturday as a day of rest, with special religious services on Sunday."[47]

T. Ratcliffe Barnett, in his book on the fervent Catholic queen of Scotland who in 1060 was first to attempt the ruin of Columba's brethren, writes, "In this matter the Scots had perhaps kept up the traditional usage of the ancient Irish Church which observed Saturday instead of Sunday as the day of rest."[48] Also it may be stated that Columba, who converted Scotland to Christianity, taught his followers that they should practice such works of piety and chastity as they could learn from the prophetical, evangelical, and apostolic writings.[49] This reveals how Patrick and his colleges made the Bible the origin and center of all education.

Enemies of the Celtic Church in Ireland

An obscurity falls upon the history of the Celtic Church in Ireland, beginning before the coming of the Danes in the ninth century and continuing for two centuries and a half during their supremacy in the Emerald Isle. It continued to deepen until King Henry II waged war against that church in 1171 in response to a papal bull. The reason for this confusion of history is that when Henry II ruined both the political and the ecclesiastical independence of Ireland he also destroyed the valuable records which would clarify what the inner spiritual life and evangelical setup of the Celtic Church was in the

[47] Flick, *The Rise of the Medieval Church,* page 237.
[48] Barnett, *Margaret of Scotland: Queen and Saint,* page 97.
[49] Bede, *Ecclesiastical History of England,* b. 3, ch. 4.

days of Patrick. Even this, however, did not have force enough to blur or obscure the glorious outburst of evangelical revival and learning which followed the work of Patrick.

Why did the Danes invade England and Ireland? The answer is found in the terrible wars prompted by the papacy and waged by Charlemagne, whose campaigns did vast damage to the Danes on the Continent. Every student knows of that Christmas Day, 800, when the pope, in the great cathedral at Rome, placed upon the head of Charlemagne the crown to indicate that he was emperor of the newly created Holy Roman Empire. With battle-ax in hand, Charlemagne continuously waged war to bring the Scandinavians into the church. This embittered the Danes. As they fled before him, they swore that they would take vengeance by ruining Christian churches wherever possible, and by slaying the clergy. This is the reason for the fanatical invasion by these Scandinavian warriors of both England and Ireland.[50]

Ravaging expeditions grew into organized dominations under famous Danish leaders. Turgesius landed with his fleet of war vessels on the coast of Ireland about the year 832. He sailed inland so that he dominated the east, west, and north of the country. His fleets sacked its centers of learning and ruined the churches.

How did the Danes succeed in overthrowing the Celtic Church? It was by first enduring, and then embracing the papacy. It must not be thought that these invaders, because they were pagans, were also ignorant and illiterate. This is far from the truth. They excelled in many lines of learning and culture.

As the years passed and bitterness toward Christianity decreased on the part of the Danes, many became nominal Christians. Being in constant conflict with centers of the Celtic Church, hostility to it was inbred in the invaders. On the other hand, the semipagan Christianity of the Danes was more powerfully impressed by the magnificent cathedrals, the colorful hierarchy, and the alluring rites and ceremonies of the papacy. It is only natural, therefore, that they should seek ordination for their clergy at the hands of Latin bishops. As the theme proceeds, the force of the following quotation from Dr. George T. Stokes will be seen: "The Danes formed one principal channel

---

[50] Stokes, *Ireland and the Celtic Church,* page 252.

through which the papal see renewed and accomplished its designs upon the independence of the Irish Church in the course of the eleventh and twelfth centuries."[51]   When the Danish bishops of Waterford were consecrated by the see of Canterbury, they ignored the Irish Church and the successors of Patrick, so that from that time on there were two churches in Ireland.[52]

Turgesius was the first to recognize the military advantages and the desirable contour of the land on which the city of Dublin now stands. With him began the founding of the city which expanded into the kingdom of Dublin.   Later on, a bishopric was established in this new capital, modeled after the papal ideal.   When the day came that the Irish wished to expel their foreign conquerors, they were unable to extricate themselves from the net of the papal religion which the invaders had begun to weave.   This leads to the story of Brian Boru.

Brian Boru Overthrows the Danish Supremacy

The guerilla fights, waged for decades between the native Irish and their foreign overlords, took on the form of a national warfare when Brian Boru emerged as one of Hibernia's greatest heroes.   First, he fought valiantly along with his brother Mahon, king of Munster, and after his brother's death, alone as successor to the kingdom.   Step by step he subdued one after another of the Danish kingdoms.   The two great battles which climaxed his career were those of Glen Mama and Clontarf, both near Dublin.   In the first he made himself master of all Ireland, up to the gates of Dublin.   In the second, Dublin was brought under the rule of a native Irish king, though he, his son, and his grandson lost their lives in the conflict.

It must not be thought that with the victories of Brian, the Danes were entirely expelled from Irish soil.   They continued for some years with varying fortunes, now weak, now strong, but never again in the ascendancy.   The power of the Danes grew weaker and weaker, but the papacy, whose entrance among the Irish the Danes had facilitated, grew stronger and stronger.   The great victory of Brian, 1014, in the battle of Clontarf, was only some fifty years before the time when William the Conqueror, under the guidance of the pope, led his Normans to the conquest of England.   The Latin clergy in Ireland, seek-

---

[51] Stokes, *Celtic Church in Ireland,* page 277.
[52] *Ibid.,* pages 308-314.

ing the ruin of the Celtic Church, gained a formidable ally in the papal
Norman kings of England. It was an easy task, upon the death of a
Celtic Church leader in Ireland, to substitute a Roman bishop from
time to time as his successor. Finally, a traitor to the Celtic Church
was found in Celsus, the Celtic archbishop of Armagh, who contrived
to make Malachy, a youth instructed in the continental school of
Bernard of Clairvaux deeply permeated by papal teaching, his successor. This Malachy "finally reduced Ireland beneath the supremacy
of Rome and introduced Roman discipline." Therefore when, a little
later, Henry II, under authorization of the papacy, brought Ireland
under English rule, the subjection of the Celtic Church was complete.

The Ruin of Patrick's Church

Showing that the introduction of the papacy into England under
the monk Augustine was religious and that full power was not secured
by Rome until William the Conqueror (A. D. 1066), Blackstone says:

> This naturally introduced some few of the papal corruptions in point
> of faith and doctrines; but we read of no civil authority claimed by the
> pope in these kingdoms until the era of the Norman conquests, when the
> then reigning pontiff having favored Duke William in his projected invasion
> of England, by blessing his host and consecrating his banners he took the
> opportunity, also, of establishing his spiritual encroachments and was even
> permitted so to do by the policy of the conqueror, in order more effectually
> to humble the Saxon clergy and aggrandize his Norman prelates; who being
> bred abroad in the doctrine and practice of slavery, had contracted a rever-
> ence and regard for it, and took pleasure in riveting the chains of a free-
> born people.[53]

The bull of Pope Adrian IV issued to King Henry II of England,
1156, authorized him to invade Ireland. A part of the bull reads thus:
"Your highness's desire of esteeming the glory of your name on earth,
and obtaining the record of eternal happiness in heaven, is laudable
and beneficial; inasmuch as your intent is, as a Catholic prince, to enlarge the limits of the church, to decree the truth of the Christian faith
to untaught and rude nations, and to eradicate vice from the field of
the Lord."

Several things are clear from this bull. First, in specifying Ireland as an untaught and rude nation, it is evident that papal doctrines,
rites, and clergy had not been dominant there. Second, in urging the

---

[53] Blackstone, *Commentaries on the Laws of England*, b. 4, ch. 8, p. 104.

king "to enlarge the limits of the church," the pope confesses that Ireland and its Christian inhabitants had not been under the dominant supremacy of the papacy. Third, in praising Henry's intent to decree the Christian faith of the Irish nation, Pope Adrian admits that papal missionaries had not carried the Romish faith to Ireland before this. In laying upon Henry II the command that he should annex the crown of Ireland upon condition that he secure a penny from every home in Ireland as the pope's revenue,[54] it is clear that the papacy was not the ancient religion of Ireland and that no Roman ties had bound that land to it before the middle of the twelfth century.

W. C. Taylor, in his *History of Ireland*, speaking of the synod of Irish princes and prelates which Henry II summoned to Cashel, says, "The bull of Pope Adrian, and its confirmation by [Pope] Alexander, were read in the assembly; the sovereignty of Ireland granted to Henry by acclamation; and several regulations made for increasing the power and privileges of the clergy, and assimilating the discipline of the Irish Church to that which the Romish see had established in Western Europe."[55]

From that time to the Reformation, the Celtic Church in Ireland was in the wilderness experience along with all other evangelical believers in Europe. Throughout the dreadful years of the Dark Ages many individuals, in churches or groups of churches, struggled to re-establish and to maintain the original purity of the apostolic teachings. No doubt under the fury of the dominion exercised by combined religious and political power, the greater number surrendered wholly or in part. Even as, during the 1260 years, the Church in the Wilderness in Mohammedan and far-off heathen lands lapsed into barbarian rites and ceremonies, so the Celtic Church in Ireland succumbed more or less to papal practices. Nevertheless, the glorious substratum endured, and when God in His mercy shed upon the world the spiritual splendor of the Reformation, many of these oppressed Christians revived and substituted the supremacy of the Bible for the domination of the hierarchy.

---

[54] O'Kelly, *Macariae Excidium or The Destruction of Cyprus*, page 242.
[55] Taylor, *History of Ireland*, vol. 1, pp. 59, 60.

CHAPTER VIII

Columba and the Church in Scotland

Columba possessed a superior education. He was familiar with Latin and Greek, secular and ecclesiastical history, the principles of jurisprudence, the law of nations, the science of medicine, and the laws of mind. He was the greatest Irishman of the Celtic race in mental powers; and he founded in Iona the most learned school in the British Islands, and probably in Western Europe for a long period.[1]

WHILE the long night of the Dark Ages covered Europe and darkness covered the people, the lamp of truth was shining brightly in Scotland and Ireland. Here arose the commanding figure of Columba. Here the virile churches, one in faith, but covering two separate islands, proclaimed the truth. Ireland on the western, and Scotland on the northwestern, brink of the known world, stood like a wall to resist the advancing menace of religious tyranny. Scotland in particular, like the Waldenses in northern Italy, found in her rugged mountains strong fortresses to assist her.

Columba, an Irishman, was born in Donegal in 521, and both of his parents were of royal stock. He founded a memorable college on the small island of Iona which was a lighthouse of truth in Europe for centuries. That the Celtic, not the Latin, race populated the British Isles was a determining factor, for the Christian churches in which Patrick had been reared received their doctrine, not from Rome, but from their brethren of the same faith in Asia Minor. Here was the link which connected the faith of Patrick and Columba with primitive Christianity.[2] The farthest lands touching the Atlantic saw the rise of a vigorous apostolic Christianity not connected with the Church of Rome, but independent of it.

The Scottish resistance to the growing European hierarchy had its origins in the work of Columba. About the time he left the schools established by Patrick in Ireland to go to Scotland, the reactionary Council of Constantinople (A. D. 553) was being held. At that coun-

---

[1] Cathcart, *The Ancient British and Irish Churches*, page 185.
[2] Moore, *The Culdee Church*, pages 23-29.

cil, the churches of the Roman Empire surrendered their freedom to the papacy. Offended at the unscriptural innovations of medieval European compromises, four large communions in the East — the Armenian, the Coptic, the Jacobite, and the Church of the East (often falsely called the Nestorian Church)—separated from the western hierarchy.[3] The news of these revolutionary happenings had come to the ears of the Celtic believers throughout the British Isles. Scotland and Ireland in the west, with the same spirit of independence which was manifested by these eastern communions toward imperial Christianity, girded themselves to meet the crisis.

In dedicating his life to the spread of Bible religion, Columba, who was of royal descent, is said to have renounced his chance to the Irish throne.[4] He was a descendant of Niall of the Nine Hostages, an Irish king so mighty that it is said of him that he held hostages for the nine kingdoms he had subdued.[5] Columba was also related to the renowned family of Riada who conquered for themselves a principality in northeastern Scotia (the ancient name for Ireland). The new state was Dalriada, from Dal, meaning "inheritance," or the kingdom of the Riadians. This relationship stood Columba well in hand when he decided to make his headquarters in Iona, because *a half a century before this,* members of the Dalradian clan had crossed over from Ireland and had secured for themselves a goodly portion of west central Caledonia, (the former name for Scotland), and called this new kingdom also Dalriada.[6] This act brought the Scots from Ireland, or Scotia. As, in the course of time, the Scots of the second kingdom of Dalriada were to conquer the large kingdom in Caledonia of the Picts to the north and west of them and then the kingdom of the Britons, or Strathclyde, to the immediate south of them, naturally the name Scotland came to ancient Caledonia.[7] For several centuries the two Dalriada kingdoms, one in Ireland and one in Scotland, existed contemporaneously. Thus this clan through Columba not only gave the spiritual leadership to Scotland, but later through their warriors also gained the political overlordship of it.

In the providence of God, Columba appeared at this moment to

---

[3] Innes, *Church and State*, pages 52, 53.
[4] Menzies, *Saint Columba of Iona*, page 1.
[5] Jamieson, *Historical Account of the Ancient Culdees of Iona*, page 21.
[6] Menzies, *Saint Columba of Iona*, Introduction, pages xxxi, 1.
[7] Maclauchlan, *Early Scottish Church*, pages 10, 135, 136.

mold these significant revolutions. Iona, the burial ground of kings and nobles, a sacred seat of the heathen Druidic learning and religion, became the center of the Culdee Church and the college of Columba. Here this great apostle developed a new chapter of Bible Christianity among a warlike and cultured pagan people.

The Education of Columba

At his birth Columba, it is said, was given two names — Crimthann, "wolf," and Colum, "dove."[8] However, in his later days of supreme devotion to Christ and to Bible truth, he was usually known by the second, Colum. In his early youth, the fame of Ireland's colleges, the outgrowth of Patrick's early organization and labors, was known far and wide. Columba, it is usually related, was first taught by Finnian of Moville. After this he removed to Leinster where he placed himself under the instruction of the bard, Gemman.[9]

Probably the most outstanding of all Columba's teachers was the renowned Finnian of Clonard, widely known for his learning. He was popular, and he placed the Bible at the foundation of all studies. According to Archbishop Ussher, his institute had an enrollment of three thousands pupils and was likened to a university.[10] Many who came there to receive their education gave themselves to the ministry of the gospel.[11] It was at Clonard that Columba became especially skillful in the art of copying and illuminating manuscripts. There he remained several years until the urgency of his spirit to help humanity, to raise up churches, and to plant mission stations sent him upon extensive labors.

Laboring in Ireland

Columba was only twenty-five years of age when he built the church at Derry, in northern Ireland, where later he planted a school. This place is now the well-known Londonderry. The youthful zeal and accomplishments of this missionary greatly impressed the historian Bede who makes special mention of Derry.[12]

During the seven years following the establishment of Derry,

---

[8] Dowden, *The Celtic Church in Scotland,* page 86.
[9] Adamnan, *Life of St. Columba,* Summary, page xv.
[10] Stokes, *Ireland and the Celtic Church,* page 101.
[11] Cathcart, *The Ancient British and Irish Churches,* page 183.
[12] Bede, *Ecclesiastical History of England,* b. 3, ch. 4.

Columba founded many churches and Biblical institutes. He is credited with bringing into existence during this period more than three hundred churches. About one-third of these were the so-called "monasteries," or church schools. Happy in his activity for God, he was constantly traveling. The sick and the infirm blessed his name, while the poor always felt that in him they had a friend. Tall of stature, he had a powerful voice which could be heard at a great distance. No journey was too great, and no labor too arduous for him to undertake while serving the needs of the people. In Ireland, where the chieftains were constantly waging war against one another, Columba commanded respect enough to travel in safety. He was devoted to the study of the Scriptures. His biographer mentions that he spent much time in writing, that is, in transcribing portions of the Bible. He is credited with having copied three hundred New Testaments with his own hands. He was the author, not only of Latin hymns, but also of poems in his native Irish tongue. A careful examination of his writings shows that in many places he uses the Itala version of the Bible. Of him Adamnan says: "He could not pass the space even of a single hour without applying himself either to prayer, or reading, or writing, or else to some manual labor."[13]

Journeys Into Scotland

There are probably three reasons why Columba chose Scotland as his mission field. In the first place, a large part of the island, especially the country of the Picts, was still pagan. Columba longed for a mission field and a life of service. Secondly, about fifty years previous to this his own countrymen, the Dalradians, had won a kingdom in the west central portion of what is now called Scotland. Here was a door open in a dark land. Thirdly, Columba saw that he could there establish a center which would be mighty in its influence not only in Scotland, but also in England, Wales, and Ireland.

After he sailed from his beloved Derry, with about two hundred of his companions, he was tempted to locate on a near-by island, when he discovered that from its highlands he could discern the coasts of Ireland. He then gave the word to sail on. He finally chose the small island of Iona, whose native name was Hy, having the large island of

---

[13]Adamnan, *Life of St. Columba,* Summary, page li.

Mull lying between it and the mainland.[14] Here he and his company disembarked in 563. In all probability, the lord of the island of Mull, being a relative of his, granted to him ownership of Iona. His followers held the island for six hundred forty-one years, until they were driven out of it in 1204 by the Benedictine monks.[15]

Pioneering in all its aspects was the story of Iona. Dwellings had to be built; crops had to be planted. In the settlement of Iona and of other centers founded by Columba and his disciples, apparently no effort was made for pomp and ostentation. These simple missionaries allowed no entanglements either in politics or worldly affairs to hinder them from obeying the heavenly vision. Although Columba was needed to direct and oversee the establishment of these new ventures for Christ, he found time, nevertheless, to convert many persons on the large neighboring island of Mull.

He founded a Christian school and training institute which later attained the highest reputation for the pursuit of Biblical study and science.[16] His work made this center so venerated that its abbots had the control of the bordering tribes and churches, and even their pastors (then called bishops), acknowledged the authority of these abbots. He built up in Iona a glorious center of evangelization which has made the island famous for all time. Here are buried not only kings of Scotland, but also kings of Ireland, France, Denmark, and Norway. Even to this day thousands of visitors come annually to this hallowed soil.[17]

The Mission Center at Iona

The spirit of God wrought mightily in Columba, and in humility he chose to dwell in a rude shelter of pioneer construction. The humble abode of his energetic and learned co-workers at Iona proves that in their hearts they had brought into subjection the restless spirit of the age. Even a generation later when one of the renowned apostles of Iona erected another mission station in northwestern England, it

---

[14] Bede, *Ecclesiastical History of England,* b. 3, chs. 3, 4.
[15] Menzies, *Saint Columba of Iona,* Appendix, page 215.
[16] Neander, *General History of the Christian Religion and Church,* vol. 3, p. 10.
[17] On my visit to Iona, I was moved not so much by the sight of the broken remnants of papal edifices which marked the later domination of Rome, nor by the tombs of kings and nobles, but by the holy ground where Columba and his successors prayed and sacrificed to save a heathen world.

is related that, "he built a church after the manner of the Scots, not of stone, but of hewn oak, and covered it with reeds."[18] Unlike the ambassadors of imperial Christianity, who loved the associations of capitals and courts, these missionaries chose the wilderness if it might be their happy lot to serve God.

Much ground was required to support the Iona mission. Many acres of land, orchards, and meadows were maintained by the students and faculty who combined manual labor with study. A considerable portion of the day was spent in gathering and winnowing the grain, feeding the lambs and the calves, working in the gardens, in the bakehouse, and in mechanical pursuits. These duties were alternated with classes of instruction by learned teachers and also by spending hours in prayer and in singing psalms. The care with which these theological students were trained to be the guardians of learning as well as the teachers of the gospel may be gathered from the fact that frequently eighteen years of study were required of them before they were ordained.[19] In other words, Iona was not a monastery, but a great mission institute. It can be likened to the schools of the prophets of the Old Testament, or to the wonderful training centers of the Church of the East.

Doctrines of the Church in Scotland

The fact that Ireland lay outside the bounds of the Roman Empire kept it from the saint worship, image worship, and relic worship which flooded the state church at that time. And at Iona there is no record of the theological students' digging for relics, or sending to Rome for relics which were reputed to have belonged to some martyred Christian. There were no processions in which relics were displayed, no burning of incense or candles before a tomb. In fact, at the time when the apostle to the Picts had erected his spiritual lighthouse in Scottish Dalriada, England had yet been untouched by papal monasteries of the continental type.

Happily, Columba had more than a generation in which to work before the influence of rulers on the Continent brought another type of Christianity to the shores of England. He built his church on the Bible and the Bible only. He could look to the authentic copy of the

---

[18] Bede, *Ecclesiastical History of England*, b. 3, ch. 25.
[19] Moore, *The Culdee Church*, page 48.

Confession of Patrick, his great predecessor, who in this short document had used twenty-five quotations from the Holy Scriptures.[20] Columba taught his followers never to receive as religious truth any doctrine not sustained by proofs drawn from the Sacred Writings. Bede expressly declares that Columba sailed away from Ireland to Scotland for the definite purpose of converting heathen to the word of God.[21] It is said of Baithen, the successor of Columba at Iona, that he had no equal this side of the Alps in his knowledge of the Sacred Scriptures and in his understanding of science.[22]

The Columban system of institutions was a confederation of spiritual centers held together by invisible bonds of grace and truth, each locality looking to the brotherhood as the final source of authority. It had no pope, and it had no descending steps of clergy like archbishop, bishop, priest, and deacon. The headman of each locality was generally the abbot of the mission institute.[23] These centers of spiritual life and training grew into well-organized institutions splendidly adapted to the spreading of Bible truths.

For many centuries Iona was recognized as the leading center, whose chief officer besides being called an abbot, was also known as the coarb, or spiritual successor, of Columba.[24] While there was a term resembling the word "bishop" sometimes used to designate the clergy, it did not mean a bishop in the twentieth-century acceptation of the term.[25] The word "Culdee," meaning "man of God," was later used to designate the Columban church.

Maclauchlan states that, generally speaking, most of the features which can be shown to have characterized the Scottish Church, even at the later period, were such that no Protestant could censure them.[26] Success attended these consecrated men as they pioneered in the conversion of the northern and western parts of Scotland, and Christianized the center of Scotland and the eastern portion of England by Iona's colonies. The remains of places of worship, which still stand in the north and are found to extend to the farthest distance of the

[20] DeVinne, *History of the Irish Primitive Church,* page 47.
[21] Bede, *Ecclesiastical History of England,* b. 3, ch. 4.
[22] Fitzpatrick, *Ireland and the Making of Britain,* page 21.
[23] Killen, *The Old Catholic Church,* page 294.
[24] Maclauchlan, *Early Scottish Church,* page 428.
[25] Jamieson, *Historical Account of the Ancient Culdees of Iona,* page 36.
[26] Maclauchlan, *Early Scottish Church,* page 327.

Hebrides, testify to the all-pervading influence of the Culdee Church.[27]

> There was a continual stream of missionaries from the churches of Ireland and Scotland flowing toward the continental church, of which we have ample evidence in the numerous Gaelic MSS. belonging to these churches found in continental monasteries.[28]

Bible Manuscripts and Bible Studies

If it be true that Columba with his own hand copied three hundred New Testaments, as well as portions of the Old Testament, what must have been the output of Iona when all the workers assigned to the making of manuscripts produced their contribution? It must not be forgotten that Columba, while supervising the institutions in Scotland, never relinquished the care of the many training centers he had established in Ireland during the first forty years of his life. It is small wonder that the Irish and Scottish Churches covered the British Isles and the continent of Europe with their thousands of missionary centers in a short period.

Lucy Menzies, in her life of Columba, gives the following excellent presentation of the copying done by the Scottish Church:

> In this as in everything connected with the spread of Christianity in Scotland, we have to look to Ireland for the history and development of the art. Letters were known in Ireland before St. Patrick's day; he used to instruct his disciples in the art of writing. The characters and designs used by these early scribes were probably of Byzantine origin and would come to Ireland from Ravenna through Gaul. The Irish adapted them to their own idea of beauty, but though early Irish manuscripts have features peculiar to Ireland, similar interlacings are found in early Italian churches, especially in those of Ravenna. These interlacings symbolized life and immortality, having neither beginning nor end. Designs of interlaced ribbon work, plaited rushes, bands, cords, and knots are common to the earliest art of various peoples, and when the first missionaries came to Ireland bringing copies of the Gospels, they naturally brought this art with them. The object of the writing was, of course, to multiply copies of the Scriptures. . . . There must have been at Iona a separate room or hut where the writing materials were kept, a library where those engaged in transcribing the Scriptures might work, where the *polaires* containing the finished copies hung on the walls and where the valuable manuscripts were kept.[29]

---

[27] Maclauchlan, *Early Scottish Church*, page 336.
[28] *Ibid.*, page 380.
[29] Menzies, *Saint Columba of Iona*, pages 68, 70.

The youth in the Culdee schools clung to the fundamental Christian doctrines, such as the divinity of Christ, baptism, the atonement, inspiration of the Scriptures, and the prophecies connected with the last days. They did not accept the doctrines of infallibility, celibacy, transubstantiation, the confessional, the mass, relic worship, image adoration, and the primacy of Peter. As Killen says:

> The monastery was, in fact, a college where all the branches of learning then known were diligently cultivated; where astronomy was studied; where Greek as well as Latin literature entered into the curriculum; where the sons of kings and nobles received tuition; and where pious and promising youths were training up for the sacred office. . . . But theology was the subject with which the attention of the teachers of the monastery was chiefly occupied; the Bible was their daily textbook; their pupils were required to commit much of it to memory.[30]

The last hours of Columba are recorded as follows:

> Having continued his labors in Scotland thirty-four years, he clearly and openly foretold his death, and on Saturday, the ninth of June, said to his disciple Diermit: "This day is called the Sabbath, that is, the day of rest, and such will it truly be to me; for it will put an end to my labors."[31]

The Century After Columba's Death

It is written of Saul in the divine word that "there went with him a band of men, whose hearts God had touched." In like manner some members of the noble galaxy surrounding Columba were so filled with the flame of living fire that they subdued unconquerable warriors of that northern land for Christ. Standing first among these contemporaries of Columba was Baithen. Unwilling always to be sheltered under the wing of Iona, the parent institution, he obtained leave to sail westward to the island of Tiree where he built a subordinate training center. Then, after having spread the influence of Iona over northwestern Scotland, he returned to the original center to become its head after Columba died. Although privileged to occupy the abbot's seat for only four years prior to his death, he obtained widespread fame for remarkable learning and courageous labors.

It would be thrilling to read how Kenneth, Ciaran, Colmonnel, Donnan, Molaise, and others pushed their way southward into the promontories of Kintyre; to the Western Isles, or Hebrides; to the

---

[30] Killen, *The Old Catholic Church,* page 292.
[31] Butler, *Lives of the Saints,* vol. 6, p. 139.

beautiful counties of Fife, Forfarshire, Aberdeen, which look out toward the waters of Norway; and above all, to northern Scotland, especially the counties of Caithness, Sutherland, and Ross. Here the members of the Celtic Church converted the heathen and built churches; they founded institutions copied after the model of Iona; they distributed Bibles, taught the people to read, and fired their converts with their own missionary zeal. If Iona was the center of the northern Picts, so Abernethy became the same to the southern Picts. They pushed farther south into the Anglo-Saxon kingdom of Northumbria.

As early as the middle of the seventh century, or about one hundred years after the founding of Iona, several large and influential mission schools had sprung up in the British Isles.[32] Probably next to Iona in fame is Lindisfarne on the northeastern coast of England. This spiritual center is prominently connected with Aidan whose work is considered in Chapter XII.

Battling Against the Northmen and the Papacy

The four hundred years following the establishment of Iona are noted for three events in England and Scotland. First, there was intense rivalry and warfare between the seven kingdoms of England, known as the Heptarchy, and the three kingdoms of Scotland. Second, all three countries — England, Ireland, and Scotland — were harassed, invaded, and in the case of England and Ireland, conquered, by the Northmen, especially the Danes. Third, and probably the most far-reaching event, was the intense struggle waged between the papacy and the Celtic Church. In Scotland the kingdoms of the Picts and the Britons were finally absorbed by the ever-increasing Scots. If England suffered such serious consequences at the hands of the Normans and Ireland at the hands of the Danes, it can readily be seen how difficult must have been the struggle of the Celtic Church to hold its own against the power of the papacy when backed by the all-powerful papal states of the Continent.

Within the one hundred twenty-five years after the death of Columba, the Picts had been swayed enough by the mighty influence of Rome to adopt the Roman Easter. Nevertheless, the change in Easter did not represent a complete surrender to the papacy. About

---

[32]Maclauchlan, *Early Scottish Church,* page 226.

the same time Nechtan, the Pictish king, expelled the Columban clergy. When, however, the conquering Kenneth MacAlpine, king of the Scots, in 846, united under the one crown the Scots and the Picts, he brought the Columban clergy back in honor. He was the king who removed the seat of the government from Iona to Forteviot, the ancient capital of the Pictish kingdom. In his day the Danes were furiously assaulting the coasts, making inroads among the Western Isles, while they practically seized supreme power in both Ireland and England. Fierce warriors as they were, they soon learned that they were no match for the Scots. Scotland must have been a wealthy country at this time because, in those northern latitudes, it attracted the century-long invasion of the Northmen. It is interesting to add that in the midst of these commotions Andrew became the patron saint of Scotland, while the thistle was chosen for its national emblem. The latter was selected because of a historic incident: When the Danes were about to make a surprise attack, a warrior planting his foot on the thistle uttered a cry of pain loud enough to be heard by the fighting Scots.

Although the Danes frequently burned and pillaged Iona, the veneration for it was so great and the pilgrimages made to it so many that it could not long remain in a devastated condition. It was a learned and righteous clergy which directed the Culdee Church, and they were so beloved by the people that this communion was deeply rooted in the affections of all. It must be kept in mind that through the two centuries that the Northmen fought to plant themselves in Scotland, the Danes were still heathen. It is repeatedly recorded how devout kings, warriors, and people would seize the remains of Columba and carry them to a place of safety, sometimes in Ireland, and sometimes further east in Scotland. For some time the bishop of Armagh in Ireland stood forth as the successor both of Columba and Patrick, the two offices often being united in the same person. Through these years as one kingdom sought to conquer another, the warring powers would naturally call for allies. Here was the chance of the papacy. As the centuries passed, the Celtic Church and the civil rulers who were pro-Celtic would look across to the Continent, but they could discern no great nation which had not made an alliance with Rome.

The dates, 1058 and 1066, stand for startling changes. There were only eight years between the time when Malcolm III became king of

Scotland, and the year that William the Norman conquered England. By the time Malcolm III had reached the throne, the aggressive Scots had succeeded in absorbing Strathclyde, the northwest kingdom of the Britons. Vigorously they had extended their territory southward to the River Tweed. As the Northmen were still in possession of the Western Isles, they had driven a wedge between Ireland and Scotland. Since it was the papacy that abetted the Norman invasion of England by William, the church of Columba in Scotland found herself alone without any strong political backing in Ireland, England, or on the Continent.

Moreover, Malcolm III, or Malcolm Canmore (that is, "large head"), had been educated in England in company with the Roman Catholic king, Edward the Confessor. When he came to the throne of Scotland he was the least imbued with the Celtic atmosphere and Celtic ideas of any of his predecessors. Yet as late as 1058, the Scottish Church remained largely as it had been modeled by its early teachers. But the crowning of Malcolm brought these believers in early Christianity into a fierce struggle. Malcolm III took Margaret as his second wife, a girl who had been determined to enter a nunnery. She was a member of one of the former royal houses of England. In exile in Hungary, she and her brothers were brought up in a strong Catholic atmosphere. Malcolm III was passionately devoted to her because she had renounced her plan to become a nun to marry him. However, in return she took charge of religious affairs and, instructed by some of the ablest men of the papal church from England and the Continent, set in motion the force which for three centuries placed the church of Columba in the shadows.

Queen Margaret and the Scottish Church

Margaret found the Scottish Church a church of the people; she determined to make it the church of the monarch. The passion of her life might be summed up in one word — Rome. As Dr. Barnett writes: "Hungary was a strongly Roman Catholic country. . . . Here we touch the first vital source from which Queen Margaret drew her passionate attachment to the Roman Church." [33] And again he writes, "Zeal for the church literally consumed her." [34] What her pur-

---

[33] Barnett, *Margaret of Scotland: Queen and Saint,* page 7.
[34] *Ibid.,* page 87.

poses were in marrying Malcolm III, king of Scotland, this same
writer states further, "Margaret very soon after her marriage is setting
about a movement to Romanize and Anglicize the ancient Celtic
Church in Scotland."[35] Still another quotation from the same author
helps to clarify the vast and determined purpose of this queen:

> It will be readily understood, therefore, that this saintly queen who had
> been brought up among the comparative magnificence of monastic religion,
> first in Hungary, and then in England where buildings like Westminster
> Abbey were being conceived, would be anxious to bring the church in the
> land of her adoption into line with all-powerful Rome.[36]

The contest which now opened was a strife between the throne and
the people. In herself the queen possessed the weapon of a keen
intellect, a strong memory, a readiness in subtle expression, and a
polemic training in the defense of papal doctrines. She also brought
to the battle a group of monastic scholars who could both prompt and
protect her in her attacks on the Celtic Church. When Margaret
landed on the shores of Fife with her retinue, the people witnessed
the largest vessels ever seen on Caledonian shores. The inhabitants
of these rural glades beheld the beauty of the Saxon princess. However, they placed a greater value upon the grace of God than upon the
queen's rubies and diamonds. Both the Scriptures and the life and
deeds of Columba had taught them the love of the spiritual.

To destroy the glory of Columba was impossible. Margaret
might as well attempt to degrade the apostle Paul. In five hundred
years the love of Scotland for Columba had not dulled. A more
feasible avenue to success would be to legislate against the religious
customs of the Celtic Church. Margaret never hesitated to unite
church and state. Like Constantine, she joined together that which
Christ had put asunder. Beginning with a Sunday law, she proceeded
to the demolition of the Celtic Church. How little does the public
suspect that religious legislation to enforce Easter and Sunday has
often been the method of choking the life out of a liberty-loving
church.

This procedure was used by Margaret. The queen called an
ecclesiastical congress, and for three days she sat in the chair. She

---

[35] Barnett, *Margaret of Scotland: Queen and Saint,* page 41.
[36] *Ibid.,* page 87.

argued, cajoled, commanded, and within a soft glove manipulated an iron hand. The blunt, impatient, warlike king stood by her side with his hand on the hilt of the sword. Did not the emperor Constantine support the episcopal chair at the great Council of Nicaea, in 325, when a pompous church became the spouse of the Roman Empire? Did not King Oswy preside in northern England at the Council of Whitby (A. D. 664), when a terrible blow was struck at the Celtic Church amid the Anglo-Saxons? And so Malcolm's fervent love for his consort led him to place the full power of the state behind the queen.

Problems of the Council

Though details are lacking, it is not difficult to picture the leaders of Columba's church in Scotland as, for three days, they were obliged to listen to the proceedings of Margaret's council. There were points of difference as is recorded in her *Life*, written by her priestly confessor, Turgot.[37] The first two points were relative to the agelong controversy about Easter. It was all a matter of religious opinion, with which the government had no right to concern itself. As to the third point, on the celebration of the mass, some authorities think this was an indignant threat, because the Culdees conducted the services of the Lord's Supper not in Latin, as Rome did, but in the native language.

The question of Sabbath and Sunday was particularly contested. As shown previously in quotations from Drs. Flick and Barnett,[38] the traditional practice of the Celtic Church was to observe Saturday instead of Sunday as the day of rest. This position is supported by a host of authors. The Roman Catholic historian, Bellesheim, gives the claim of the queen and describes the practice of the Scots as follows:

> The queen further protested against the prevailing abuse of Sunday desecration. "Let us," she said, "venerate the Lord's day, inasmuch as upon it our Saviour rose from the dead: let us do not servile work on that day.". . . The Scots in this matter had no doubt kept up the traditional practice of the ancient monastic Church of Ireland, which observed Saturday rather than Sunday as a day of rest.[39]

---

[37] Barnett, *Margaret of Scotland: Queen and Saint,* page 89.

[38] See Chapter VII, entitled, "Patrick, Organizer of the Church in the Wilderness in Ireland."

[39] Bellesheim, *History of the Catholic Church of Scotland,* vol. 1, pp. 249, 250.

Andrew Lang writing up on the general practice of the Celtic Church says: "They worked on Sunday, but kept Saturday in a sabbatical manner."[40] Another author states:

> It seems to have been customary in the Celtic churches of early times, in Ireland as well as Scotland, to keep Saturday the Jewish Sabbath, as a day of rest from labor. They obeyed the fourth commandment literally upon the seventh day of the week.[41]

The historian Skene in commenting upon the work of Queen Margaret also reveals the prominence of the Sabbath question as follows:

> Her next point was that they did not duly reverence the Lord's day, but in this latter instance they seemed to have followed a custom of which we find traces in the early monastic Church of Ireland, by which they held Saturday to be the Sabbath on which they rested from all their labors, and on Sunday on the Lord's day, they celebrated the resurrection.[42]

As pointed out in the story of Patrick, the opposition to the Ten Commandments failed to recognize that the culminating reason for the death of Christ upon the cross was that while becoming man's substitute He was to uphold the moral law. The papal church denies the death of Christ on the cross as man's substitute and surety.[43] Columba, however, did recognize this truth. A verse from the poem by him addressed to his Redeemer reads as follows:

> As Thou didst suffer on the cross
> To save a guilty race
> Show me Thy power, with Thy love
> And glory grant, with grace.[44]

Nothing so quickly leads to persecution as Sunday laws. In a land like Scotland there could be the Anglo-Saxon sect observing Sunday, the Celtic Church consecrating Saturday from the days of the apostles, Moslems observing Friday, and unbelievers celebrating no day. A law which would single out any one certain day of the week and exalt it to sacredness would be sectarian legislation. Soon the favored sect would indulge in feelings of superiority and point the finger of scorn

[40] Lang, *A History of Scotland*, vol. 1, p. 96.
[41] Moffat, *The Church in Scotland*, page 140.
[42] Skene, *Celtic Scotland*, vol. 2, p. 349.
[43] See Note 53, p. 60, of this book.
[44] Smith, *The Life of Columba*, page 142.

at those conscientiously observing another day. Bitterness would set in speedily, followed by persecution.

In this way the Culdees were ordered to conform or to depart. When King David, the son of Margaret, had confiscated their Loch Leven lands, he ordered them to conform to the rites of the Sunday-keeping monks, on whom he had conferred the dispossessed property, or to be expelled.[45] Needless to say, they were expelled. This was in the year 1130.

Scotland Subsequent to the Papal Penetration

The unscrupulousness of the victors in destroying or in misrepresenting the records of the past has placed a false face over the true story of the Celtic Church.[46] The gulf between that church and the papacy was great even as late as 1120. A severe difference arose between King Alexander, another son of Margaret, and Eadmer, a newly appointed head to the bishopric of Saint Andrews. When he asked counsel of two Canterbury monks, they made a remarkable statement, "For they say that Eadmer cannot accommodate himself to the usages of the Scottish Church without dishonoring his character and hazarding his salvation."[47] Although Rome admits that as late as 1120 the usages of the Culdees were so far from those of Rome that a bishop would endanger his eternal salvation to follow them, yet at the same time she did to Scotland's hero as she had done to Patrick — enrolled Columba as a Roman saint.

> It is a remarkable fact that those very regions in which the Iro-Scottish mission work was most successful during the sixth and seventh centuries were precisely the regions in which the evangelical sects of the later times flourished most.[48]

The transformations in character and practices wrought by Columba and his successors elevated the condition of women, brought loving attention to the children, produced Bible-loving believers, brought proper relations between church and state, and breathed an enduring missionary life into a vigorous western people. In Scotland the seeds were sown plentifully and deep. There was a rich evan-

---

[45] Maclauchlan, *Early Scottish Church,* pages 400-403.
[46] *Ibid.,* page 390.
[47] *Ibid.,* page 395.
[48] Newman, *A Manual of Church History,* vol. 1, p. 414.

gelical subsoil. This enrichment endured long, although the growth was later covered by a layer of papal practices and traditions. When the Reformation came to this realm, it was to a large extent a reversal of the royal establishment of popery in Scotland. The papacy had been unable to wholly exterminate the faith and simpler system of the ancient Culdees, especially in those districts which were the earliest abodes and latest retreats of primitive Christianity. As there were reformers in nearly every other country in Europe before the Reformation, it could not be far wrong to conclude that they also continued to exist in that country which was the last to register its public protest against the usurpation of the Church of Rome.

"No religion ever has been destroyed by persecution if the people confessing it were not destroyed." The ancient faith of Columba was handed down from father to son enshrouded in lasting love and affection. The sufferings which the Scots underwent at the hand of the usurping religion also deepened their faith even as expression deepens impression. Encroachments of the Romanists were firmly resisted. As appears later, individuals of the Waldensian communion as well as followers of Wycliffe were found in Scotland during the days of papal supremacy there. The final and permanent uprising against religious tyranny came when the Reformation secured this land as one of her greatest allies. It is not an injustice to history to say that Scotland twice saved the world for the Reformation. At length the Church in the Wilderness triumphed, due in no small degree to the impetus given it by the wonderful organization and godly life of Columba.

CHAPTER IX

Papas, First Head of the Church in Asia

The Nestorian Christians are the small, but venerable, remnant of a once great and influential Christian church. They are the oldest of Christian sects; and, in their better days, were numerous through all the vast regions from Palestine to China; and they carried the gospel into China itself.[1]

IN THE stories of Vigilantius and Patrick a survey was made of the true church in central Europe and in Ireland. The story of Papas (spelled Papas by Smith and Wace, Papa by Wigram, Phapas by others) takes us eastward to a vast, densely populated region which was already the home of unnumbered Christian churches. When Papas was chosen supreme head of the Church of the East in 285, no general director of an extensive Christian organization had before been thought of as far as history shows. Papas was a contemporary of Lucian, and like him, a forerunner of Patrick and of Vigilantius. From the facts related in this chapter, one can see that these latter two must have been strongly influenced in their work by the experience of Papas and the Church of the East.

In the story of Papas an attempt is made to tell when and where the Church of the East was organized. As this church arose it was faced with strong counterfeit religions. The Church of the East is often called the Assyrian Church because it lies in the territory once called Assyria. This region stretches along the Tigris and Euphrates Rivers where once were the ancient realms of Assyria and Babylon. It is often called Mesopotamia, as well as Assyria. This church is many times wrongly called the Nestorian Church. And because Seleucia, its headquarters, is only about forty miles from the former city of Babylon, it has been termed the Church of Babylon, and also the Chaldean Church.

Papas was chosen to be the head of the new organization when all the world was astir. The greatness of his vision meant much to the Church in the Wilderness. At the time of his election, he had been church director in the region lying around Seleucia. The creation of

---

[1] Perkins, *A Residence of Eight Years in Persia*, page 1.

the new office elevated him from provincial director to the position of head over all the Church of the East. The unity abiding in that body was so strong that the directors of church provinces from Assyria to China confirmed this choice, recognizing and submitting to the supreme authority of Papas. He came to influence Syrian, or Assyrian, Christianity when a leader was needed who would not only direct the growing work in the Orient, but also show how the Church of the East should relate itself to Christianity in Europe. Papas is recognized as a learned man, versed in Persian and Syrian literature.[2]

Transforming Heathenism Without Being Transformed

Only a hundred years after the death of the apostle John, the Assyrian Christians had planted their churches among the Parthians, Persians, Medes, Bactrians, Scythians, Turks, and Huns.[3] One circumstance which made this possible was the conversion of thousands of listeners on the Day of Pentecost who returned with the gospel to the Parthians, Medes, Elamites, Arabians, and dwellers in Mesopotamia.[4] The truths of Christianity broke down entrenched polygamy among the Parthians. Their church doors were opened only to those Parthians who had but one wife. The "motions of sin in the flesh" vanished in the converts who walked no longer after the flesh, but after the spirit. Among their Persian converts, they had found incest universally practiced. Fathers married their daughters, and sons took their mothers to wife. This practice was part of Zoroastrianism, the state religion.[5] The anger of the state, as well as the wrath of the mobeds, the Magian priests, was brought down on anyone who spoke against it. All this was changed among the Christians.

Preaching the high standards of the New Testament also elevated the industrial life of the Medes, Bactrians, Huns, and Scythians. The powers of darkness fell before the children of light! Bardesanes, writing about 180, puts it this way:

> We are called Christians by the one name of the Messiah. As regards our customs our brethren abstain from everything that is contrary to their profession, e. g., Parthian Christians do not take two wives. Jewish

---

[2] Bar Hebraeus, *Chronicon Ecclesiasticum*, vol. 3, p. 27.
[3] *Recognitions* of Clement, book 9, and Tertullian, *An Answer to the Jews*, chapter 7, found in *Ante-Nicene Fathers*, volumes 8, 3.
[4] Acts 2:9-11.
[5] Prideaux, *The Old and New Testament Connected*, vol. 1, p. 203.

Christians are not circumcised. Our Bactrian sisters do not practice promiscuity with strangers. Persians do not take their daughters to wife. Medes do not desert their dying relations or bury them alive. Christians in Edessa do not kill their wives or sisters who commit fornication but keep them apart and commit them to the judgment of God. Christians in Hatra do not stone thieves.[6]

Particular attention is called to the statement in the foregoing quotation, "Jewish Christians are not circumcised." This refutes the charge that Christians who sanctified Saturday also practiced circumcision.

The successes of the Assyrian Christians among the Scythians constituted a moral revolution. That vast, undefined region, lying north and east of the Black and Caspian Seas, generally known as Scythia, was a cradle of nations. Over and over again, successive waves of fierce warriors drove westward through the civilized parts of Asia. Often they settled in the territory they conquered and founded new kingdoms.

One Scythian tribe in particular may be noted. It seized the territory of northwestern India, which was then ruled by the successors of Alexander the Great, and founded the Kushan dynasty (A. D. 45-225). It had in its list several notable kings, one of which, fervently devoted to Buddhism, called a famous council of Buddhist priests with the intent of promoting unity among the monks and of converting the whole world to the new religion of India. One chief object sought in this conference was to bring uniformity among the Buddhist monks on the observance of their weekly Sabbath. A world convention held at Vaisali reveals how the Old Testament had impressed upon Buddha and his followers the weekly observance of a sacred day. Of this council Arthur Lloyd writes:

> Was it permissible for brethren belonging to the same community to keep the sabbaths separately? . . . We can see how strong was the current of party feeling from the question about the sabbath. The opposing parties could evidently no longer meet together for the joint celebration of the customary observances, and the tension between the monks of the east and the west was very great.[7]

Thus it is plainly seen how the field had been prepared for the coming of Christianity.

---

[6] Stewart, *Nestorian Missionary Enterprises*, page 78.
[7] Lloyd, *The Creed of Half Japan*, page 23.

The missionaries from Assyria did not recoil from entering the kingdoms founded by the Scythians in India and Scythia, nor did they fail to persevere in their attempts to evangelize the numerous tribes to the north. They pitched their tents alongside these wandering peoples on the plains of Tartary. There they planted thousands of Christian centers and achieved marvelous successes in missionary endeavors.[8]

Seleucia, Headquarters of the Church

To understand the might of the Church of the East over which Papas was elected first supreme head, consideration should be given to the twin cities of Seleucia and Ctesiphon, the first center of this strong organization. It must be remembered that in the days of the apostles it was the Parthian Empire which lay east of Syria and Asia Minor. This empire was destined to endure for nearly five hundred years (250 B. C. to A. D. 226). It continued long enough to see the Romans come up and subjugate the weak successors of Alexander. The Romans, however, dreaded a clash with the Parthians because of their crushing cavalry. Had the Parthians put down Zoroastrianism, a religion which had been strong and crafty and determined to rule the state since the days of the Persian Empire, and had the Parthians been more avaricious of power, they might have continued to be dreaded conquerors.[9] But they failed to do this. The Persians overthrew them in 226, and the new empire also set up its capital at Seleucia. When Papas was elected supreme leader of the church, he moved its headquarters there. Thus during the centuries that Seleucia and Ctesiphon comprised the seat of government, first of the Parthians and then of the Persian Empire, New Testament believers looked to this place as their earthly spiritual center.[10]

It was a region to stir the imagination. Not far from the churches along the Euphrates River the Garden of Eden had cradled the human race. In this neighborhood the ark had rested after the Flood. Near by, Abraham and his fellow pilgrims had paused as they journeyed from Ur of the Chaldees to the land of Canaan. Had the apostle John

---

[8] See the author's discussion in Chapters XVII to XXIII.

[9] Rawlinson, *The Seven Great Monarchies of the Ancient Eastern World*, vol. 3, ("The Sixth Monarchy"), pp. 207-211.

[10] While the writer was at Bagdad, he visited what remained of Seleucia and Ctesiphon. These ruins are only a few miles from Bagdad.

in his old age visited Edessa, he would have seen one of the fairest and most progressive cities of his day.[11]

Assyrian Church Leaders Before Papas

The century and a half between the death of the apostle John and the time of Papas was full of interest for the believers in the east. Not only there, but also in the west, movements of vast import were taking place in the Christian world. Because of Parthia's tolerant spirit, no iron monarchy held the nations of the Middle East in its viselike grip as the Roman Empire held Europe. The roads were open for the youth who bade father and mother farewell as they responded to the Macedonian call. Travelers paused at the famous cities of Edessa or Arbela as they passed on their way from the Celts of Ireland to the Celts of Turkistan or Mongolia. Neither the hoarfrosts in the tableland nor the monsoons of India could restrain the zealous evangelists of the Syrian missions. In their hands they held that fountain of inspiration, the Peshitta, the Syriac translation of the Bible. Burkitt says: "The place that is occupied among English-speaking Christians by the Authorised Version is occupied in the Syriac churches by the Peshitta."[12] That version was to have a circulation nearly as great as the Authorized Version in the West. The Christians memorized it, they recited it, they sang it. Mongolian, Manchu, Tartar, Hindu, Malay, and Filipino heard with astonishment the message as it fell from their lips.

The tolerant attitude of the Parthian Empire, until its overthrow in 226, facilitated freedom of movement. No favored religion drove the state to inaugurate persecution. It is true that Zoroastrianism in its homeland of Persia proper was arrogant. Nevertheless, although it was powerful, it was not considered the imperial religion, the *religio licita*, of this region.

The subkingdom of Adiabene, being under the Parthian Empire, was permitted to live its own life. However, the five successive provincial directors in this realm before Papas suffered for their faith.[13] Samson was put to death because of the opposition of the Zoroastrians. His successor, Isaac, was imprisoned for some time in a pit because

---

[11] Wigram and Wigram, *The Cradle of Mankind,* page 17.
[12] Burkitt, *Early Eastern Christianity,* page 41.
[13] Wigram, *Introduction to the History of the Assyrian Church,* pages 27-34.

he had sheltered a prominent man who was a convert from Magianism. At the time of Noah (A. D. 163-179), the Zoroastrians invented a new and despicable kind of persecution. Kidnaping the daughters of the Christians, they sought to win from the maidens some expression favorable to their religion of sun worship. Once that was done, they claimed these children as converts and took them into a life of captivity.

A royal decree of toleration was about to be issued when the death of the Parthian monarch frustrated its publication. The last directing pastor in Adiabene spans the closing years of the Parthian Empire. Then came the vast movement to elect a head of the entire Church of the East. There must have been considerable stir when Papas was chosen.[14] This united action brought together spiritual leaders from many large church provinces and thus new life and hope were brought to the believers from Syria to China.

Toward the end of the second century, while the Christians of the East were busily pushing the work of evangelization from Asia Minor to Scythia, they were suddenly startled by the order from Victor I, bishop of Rome, excommunicating them. In clinging to certain practices, they followed the Scriptures; they had been adverse to the novel theories and practices which their brethren in the Roman Empire had been introducing. The subtle spiritual dangers to the true church in the West were more threatening than the physical dangers assailing the Church of the East. To understand this first usurpation whereby the ecclesiastical power at Rome alienated eastern Christians, a short explanation is necessary.

Separation of the Churches

A division between church members who sought world leadership and those who humbly followed Jesus was growing in Europe. The majority of writings of Christian authors acceptable to the West, which have come down to us from the centuries immediately following the apostles, reflect the mixture of Christianity and pagan philosophy. This is especially true of the allegorizing teachers and graduates of the church college of Alexandria.

Many eminent theologians, particularly Protestant, speak against accepting the writings of the so-called apostolic fathers with too much

---

[14] Bar Hebraeus, *Chronicon Ecclesiasticum,* vol. 3, p. 27.

authority. Augustus Neander says that they have "come down to us in a condition very little worthy of confidence."[15]   John L. Mosheim testifies that they all believed the language of the Scriptures to contain two meanings, the one plain, the other hidden; that they attached more value to the hidden meaning, thus throwing obscurity over the Sacred Writings.[16]   Archdeacon Frederic W. Farrar writes: "There are but few of them whose pages are not rife with errors." "Their acquaintance with the Old Testament is incorrect, popular, and full of mistakes."[17]   While Martin Luther, who had studied deeply into the writings of those allegorizing, mystical church fathers, declared that God's word when it is expounded by them is like straining milk through a coal sack.[18]   Adam Clarke testifies that "there is not a truth in the most orthodox creed, that cannot be proved by their authority, nor a heresy that has disgraced the Romish Church, that may not challenge them as its abettors."[19]

In the second century the aims of the sun-worshiping emperors and those of the Alexandrian theologians ran parallel. There was an ambitious scheme on foot to blend all religions into one of which "the sun was to be the central object of adoration."[20]   Speaking of the influence of pagan philosophy on early church writers, Schaff says, "We can trace it . . . even in St. Augustine, who confessed that it kindled in him an incredible fire."[21]

Approving in their hearts the conciliating attitude of the pagan emperors and the mass methods of Alexandria's evangelism, the bishops of Rome decided to eclipse any public attraction which pagan festivals could offer. Seated in the empire's capital, from the height of their pedestal of influence, they determined to bring together Easter, a yearly festival, and Sunday, a weekly holiday sacred to the worship of the sun, to make the greatest church festival of the year.

The controversy over Easter, which was to rage for centuries, now began. God had ordained that the Passover of the Old Testament should be celebrated in the spring of the year on the fourteenth day

---

[15] Neander, *General History of the Christian Religion and Church,* vol. 1, p. 657.
[16] Mosheim, *Institutes of Ecclesiastical History,* b. 1, cent. 3, pt. 2, ch. 3, par. 5.
[17] Farrar, *History of Interpretation,* pages 162, 165.
[18] Luther, *Table Talk,* page 228.
[19] Clarke, *Commentary,* on Proverbs 8.
[20] Milman, *The History of Christianity,* vol. 2, pp. 175, 176.
[21] Schaff, *History of the Christian Church,* 2d Period, vol. 2, par. 173.

of the first Bible month. Heathenism in the centuries before Christ had a counterfeit yearly holiday celebrating the spring equinox of the sun. It was called "Eostre" from the Scandinavian word for the goddess of spring, from whence we get our word "Easter." Since the resurrection of Christ had occurred at the time of the Old Testament Passover, a custom developed of celebrating it yearly, though neither Christ nor the New Testament provided for it.[22] This rivaled the pagan spring festival. However, the fourteenth day of the month of the Passover could fall, as now, on any day of the week. The eastern churches celebrated the resurrection of Christ annually two days after the Passover feast. They commemorated the resurrection on whatever day of the week the sixteenth day of the month fell. This was in harmony with the way the Bible regulated the Old Testament Passover feast.

In addition to their yearly spring festival at Eastertime, sun worshipers also had a weekly festival holiday. As was previously pointed out, the first day of the week had widespread recognition as being sacred to the sun. The bishop of Rome, seeking to outrival pagan pomp, assaulted those churches which celebrated Easter as a movable feast. He determined to force Easter to come on the same day of the week each year, namely, Sunday.[23]

By this he would create a precedent which only a devout and scholarly opposition could expose. By this he would appeal to the popular prejudices of his age, be they ever so incorrect. By this he would claim to be the lord of the calendar, that instrument so indispensable to civilized nations. By this he would assert the right to appoint church festivals and holy days. By this he would confuse and perplex other church communions, more simple and scriptural than he. Only those who have read carefully the history of the growth of papal power will ever know how powerfully the controversy concerning Easter served in the hands of the bishops of Rome.

Victor I, the bishop of Rome, assembled provincial synods up and down the Mediterranean coasts to come to an agreement on the date of Easter. Clement, at the head of the school of Alexandria, brought decision in favor of Rome's attitude by publishing a summary of

---

[22] Killen, *The Old Catholic Church*, page 275.
[23] Bower, *The History of the Popes*, vol. 1, p. 18; also, Hefele, *History of the Christian Councils*, vol. 1, pp. 300-313.

traditions he had collected in favor of Sunday observance.[24] Clement went further. There is no record of a writer daring to call Sunday the Lord's day before him. This Clement did. At the same time Victor proclaimed it to all the nations around the Mediterranean. He knew that the pagans would agree to a fixed yearly spring festival and that those Christians who were becoming worldly would do the same. Therefore, he issued his decree ordering the clergy everywhere to observe Easter on the first Sunday following the first full moon after the spring equinox. A lordly command issuing from one bishop over others was something new in the world. Christian clergy, up to that time, had had their provincial synods. Generally, they had followed the decrees obtained by a majority vote in these regional gatherings. Never before Victor I, had any bishop dared to pass over the head of the provincial synods to command other clergy to obey his decrees. The shock was so astonishing and the resistance to it so pronounced that the historian Archibald Bower describes this assumption of power as "the first essay of papal usurpation." [25]

The Church of the East answered the lordly requisition, declaring with great spirit and resolution that they would by no means depart from the custom handed down to them. Then the thunders of excommunication began to roar. Victor, exasperated, broke communication with them, pronounced the clergy of the East unworthy of the name of brethren, and excluded them from all fellowship with the church at Rome.[26] Here was a gulf created between the eastern and the western churches, a gulf which widened as the bishop of Rome grew in power. When Papas was elected as supreme head over the Assyrian communion, he found himself and his church anathematized, excommunicated.

Zoroastrianism Attacks the Church

The Church of the East, excommunicated by the West, was left alone to work out its own destiny. In addition to lying under the ban of Rome, it constantly encountered the persistent opposition of Zoroastrianism, the state religion of Persia, the home of its origin. Zoroaster was the founder of Zoroastrianism, which in its later de-

[24] Shotwell and Loomis, *The See of Peter*, page 276.
[25] Bower, *The History of the Popes*, vol. 1, p. 18.
[26] Mosheim, *Institutes of Ecclesiastical History*, b. 1, cent. 2, pt. 2, ch. 4, par 11.

velopment was called Mithraism. When the attention of a traveler in Persia today is directed to the fire temples which dot the land, he is at once convinced of the former power of Zoroastrianism. Many ruins of these famous fire temples can be found on the Iranian plains.[27] The traveler may likewise visit Malabar Hill, Bombay, India, the well-known spot where the Parsees, descendants of the ancient faith of Persia, dispose of their dead. His chief interest will not be in those cement towers of silence on which the vultures perch, ready to feast upon the lifeless human bodies. He may gaze instead in rapt meditation upon the temple where the robed priest sits near the sacred flame, feeding it sandalwood. The Parsees fled to India after the rapid advance of the armies of the newly born Mohammedanism had struck down the great Persian Empire. They took with them, they claim, the sacred flame. Until their exodus, Persia had been bound together by the almost invincible religion of Mithra, sun-god of Zoroastrianism.

With its alluring philosophy, its deities connected by interesting fantasies with the movements of the stars and planets, its sacred books, its chanted music, its intriguing mysteries, its holy days, and its white-robed hierarchy, Mithraism held sway over the Parthian and Persian Empires for many centuries until its conquest by Mohammedanism in 636. It all but seized the Roman Empire in its permanent grip.

Zoroaster's Imitation of Bible Doctrines

Historians have been astonished by the remarkable similarity between the religion of the Bible and the entrancing mysteries from the Iranian tableland. While these writers are divided over the facts concerning Zoroaster, we will present strong evidence to show that he, like other certain world-wide religious impostors, appears on the pages of the past as a counterfeiter of the Old Testament in general and in particular of the fertile visions granted to the prophet Daniel. The reader will be interested in the statements now offered.

The learned Prideaux speaks plainly of Zoroaster's activities, as a subordinate of the prophet Daniel who was a prime minister of both the Babylonian and Persian Empires. After discussing the different

---

[27] Jackson, *Persia, Past and Present,* pages 133, 153, 253, 281, 336, 366. When the writer visited Malabar Hill, he was told that each white-robed priest serves six hours, thus dividing the twenty-four-hour watch among four priests.

theories of superficial writers concerning this Persian religious mystic, he writes:

> But the Oriental writers, who should best know, all unanimously agree, that there was but one Zerdusht or Zoroastres; and that the time in which he flourished, was while Darius Hystaspes was king of Persia. . . . It must therefore be Daniel under whom this impostor served. . . . And, no doubt, his seeing that great, good, and wise man arrive at such a height and dignity in the empire, by being a true prophet of God, was that which did set this crafty wretch upon the design of being a false one. . . . All which plainly shows the author of this doctrine [Zoroastrianism] to have been well versed in the sacred writings of the Jewish religion out of which it manifestly appears to have been all taken; only the crafty impostor took care to dress it up in such a style and form, as would make it best agree with that old religion of the Medes and Persians which he grafted it upon.[28]

The above hypothesis is supported by the following statements from E. A. Gordon, an Orientalist of wide renown. In reading these testimonies we must remember that Daniel, Ezekiel, and Jeremiah were brought up together as boys and as prophets were prophesying at the same time. Thus, we can see more clearly the possible contacts of Zoroaster with Daniel.

"Note that the Persian sage, Zoroaster, is said to have conferred with Jeremiah, another prophet of the Hebrew exile."

"In the fifth century B. c. Ezekiel gives a wonderful account of the caravan traffic with Tyre in his day, which was also that of Confucius, Lao-tze, Gautama Buddha, and Pythagoras."[29]

In answer to those historians who advocate the hypothesis that the Persian impostor was a legendary character, *The Catholic Encyclopedia* says the following about Zoroaster: "It can no longer be doubted that Zoroaster was a real historical personage. The attempts of some scholars to represent him as a mythical being have failed, even though much that is related about his life is legendary, as in the case of Buddha."[30]

So marked is the similarity between the visions of Daniel and the dreams of Zoroaster that some Biblical commentators who lean

[28] Prideaux, *The Old and New Testament Connected,* vol. 1, pp. 194-197.

[29] Gordon, *"World Healers,"* pages 41, 450.

[30] *The Catholic Encyclopedia,* art. "Avesta."

toward modernism have suggested that Daniel copied his visions from the Persian prophet. Others have confused him with the prophet Daniel. Other writers have thought that both had a common origin, and that the truths of the Old Testament, particularly the prophecies of Daniel, either came from Zoroastrians or were adopted from the Old Testament by Zoroaster.[31]

The following doctrines from the prophet Daniel reappear in the teachings of Zoroaster: one supreme God, the coming of the Messiah, the existence of angels and their revelations to man,[32] the resurrection of the dead, the judgment of all mankind, and Adam and Eve—the first parents. There is a collection of "sacred" volumes—writings composed by Zoroaster — which was called the *Book of Abraham*. The same observances about meats, clean and unclean, are found as were given to Moses. There are commands for the payment of tithe, the ordaining of one high priest over all, and references to Joseph, Moses, and Solomon in the same way as they are presented in the Old Testament. Zoroaster also hated idolatry.

As the Jews had a visible Shekinah of glory, indicating the presence of God in the temple, so Zoroaster taught his priests to behold in the sun and in the sacred fire in the fire temples, the dwelling place of their supreme god. Zoroaster also instituted a priesthood similar to the Jewish priesthood.

In the larger fire temples the priests watched in relays and fed the sacred flame throughout the twenty-four hours of the day. The druidesses of pagan Ireland and the vestal virgins of pagan Rome, both vowed to perpetual virginity, kept the sacred temple fires continually burning for centuries.[33]

Zoroaster arranged the performance of his religion so that it was accompanied by pomp and color. The priests were arrayed in long, white robes and had tall, peaked caps upon their heads. They marched in procession on the stated days of solemn assemblies. Everything was done to make their services impressive. On these occasions libations were poured on the ground, sacred hymns were sung, and portions of the sacred writings of Zoroaster were read. For financial

---

[31] Hopkins, *History of Religions,* pages 408, 409.

[32] Rawlinson, *The Seven Great Monarchies of the Ancient Eastern World,* vol. 3, p. 586.

[33] Killen, *Ecclesiastical History of Ireland,* vol. 1, p. 29.

support they received offerings, and also possessed considerable endowments.[34]

The revelations of the Old Testament had disclosed the Trinity. "In a disfigured and uncouth semblance" Zoroaster proclaimed his species of a trinity.[35] He placed at the head of his celestial hierarchy Ormazd (or Ahura-Mazda), the great wise spirit, and Ahriman, the supreme evil spirit, who was the coeval and rival god of darkness dwelling in the bottomless pit of night. With them he associated in a marked way, Mithra, the god of light, who was the sun and an embodiment of sun worship. As the sun was neither in the heavens nor on earth, but swung in an intermediate position between heaven and earth, so Mithra was the great mediator. When Mithraism had overspread the Roman Empire, Mithra was said to be the champion of sinners, the companion after death, and the guide of the soul into the heaven of heavens.

Ezra, Nehemiah, and Esther had witnessed the domination of the cult of Zoroaster in the Persian Empire. This same religion captivated province after province of the Roman Empire until, through the popularizing of its sun-god, Mithra, it threatened to stifle Christianity.

The devotion to Mithra was astonishingly far-reaching. A long line of Mithraea, or temples of the god, stretched from southern France along the Rhine River, extending over into the territory of the Germanic tribes. Perhaps no political divisions of the state did more to bring glory to the Oriental deity than the Germanic provinces of the empire. The city of Rome itself abounds with the monuments of Mithra.[36] It is an evidence of the great strength of Mithraism that pagan Rome, and later papal Rome, was seen surrendering to the religion of the Persians, its enemies.

It was difficult for Christianity in its pioneer days to face a religion which for six hundred years had been the dominant cult of the Persian and Parthian Empires. A spiritual opposition, however, more serious than persecution devolved upon the early evangelists of Christianity because many outward features and beliefs of Zoroas-

---

[34] Rawlinson, *The Seven Great Monarchies of the Ancient Eastern World*, vol. 3, p. 588.
[35] Edgar, *The Variations of Popery*, page 296.
[36] Cumont, *The Mysteries of Mithra*, pages 79-81.

trianism appeared identical to those of the apostolic church. This anti-Christian religion began to tell of Mithra the mediator, of his terrestrial mission to defend the faithful, of his ascension to heaven, of the baptism he instituted, of his second coming followed by the restoration of all things and the final unending reign of the righteous. Resemblances between Christianity and Zoroastrianism were so great that when the early Christians had multiplied enough to face their opponent, each body was in a position to look upon the other as a counterfeit.

The Sun-Worshiping Creed of Zoroaster

In tying the seasonable observances of its cult to the planets and the stars, Zoroastrianism had opened a field more sure for flights of speculation than the legends of older mythologies. The worst obstacle, however, which the early church had to meet was the exalted character given to Sunday by the Persian devotees. The great defect in many of the ancient religions was that they neglected to assemble their followers one day in seven to hear expounded the laws of their founders. This Moses had commanded his people to do.[37] Zoroastrianism did not neglect this principle. It emphasized the sacredness of one day in seven. Since it was pre-eminently a religion of sun worship, what was more appropriate than to choose Sunday, the day of the sun, as the holy day?[38]

To enhance Sunday observance, the magi, or Persian wise men, taught that the five planets, all that were known in their day, with the sun and the moon, were deities. A day of the week was dedicated to each one of these seven heavenly bodies. Thus Sunday was devoted to Mithra, or the sun, the greatest of all gods of Zoroastrianism.

Their baptismal service, called the "tauroholium," was an example of the Mithraistic rites so abhorrent to the followers of Jesus. The novitiate was made to lie naked on the floor of a lower chamber whose roof was of latticework. In the upper chamber a bull was slain, and the blood dripped through the latticework onto the candidate below. We have already mentioned the practice of incest. Since Mithra was said to have been born in this way, the revolting practice persisted

---

[37] Josephus, *Antiquities of the Jews*, b. 1, ch. 1, par. 1.

[38] Cumont, *The Mysteries of Mithra*, pages 167, 191; also Tertullian, *Apology*, chapter 16, found in *Ante-Nicene Fathers*, volume 3.

through the centuries. In addition to the Persian sacrifices, oblations were used, such as pouring oil or honey or milk onto the ground. As the followers advanced through the seven stages or degrees upward in the cult of Mithraism, many purifications and flagellations were demanded. We have noted the unparalleled rapidity and strength with which Mithraism captured the provinces of the Roman Empire. It was in the homeland of Persia, the center and source of the counterfeit, where the first missionaries of the Christian faith stormed its citadel. Thus, in the opposition of the western ecclesiastical power in Europe and in the powerful antagonist of Zoroastrianism in the East there was an almost insurmountable obstacle to be overcome by the Church of the East. It was providential that at this critical time while the church was extending its vast program toward the East, it unified its forces and found in Papas a strong leader.

The Church Meets Buddha's Counterfeit

In the centuries before Christ and immediately thereafter, the civilized nations became acquainted with one another through navigation, treaties, commerce, and travel.[39] Rome, Greece, Persia, and China were all interested in building and maintaining good roads, and determined to reach out for the other's territory. By the time of Pompey, about 50 B. C., the Roman rule had been extended to the western shores of the Caspian Sea, where the boundary of China was to be found.[40] From the time of Alexander's conquest of northern India (325 B. C.) there was considerable intercourse between Egypt and India.[41] The carrying into captivity of the Jews—that of the two tribes of the south, beginning 606 B. C., and that of the ten tribes of the north, beginning about 800—and their being scattered throughout all nations, were other means of intercommunication between Oriental nations in Old Testament times. The Jesuit scholar, M. L. Huc, has pointed out that the Jews proceeded in numerous caravans to Persia, India, Tibet, and even China; that this had the effect of disseminating their books, their doctrines, and their prophecies among all the inhabitants of Asia; that the Jews were scattered into all cities; and that it

---

[39] Howells, *The Soul of India,* pages 534, 535.
[40] Huc, *Christianity in China, Tartary, and Thibet,* vol. 1, p. 9.
[41] Howells, *The Soul of India,* page 535.

was not easy to find a spot of the earth which had not received them and where they had not settled.[42]

This intercourse of Oriental nations is thus expressed by another writer:

> Throughout the Han Dynasty commercial relations existed between Rome and China, the two greatest and most powerful empires of antiquity. In the first century, Strabo saw 120 ships in a Red Sea port, ready to sail to India; and, up to the opening of the third century, maritime expeditions left Egyptian and Persian ports via the Red Sea and Indian Ocean for Canton and other south China ports.[43]

Khotan, a great city of Turkestan, far west from China proper, was founded by the Chinese emperor who built China's Great Wall (c. 214 B. C.). It was the capital of Turkestan, a country as large as France and very rich in resources. It was the central city where Chinese and Aryans met. Turkestan had highways, inns, and transportation facilities that made trade and communication possible between China and Persia and India.

The following significant link in history is most interesting. Historians point out that Darius the Great, son of Hystaspes, conquered northwestern India about the time that Buddha made his famous visit to King Ajatasatru, whose dynasty reigned over wide dominions in northeastern India.[44] Here was a way for Zoroaster's teachings to mingle with those of Buddha. The part of India conquered by Persia was ruled as the twentieth satrapy, or province, and was considered the richest district in the Persian Empire. It furnished the largest bullion revenue of the empire's Asiatic provinces. A contingent of India's archers fought in the Persian army which marched against Greece.[45] This overlapping of Persia and India made Zoroastrianism available for the Hindu people.

The given name of Buddha was Gautama. The word Buddha means "the enlightened." Ernest de Bunsen says, "The doctrines of Zoroaster were as well known by Gautama as by the initiated Hindus, though they hid this knowledge more or less from the people."[46] Bun-

---

[42] Huc, *Christianity in China, Tartary, and Thibet,* vol. 1, pages 2, 3.
[43] Gordon, *"World Healers,"* page 40.
[44] Smith, *Early History of India,* pages 34, 40.
[45] *Ibid,* pages 39, 40.
[46] Bunsen, *The Angel-Messiah of Buddhists, Essenes, and Christians,* page 10.

sen further says, "The Buddhistic reform was based on Zoroastrian doctrines."[47] Pythagoras of Greece followed Zoroaster. Since Confucianism in China in its close resemblance to Buddhism apparently followed Old Testament teachings and was similar to Pythagorean philosophy, agreements in these three religions can be found.[48] Their differences are chiefly on the difference of emphasis. Buddha of India placed his emphasis on the world to come; Confucius of China on a religion of home and state; and Pythagoras of Greece on the mind and soul. The first was pantheistic, the second was nationalistic, and the third was spiritistic. In this manner these religious leaders influenced nations and caught them in their bewitching, false applications of divine revelations.

Until the time of Buddha, about 500 b. c., India had been in the grip of Brahmanism, loaded with the caste system and given over to idolatry. The new religion of Buddha swept successfully into this subcontinent. Buddhism changed idolatry from the worship of millions of gods to the worship of Buddha himself.[49] Its teaching is permeated with doctrines and ceremonies counterfeiting the revealed religion of the Old Testament. In Buddhism one can find visions, miracles, a priesthood, a carnal ten commandments, processions, temples, images, and feast days.[50] The great Buddha festival of the fifteenth day of the seventh month should be noted as being the precise date of the Biblical Feast of Tabernacles.[51] In this, Buddha probably followed Zoroaster.[52] Later striking evidences will be given of how Buddhism subsequently saved itself from world rejection by counterfeiting the history and doctrines of Christ.[53]

The relation of Buddha to the seventh-day Sabbath is expressed by Arthur Lloyd in these words:

> To us it will seem easy to conjecture the quarter from which he got his idea of a weekly Sabbath, and the fact that the Order of Monks kept their

---

[47] Bunsen, *The Angel-Messiah of Buddhists, Essenes, and Christians*, page 80.

[48] See the author's discussion in Chapter XXI, entitled, "Adam and the Church in China." On agreement between Pythagorism and Confucianism see *The Encyclopedia Britannica*, 9th ed., art. "Confucius."

[49] Gordon, *"World Healers,"* pages 10, 31, 66, 138, 151, 165.

[50] Beal, *Buddhists' Records of the Western World*, vol. 1, pp. i-l (Introduction).

[51] Reichelt, *Truth and Tradition in Chinese Buddhism*, page 97.

[52] Fluegel, *The Zend-Avesta and Eastern Religions*, page 101.

[53] See the author's discussion in Chapter XXIII, entitled, "The Church in Japan and the Philippines."

Sabbath days for many centuries after the nirvana will make it easier for us to recognize and admit the doctrine held by a large section of northern Buddhists that Buddha also taught, personally and during his earthly life, the salvation worked out for many by another Buddha, who is boundless in life, light, and compassion, and whom Japan knows as Amitabha.[54]

The Church of the East Combats Hinduism

Hinduism, which had already attempted to meet the challenge of the Old Testament teachings and the Buddhist reform, bestirred itself again to oppose the Church of the East. In the days of the prophet Daniel the full light of God's truth broke upon the people of the Ganges. They were engaged in the sensual worship of their idols. Immorality and degeneracy had seized upon them with terrible force. They were destined to perish in their own corruption should salvation not reach them from some other quarter. The Jews of the ten tribes, more than a century before Daniel, had been taken into captivity. In the providence of God they had been scattered into many lands; yet they were still God's chosen people. Fired by the wonderful new revelations vouchsafed to the prophet Daniel, they preached with a ringing challenge to the animistic gods of India. Hebrew literature poured across the Himalyas telling of God the Father, the Holy Spirit, and a third Person of whom the psalmist declared: "The Lord said unto my Lord, Sit Thou at My right hand."[55] The Jews settled in India.[56] One Orientalist finds convincing evidence that the Afghans were descended from the lost tribes. In the country of the Afghans among the innumerable descendants of the Jewish captivities Buddha's race ruled. There stirring events of Buddha's ministry took place.[57]

The Brahmans hastened to develop a new philosophy of the deity. Historians show that at this time (c. 500 b. c.) the Hindu priests changed their teachings and adopted the adorable conception of a loving heavenly Father.[58] A new literature sprang up, and innumerable tractates were written to place Brahma (the creator), Vishnu

---

[54] Lloyd, *The Creed of Half Japan,* page 16.
[55] Psalm 110:1.
[56] Edersheim, *The Life and Times of Jesus the Messiah,* vol. 1, pp. 12-14; also Gordon, *"World Healers,"* page 229.
[57] The writer visited the synagogue in Cochin, India, whose leaders believe that their ancestors started eastward from Palestine long before Christ.
[58] Hunter, *The Indian Empire,* pages 99, 113; also Smith, *The Oxford History of India,* pages 56, 57.

(the preserver), and Siva (the destroyer), the Hindu trinity, on a par with Jehovah. These more abstract and less materialistic concepts of religion were the beliefs of the Brahmans and the educated classes, but they left the masses to their coarse idolatry. The Brahmans aimed to control the idolatry of the ignorant populace by using powerful doctrines of fear and favor.

Nothing had aroused the Jews in captivity to such a pitch of enthusiasm as the visions of Daniel disclosing the coming of their Messiah. The Hebrew prophet made it clear that this Anointed One was to be a suffering mediator, a substitute in His death for sinners.[59] While the Brahmans did not grasp this phase of the Messiah's mission any more than did the Pharisees, they were aroused to the significant appeal which a divine mediator would have upon the masses. Therefore, they invented new teachings without acknowledging the source of their inspiration. They began to teach a Hindu trinity, a rival to the Old Testament Godhead. An illustration of this can be seen outside of Bombay, in the rock-cave temple on the island of Elephanta, visited annually by thousands of pilgrims and travelers.[60]

Besides giving to their votaries the three-heads-on-one-body type of trinity, the priests employed the heathen doctrines of pantheism, nirvana, and transmigration. In pantheism they taught that the Godhead was the sum total of the universe. Material things, as one saw them, did not exist. Every visible object was an illusion, all things were but fleeting manifestations of divinity. They were without essential reality. Only one thing was real—Brahma, the Absolute, the Infinite, the Indescribable, the All.

The doctrine of transmigration struck terror to the hearts of the people of India. It contemplated a never-ending succession of funerals and subsequent rebirths into lower animal or plant forms of life. Existence in this present life for the Hindu masses meant at the best only one misery after another. Death, however, held no release for them. Instead of bringing relief to life's sufferings, the soul must descend to earth again to become a snake, a dog, or a filthy swine. If any hope existed in a chance to choose the lesser of two evils in the

---

[59] Daniel 9:24-26; 7:27.
[60] The writer made a special trip to the island of Elephanta, and ascended the hill amid many votaries on their way to worship Hinduism's triune god. He took photographs of the immense stone representing the heathen trinity or three heads on one body, three persons in one substance.

world to come, they must obey the priests in this life. Hence, the power of the Brahmans.

The third doctrine, nirvana, was the belief in the utter absorption of existence at death. It meant the annihilation of the man, the self, by complete union with Brahma. It contemplated the melting away of all conscious entities into the passionless peace and rippleless thought of deity. The most blessed existence was the utter dissolution of all existence. The trinity would gather up into itself for endless years all the untold personalities of the universe. Heaven was not a place, it was a state of mind. It was heresy to the Hindu to say that eternity would be filled with holy, happy beings such as the Old Testament described. According to Hinduism, thrones, principalities, angels, demons, and mediators would all perish. They were all phantasies of the spirit; they did not really exist.

The New Revolution in Hinduism

Such was India 500 years after Daniel when the Church of the East entered that unhappy land. Of all the difficult situations Christianity ever faced in the Orient, the one in India was without rival. Fearless in the strength of the Holy Spirit, apostolic fervor at once challenged hidebound heathenism. Now unified under the organization completed by Papas, the church went forth to conquer for Christ. God gave wonderful success. With the sickle of truth the witnesses for Jesus gleaned golden grain for the heavenly garner. Year after year, decade after decade, Christianity revealed itself as a conquering force in India.

Then an amazing revolution occurred. The Brahmans awoke with a start. They realized that new truths were wrenching their power from them. They doubtless reasoned thus, "Why sit we here as fools? Have we not seen the church at Rome in the west build up a successful rival to the New Testament church? Let us outrun both Rome and the simpler bodies of Christianity. Let us fabricate such a dazzling scheme of imitation that all other religions, even our own former teaching, will be completely eclipsed." Then about 600 they invented the Krishna legend, and in support of it they falsified their chronology.

The power of the gospel to challenge error is revealed in the stirring among the Hindu leaders. The pagan priests were aware that it meant the end of their power unless they fabricated new weapons.

Success depended upon their ability to imitate. They must make the same powerful appeals to the human emotions which for the first time had been brought to the world through Jesus Christ. They must revamp their religious duties and copy or counterfeit the services of the true church.

To build a defense against the gospel, they were obliged to do three things. First, they must invent a god of their own who entered a human body. This could compete with the story of the birth of Jesus in the flesh, which was winning hearts everywhere. Secondly, they must give this counterfeit messiah a name similar to Christ, with similar events of His life and parallel teachings. Thirdly, they must arrange their chronology with Hindu astronomy to throw the date of this fabricated incarnation centuries previous to the birth of Jesus in order to make Christianity appear to have been copied from Hinduism. New literature was provided to give success to the venture.

The deity they chose to incarnate was Krishna, a name much like that of Christ. Books written by pagans, previous to the coming of Christianity, had told of the descents of the gods among men. These however, had been simply the manifestation of some part or some attribute of the divinity. The new doctrine of incarnation which now sprang up produced a complete round of literature and theology concerning the wondrous birth of Vishnu, the supreme deity, who came in human flesh under the name "Krishna."[61] "He descended in all the fullness of the godhead, so much so that Vishnu is sometimes confounded with Brahma, the latter becoming incarnate in Krishna as 'the very supreme Brahma.' "[62] Many epics were written to glorify the exploits of this god who had descended to share the joys and sorrows of humanity. In the hearts of millions, Krishna has come to occupy the place of Vishnu himself. Even as Christians may direct their prayers to Christ instead of to God, so Hindus may direct their prayers to Krishna rather than to Vishnu, the supreme deity.

Great credit is due to John Bentley who, in 1825, detected this fraud of the Brahmans after it had been accepted for twelve hundred years. The similarity between the name of Christ and Krishna had long been noticed. Writers had listed the many agreements between

---

[61] M'Clintock and Strong, *Cyclopedia*, art. "Avatar."
[62] *Ibid.*, art. "Krishna."

the events of Christ's birth and life and those of Krishna.[63] When later translations of Hindu literature were published, thinkers were puzzled over the many startling similarities between the teachings of the two religions. The priests of India who claimed that the incarnation of Krishna was six hundred years before Christ, loved to boast that the New Testament was built out of the Hindu epics. Bentley solved the mystery. He obtained from the Brahmans the horoscope of Krishna, who, they said, was born at midnight of March 25, and also the positions of the sun, the moon, and the five planets among the heavenly constellations. This keen Englishman, skilled in the mathematics of astronomy, proved conclusively that the earliest date which could be claimed for the birth of Krishna was August 7, A. D. 600.[64] Subsequent writers on Hinduism have felt Bentley's findings worthy of consideration.

The following interesting details concerning Krishna are given by M'Clintock and Strong:

> Krishnaism, with all its imperfections, may be accounted as a necessary and the extreme revolt of the human heart against the unsatisfying vagaries of the godless philosophy into which Brahmanism and Buddhism had alike degenerated. The speculations of the six schools of philosophy, as enumerated by native writers, served only to bewilder the mind until the word *maya*, "illusion," was evolved as the exponent of all that belongs to the present life, while the awful mysteriousness of *nirvana* overshadowed the life to come. Man's nature asks for light upon the perplexed questions of mortal existence, but at the same time demands that which is of more moment, an anchorage for the soul in the near and tangible. . . .
>
> On the other hand, the Puranas disclose with regard to Krishna a human life, when considered from the most favorable standpoint, discreditable to the name and nature of man. It is a tissue of puerilities and licentiousness. The miraculous deeds of Krishna were rarely for an object commensurate with the idea of a divine interposition. His associations as a cowherd (gopala) with the gopis [females] — in which capacity he is most popular as an object of adoration—are no better than the amours of classic mythology.[65]

At the time the Brahmans invented the Krishna story there was no opposing power in India strong enough to prevent them from creat-

---

[63] Milman, *The History of Christianity*, vol. 1, p. 94, note.
[64] Bentley, *Historical View of Hindu Astronomy*, page 111.
[65] See M'Clintock and Strong, *Cyclopedia*, art. "Krishna;" also Kaye, *A Guide to the Old Observatories*, pages 68, 69.

ing the fraud. The Dark Ages were settling down on Europe. In the West there was neither enough interest nor ability to unmask the deception. It is a great tribute to the splendid missionary activity displayed by the Church of the East that Hinduism, fearful of losing its power, was driven to create a fraudulent counterfeit of Christ and His gospel. It proves that the evangelical church over which Papas had been elected in 285 had become a force to be reckoned with by 600.

Speaking of Cosmas, the celebrated Nestorian traveler and preacher, a well-known Oriental writer, using the word "monk" in its original meaning of pastor, indicates the vast extent of the Church of the East in 538:

> Here we will again pause a moment to consider the description given by Cosmos (who before he became a monk was an Alexandrian merchant and navigated the Mediterranean, Red Sea, Persian Gulf, and also visited India and Ceylon) of the vast extent of AN ORIENTAL CHRISTIANITY at the very date, A. D. 535, of the arrival of the Mahayana in Japan. He declares that churches with a complete liturgy were then to be found in Ceylon, Malabar, Socotra, and N. W. India (apparently identical with the St. Thomas Christians) ministered to by bishops and priests sent from the Patriarch of Seleucia; also in Bactria and amongst the Huns; in Mesopotamia, Scythia, etc.[66]

In the story of Papas we have seen the forces with which the Church of the East contended. Yet against all these powerful enemies the church under the organization begun in the days of Papas was triumphant. Each one of these counterfeit religions was obliged to adopt drastic measures to combat the inroads made by this church, a guardian of apostolic Christianity. God greatly blessed the Church of the East and preserved it for centuries until it had accomplished its mission.

---

[66] Gordon, *"World Healers,"* page 77.

CHAPTER X

How the Church Was Driven Into the Wilderness

The Goths carried back these Christian captives (from Asia Minor) into Dacia, where they were settled, and where considerable numbers embraced Christianity through their instrumentality. Ulfilas was the child of one of these Christian captives, and was trained in Christian principles.[1]

THE story of the Goths enters strongly into the interpretation of the 1260-year prophetic period. When we consider the Goths and their appearance among the nations, it brings us to the name of Ulfilas.

Pen cannot picture how completely the face of Western Europe was changed by the Teutonic invasions sweeping from the east to the south and west. These continued for at least two centuries, ending in 508 when the papacy completed its triumph over the newcomers. The inhabitants of Europe were driven into the background, as was also the general use of the Latin language, while strangers and foreign tongues reigned from the Danube to the Thames. The amount of territory of the old Roman Empire was practically halved. Profound changes took place in what remained of that empire, now limited to the eastern end of the Mediterranean. Meanwhile, in eastern Europe there was a revival of the simpler types of Christianity. The Celtic and the Gothic peoples in the West also contributed to this new evangelical era.

Great victories for Christ were won by Ulfilas (A. D. 311-383). The triumphs of this missionary were made among the nations crowded along the northern frontiers of the Roman Empire. Like Patrick of Ireland, he passed his early years in a land of captivity. Ulfilas finished his work about the time that Patrick was beginning his. There is much similarity in the beliefs and accomplishments of the two heroes.

Lucian of Antioch was at the height of his career when Ulfilas was a lad. Asia Minor, the homeland of his ancestors, was, in the early years of the church, the scene of strong opposition to those allegorizing

---

[1]Smith and Wace, *A Dictionary of Christian Biography,* art. "Ulfilas."

ecclesiastics who had been loaded with imperial favors by Constantine, and who were antagonistic to Lucian's translation of the Bible and his system of teaching. Ulfilas was called to take his choice. He decided not to walk with the allegorizers. The Gothic Bible which he gave to the nations he converted follows in the main the Received Text transmitted to us by the learned Lucian.[2] Such early contacts and associations molded the belief and plans of Ulfilas. The Goths along the north shore of the Black Sea had pushed their boats to the southern harbors and had carried away captive the ancestors of Ulfilas who resided in Asia Minor.

Constantine II, son and successor to Constantine, did not, as previously noted, partake of his father's views, and he had thrown the aegis of imperial protection around the other party which was branded by the church at Rome as Arians. To these he had granted full religious liberty. What was the attitude of Ulfilas toward the disputes over the Godhead which had convulsed the Council of Nicaea? The historian W. F. Adeney says:

> There is no reason to doubt that Ulfilas was perfectly honest in the theological position he occupied. As an earnest missionary, more concerned with practical evangelistic work than with theological controversy, he may have been thankful for a simple form of Christianity that he could make intelligible to his rough fellow countrymen more easily than one which was involved in subtle Greek metaphysics.[3]

Although the Goths refused to believe as the church at Rome did, and as a consequence have been branded as Arians, Romanism actually meant little to them. In fact, it meant little to Ulfilas, their great leader.[4] The Goths refused to go along with the mounting innovations being introduced into the church of the caesars, which church quickly branded any competitor as Arian. They were, above all, a warlike people before the coming of Ulfilas. The greatest struggle this apostle had with the Goths, as he informs us, was not so much the destruction of their idolatry as it was the banishment of their warlike temper. They, however, made great progress in replacing their passion for martial campaigns with a settled, organized government and the upbuilding of their civilization.

---

[2] Cheetham, *A History of the Christian Church*, page 423.
[3] Adeney, *The Greek and Eastern Churches*, pages 305, 306.
[4] Bradley, *The Goths*, page 59.

From 250 to about 500, the Teutonic masses poured over the provinces of western Europe and formed ten new nations. Among these ten were the two branches of the Goths — the Visigoths, or western Goths, and the Ostrogoths, or eastern Goths. Other invading tribes were the Franks, the Burgundians, the Vandals, the Anglo-Saxons, the Alamanni, the Heruli, and the Suevi. These were destined to become powerful nations of western Europe. The invading hosts settled in the Roman Empire, forming such kingdoms as England, France, Germany, Switzerland, Spain, Italy, and Portugal. Three other kingdoms arose from the migrations, and if they had not been conquered, the Heruli might now be ruling over central and southern Italy, the Vandals over northern Africa, and the Ostrogoths in southern Europe.

For two centuries these questions hung in the balance: Would these new nations cling to their ancient Germanic paganism? Would they become converts to Celtic Christianity? Would they fall under the dominion of the church at Rome? It is a gripping story that reveals how they were converted, some at first to Gothic, but later all to Celtic, Christianity before they were subdued by hostile nations whose armies were urged on by the papacy.

Because Ulfilas belonged to the church which had refused to accept the extreme speculations concerning the Trinity, there was a gulf between his converts and those who followed Rome. Brought up in captivity, he had not witnessed the stirring scenes of the Council of Nicaea (A. D. 325). In that famous historic assembly the church at Rome and the emperor rejected the views of Arius, and condemnation was pronounced upon those who recoiled from accepting the council's decision. Whether the teachings of Arius were such as are usually represented to us or not, who can say ? Phillipus Limborch doubts that Arius himself ever held that Christ was created instead of being begotten.[5]

Because of Constantine's favor, the party of the church at Rome was dominant. After Constantine's death, however, emperors for nearly a half century played loosely with the opponents of the Roman Church and often lifted the ban on the opposing groups. In fact, there were times when it looked as if the views of those who rejected the extreme Trinitarian speculations would become permanently domi-

---

[5] Limborch, *The History of the Inquisition,* page 95.

nant in the empire. Consequently when thousands of churches and church leaders of the opposition were stigmatized as Arians, it is not surprising to find Ulfilas standing for these beliefs.

Since the Goths had no written language, Ulfilas was compelled to invent an alphabet. He reduced Gothic sounds to writing. The first great piece of literature which the people of these vast nations, lying north of the empire's frontiers, looked upon was the Bible. It became the bond of union amongst the Gothic peoples. It was the parent of Teutonic literature. It was the forerunner of a Luther, a Shakespeare, and a Goethe. But, as Massmann observes, there is no trace of what was called Arianism in the surviving remains of the Gothic translation of the New Testament.[6]

Since his ancestors were from Asia Minor (the provinces where the apostle Peter had been especially instructed by God to plant the gospel), Ulfilas was undoubtedly influenced by the doctrines of the apostle to the Jews; and he rejected the liberal and unscriptural teachings which had flooded many western churches. He was a believer in the divine revelation of the Old Testament, as well as that of the New Testament. He impressed upon the Gothic people a simple, democratic Christianity. Like Patrick and Columba, he apparently kept the seventh day as the Sabbath. This may be seen in the following quotation concerning the great Theodoric, a subsequent king of the Goths (A. D. 454-526), taken from the historian Sidonius Apollinaris. Sidonius was not only a bishop of the church in France, but was also the son-in-law of the Roman emperor. He was in France when the great invasions of the Goths took place. Therefore, he was well informed on the practices of the Goths. He writes:

> It is a fact that formerly those who dwelt in the east were accustomed as a church to sanctify the Sabbath in the same manner as the Lord's day, and to hold sacred assemblies; wherefore Asterius, bishop of Amasia in Pontus, in a homily on incompatibility called Sabbath and Sunday a beautiful span, and Gregory of Nyssa in a certain sermon calls these days brethren and therefore censures the luxury and the Sabbatarian pleasures; while on the other hand, the people of the west, contending for the Lord's day, have neglected the celebration of the Sabbath, as being peculiar to the Jews. Whence Tertullian in his apology: "We are only next to those who see in the Sabbath a day only for rest and relaxation." It is, therefore,

---

[6]Milman, *The History of Christianity,* vol. 3, p. 58, note.

possible for the Goths to have thought, as pupils of the discipline of the Greeks, that they should sanctify the Sabbath after the manner of the Greeks.[7]

From a scholar and traveler describing the Muscovite Russian Church (Christians still dwelling in the region where tribes formerly had been affected by the teachings of Ulfilas) we learn that after their conversion they "ever since continued of the Greeke Communion and Religion; . . . reputing it unlawfull to fast on Saturdaies."[8]

This same author, describing the doctrine of the Greek Orthodox Church, says:

> They admit Priests' Marriages. . . . That they reject the religious use of Massie, Images, or Statues, admitting yet Pictures or plaine Images in their Churches. That they solemnize Saturday (the old Sabbath) festivally, and eat therein flesh, forbidding as unlawfull, to fast any Saturday in the yeare except Easter Eve.[9]

The papacy for many centuries commanded fasting on Saturday, and this created a dislike among the unthinking church members for the sacredness of the day.[10]

Conversion of the Goths by Ulfilas

It would be impossible to obtain a correct understanding of the events which drove the church into the wilderness without realizing the large part in the drama which circled about the Goths. Tribe after tribe of the Teutons — the practically unknown peoples living north of the Danube — possessed the power of making crushing blows against settled states. Masses of humanity, capable of being mobilized into destructive invading armies, hung upon the confines of the Roman Empire. The revolution wrought by their migrations and decisive victories in battle will appear as we evaluate their place in history. To the surprise of all, the Goths had been won to the gospel in an astonishingly short time, not by the persuasion of Rome, but by Ulfilas. While the church at Rome was grasping after secular power, these churches were alive with missionary zeal.

---

[7] Apollinaris, *Epistolae,* lib. 1, epistola 2, found in Migne, *Patrologia Latina,* vol. 58, p. 448.

[8] Purchas, *His Pilgrimes,* vol. 1, pp. 355, 356.

[9] *Ibid.,* vol. 1, p. 350.

[10] See the author's discussion in Chapter xv, entitled, "Early Waldensian Heroes," page 273, also in Chapter xvi, entitled, "The Church of the Waldenses," pages 307, 308.

Onward then came those mighty armies of the invading hosts. Giant men seated on war steeds preceded the covered wagons in which were women, children, and earthly possessions. Province after province fell before their powerful battle-axes. The Roman populace either perished or fled to mountains and dens. Finally, in 409, the invaders arrived before Rome. After conquering the city which for centuries had terrified the world, they retired. But they returned after several decades for the final conquest of Italy.

The Goths and the Vandals did not fight because of a bloodthirsty temperament, but because they were blocked by the Romans when driven westward by the wild masses from Scythia and Siberia. The historian Walter F. Adeney has pictured the spirit and methods of the Goths when they sacked Rome in 410:

> In the first place, it was a great thing for Europe that when the Goths poured over Italy and even captured Rome they came as a Christian people, reverencing and sparing the churches, and abstaining from those barbarities that accompanied the invasion of Britain by the heathen Saxons. But, in the second place, many of these simple Gothic Christians learned to their surprise that they were heretics, and that only when their efforts toward fraternizing with their fellow Christians in the orthodox Church were angrily resented.[11]

The following words from Thomas Hodgkin show how superior were these invading hosts to the corrupt condition of the state church in northern Africa, when the Vandals who also refused Rome's state-prescribed doctrines seized the homeland of Tertullian and Cyprian:

> Augustine had said: "I came from my native town to Carthage, and everywhere around me roared the furnace of unholy love. . . . Houses of ill-fame swarming in each street and square, and haunted by men of the highest rank, and what should have been venerable age; chastity outside the ranks of the clergy a thing unknown and unbelieved, and by no means universal within that enclosure; the darker vices, the sins of Sodom and Gomorrah, practiced, avowed, gloried in"— such is the picture which the Gaulish presbyter draws of the capital of Africa.
>
> Into this city of sin marched the Vandal army, one might almost say, when one reads the history of their doings, the army of the Puritans. With all their cruelty and all their greed they kept themselves unspotted by the licentiousness of the splendid city. They banished the men who were earning their living by ministering to the vilest lusts. They rooted out

---

[11]Adeney, *The Greek and Eastern Churches,* page 306.

10

prostitution with a wise yet not a cruel hand. In short, Carthage, under the rule of the Vandals, was a city transformed, barbarous but moral.[12]

At this point it should be clearly stated that the Goths are not being presented as constituting the Church in the Wilderness. However, they certainly were not in sympathy with the church at Rome. They were a people in which truth was struggling to come to the surface. But, on the other hand, the religious power predicted in Daniel 8:12 was to cast down the truth to the ground, and so to practice and prosper.[13]

The 1260-Year Prophecy of the Little Horn

Thus he said, The fourth beast shall be the fourth kingdom upon earth, which shall be diverse from all kingdoms, and shall devour the whole earth, and shall tread it down, and break it in pieces. And the ten horns out of this kingdom are ten kings that shall arise: and another shall rise after them; and he shall be diverse from the first, and he shall subdue three kings. And he shall speak great words against the Most High, and shall wear out the saints of the Most High, and think to change times and laws: and they shall be given into his hand until a time and times and the dividing of time. But the judgment shall sit, and they shall take away his dominion, to consume and to destroy it unto the end.[14]

The chain of prophecy in Daniel 7 reveals by the means of animal symbols, the succession of world events from the time of the prophetic writer until the second coming of Christ. On the head of the fourth beast of Daniel's prophecy, which beast is often interpreted to be the fourth universal monarchy, the Roman Empire, are seen ten horns. Commentators correctly conclude that these are the ten Germanic kingdoms which invaded, broke up, and took possession of the western part of the Roman Empire, or the original territory of the fourth beast. The rise of the "little horn," its growth in power, its plucking up of three of the ten horns, and its stout words against God, accompanied by the 1260-year persecution of the saints, must now claim attention.

Clovis was king of the Franks, one of the pagan tribes which had previously crossed the empire's frontiers into the province of Gaul. His father before him had worked devotedly with Rome's bishops.

---

[12] Hodgkin, *Italy and Her Invaders,* vol. 1, pt. 2, pp. 931, 932.
[13] Daniel 8:12.
[14] Daniel 7:23-26.

Clovis met and successfully overthrew the feeble resistance of the empire's army. His next formidable enemy was the pagan Alamanni, later to be called the Germans.[15] He had a long and bloody battle with them in which he successfully resisted their invasion. Previous to this, he had married Clotilda, daughter of the king of the Burgundians, and a devout Catholic.

Observing the power and influence of the papacy, and anxious to avail himself of papal support, he professed conversion in 496, and his entire following united with him in adherence to Catholicism, three thousand of whom were baptized along with himself soon after his conversion. As he expected, the Catholics rallied around him as the only Catholic prince in the West.[16]

The Teutonic kingdoms which had occupied other Roman provinces, as well as France, were either continuing in their idolatry or were converts to Christianity as taught by Ulfilas. They are usually catalogued as Arians. After his political conversion to Christianity as championed by the church at Rome, Clovis defeated the Burgundians, which people at this time were divided between paganism and Christianity. The desire to spread his new religion and to ruin Christian kingdoms which refused the new doctrines seemed to be the aim of his warlike temper. The barbarity and cruelty of his subsequent acts proved how much his conversion was political and not a surrender to truth in the heart. There is no question but that his new profession served the purpose of establishing and enlarging his kingdom, and for this reason he renounced idolatry for the Christianity of the church at Rome.[17]

The climax of his rise to fame and power was attained when he reached out to take the rich and beautiful lands of southern France from the kingdom of the Visigoths. Step by step, supported by Rome and by the influence of the emperor of Constantinople, Clovis drove them back until the great and decisive battle of 507-508 was waged. It was decisive because neighboring pagan kingdoms that hated him were ready to rush in against him if he lost. Rome watched with anxious heart the outcome of this decisive battle, for she well knew

---

[15] Gibbon, *Decline and Fall of the Roman Empire*, ch. 38, par. 5.
[16] Newman, *A Manual of Church History*, vol. 1, p. 404.
[17] Mosheim, *Institutes of Ecclesiastical History*, b. 2, cent. 5, pt. 1, ch. 1, pars. 4, 5.

that her hopes of expansion in this world were vain if her only prince in the West failed.

The emperor at Constantinople also followed with breathless attention the news of this war. The emperor, faced by powerful enemies on the east and north, saw little future for the type of Christianity he was championing if Clovis failed to give the Franks a permanent place under the sun by this final victory.

The army of the Visigoths was routed by the Franks in the encounter of 507. It was necessary for Clovis to destroy the sources of further supply. He struck while the iron was hot, and in 508 pursued the Visigoths to their southern strongholds and overcame them. Clovis was named consul by the emperor;[18] while by the church at Rome he was called the first Catholic Majesty and his successor "the Eldest Son of the Church." The "little horn" was now in process of uprooting other horns. How great was the significance on the course of the world's history of the culmination in 508 of the establishment of the first Catholic kingdom in the West, let witnesses testify. Says R. W. Church:

> The Frank king threw his sword into the scale against the Arian cause, and became the champion and hope of the Catholic population all over Gaul.
> The *invaders* had at length arrived, *who were to remain.* It was decided that *the Franks, and not the Goths,* were to direct the future destinies of Gaul and Germany, and that the *Catholic faith,* and not Arianism, was to be the religion of these great realms.[19]

Again, from Dr. David J. Hill, former United States ambassador to Germany:

> Up to the time of Clovis the invading hordes of the East had moved steadily westward. . . . Thenceforth that tide was to be turned backward, and conquest was to proceed in the opposite direction. The Franks alone, of all the *barbarian races* which had invaded the empire, were not wholly absorbed by it; but kept, as it were, an open channel of communication with the great Germanic background. It was the Franks who, turning their faces eastward, not only *checked further advances of the barbarians,* but . . . were to become the defenders of Christendom.[20]

---

[18] Ayer, *A Source Book for Ancient Church History,* page 575.
[19] Church, *The Beginning of the Middle Ages,* pages 38, 39.
[20] Hill, *History of Diplomacy in the International Development of Europe,* vol. 1, p. 55.

As Prof. George Adams writes:

> This question Clovis settled, not long after the beginning of his career, by his conversion to Catholic Christianity. . . . In these three ways, therefore, the work of Clovis was of creative influence upon the future. He brought together the Roman and the German upon equal terms, each preserving the sources of his strength to form a new civilization. He founded a political power which was to unite nearly all the continent in itself, and to BRING THE PERIOD OF THE INVASIONS TO AN END.[21]

Thus it was Clovis, king of the Franks, who in 508 put an end to the prospect that paganism might eventually be supreme.

> He [Clovis] had on all occasions shown himself the heartless ruffian, the greedy conqueror, the bloodthirsty tyrant; but by his conversion he had led the way to the triumph of Catholicism; he had saved the Roman Church from the Scylla and Charybdis of heresy and paganism.[22]

Through Clovis a new era began. We quote now from Lewis Sergeant:

> But after all the changes, it was the Franks who constantly grew strong, who built up a law, a church, and an empire. . . . The baptism of Clovis, which implied the general conversion of the Franks to Christianity, set the crown on a century of striking successes for the western church.[23]

Subjugation of the Goths by Emperor Justinian

Thirty years after the victory of 508 the papacy was elevated to universal supremacy by Justinian. The stage was already set. The victory of Clovis over the Visigoths in 508 which broke the centuries of pagan dominion did not necessarily eradicate paganism scattered elsewhere. Thirty years later (A. D. 538) dominion passed to the papacy, a theocracy which persecuted more severely than did paganism. It is generally recognized that a union of church and state is more intolerant than a political state.

Fired by the victory of Clovis, the ecclesiastical power of Rome was stirring everywhere. In northern Africa they were disturbing the peace of the Christian kingdom of the Vandals, and in Spain they were rising against the Visigoths. Everywhere, says Milman, the

---

[21] Adams, *Civilization During the Middle Ages,* pages 141, 142.
[22] *The Historians' History of the World,* vol. 7, p. 477.
[23] Sergeant, *The Franks,* page 120.

ecclesiastics were increasing their power as mediators, negotiators of treaties, or as agents in the submission or revolt of cities.[24]

The Church Forced Into the Wilderness

Justinian determined to make the rule of the papacy universal within his dominion. In 532 he issued his famous edict which laid the foundation for the persecutions of the church which maintained the apostolic faith during the 1260 years. The distinction between the important dates of 532, 533, and 538 should now be considered.

Archibald Bower says of the edict of Justinian:

> By an edict which he issued to unite all men in one faith, whether Jews, Gentiles, or Christians, such as did not, in the term of three months, embrace and profess the Catholic faith, were declared infamous, and, as such, excluded from all employments both civil and military, rendered incapable of leaving anything by will, and their estates confiscated, whether real or personal. These were convincing arguments of the truth of the Catholic faith; but many, however, withstood them; and against such as did, the imperial edict was executed with the utmost rigor. Great numbers were driven from their habitations with their wives and children, stripped and naked. Others betook themselves to flight, carrying with them what they could conceal, for their support and maintenance; but they were plundered of the little they had, and many of them inhumanly massacred by the Catholic peasants, or the soldiery, who guarded the passes.[25]

The emperor prescribed the faith of every man, and that faith consisted of the doctrines of Rome. There was no protest from the pope. The world dominion of paganism had come to an end; but a dominion more damaging to primitive Christianity, more blighting to the intellect, had taken its place. The edict of Justinian in 532 extended over the whole empire as far as it then stretched. When, however, northern Africa and Italy were conquered, this edict followed the imperial arms. The severe and ruinous application of the decree did not cease when the three months specified in it ceased. It set the pace for the 1260-year period brought to view by the prophet Daniel.

By the decree of 532 Justinian reduced all true and sincere believers to the direst condition. But by the decree of 533 he exalted the papacy to the highest earthly position possible. This exaltation, how-

---

[24] Milman, *History of Latin Christianity*, vol. 1, b. 3, ch. 3, par. 2.
[25] Bower, *The History of the Popes*, vol. 1, p. 334.

ever, was in decree only, until success in war put it into effect. It, therefore, at first could apply only to his own territory. On the other hand, both decrees applied in Europe when in 538 the Ostrogoths in Italy were crushed and more power was given to the papacy.

Justinian wrote to the pope in 533: "We have made no delay in subjecting and uniting to Your Holiness all the priests of the whole East." In the same letter he also said: "We cannot suffer that anything which relates to the state of the church, however manifest and unquestionable, should be moved, without the knowledge of Your Holiness, who are THE HEAD OF ALL THE HOLY CHURCHES." [26]

When the news came of the success of his general in crushing the Vandals in Africa in 534, Justinian was elated. Then, as the historian Gibbon says: "Impatient to abolish the temporal and spiritual tyranny of the Vandals, he proceeded without delay to the full establishment of the Catholic Church." [27]

An opening having presented itself to declare war on the Ostrogoths, Justinian dispatched his general, Belisarius, against them. After a series of victories, the general entered Rome with his army. The Ostrogoths came 150,000 strong to lay siege against Justinian's army, but they were outgeneraled. They could make no headway against the city; while behind them, the hostility of the people depressed them. "The whole nation of the Ostrogoths had been assembled for the attack," says Thomas Hodgkin, "and was almost consumed in the siege." "One year and nine days after the commencement of the siege," he further says, "an army so lately strong and triumphant, burnt their tents and recrossed the Milvian Bridge." "With heavy hearts the barbarians must have thought, as they turned them northwards, upon the many graves of gallant men which they were leaving on that fatal plain. Some of them must have suspected the melancholy truth that they had dug one grave, deeper and wider than all, the grave of the Gothic monarchy in Italy." [28]

Because of the events of this year, 538, the papacy had gained a temporal foothold. It could progressively claim independent sovereignty and so was more able to carry out its program to secure supreme rule. Making the papal hierarchy supreme in Italy would ultimately

---

[26] Croly, *The Apocalypse of St. John*, pages 167, 168.
[27] Gibbon, *Decline and Fall of the Roman Empire*, ch. 41, par. 11.
[28] Hodgkin, *Italy and Her Invaders*, vol. 4, ch. 9, pp. 251, 252.

create a dual sovereignty there, and establish a precedent for the same methods among other nations. The ruin of the Ostrogothic power blocked the way for a united Italy to put a king of its own on the throne.

The historian Milman, commenting upon the destruction of the Ostrogoths, writes:

> The conquest of Italy by the Greeks was, to a great extent at least, the work of the Catholic clergy. . . . The overthrow of the Gothic kingdom was to Italy an unmitigated evil. . . . In their overthrow began the fatal policy of the Roman See, fatal at least to Italy, . . . which never would permit a powerful native kingdom to unite Italy, or a very large part of it, under one dominion. Whatever it may have been to Christendom, the Papacy has been the eternal, implacable foe of Italian independence and Italian unity.[29]

It makes little difference whether the self-appointed successor of Peter rules over ten square miles or ten million square miles. If he rules, he is as verily a king as any other sovereign. Today, he is the emperor of the Vatican empire. He appoints his ambassadors, coins his money, has his own postal service. Yet why should he be made a king any more than the head of any of the Protestant churches? Such a kingship requires a union of church and state. Such a kingdom was especially condemned by Jesus.

Justinian declared the pope to be "THE HEAD OF ALL THE HOLY CHURCHES." Though the popes forgot that this title was given by fallible man, not by God, they have never forgotten to claim that power. The bitter injustice done to the Italian people by Justinian's enthronement of the papacy in their midst, which created a sovereignty within a sovereignty, may be seen in the character of the emperor. What kind of man was Justinian? Gibbon declares:

> The reign of Justinian was a uniform yet various scene of persecution; and he appears to have surpassed his indolent predecessors, both in the contrivance of his laws and the rigor of their execution. The insufficient term of three months was assigned for the conversion or exile of all heretics; and if he still connived at their precarious stay, they were deprived, under his iron yoke, not only of the benefits of society, but of the common birthright of men and Christians.[30]

---

[29] Milman, *History of Latin Christianity*, vol. 1, b. 3, ch. 4, par. 20.
[30] Gibbon, *Decline and Fall of the Roman Empire*, ch. 47, par. 24.

The papacy has always held that her tradition is of equal authority with the Scriptures. Having "eyes like the eyes of man,"[31] the papacy cried out, More power, more power. She immediately turned her wrath upon the refugees in Italy who had fled out of the East from the decree of Justinian in order to find security under the tolerant rule of the Ostrogothic king Theodoric.

These joined the Waldenses who were convinced that the papacy was the "little horn" of Daniel, and the "man of sin" of Paul's writings.[32] The Church of Rome accepted the persecuting policy of Justinian, even as she had accepted the exalted title he bestowed upon her. Then to the true church were given two wings of a great eagle that she might fly from the "great tribulation, such as was not since the beginning of the world to this time, no, nor ever shall be."[33] The Dark Ages began. Implacable and unrelenting persecution was the resort of the church and state system. Wielding a power greater than that ever exercised by the caesars, Romanism pursued the church farther and farther into the wilderness. Nevertheless, affliction and trials caused the persecuted church to live on, shining brighter and brighter until, at the hand of God's providence, her persecutor received a "deadly wound" when the 1260 years ended.[34]

Ulfilas passed on. The church of the emperors, which he had ignored and whose teachings he refused to impart to the hordes of the north, later destroyed the sovereignty of those nations who professed his faith. They were conquered neither by New Testament teaching nor by missionary effort, but by the sword. Though independent rule was taken away from the Goths, the Gothic people lived on. They were in subjection, but they evinced no great love for the mysterious articles of faith taught by the lash of the whip. Deprived of martial weapons, they became an easy prey to the rapidly advancing Franks. Nevertheless, one can follow the stirring movements among their de-

---

[31] Daniel 7:8.

[32] Daniel 7:8, 20; 2 Thessalonians 2:3. See the author's discussion on the Waldenses in Chapters xv and xvi.

[33] Matthew 24:21.

[34] Revelation 13:3, 5. Since 1260 years added to 538 brings us to 1798, one is led to ask, What were the events clustering about 1798? In that year the pope was taken prisoner by the armies of the French Revolution, the college of cardinals was abolished, and religious liberty was proclaimed in the city of Rome. See the author's discussion in Chapter xxiv, entitled, "The Remnant Church Succeeds the Church in the Wilderness."

scendants as they listened to men mighty in the prophecies and faith of Jesus. The days dawned when others came in the spirit and power of Ulfilas. Such contributed their part when the hour came to have the Bible once more exalted as the center of all Christian life and belief.[35]

[35] Favyn, *Histoire de Navarre,* pages 713-715.

CHAPTER XI

Dinooth and the Church in Wales

The abbot of the most distinguished British monastery, at Bangor, Deynoch[1] by name, whose opinion in ecclesiastical affairs had the most weight with his countrymen, when urged by Augustin to submit in all things to the ordinances of the Roman Church, gave him the following remarkable answer: "We are all ready to listen to the church of God, to the pope at Rome, and to every pious Christian, that so we may show to each, according to his station, perfect love, and uphold him by word and deed. We know not, that any other obedience can be required of us towards him whom you call the pope or the father of fathers."[2]

THE heroic figure of Dinooth (c. A. D. 530-610) sheds glory upon the history of Christianity in Wales. He stamped his personality upon the life of the Welsh nation, and he gave direction to the thought of his country's church. In his lifetime occurs the first desperate encounter between an able leader of the Celtic Church and the agents of the papacy. He became director of Celtic Christianity in England and Wales about the time the 1260-year period was beginning in 538. He led the Celtic Church in its critical encounter with Augustine, the founder of the papal church in England.

The Welsh still consider the sixth century as the most brilliant period of their history.[3] Columba was finishing his work in Scotland when Dinooth was at the height of his career. Since these two were leaders of the same faith during victorious years of Celtic Church advance in the British Isles, Dinooth learned from Columba, and followed his program of evangelization.

Add to the names of these pioneers that of Aidan, a famous leader of Celtic Christianity in England in the generation following Dinooth, and one can see the unity, as well as the abundant evangelism, that this church displayed. To obtain a close-up view of the environment in which Dinooth carried on his great work, it is necessary to examine the history of the British Isles as they experienced three inundating waves of penetration.

---

[1]Variously spelled Dinooth, Dinodh, and Dinuth.
[2]Neander, *General History of the Christian Religion and Church*, vol. 3, p. 17.
[3]Killen, *The Old Catholic Church*, page 272.

Wales was the first of the nations of Great Britain to feel weapons of aggression directed against the Celtic Church after the arrival of the papacy. Welsh believers exemplified the bravery of others who laid down their lives for their faith. The Celtic people were renowned for their courage, and they almost exhausted the conquering forces of the Roman Empire when army after army melted away before the native tribes of the Welsh mountains.[4]

The Welsh, a part of the great Celtic branch of the human family,[5] were originally pagan in their religion. Some practiced polytheism, while others followed druidism. The schools of the druids are famous in history for their scholarship and literary training.

The Arrival of Christianity

Christianity early entered the British Isles. Even in the days of the apostles the message may have reached them, for Mosheim writes, "Whether any apostle, or any companion of an apostle, ever visited Britain, cannot be determined; yet the balance of probability rather inclines towards the affirmative."[6]

Origen about A. D. 225 spoke concerning Britain as follows: "When did Britain previous to the coming of the Christ agree to the worship of one God? When the Moors? When the whole world? Now, however, through the church all men call upon the God of Israel."[7]

During the four hundred years that Britain was under the Roman Empire, the followers of the gospel there knew nothing of the ecclesiastical domination and pompous ritual of Rome. The truth was practiced in apostolic simplicity. The British were first evangelized, not by Rome, but by their brethren in Asia Minor who had continued in primitive Christianity.[8] Columbanus, who was of the same faith as Dinooth, declared that his church had received nought but the doctrines of the Lord and the apostles.[9] Therefore, as shall later be seen in his conflict with papal leaders, we must conclude that early British Christianity was apostolic and not papal.

The invasions of the Goths and the sack of Rome brought a crisis

---

[4] Green, *A Short History of the English People,* vol. 1, pp. 28-30.

[5] Fitzpatrick, *Ireland and the Making of Britain,* page 160.

[6] Mosheim, *Institutes of Ecclesiastical History,* b. 1, cent. 2, pt. 1, ch. 1, par. 4, note 8.

[7] Origen, *In Ezechielem,* Homilia 4, found in Migne *Patrologia Graeca,* vol. 13, p. 698.

[8] Yeates, *East Indian Church History,* page 226 and note 1.

[9] Fitzpatrick, *Ireland and the Foundations of Europe,* pages 58, 59.

to the Celtic Church in England and Wales. The defense policy of the empire was forced to a radical change. The order was given at once for the imperial legions to abandon Britain, as they were needed on the Continent nearer home. The frontier of the empire contracted, leaving the British to their fate. At once the fierce Picts from Scotland and the Saxons from Scandinavia swept down upon the island. And, when about 449 the surge of invasion of the Anglo-Saxons began, the hatred of the foreigners against the Britons spent its fury on the British Church. Ultimately, paganism was dominant from the English Channel to the border of Scotland — Wales alone being able to stand its ground.

Step by step the Anglo-Saxons conquered and settled England. It took them almost two hundred years to do what the Romans did in a few years. Never was there more noble, sacrificing, and persistent resistance to despoilers. The overrunning of Italy and Spain was a migrating movement, but England was won only inch by inch and foot by foot. The defenders were farmers and herdsmen as well as fighters, but the pagan invaders took their lands. Christian churches were demolished or replaced by heathen temples. During all these conflicts in England, however, Celtic Christianity was expanding and growing stronger in Ireland, Scotland, and Wales.

While the pagan Anglo-Saxons were pressing the Celtic Church back to Wales, a revolution had taken place in France which would ultimately affect Christianity throughout Great Britain. The pagan Franks, coveting the rich lands in southern France possessed by the Christian Visigoths, underwent a political conversion to Rome, strongly supported by the bishop of Rome and the Roman emperor. The Franks conquered the Visigoths in 508. This made their new faith dominant in France, and foreshadowed a similar advance into England. Before the revolution in Gaul was fully consummated, the conquering Anglo-Saxons in England had coalesced into a number of strong confederacies. Finally, there emerged a number of kingdoms, usually under the number of seven, spoken of as the Heptarchy. Of these, the kingdom of Kent was the first to engage attention because of its early strong lead and of its relationship with the church at Rome.

The king of Kent at this time (A. D. 560-616) was Ethelbert, who had married Bertha, the daughter of the Roman Catholic king of the

Franks. Immediately a powerful advantage was given to the papacy, since this zealous princess had the support not only of the strong nations of Gaul and Italy, but also of the Eastern Empire, whose emperor was in alliance with the papacy. Bertha consented to this marriage only on condition that she could be accompanied to England by her chaplain.

Augustine in Great Britain

When Augustine and his monks landed on the island (A. D. 597), political conditions favored his coming. The papacy had sought for more than two hundred years to pierce the apostolic Christianity which prevailed throughout Great Britain. By misrepresentations and by the sword it had persecuted the evangelical dissenters in northern Italy. It also hated the similar organization in Great Britain. Now, at last, it had found an ally. The previous stubborn resistance of the Celtic Britons to the Germanic Anglo-Saxon invaders had permeated the latter with rage toward their victims. The religious hatred embosomed in the papacy was now joined to the racial hatred of the Anglo-Saxons.

On landing, Augustine went to Canterbury, the metropolis of Kent. He and his companions drew near, "furnished with divine, not with magic virtue, bearing a silver cross for their banner, and the image of our Lord and Saviour painted on a board; and singing the litany."[10] It was a severe affliction upon the Christianity introduced among the Anglo-Saxons to make them believe that the ineffable Eternal could be represented by an image on a board, and to teach them license with God's commandment against images while proclaiming obedience to Christ, for had not the prophet declared of God: "'To whom then will ye liken Me?"[11]

These newcomers were given permission to teach openly, to repair and to reopen the churches which the pagan Anglo-Saxons had destroyed. How political and therefore how superficial Augustine's wholesale baptism of ten thousand Kentish subjects was, became apparent when shortly after the death of the king the kingdom lapsed into paganism.[12] Due probably to the influence of Augustine, a re-

---

[10] Bede, *Ecclesiastical History of England*, b. 1, ch. 25.
[11] Isaiah 40:25.
[12] Fitzpatrick, *Ireland and the Making of Britain*, page 9.

vision of the old laws had been made in which an ordinary penalty was prescribed for offenses against ordinary citizens, a ninefold penalty for an offense against the king, but an elevenfold penalty for an offense against the bishop and a twelvefold penalty for an offense against a church building.

Then followed more strategic marriages. Probably the greatest line of success achieved by Augustine was the marriage of the Roman Catholic princess Aethelberg, daughter of Ethelbert, to the pagan king, Edwin, ruler of Northumbria, and later the marriage of the Roman Catholic princess Eanfled, granddaughter of King Ethelbert to the Northumbrian king, Oswy, grandson of Edwin, who had embraced the British faith under the influence of his saintly father, King Oswald, a student of Columba's celebrated training school at Iona. These three, Bertha, Aethelberg, and Eanfled, represented Rome's policy of marrying Catholic princesses to the ruler of the country whose faith was to be overthrown. Of these three, Eanfled had the most influence, as is related later, when she turned away the heart of her husband, King Oswy of Northumbria, from following the Celtic Church after he, for ten years as king, had walked in the footsteps of his noble father.

King Arthur and Early Welsh Heroes

One name around which romance has built a voluminous literature is that of King Arthur, the Welsh hero. This George Washington of his country must have fought many fierce battles to throw back the Anglo-Saxons. Evidently Arthur was the sword of the Lord in defense of the British Church. He is credited with building or repairing many churches, as well as with successful battling. The historian Gibbon says:

> But every British name is effaced by the illustrious name of ARTHUR, the hereditary prince of the Silures, in South Wales, and the elective king or general of the nation. According to the most rational account, he defeated, in twelve successive battles, the Angles of the north and the Saxons of the west; but the declining age of the hero was embittered by popular ingratitude and domestic misfortunes.[13]

The splendid growth of the Celtic Church during the period which elapsed between the time of King Arthur and the landing of Augustine,

---

[13] Gibbon, *Decline and Fall of the Roman Empire*, ch. 38, par. 38.

brought serious misgivings to the papal church. Dr. A. Ebrard says of Pope Gregory I: "A Rome-free British Irish church and mission in the British Islands already existed. He invested Augustine with jurisdiction over all the bishops of the British Church."[14] The fact that Pope Gregory commissioned Augustine to be archbishop over British bishops as well as over the Roman Catholics proves that the pontiff planned the extinction of the Celtic Church.

Augustine influenced King Ethelbert of Kent to summon the Celtic teachers from the nearest provinces of the Britons to Augustine's Oak, a place probably located on the banks of the Severn. The summons was sent to the famous Celtic training school at Bangor in Wales. Bede relates that the large enrollment of ministerial students at this college necessitated its being separated into seven divisions with a dean over each. None of the different parts contained less than three hundred men, all of whom lived by the labor of their hands.[15]

Dinooth, as president of his college, would, according to the organization of the Celtic Church in that period, be supreme director also of the churches in Wales. If Dinooth would attend the proposed conference, Augustine would have opportunity to encounter a learned representative of early British Christianity.

To Augustine's Oak, therefore, came delegations of the doctors or teachers from Bangor, Wales, which college might be looked upon as the ecclesiastical center of the Britons.[16] The Roman Catholics began by accusing the Celtic pastors of doing many things against the unity of the church. Augustine requested them to abandon their method of keeping Easter, to preserve Catholic unity, and to undertake in common the preaching of the gospel to the pagans. A long disputation followed. It was clearly evident to those pastors, whose church had an origin independent of the papacy and had never had any connection with Rome, that the unity demanded of them meant the loss of their identity. They refused to be swayed by the exhortations and rebukes of Augustine and his companions. They gave answer that it was their preference to follow their own Christian

---

[14] Ebrard, *Bonifatius, der Zerstörer des Columbanischen Kirchentums auf dem Festlande,* page 16.
[15] Bede, *Ecclesiastical History of England,* b. 2, ch. 2.
[16] The writer, while traveling in Wales, saw ancient church buildings still standing in the neighborhood of Bangor.

practices. The Britons promptly declared, "that they could not depart from their ancient customs without the consent and leave of their people."[17] Therefore a second conference was arranged.

Second Conference on Church Doctrines

To this second meeting came seven bishops, as Bede calls them, and many learned men of the Britons. Before these delegates left for this conference they visited one of their ancient men noted for his sanctity and wisdom to ask his advice. He counseled them to let Augustine and his party arrive at the place of meeting first. If, when the Britons arrived, Augustine arose and received them with the meekness and humility of Christ, they were to look upon him as heaven's messenger. If, however, he displayed haughtiness and arrogance, it was a sign that they were to refuse to fellowship with him or accept his authority.

When they did arrive at the place of meeting, Augustine was already there and, retaining his seat, did not deign to rise. Whereupon, the Britons charged him with pride, answering all his arguments. Augustine commanded them to keep Easter according to the Church of Rome, to give up their evangelical unity, and to become Romanists. The Britons fully and determinedly rejected Augustine's claims to the superior authority of his church and the supremacy of the pope who sent him. They declared that "they would do none of those things, nor receive him as their archbishop."[18] Consequently, Augustine predicted their ruin, saying that "if you will not join with us in unity, you shall from your enemies suffer the vengeance of death."[19]

James Ussher writes of this interview: "The Welsh Chroniclers further relate that Dinooth the abbot of Bangor produced divers arguments at that time to show that they owed him no subjection." From the same authority we further learn that the Welsh made answer to Rome's monks that they adhered to what their holy fathers held before them, who were the friends of God and the followers of the apostles, and therefore they ought not to substitute for them any new dogmatists.[20]

---

[17] Bede, *Ecclesiastical History of England*, b. 2, ch. 2.
[18] *Ibid.*, b. 2, ch. 2.
[19] Killen, *The Old Catholic Church*, page 276.
[20] Ussher, *Discourse on the Religion Anciently Professed by the Irish and British*, page 106; also Lane, *Illustrated Notes on English Church History*, vol 1, pp. 54, 55.

Soon after this contest between Dinooth and Augustine the Welsh clergy lived to see the terrible slaughter of their young ministerial candidates in the war waged upon the Britons and the British Church in Wales. Aethelfrith, king of Northumbria, raised a great army to war against them. As he prepared to attack, he noticed a special company of about twelve hundred young men engaged in prayer. These were from the famous training college of Bangor, Wales. Though these young men were opposed to bearing arms, they were wont to pray for the soldiers of their own nation who were fighting for national existence. Upon learning who these twelve hundred were, Aethelfrith shouted that their prayers showed on what side they stood, even if they did not bear arms, and that he would slay them first. By his wicked command practically all of them were exterminated. So great was the slaughter that the papal historian Bede thinks he sees in this a fulfillment of Augustine's malediction.

Ussher has recorded some of the poems of the leading Welsh bard, Taliessin, poet laureate we may say, who wrote:

> Woe unto him who doth not keep
> From Romish wolves his holy sheep.

All must admire the spirit of the Welsh church leaders. Their lot was hard enough with the fierce Anglo-Saxon armies constantly harassing them. Added to that were the demands of the papal emissaries and of the organization backed by the king of France and the Roman emperor. The gulf between the two types of believers was deep and wide. This same Pope Gregory who sent Augustine to Britain had issued a bull declaring that the decrees of the first four general councils of the church were of equal inspiration with the gospels. This was an unacceptable man-made enlargement of the Scriptures. The Celtic Church rejected it and clung to the Bible and the Bible only.

In the second place the Welsh would not accept what Augustine did in Kent. On the advice of Gregory, he proceeded to sanctify, not abolish, the idolatrous festivals he found there. It was the practice of the apostles and their immediate successors wherever possible to abolish pagan sacrifices which, they declared, were sacrificed to devils.[21] Images of no kind were permitted in the churches of primitive Christianity during the first three hundred years.

---

[21] Bower, *The History of the Popes*, vol. 1, pages 416, 417.

Then, the pressure to accept the supremacy of a foreign Italian bishop as ordained of God to be a universal head of the church by virtue of apostolic succession, was offensive to the Welsh Church which had received its faith in direct descent from the apostles. A fourth point was the new conception of the office of the bishop. The Celtic Church retained the original understanding of the New Testament that a bishop was a pastor over a church, a presbyter, and not a spiritual overlord who held his authority from a superior in the Roman Catholic hierarchy.

A fifth reason for the difference between the Welsh Church and the papacy was the increasing demand by Rome for celibacy of the clergy. The Church in the Wilderness always maintained the original God-given freedom of its officers to marry. At times when dangers, exposure, and travel were the lot of the missionaries, they often chose the single life. These cases were the exception and certainly were never made the *sine qua non* of entrance into the ministry. The papacy, even in the days of its greatest power, was never able to force celibacy onto the Welsh clergy, though she made many attempts to accomplish it.[22]

Then came the controversy over the Sabbath. The historian A. C. Flick says that the Celtic Church observed the seventh day as the Sabbath.[23] The believers resented the effort to stigmatize them as Judaizers because they conscientiously believed the seventh day of the fourth commandment to be still binding. Moreover, this same Pope Gregory had issued an official pronouncement against a section of the city of Rome itself because the Christian believers there rested and worshiped on the Sabbath.[24] When the facts reveal that at this time, the seventh century, there were still more Christian churches throughout the world sanctifying the seventh day, the day which God sanctified in the fourth commandment of the Decalogue rather than Sunday, we can fully understand those apostolic churches that refused to worship on another day.

There is much evidence that the Sabbath prevailed in Wales universally until A. D. 1115, when the first Roman bishop was seated at St. David's.

---

[22] Bund, *The Celtic Church of Wales,* page 297.
[23] Flick, *The Rise of the Medieval Church,* page 237.
[24] *Epistles of Pope Gregory* I, coll. 13, ep. 1, found in *Nicene and Post-Nicene Fathers,* 2d Series, vol. 13.

The old Welsh Sabbathkeeping churches did not even then altogether bow the knee to Rome, but fled to their hiding places "where the ordinances of the gospel to this day have been administered in their primitive mode without being adulterated by the corrupt Church of Rome." [25]

The Welsh and the papists led by Augustine disagreed. The Welsh Church continued independent. Nothing would ever now satisfy Rome but the obliteration of the Celtic Church.

The change came when William the Conqueror landed in England with his Norman warriors and overthrew the Anglo-Saxon power. Here is a truly interesting parallel. When the Franks, still pagans, crossed the Rhine to overthrow Gaul, the papacy co-operated with the new pagan tribes, relying upon her great alliance with the Eastern emperor to so influence the invaders that, in ruining Gaul, they would also ruin the Celtic Church. And such came to pass as we present later in studying the widespread work in Europe of the Celtic missionaries from Ireland and Scotland. Likewise, William the Conqueror had the full assurance of the help of the pope, and the understanding that he would have this continued support, on condition that the Celtic Church must go. [26]

It is sad to follow step by step the policy pursued to displace the Celtic Church in Wales. One is thrilled by the spirit of independence and fidelity to apostolic truths which was shown by its members in the following centuries. Dinooth is a type of the splendid leadership given the native church. Had the entire conflict come immediately after William the Conqueror landed, instead of the prolonged wearing away, undoubtedly the early Celtic Church would still be there. Little by little, however, by intrigue, by flatteries, by threats, supported at every turn by England's armed power and seconded by the strong papal influences in Italy and France, the papal clergy succeeded after seven centuries in obtaining the mastery.

Steps in Subjection

In analyzing the different steps in securing this subjection, we might present them as follows: First, some of the Celtic clergy were persuaded to seek ordination from the papal primate of England, the archbishop of Canterbury. Secondly, the bishop of England assumed

---

[25] Lewis, *Seventh Day Baptists in Europe and America*, vol. 1, p. 29.
[26] Stokes, *Celtic Church in Ireland*, page 165.

the power to nominate the clergy of Wales. Thirdly, England, by right of conquest succeeding certain wars, claimed definite pieces of territory within the Welsh realm in which she would build a Catholic monastery and set over the community a Catholic bishop. Fourthly, whenever a Norman bishop was placed in Wales, he astutely followed the policy of claiming the lands belonging to any near-by landed noble who owed unpaid revenues. Fifthly, continued efforts were made by the papal clergy of England to drive a wedge between the Celtic clergy in Wales and the Welsh princes. Sixthly, as this went on, they had persuaded the Welsh princes that it was to their advantage to divorce their interests from those of the native church. Seventhly, when a sufficient number of papal clergy had gained a foothold in Wales, they began to hold regional synods or conventions. Eighthly, another step in advance was made when the native clergy submitted to a tour of visitation by a Catholic bishop.

A new turn in affairs came with the victories of King Edward I. This aggressive warrior who overthrew Sir William Wallace of Scotland as well as Prince Llewellyn of Wales, asserted his claim to be the head of the Welsh Church, and also to be the sovereign lord over Wales. By statutory legislation he decreed that English law should be the code of procedure wherever the crown had visited the states in Wales. In other territories he was willing that the old Celtic ecclesiastical measures should prevail in the church while English civil law ruled in secular matters. Thus from 1272 until King Henry VIII, Wales was no longer under Welsh law both civilly and religiously, but was under three different codes.

Under Henry VIII all this was swept aside. This monarch, who had brought into existence the Church of England, ordered that the civil and religious laws of England should be supreme throughout Wales. This had an immense effect in tearing down Welsh customs and in overthrowing the influence of the Celtic Church. It placed the Welsh clergy in the difficult position of either surrendering their convictions and practices of centuries, or being found in rebellion against the supreme law of the land. This situation has continued from then until now. It had the tendency to embitter a people who had never been too fond of their neighboring Anglo-Saxon kingdom. These changes were forced upon them and were never heartily accepted, so that when the Methodist revival in the eighteenth century swept

Wales, it found a nation always resentful of ritualism, ready to return to evangelism.

The Celtic Church of Wales, not the papal, is the connecting link in that land between apostolic Christianity and latter-day Protestantism. Although centuries have passed, the old religious characteristics of the people still remain. Ecclesiasticism which was forced upon them is no deeper than a thin veneer. The deadly struggle between these Celtic and Roman churches may be summed up in the words of J. W. Willis Bund:

> The issue was at once shifted from a fight between Christianity and paganism to a fight, a deadly fight, between the Latin and the Celtic Churches. In the north of England the Latin Church was victorious. She forced the Celtic missionaries to retire to Scotland or Ireland, and nominally brought England under the rule of Rome. But in Wales the result was different. Here the Latin Church was repulsed, if not defeated; here Celtic Christianity long maintained its position with its peculiar ideas and exceptional beliefs.[27]

---

[27] Bund, *The Celtic Church of Wales,* page 5.

CHAPTER XII

Aidan and the Church in England

Not Augustine at Canterbury, but devoted Irish Gaels in every valley of the Heptarchy—Aidan, Finan, Colman, Maeldubh, Diuma and the others — first carried the evangel of Christian culture to the savage English tribes.[1]

PATRICK in Ireland, Columba in Scotland, and Dinooth in Wales were apostles to a people using the Celtic tongue. Aidan, on the other hand, a disciple of Columba's Celtic school, was called to be an apostle to a different race — the pagan Anglo-Saxons of England. During its six hundred-year Anglo-Saxon period, the conversion of England stood as a monument to the missionary zeal of Aidan.

The pagans in conquering Britain by the sword had all but destroyed the primitive British Church. Nearly two hundred years later this same evangelical church not connected with Rome, through Aidan and his successors, subdued practically two thirds of their heathen conquerors by the power of the gospel.[2]

The seven kingdoms, the Heptarchy, into which England was divided in Aidan's days, were as jealous of one another as are the Balkan States today. Mercia in the center was the largest. The next largest, occupying the northeast portion of the realm, was Northumbria, where Aidan began his great work. South of Northumbria along the coast were (in succession) East Anglia; Essex, the kingdom of the East Saxons; Kent; and Sussex, the kingdom of the South Saxons. To the southwest of these lay the seventh member of the Heptarchy, Wessex, the kingdom of the West Saxons.

The Character and Education of Aidan

To the west and north of these seven pagan Anglo-Saxon kingdoms lay the Celtic Christian lands of Wales, Ireland, and Scotland; and to the southeast across the English Channel was the kingdom of the Franks which was ruled over by papal sovereigns.

Aidan came from Iona, which had grown into a well-equipped

---

[1] Fitzpatrick, *Ireland and the Foundations of Europe,* page 14.
[2] Soames, *The Anglo-Saxon Church,* pages 57, 58.

university.[3] Scholars of renown filled its chairs of instruction. This fact so impressed Dr. Samuel Johnson, the interesting figure in English literature, that he wrote: "We were now treading that illustrious island, which was once the luminary of the Caledonian regions, whence savage clans and roving barbarians derived the benefits of knowledge, and the blessings of religion."[4] Many travelers of the high seas occupied the guesthouse at Iona during the student life of Aidan, so that he devoured eagerly the knowledge imparted by the navigators from Iceland in the north, from the Holy Land in the south, and from other distant parts of the world.[5] He must also have known considerable about the seven kingdoms of pagan England, since many Angles came into Caledonia, either as fugitives or as captives taken by the warring Scots.

Two events occurred which singled out the call of Aidan as one of an unusual nature. The assembly of Iona selected one of their students to go in answer to the request from King Oswald of Northumbria for an evangelist. Though distinguished for the austerity of his life and for his learning, the one selected quickly returned home, complaining, like the ten spies of old, of the fierce people and the great obstacles to overcome. He lacked the faith to serve, however much he loved to shine. Another student in the assembly who advocated love, gentleness, and patience in winning the Anglo-Saxons, was chosen. This was the youthful Aidan.

The second unusual factor in the case was the remarkable career of Oswald, ruler of the land to which Aidan was called. In early youth Oswald knew of the national hatred of his pagan people for the Britons which led to the slaughter of the twelve hundred students.[6] He had also witnessed the conversion of his pagan father to the superficial Christianity advocated by Paulinus, a priest sent from Kent. Later the priest fled when, at the death of Oswald's father, the Northumbrians lapsed into idolatry. Oswald himself was compelled to flee his own land and find an asylum at Iona. Then the love of his countrymen for his family revived, and Oswald was summoned to the

---

[3] Lloyd, "Historical Account of Church Government," quoted in Stillingfleet, *The Antiquities of the British Churches,* vol. 2, pp. 157, 158.

[4] Boswell, *The Life of Samuel Johnson,* vol. 3, p. 147, note.

[5] Fitzpatrick, *Ireland and the Foundations of Europe,* pages 26, 154.

[6] See the author's discussion in Chapter XI, entitled, "Dinooth and the Church in Wales."

throne.   Paulinus, the Roman bishop, was still alive and near at hand, but Oswald wanted his people in Northumbria to walk in the ways of Columba, so he passed this priest by and sent to Iona for a leader.

Rome's Mission to the Kingdom of Kent

Northumbria was not the only Anglo-Saxon kingdom which, after it had lapsed from Romanism into idolatry, was won to Christ by the Celtic Church.   In fact, the history of the whole 1260-year period reveals that it was the Church in the Wilderness in papal lands that helped, by virtue of its competition, to keep Roman Catholicism alive. When it was removed or destroyed in certain areas, the standards of Christianity began quickly to fall.   Such was the case in Essex, Mercia, East Anglia, and Kent.   To understand this and to follow the great work of Aidan and his successors, consideration should be given to the labors of Augustine and his forty monks who came from Rome to Canterbury in 597.

The following instruction from Pope Gregory to Augustine after the latter through the efforts of Bertha, the Catholic wife of the pagan king, Ethelbert, had secured for him and his monks a footing in Kent is worthy of notice:

> At first it was Gregory's intention, which he intimated, indeed, to King Ethelbert, to have all the temples of idolatry destroyed; but on maturer reflection, he altered his mind, and dispatched a letter after the abbot Mellitus, in which he declared, that the idol temples, if well built, ought not to be destroyed, but sprinkled with holy water, and sanctified by holy relics, should be converted into temples of the living God; so that the people might be more easily induced to assemble in their accustomed places.   Moreover, the festivals in honor of the idols, of which the rude people had been deprived, should be replaced by others, either on the anniversaries of the consecration of churches, or on days devoted to the memory of the saints, whose relics were deposited in them.   On such days, the people should be taught to erect arbors around the churches, in which to celebrate their festive meals, and thus be holden to thank the giver of all good for these temporal gifts.   Being thus allowed to indulge in some sensual enjoyments, they could be the more easily led to those which are inward and spiritual.[7]

As to the methods Augustine employed, the following is from the historian Albert Henry Newman:

[7] Neander, *General History of the Christian Religion and Church*, vol. 3, p. 15.

By making a parade of ascetical life, by pretended miracles, and by promises of earthly advantages, they succeeded in converting Ethelbert, king of the Saxons, who with about ten thousand followers received baptism in a river at the hands of the missionaries. A firm alliance having been formed between the king and the Roman See, the missionaries addressed themselves to the far more difficult task of subjecting the British Christians to Rome. When all other means proved unavailing, they persuaded the Saxon king to make an expedition against them. Three thousand of the British Christians were slaughtered on one occasion. For centuries the Christians of the old British type, in Wales, Scotland, and Ireland, as well as in various parts of Germany, resisted with all their might the encroachments of Rome, and it is probable that Christianity of this type was never wholly exterminated.[8]

Aidan's Missionary Labors

In direct contrast to the method employed by Augustine in Kent stands the manner in which Aidan labored for Northumbria. John Lingard, a defender of the papacy, writes:

As soon as he had received the episcopal ordination, he repaired to the court of Oswald. His arrival was a subject of general exultation; and the king condescended to explain in Saxon the instructions which the missionary delivered in his native language. But the success of Aidan was owing no less to his virtues than to his preaching. The severe austerity of his life, his profound contempt of riches, and his unwearied application to the duties of his profession, won the esteem, while his arguments convinced the understanding of his hearers. Each day the number of proselytes increased; and, within a few years, the church of Northumbria was fixed on a solid and permanent foundation.[9]

The character of Aidan was well balanced. In religious fervor he was second to none of the great church leaders. His industry was amazing. He was never idle. In him was that flame of living fire which blazed forth so gloriously in many of the young missionaries sent from the schools of Patrick and Columba. Of him Bede says:

It was the highest commendation of his doctrine, with all men, that he taught no otherwise than he and his followers had lived; for he neither sought nor loved anything of this world, but delighted in distributing immediately among the poor whatsoever was given him by the kings or rich men of the world. He was wont to traverse both town and country on foot, never on horseback, unless compelled by some urgent necessity; and

---

[8] Newman, *A Manual of Church History*, vol. 1, p. 411.
[9] Lingard, *The Antiquities of the Anglo-Saxon Church*, vol. 1, pp. 27, 28.

wherever in his way he saw any, either rich or poor, he invited them, if infidels, to embrace the mystery of the faith; or if they were believers, to strengthen them in the faith, and to stir them up by words and actions to alms and good works.[10]

The good work spread to the other Anglo-Saxon kingdoms. What thrilling encouragement this evangelical movement among these pagan neighbors must have given to those of like faith who in Persia and the Far East were laboring for the conversion of the heathen! One medieval historian breaks forth in admiration as he attempts to tell what God had done for King Oswald. He enumerates all the nations—the Britons, the Scots, the Picts, and the English—and the provinces of Britain that were brought under Oswald's dominion.[11]

Aidan was a man of prayer. He withdrew into his closet and shut the door. On bended knees he poured forth his fervent supplications to God. He had a clear perception of truth and duty, and he exercised a saving, transforming influence upon all who were about him.

He exhibited great tenderness in his labors for the sinner and in his effort to relieve the poor and afflicted. "He is said to have been deeply concerned for the welfare of the poor and to have devoted much attention to ransoming slaves."[12] Bede, while expressing plainly his disapproval of Aidan's refusal to accept papal doctrines, takes great pleasure in saying that this missionary was careful to omit none of the things which he found in the apostolic and prophetic writings, but that to the utmost of his power he endeavored to perform them all.[13]

Aidan was also a founder of church schools and training colleges. At the beginning of his ministry, King Oswald assigned to him the island of Lindisfarne. This was situated on the eastern coast of Northumbria near to the capital of the kingdom, but sufficiently off the main thoroughfare to give the proper surroundings to an educational center. Taking Iona as a model, Aidan did for England through this mother college what Columba had done for Scotland. The fields were used to give work to support the students, as well as to furnish the food for faculty and pupils. It was the purpose of the Celtic

[10] Bede, *Ecclesiastical History of England,* b. 3, ch. 5.
[11] *Ibid.,* b. 3, ch. 6.
[12] Latourette, *The Thousand Years of Uncertainty,* page 57.
[13] Bede, *Ecclesiastical History of England,* b. 3, ch. 17.

Church to plant many centers rather than to concentrate numbers and wealth in some ecclesiastical capital. Aidan and his followers limited the buildings to the necessities of the school.

Of the location of Lindisfarne and its influence in creating similar institutions, John Lingard says that in all his toil, Aidan kept his eyes fixed on his patron, Columba.[14] From Aidan's first institution, similar training centers were established in the kingdoms of Bernicia, Deira, Mercia, and East Anglia. Aidan's work was a triumph for truth. First, paganism was swept away and replaced by religion founded on New Testament doctrines.

Only thirty years was spanned by Aidan and his immediate successors, Finan and Colman. In apportioning these years, Bede gives seventeen to Aidan, ten to Finan, and three to Colman.[15] And yet in that brief period the Celtic Church grew and prospered so that John Meissner says, "The original Celtic Christianity had thus a very powerful hold on the country at the time when the first Roman emissary landed in Kent."[16] Edward Hulme writes that " 'Aidan was the apostle of England.' "[17]

Celtic Church Training Centers

The chief instrument of Aidan's success was the training school. In naming these evangelical colleges, many writers call them "monasteries," using the term in its ancient sense. W. M. Hetherington presents as additional proof that the East was the homeland of early British Christianity, that the terms "monk" and "monastery" as used by the ecclesiastical writers of that age did not mean segregated congregations of unmarried men as writers generally now use the expressions. These words meant, rather, that the pupils of the British theological seminaries were married men and were frequently succeeded in their offices and duties by their own sons. This author further claims that wherever the Culdees or Celtic Christians founded new settlements, the presiding officer of the board of directors was chosen by election, not appointed by some foreign superior. "He was, in fact, nothing more than 'the first among equals.' "[18]

---

[14] Lingard, *The Antiquities of the Anglo-Saxon Church,* vol. 1, p. 155.
[15] Bede, *Ecclesiastical History of England,* b. 3, ch. 26.
[16] Meissner, *The Celtic Church in England,* page 4.
[17] Hulme, *A History of the British People,* page 33.
[18] Hetherington, *History of the Church of Scotland,* vol. 1, pp. 11, 12.

Archbishop James Ussher writes that "our monasteries in ancient times were the seminaries of the ministry: being as it were, so many colleges of learned divines, whereunto the people did usually resort for instruction, and from whence the church was wont continually to be supplied with able ministers."[19] Furthermore, the learned Joseph Bingham takes considerable pains to prove by past authorities that "monk" and "monastery" originally had different meanings from those usually given to the words now.[20]

Soon after the establishment of Lindisfarne, Aidan founded Melrose on the Tweed River as a second training field. Although for centuries since then the shadows have daily crept across the vacant fields where once stood this Columban college, yet splendid memorials still remain to show its noble contribution to civilization.[21]

Whitby as a Training Center

Another such institute, probably the most famous of all Columban spiritual headquarters in England, was Whitby in the kingdom of Northumbria. Two celebrated names — Hilda and Caedmon — are connected with this history-making center. Whitby is remembered particularly because of the celebrated abbess Hilda. She was of royal descent, and from the age of thirteen was well known for her piety and consecration to the Christian faith. When paganism again arose in Northumbria after the superficial work done by Augustine, Hilda left the country and went to the south, probably to East Anglia. Then came the great news that King Oswald was on the throne of her native land. Having distinguished herself by a noble work in two training centers, she returned to Northumbria and undertook either to build or to arrange a Bible seminary at Whitby. Bede relates that Aidan and other religious men knew her and honored her work. Because of her innate wisdom and inclination to the service of God, they frequently visited with her and diligently instructed her in the doctrines. Even kings and princes asked and received her advice.[22] She put the seminary at Whitby under efficient and scholarly discipline. This establishment was very large, having two separate divisions, one for each sex. This latter arrangement was unusual. She obliged all those

---

[19] Ussher, *The Whole Works,* vol. 4, p. 297.
[20] Bingham, *The Antiquities of the Christian Church,* b. 7, ch. 2, sec. 6.
[21] Bede, *Ecclesiastical History of England,* b. 4, ch. 27.
[22] *Ibid.,* b. 4, ch. 23.

who were under her direction to attend much to the reading of the Bible and to learn how to teach scriptural truths.

There is ample evidence that this was the type of training center established throughout the world by the Church in the Wilderness. A specialty was made of studying and copying the Holy Scriptures. Farming and other trades were taught. To the girls instruction was given suitable to their later life. Whitby became the nursery of eminent men, graduating five who became provincial directors, and giving to the world Caedmon, the first of English religious poets. Dugdale says that Hilda "was a professed enemy to the extension of the papal jurisdiction in this country, and opposed with all her might the tonsure of priests and the celebration of Easter according to the Roman ritual."[23] In the crisis precipitated in the national convocation, when the contending papal and the British delegates met at Whitby in 664, Hilda was found on the side of the successor of Aidan. Many other training centers besides Whitby were established by the Scots in Great Britain and Ireland.

Caedmon

The grace of the Lord made use of a simple custom in one of these training centers to bring forth a leader. It seems that at certain entertainments a harp would be passed around from one individual to another and each was expected to compose an impromptu poem and play the harp in accompaniment. Caedmon, being a simple cowherd, felt so deeply his inferiority that one night when the harp was passed to him he refused to make an attempt, and retired to the stable where he had charge of the cattle. It seemed that a man appeared to him in his sleep and greeted him, saying, "Sing, Caedmon, some song to me." He answered that he could not, and it was because of this that he had left the feast. The visitor answered him, "However, you will sing to me." "What shall I sing?" asked the humble youth. "The beginning of created things," commanded the voice. Immediately he began to sing and compose to the praise of God. When this was reported, Hilda, always seeking for gifts among her students, requested him to relate the dream and repeat the words he had heard. Bede says, "They all concluded, that heavenly grace had been conferred upon him by our Lord."

---

[23] Quoted in M'Clintock and Strong, *Cyclopedia*, art. "Hilda."

The students of the abbey delighted themselves in exercising the gift they had discovered in Caedmon.   They gave him passages from the Holy Scriptures which, when translated into English, he immediately converted into harmonious verse and sweetly repeated to his masters.   Bede writes:

> He sang the creation of the world, the origin of man, and all the history of Genesis: and made many verses on the departure of the children of Israel out of Egypt, and their entering into the Land of Promise, with many other histories from Holy Writ; the incarnation, passion, resurrection of our Lord, and His ascension into heaven; the coming of the Holy Ghost, and the preaching of the apostles; also the terror of future judgment, the horror of the pains of hell, and the delights of heaven; besides many more about the Divine benefits and judgments, by which He endeavored to turn away all men from the love of vice, and to excite in them the love of, and application to, good actions.[24]

The sermons wrought into verse by Caedmon captured the hearts of England.   Caedmon loved sacred subjects.   Composed in the people's language, these elevating themes could be sung by all circles. For the first time the common people enjoyed the wonderful words of life in hymns they could understand.   In those days when there was no printing press, Caedmon, through singing, gave the message that Aidan and his disciples set forth by preaching.

Finan

At Aidan's death Finan was chosen in his place.   He carried forward the work ably begun by his predecessor.

When Finan evangelized the kingdom of Mercia, it held a dominant position in the Heptarchy, for it was located in the center of England and was inhabited by a brave, warlike people.   Through the influence of the warlike ruler, Penda, the kingdom was given to idolatry.   Now, Penda's son, Peada,—a most exemplary young man, open-minded and resourceful,—was in love with Elfleda, the daughter of King Oswy of Northumbria, who was brother of Oswald.   When he sought the hand of the girl in marriage, the father refused on the basis that he was not a Christian; but he requested Peada to receive instruction in the teachings of Christ and to work for the conversion of the southern part of Mercia over which his father had set him as

---

[24] Bede, *Ecclesiastical History of England*, b. 4, ch. 24.

ruler. When he learned of the gospel and was taught concerning the resurrection and the future immortal life, he rejoiced in his new-found light and informed Elfleda's father that it was his great desire to become a Christian whether he secured the girl or not. Thereupon Finan was sent to Peada with a large retinue of earls, soldiers, and servants. After Finan had baptized the young prince, he left behind to further instruct him and his people, four pastors of the Celtic Church—Cedd, Adda, Betti, and Diuma. The last-named minister was of Scottish blood while the others were English. When these pastors arrived in the province of the prince, they preached the word of God, which was gladly received by many of the nobility as well as by the common people. Many renounced their idolatry and were baptized.

The East Saxons

From the kingdom of Mercia we turn to Essex. A study of the religion of the East Saxons reveals again the superficial work of papal missionaries. Following his first success in Kent, Augustine ordained Mellitus as bishop to Sabert, king of the East Saxons. Many were baptized, and it looked as if Mellitus had done a good work. Upon the death of Sabert, however, his three pagan sons immediately made an open profession of idolatry which previously they had renounced. They granted liberty to the people to serve idols. And when they saw the Roman bishop celebrating mass and giving the wafer to the people, they argued with the priest. Finally, they forced the bishop and his followers to depart from the kingdom. Immediately Mellitus fled to the two papal bishops of the kingdom of Kent. All three agreed it would be best for them to leave England, so they withdrew into France.

Under Finan the Christian faith was again established among the East Saxons, and this time the Celtic Church brought the message. The Essex king, Sigebert, and his friends were baptized. After his baptism, the king called Celtic missionaries to his kingdom. Thus the Celtic Church was the instrument in God's hand of making Christianity prevail over idolatry in the kingdom of Essex.

Finan recognized how God was working with the church missionaries in Essex. Following the example of Columba and Aidan before him, he established a theological training center at Tillbery.

It has been shown how the three kingdoms of Northumbria, Mercia, and Essex were brought back from their idolatry to the faith of the Celtic Church through the consecrated labors of the Scots. Speaking of the magnificent work done by the Celtic Church in these kingdoms, the historian Rapin de Thoyras writes:

> Austin [Augustine] has had the honor of converting the English, when in the main the progress he made was not very considerable. 'Tis true he preached to the Saxons of Kent, as Mellitus did to those of Essex, and that with good success. . . .
>
> Augustine in the height of his success, for which he is so greatly honored, established but two bishops only, Justus at Rochester (in his own Kent), and Mellitus at London, though the pope had expressly ordered him to settle bishops wherever there should be occasion. . . . This is clear evidence, that the progress ascribed to him was not so considerable as Gregory imagines. . . . It is therefore surprisingly strange that the conversion of the English should be ascribed to Augustine, rather than to Aidan, to Finan, to Colman, to Cedd, to Diuma, and the other Scotch monks, who undoubtedly labored much more abundantly than he. But here lies the case. These last had not their orders from Rome, and therefore must not be allowed any share in the glory of this work.[25]

The historian Henry Soames writes upon the same theme:

> Only two counties, therefore, north of the Thames . . . were ever under Roman superintendence during their transition from paganism to Christianity, and these two were largely indebted to domestic [Scottish] zeal for their conversion. Every other county, from London to Edinburgh, has the full gratification of pointing to the ancient church of Britain as its nursing mother in Christ's holy faith.[26]

The Church in Kent, Wessex, East Anglia, and Sussex

What now should be said of the four other kingdoms — Kent, East Anglia, Sussex, and Wessex? Kent, being the kingdom in the southeastern part of the island and farthest away from the missionary advance of the Scots, had early been entered by Augustine. The Christianity which prevailed in this province, therefore, was of the papal type. Wessex, kingdom of the West Saxons, was farthest away from either the Scottish or the papal advance; therefore it long resisted any profession of Christianity.

---

[25] Thoyras, *History of England*, vol. 1, p. 69.
[26] Soames, *The Anglo-Saxon Church*, pages 58, 59.

As to the country of the East Angles, here again it was the influence of Scottish missionaries which reclaimed it to Christianity when, after the departure of the Roman monks, it had fallen into idolatry. A few years after this lapse into paganism a Scottish pastor labored so diligently among them that great numbers of the apostates were led to renounce their errors and return to the faith.[27] As for Sussex, kingdom of the South Saxons, it was greatly indebted to the Celtic Church for the knowledge of Christ. Their king had been baptized in the province of the Mercians by the evangelical Scots. Even in the Roman Catholic province of the West Saxons it was the labors of Scottish missionaries which efficiently helped the Anglo-Saxons there to depart from their paganism and embrace the gospel.

"It is no exaggeration to say that, with the exception of Kent and Sussex, the whole English race received the foundation of their faith from Celtic missionaries, and even in Sussex it is known that Irish missionaries were at work before the arrival of Wilfrid."[28] As the celebrated Count de Montalembert, French Catholic scholar, wrote, "Northumbrian Christianity spread over the southern kingdoms."[29]

Colman

At the death of Finan, Colman was chosen as his successor to lead the Celtic Church. Bede says that he was sent from Scotland.[30] Colman came to preach the word of God to the English nation.[31] The Scots sent him to Lindisfarne, therefore his consecration and his field of labor were identical with those of Aidan and Finan — the kingdom of Northumbria. Since, however, at that time Oswy, king of Northumbria, was a leader among other kingdoms of England, Colman would naturally be a leader of leaders. He possessed the meekness of Christ. Step by step British Christianity successfully met entrenched paganism and decadent Romanism and advanced into province after province.

Suddenly the wind changed; the intrigues of the Roman Catholic queen of Oswy succeeded. When Colman had been in office only three years, the actions of the queen precipitated the Council of Whitby.

---

[27] Bede, *Ecclesiastical History of England*, b. 3, ch. 19.
[28] Meissner, *The Celtic Church in England*, page 4.
[29] Montalembert, *Monks of the West*, vol. 4, p. 88.
[30] Bede, *Ecclesiastical History of England*, b. 3, ch. 25.
[31] *Ibid.*, b. 4, ch. 4.

Three things were against Colman: first, the short time in which he had been in office; secondly, the fact that his antagonist, Wilfrid, had been drilled in the ways of the papacy; and lastly, the intrigue of the Roman Catholic queen.

The main question in dispute was the same as that between Augustine and Dinooth, the same which had led Victor I, the Roman bishop, to excommunicate the clergy of the East—the date of the observance of Easter. In other lands the sword was used against those who refused to accept the practices of Rome.[32] Eanfled, the Roman Catholic queen of Oswy, was determined to bend the king to the practices of Rome.

The queen's chaplain, Wilfrid, was one of the most determined opponents of the Celtic Church. He had been sent to Rome where for four years he had looked upon the gorgeous rites and temples of the papacy. During this time he had been drilled in the arguments and traditions designed to spread Rome's authority, and he returned to Northumbria with the purpose of forcing the Celtic Church to come into line with papal practices.[33] Public debate is exactly what Wilfrid sought, in order that a decision might be proclaimed in favor of the papacy. The weakness of the king assured this victory in advance. Oswy decreed that both parties should meet in open forum. The place chosen was Whitby. Oswy presided over the council. Colman, his Scottish clerks, the abbess Hilda and her followers, and Bishop Cedd were on the side of the Scots. The king, his son, Prince Alchfrid, the queen, and two able Roman priests besides Wilfrid were on the side of Rome.[34]

None can read the report of the discussion as handed down by the papal historian Bede without realizing how skillfully Colman answered the arguments in the case. However, Wilfrid artfully brought the debate around to the supremacy of Peter. It is informing to know that, although this question was in nowise the real point at issue, the Roman divines heaped derision on the great Columba as Wilfrid shouted:

> As for you and your companions, you certainly sin if having heard the decrees of the apostolic see and of the universal church you refuse to

---

[32] Green, *A Handbook of Church History,* page 433.
[33] Terry, *A History of England,* page 44.
[34] Bede, *Ecclesiastical History of England,* b. 3, ch. 25.

follow them; for though your fathers were holy, do you think their small number, in a corner of the remotest island, is to be preferred before the universal church of Christ? And if that Columba of yours was a holy man and powerful in miracles, yet, could he be preferred before the most blessed prince of the apostles, to whom our Lord said, "Thou art Peter, and upon this rock I will build My church, and the gates of hell shall not prevail against it; and to thee I will give the keys of the kingdom of heaven?"[35]

Immediately the king broke in: "Is it true, Colman, that these words were spoken to Peter by our Lord?" When Colman replied in the affirmative, endeavoring at the same time to show the fallacy and weakness of using the incident of the keys as a basis for church supremacy, his remarks were considered beside the point. The king led the audience to increasing indecision, until they finally renounced their former custom and decided to conform to the pretended superiority of the papal Easter.[36]

It is not difficult to see why King Oswy surrendered to the pressure of the queen and her chaplain. Through alliance with the kings of Europe, Rome was laying broad and deep the foundations of her theocracy. The new line of kings, descendants of Charlemagne, was rising to dominance on the Continent and carrying the papacy along with them. The decrees of the general councils of the papacy were supreme. Kings of even greater resolution than Oswy would have weakened before the pressure.

The Four Centuries Following Whitby

Some have asked why Colman and his accompanying workers immediately left for the island of Iona. How could he have done otherwise? If he had rallied his forces to fight the king and the foreign priests, such a plan might have torn down the church organization which had been so ably built up by Aidan and Finan. He remembered that when the first fierce persecutions fell upon the infant church in Jerusalem the apostles left the city, so that the assaulting opposition was turned aside from the church. Thus, we can see the wisdom of Colman in departing immediately with his co-workers.

"During the four dark centuries that followed the Council of Whitby, the northward extension of the Roman Church was checked

---

[35] Stokes, *Ireland and the Celtic Church,* pages 163, 164.
[36] Bede, *Ecclesiastical History of England,* b. 3, ch. 25.

by racial warfare and pagan invasions which built up additional barriers between the north and the south."[37]

In the providence of God, Colman's departure could not have been better timed. The papacy was not permitted a widespread enjoyment of her questionable victory at the Council of Whitby, as many historians have stated. Before Wilfrid and his successors could accomplish the destruction of the Celtic Church, the design for which he had trained at Rome, the Danes swept down upon England bringing with them a new flood of paganism.

However, when the leaders of the British Church had departed, the representatives of Romanism immediately seized the spiritual overlordship of the realm. The year following Whitby, Pope Vitalian wrote a letter to King Oswy concerning the appointment of an archbishop for Canterbury, in which he said, "By the protecting hand of God you have been converted to the true and apostolic faith." Pope Vitalian told the king that he would root out the enemy tares.[38] He further promised to send the relics of the apostles Peter and Paul along with the letter. Not long afterward, the king's son, Alchfrid, discovered and banished the Scottish sect.[39] This injustice was inflicted by King Alchfrid upon the Scottish believers with the approbation of his father, Oswy, because the Scots refused to conform to a church which sanctioned relic worship.

Although the papacy had secured the ascendancy in England, God did not permit the truth to die. The seed sown by Aidan, Finan, and Colman, though dormant, was not lifeless. The faith represented by the Celtic leaders remained powerful in Scotland, Ireland, Wales, and in the southwestern part of England. Followers of the truth persisted down through the centuries, so that when Wycliffe began his marvelous revival centuries later, his followers are thought by some to have been those who had maintained from generation to generation the doctrines of Aidan.

During the four hundred years from Whitby to the Norman conquest the papacy in England proper was never able to overcome totally the paganism of the Danes or the inspiring courage of Celtic believers. Therefore, the Church of Rome saw that if it was to win, a

[37] Barnett, *Margaret of Scotland: Queen and Saint,* page 75.
[38] Bede, *Ecclesiastical History of England,* b. 3, ch. 29.
[39] *Ibid.,* b. 5, ch. 19.

new plan of battle must be devised. Time and circumstances placed in its hands a leader destined to bring about a change in the British Isles. This champion was William of Normandy.

The Papacy and William the Conqueror

The papacy favored the conquest of England by William of Normandy.[40] There were three reasons for this. The Danes in conquering Anglo-Saxon England (c. A. D. 820) were imbued with such a pagan background that Rome could never expect a strong ascendancy through them even though in later years they had leanings toward that faith. This might even have meant a victory for the ancient Celtic Church which had already shown itself spiritually able to win both Anglo-Saxons and Danes. Therefore, the papacy welcomed the hour when a strong Norman leader in France had an apparent claim to the throne of England. In the second place, something had to be done to break the power of the Celtic Church, particularly in Scotland and Ireland. Finally, it was necessary to have a new race upon which to build. The Normans, whose fatherland was France, were living under the leadership of the people whom the pope had entitled "the eldest daughter of the church." They had enthusiasm for the political combination of colorful superstition, a tryannical caste system, and regal pomp. If the Normans could lay an iron hand upon Saxon and Danish England, the whole of the British Isles might be brought fully under the papal flag.

When William of Normandy landed in England in 1066 with his warriors, the Danish king, Harold, had just been called to fight in the north a terrific battle with a rebellious rival. Obliged to move south by forced marches to meet the Norman invaders, his wearied army drew up on the heights of Hastings. But it could not withstand the invaders, and the battle was won by the Normans.

The victory at Hastings brought new leadership for the Roman Church in England. A powerful reorganization of English life, customs, and institutions followed. Nevertheless, three hundred years passed before the combined powers of continental Roman Catholicism and Norman prowess could bring Ireland and Scotland under the dominance of the papacy. Wales was not subdued. Even then the

---

[40] Thatcher and Schwill, *Europe in the Middle Ages,* page 206.

spiritual conquest was one of might and not of right.   Swayed by fear and awed by authority, the people accepted the customs of the Normans and made a superficial profession of accepting the papal doctrines.   The deeper convictions of truth and liberty which prevailed in the days of the Celtic Church were smothered under the weight of the invaders.   The great work of Aidan was apparently buried in utter darkness.   Yet, centuries later when the Reformation challenged the supremacy of Rome, the seed sown by Aidan, Finan, and Colman sprang forth to newness of life.   The Church of the Wilderness bestirred herself, and a new day dawned not only for England, but for the world.

CHAPTER XIII

Columbanus and the Church in Europe

Columbanus proved to be the great avant-courier of the rebirth of civilization in Europe. During the five hundred years that followed there was hardly a generation that did not see the vineyards crowded with Irish laborers, that did not hear the voice of some authoritative personality of the Gael ringing in the ears of princes and peoples.[1]

A S THE tide of Celtic missionary work rolled on, it brought forth a leader who did more for the reconversion of Europe than anyone who followed him. Columbanus (some write his name Columban) was the apostle to the Europe submerged by the influence of Clovis and the northern pagans. Patrick took the ancient pagan civilization of Ireland and forged it into a crusading Christianity; Columba through his college at Iona lifted Scotland from darkness to a leadership of light; but Columbanus was to impress the teachings of Christ on France, Germany, Switzerland, and Italy.

The Holy Spirit bestowed upon Columbanus many spiritual gifts as he surrendered his heart to the Saviour. With his training came an inescapable burden to carry the gospel which he learned to the Continent in its then chaotic condition.

The environment into which Columbanus (A. D. 543-615) was born was the finest there was anywhere in the West. The overflowing of the Teutonic invasions which had torn down the structure of Roman civilizations in Europe had left Ireland and Scotland untouched. There the best in Celtic, Roman, and Christian culture had been preserved, organized, and nurtured by Patrick, Columba, and a generation of enthusiastic scholars. Columbanus breathed this atmosphere, and by masterly self-discipline was, like Moses in the court of Pharaoh or Paul in the seminaries of the Pharisees, "learned in all the wisdom"[2] of his day. He was tall, sinewy, and handsome. "His fine figure and his splendid color," says his biographer Jonas, "aroused against him the lust of lascivious maidens."[3]

---

[1] Fitzpatrick, *Ireland and the Foundations of Europe,* page 15.
[2] Acts 7:22.
[3] Jonas, *Vita Columbani,* found in Migne, *Patrologia Latina,* vol. 87, p. 1015.

Columbanus spent several years in study in the halls of learning at Bangor. Here he devotedly studied the Scriptures. The music of sacred song charmed his soul, and he perfected his gift of writing poetry. From Bangor he could look across the waters of the Irish Channel to England which was still in the grip of the pagan Anglo-Saxons. Northward he could behold the marvelous transformations wrought in Scotland by Columba. Farther to the east lay France in wretched moral condition. The apostolic spirit burned within Columbanus as he heard the stories of the miserable state of Gaul, and he decided to go forth to evangelize France in the missionary spirit of Celtic Christianity.

Missionary Endeavors in France

The arrival of Columbanus in Gaul brought the dawn of a new day for Europe. In the many centers of civilization which he and his followers created, he implanted the spirit of Christianity in the hearts of the people.[4] The power of the gospel continued for centuries in spite of papal supremacy.[5] In fact, the Church of Rome, in order to save its prestige, was compelled to assail the Columban Order and Rule, and to favor the Benedictine. The best in European civilization still owes its rebuilding to Columbanus, his companions, and his followers; other European evangelicals co-operated.[6]

For years before the coming of Columbanus there had been savage, fratricidal warfare among the descendants of Clovis. As for the populace, they had a form of religion but no conception of true piety; and with no solid guiding principles, they were like the heathen. Immorality and degradation abounded. Columbanus and his associates reckoned not on political might, but on the power of the love of God in their hearts to convince the population. They relied upon the Holy Spirit in noble lives to cause the masses to hunger and thirst after righteousness.

The learning of Columbanus had won him high favor with the reigning descendants of Clovis. King Guntram hailed his arrival with joy. Clarence W. Bispham says: "Here are Irish missionaries in new surroundings. Before this they were in strife with the heathen. Now

---

[4] Bispham, *Columban — Saint, Monk, Missionary*, page 44.
[5] Newman, *A Manual of Church History*, vol. 1, p. 414.
[6] Smith and Wace, *A Dictionary of Christian Biography*, art. "Columbanus."

they begin to battle against a corrupt and debased Christianity."[7]
Or, as Jonas, the biographer of Columbanus who learned from his
associates the facts of his life, wrote: "The creed alone remained.
But the remedy of repentance and the love of mortifying the lusts of
the flesh were to be found only in a few."[8] So King Guntram besought
him to settle in his realm, saying: "If you wish to take the cross of
Christ and follow Him, seek the quiet of a retreat. Only be careful,
for the increase of your own reward and our spiritual good, to remain
in our kingdom and not to go to neighboring peoples." The missionaries accepted the offer of an old, half-ruined fort at Anagrates (the
present Anegray), which dated from Roman days, as the site for their
first mission.

The First Three Centers in France

The beginnings at Anagrates in the wilderness of the Vosges were
difficult. While the buildings were being erected and before the first
fruits of the ground could appear, the Irish missionaries knew what
suffering meant. Food at times was so scarce that they lived on ber-
ries, on the bark of trees, and on whatever they could find on the
ground. On one occasion King Guntram, hearing of their distress,
commanded food to be brought to them. Yet they stood faithfully at
their post of duty. All they asked was an opportunity for manual
labor and the solitude in which to study the Scriptures. These tall,
powerful men dressed in their long, coarse gowns, their books slung
over their shoulders in leather satchels, and carrying staves in their
hands, must have made a deep impression on the native population.
Of their exemplary life and saving example, Jonas again writes:

> Modesty and sobriety, gentleness and mildness shone forth in them all.
> The evils of sloth and of unruly tempers were expelled. Pride and haughti-
> ness were expiated by severe punishments. Scorn and envy were driven
> out by faithful diligence. So great was the strength of their patience, love,
> and mildness that no one could doubt that the God of mercy dwelt among
> them.[9]

At times Columbanus would retire apart and live for days by himself. He had no companion but the Bible which he no doubt had

---

[7] Bispham, *Columban — Saint, Monk, Missionary*, page 19.
[8] Jonas, *Vita Columbani*, found in Migne, *Patrologia Latina*, vol. 87, pp. 1017, 1018.
[9] *Ibid.*, vol. 87, p. 1018.

transcribed by his own hand at Bangor. He trusted God for food and for care against the elements. He was looked upon as a prince over the wild beasts. From these retreats he came forth like the prophets of old, strengthened and refreshed for his labors.

Wide-spreading influence quickly came to the new mission. The youth of the land, many of whom were from noble families, flocked to the young training center. It was not now necessary to travel abroad to attend the colleges of the Emerald Isle. Here was a faculty of thirteen Irish teachers in their own land, bringing the sanctity, the learning, and the manual skill of their famous Celtic seminaries. A hundred years earlier Clovis had made a political union with the papacy in order to gain the support of the eastern emperor; but this had turned out to be a detriment, not a stimulant. And no wonder, for in the days of Columbanus the pope of Rome was Gregory I, called Gregory the Great, well known as an enemy of classical learning.[10] Many authorities upbraid this pontiff because he drove the mathematicians out of Rome, proscribed Greek, and denounced learning.[11]

Anagrates soon became too small. The number of candidates for admission into the new settlement increased greatly. The influence of Columbanus became widespread. The sincerity and consecration of the Irish camp was so superior to anything of that nature on the Continent that it was like introducing a new religion. The inhabitants of storm-swept Europe turned their eyes to the place whence came inspiring reports, and doors of opportunity were opened to the evangelists. This determined Columbanus to open another center for the spread of the gospel.

He met with the hearty co-operation of King Guntram. The ruler of Burgundy gladly granted them a site at Luxeuil, situated at the foot of the Vosges mountains, where the forests of the mountains had invaded the plain. Here were the ruins of old Roman villas, overgrown by the tangled underbrush. This wilderness abounded in bears, wolves, foxes, and other wild life. But under the sturdy blows of these missionaries of the Church in the Wilderness all this changed. The forest was felled and the land was cleared. The plowshares broke up the fallow ground, and soon fields of waving grain were seen. As

---

[10] M'Clintock and Strong, *Cyclopedia*, art. "Gregory."

[11] Draper, *History of the Intellectual Development of Europe*, page 264.

accommodations were provided, the noble youth of the land flocked to Columbanus as postulants in the new brotherhood. Luxeuil was destined to become the mother of numerous centers of civilization in Europe.[12] As these missionaries worked, they would reply to questions: "We be Irish, dwelling at the very ends of the earth. We be men, who receive naught but the doctrine of the apostles and evangelists."

Again there was rapid growth and crowded conditions at Luxeuil as there had been at Anagrates. Columbanus founded a third training center at Fontaines, so named by him because of the warm medicinal springs issuing from the ground. Located within a radius of about twenty miles, these three settlements formed the evangelical center of the work of the Church in the Wilderness in France. Everywhere the people rallied around them. Fresh ideas of truth triumphant spread as if on the wings of the wind. There developed other leaders who trained recruits who would repeat their exploits. Also from Ireland came a continual stream of trained leaders and teachers to augment the first evangelists.[13] Thus the word of God grew mightily. Soon, however, danger of a deadly nature raised its head to threaten the growth of the church.

The Struggle With the Bishops of Rome

In Scotland and England the Irish missionaries were grappling with stark heathenism. On the Continent they were facing a more difficult situation. The gulf between the Celtic Church and the Church of Rome was greater than that between Irish Christianity and paganism. In fact, this gulf was far greater than that between Protestantism and Romanism in the days of Luther. Paganism did not have access to the culture and truth which the papacy claimed. It was not supported, as was the papacy, by the military machine of the Roman Empire of the East, created by Belisarius, the greatest fighting genius of the age. The union of a Christian church with the state is always more dangerous to liberty than the union of paganism with the state. The opposition of the bishops of Rome to the work of Columbanus, therefore, meant a struggle between liberty and despotism.

---

[12] Smith and Wace, *A Dictionary of Christian Biography,* art. "Columbanus."
[13] Fitzpatrick, *Ireland and the Making of Britain,* pages 7-14.

The condition of the papacy in this region has thus been described by a modern historian:

> The church among the Franks and Germans was in a wretched condition. Many of the church lands were in the hands of laymen. There was little or no discipline, and no control exercised over the clergy. Each priest did what was right in his own eyes. There were, at this time, many vagabond priests and monks wandering about over the country, obtaining a precarious living by imposing upon the people.[14]

Concerning the church in the era of Justinian, the same historians of the medieval period declare: "The Christianity of that day was utterly degraded, and the Christians differed very little from the other peoples about them. Mohammedanism was in part a revolt against this degradation."[15]

The priests were jealous of the influence and growth of the Celtic missions. Back of it all, however, lay their resentment at the rebuke given by Columbanus to their questionable lives. Therefore, they summoned the Irish leader in 602 to answer before a synod of Gaulish bishops. He refused to appear, but for his defense he sent an epistle begging them to refrain from interfering. The Roman Catholic historian John Healy, writes thus of the affair:

> Remonstrance was useless; they adhered tenaciously to their country's usages. Nothing could convince them that what St. Patrick and the saints of Ireland had handed down to them could by any possibility be wrong. They only wanted to be let alone. They did not desire to impose their usages on others. Why should others impose their usages on them? They had a right to be allowed to live in peace in their wilderness, for they injured no man, and they prayed for all. Thus it was that Columbanus reasoned, or rather remonstrated with a synod of French bishops that objected to his practices. His letters to them and to Pope Gregory the Great on the subject of this paschal question are still extant, but he cannot be justified in some of the expressions which he uses. He tells the bishops in effect in one place that they would be better employed in enforcing canonical discipline amongst their own clergy, than in discussing the paschal question with him and his monks. Yet here and there he speaks not only with force and freedom, but also with true humility and genuine eloquence. He implores the prelates in the most solemn language to let him and his brethren live in peace and charity in the heart of their silent woods, beside the bones of their seventeen brothers who were dead.[16]

[14] Thatcher and Schwill, *Europe in the Middle Ages,* page 242.
[15] *Ibid.,* page 338.
[16] Healy, *Insula Sanctorum et Doctorum,* pages 374, 375.

Here is an incident by which one may contrast the spirit of the two churches. One needs only to compare the letter of Columbanus with the haughty treatment of Dinooth of Celtic Wales by Augustine. On this point Clarence W. Bispham writes:

Columban's answer is in splendid contrast to Augustine's unfortunate utterance, through which he has been prophetically responsible for certain deeds of blood. In conclusion, we must recognize that the Bangor Rule of Life, though most severe, produced a meekness of character in the fiery Keltic nature that is amazing, and is in wonderful contrast to the more moderate Benedictine Rule which produced the arrogance of St. Augustine.[17]

Columbanus and Queen Brunhilda

If there ever was another Jezebel, it was Brunhilda, wife of King Sigebert of Austrasia, brother of Guntram and persecutor of Columbanus. After murdering her husband in 575, she charmed the son of his brother, Chilperic, king of Neustria. Through infatuation the lad married her. Later she led her grandson, Theuderich II, king of Burgundy, into profligate life. Theuderich had great respect for Columbanus, and for some years protected and defended him even while the Irish missionary was remonstrating with him and his dissolute grandmother for their evil ways. For fear that Theuderich would espouse a queen who would displace her, Brunhilda plotted to keep him in a life of vice.

When the Celtic apostle rebuked her for the iniquitous life of the court, she turned on him in fury; and from that time began continued persecution of the evangelical colleges founded by Columbanus. About ten years previous to this, Augustine, the monk sent to convert England, had brought a letter of introduction to Brunhilda from the pope.[18] Of Brunhilda's affiliations with the religious enemies of the Celtic Church, historians write: "Brunhilda seems to have been, according to the ideas of her time, a religious woman. She built churches, monasteries, and hospitals, and was a friend of some of the leading churchmen of her day."[19] Since the queen-dowager and the Roman Catholic bishops were hostile to Columbanus, she urged them to attack the Celtic faith and to abolish his system of education.

---

[17] Bispham, *Columban—Saint, Monk, Missionary,* page 57.
[18] Fitzpatrick, *Ireland and the Making of Britain,* page 196.
[19] Thatcher and Schwill, *Europe in the Middle Ages,* page 93.

Columbanus in Exile

By this time the fame of Columbanus had greatly increased in all the cities and provinces of France and Germany, so much so that he was highly venerated and celebrated. Even the soldiers of the king on various occasions either hesitated to execute the royal order for his banishment, or executed it so loosely that Columbanus could escape back to Luxeuil. Because he feared vengeance on his associates, the old scholar decided to depart. He first made his way with certain companions to the Loire River, which it seems he followed, intending to set sail from the port of Nantes for Ireland.

The story of his movements reads not like a departure in exile, but like a march of conquest. He did not sail from Nantes, however, but went to Soissons, the capital of Clotaire II, king of Neustria. There his position was similar to prime minister, if not one of royal power. Clotaire consulted him on all important questions of state and followed his advice, but Columbanus had a yet greater work to do. He hoped to plant new centers in Germany, Switzerland, and Italy.

As Columbanus had been honored by Clotaire II, king of Neustria, which country later expanded and became France, so he was royally treated by Theodebert, king of that Austrasia, which country later would take in portions of the territory that is now Germany. While on his way to Theodebert, he stopped at Meaux, where he was entertained by a prominent citizen, a friend of Theodebert. His godly life influenced the daughter of his host to dedicate her life to the Columbanian missions. These beginnings of Celtic Christianity were multiplied when the learned associates of Columbanus declined to proceed further east into the wilderness, and began immediately to found new settlements starting with Metz as the center.

King Theodebert was happy over the arrival of Columbanus at his court. He besought him to remain in his kingdom permanently and to carry on his work. The scholar, however, wished to do more for Europe which was in a state of barbarism.[20] As Benedict Fitzpatrick says, "The Irish were the first missionaries in Germany, and Germany had in the main been made a Christian land by them when Boniface, who has been called the Apostle of Germany, first arrived there."[21]

---

[20] Fitzpatrick, *Ireland and the Making of Britain*, page 12.
[21] *Ibid.*, page 10.

It might be well at this point to protest against crediting the Benedictine monks with the work that was done by the Irish missionaries. Fitzpatrick says, "The general belief that the Benedictines, who were the only 'rivals' of the Irish monks in the period under review, were learned men is totally erroneous. No branch of the Benedictines making learned studies their aim existed till the establishment of the Maurists in the seventeenth century."[22]

For several years Columbanus labored in Germany and Switzerland, leaving a string of missions to carry on the work he had started. However, a pagan conspiracy against him forced him to again remove to other lands. Leaving the center of Bregenz, in what is now Austria, in charge of one of his historical associates, Gallus (generally known as St. Gall),[23] Columbanus, although past seventy years of age, made his way over the towering Alps to the court of Agilulf, king of the Lombards. In this region the primitive Christian teachings of Jovinianus of the fourth century, and of Claude of the ninth century, were still persisting.[24] Here Columbanus was joyfully received. Now, we might say, the Celts and the Waldenses were joining hands in spreading the gospel. The Lombards and the descendants of the Goths had followed the simpler and more Biblical Christianity of the Church of the East and never had walked in the ways of the papacy.[25] The mighty Lombard king was glad to have this powerful spiritual leader from Ireland in his realm. In the medieval centuries these valleys were extremely populous.

Refusing to stay at the court, however, Columbanus besought the king for a place wherein to plant a new center. Agilulf was reminded of the locality of Bobbio where there was a ruined church. The Lombards at this time, because they were not affiliated with the papacy, were branded by Rome as Arians. As the papacy, supported by the armed forces of the Eastern Roman Empire, had assumed a threatening attitude toward both Celtic Christianity and to those commun-

---

[22] Fitzpatrick, *Ireland and the Making of Britain,* page 47.

[23] The writer took particular pains to visit the celebrated library at St. Gall, named in honor of Gallus, in order to inspect the Irish manuscripts still remaining there. The life and literary labors of St. Gall are worthy of the study of any student.

[24] Beuzart, *Les Heresies,* pages 6, 470. See the author's discussion in Chapters VI and XV, entitled, "Vigilantius, Leader of the Waldenses," and "Early Waldensian Heroes," respectively.

[25] Robinson, *Ecclesiastical Researches,* pages 157, 158, 164, 165, 167.

ions it chose to call Arians, there was naturally the fellowship of misery between Columbanus and King Agilulf.

John Healy writes that Bobbio "was near the Trebbia, almost at the very spot where Hannibal first felt the rigors of that fierce winter in the snows of the Apennines."[26] One is astonished at the marvelous work in clearing the forests, in arranging the buildings, in tilling the lands and producing the crops, performed anew at Bobbio. Columbanus seems to have had unusual ability in directing farm operations, in acting as physician for his associates, and in using the hides of bears to make sandals. He was specially skilled in domesticating wild animals. While he excelled in directing such labors as building highways, digging wells, constructing churches and training schools, he did not neglect learning. One scholar writes, "The Irish foundations in Germany and north Italy became the chief book-producing center on the Continent."[27] When later scholars began their search for Irish written manuscripts, St. Gall and Bobbio were found to be valuable storehouses.

Of Bobbio it is written: "Here the nucleus of what was to be the most celebrated library in Italy was formed by the manuscripts which Columban had brought from Ireland and the treatises of which he himself was the author." "The fame of Bobbio reached the shores of Ireland, and the memory of Columban was dear to the hearts of his countrymen." "A tenth-century catalogue, published by Muratori, shows that at that period every branch of knowledge, divine and human, was represented in this library."[28] Bobbio became such an evangelical training center that later the Roman Catholic Church followed the same procedure with Columbanus as she did with Patrick and Columba; she finally claimed him as one of her own.

Death of Columbanus

Columbanus did not live much more than a year after he had finished his work at Bobbio. Though there was widespread grief at his impending death, there were no regrets in his own heart. He could look back on his more than thirty years of arduous labors and recognize that he had made an indelible impress upon the Franks, Germans,

---

[26] Healy, *Insula Sanctorum et Doctorum*, page 377.
[27] Fitzpatrick, *Ireland and the Foundations of Europe*, page 24.
[28] *The Catholic Encyclopedia*, art., "Bobbio."

Suevi, Swabians, Swiss, and Lombards. He willingly laid down the work for which God had appointed him. He finished his work in 615, being at that time some seventy-two years of age. His body was buried beneath the altar of the church, and to this day his remains are kept in the crypt of the church at Bobbio. About twenty-five extant manuscripts are purported to be his writings.

Reasons for the Opposition of the Papal Bishops

There are certain writers who seek to minimize the differences between the Celtic Church and the Roman Catholic Church. Probably this is wishful thinking on their part, because they like to believe that the divine messages of the Celtic Church have passed into the rival communion, never to reappear. This viewpoint is contrary not only to the thorough examination made by a host of authorities, but also to conclusions reached by a simple consideration of the differences of life and doctrine of the two systems. George T. Stokes, speaking of the final willingness of the Celtic leaders to go along on the question of Easter, says:

> But though the Celtic Church by the beginning of the eighth century had thus consented to the universal practice of the church both east and west alike, this consent involved no submission upon other matters to the supremacy of the see of Rome. Nay, rather, we shall see hereafter that down to the twelfth century the Celtic Church differed from Rome on very important questions, which indeed formed a pretext for the conquest of this country by the Normans.[29]

What were these important questions upon which the Celtic Church for centuries differed from the Roman? It was on such vital questions as the supreme authority of the Scriptures, the supremacy of the pope, the celibacy of the clergy, auricular confession, transubstantiation, the Trinity, and the binding claims of the moral law. Many other differences might be mentioned. Considering the unrelenting hostility of the papacy to the Celtic Church, it is clear that one or the other of the two communions must either die or surrender.

The absence of learning in the papal church and its abundant presence in the Celtic Church in the days after the fall of imperial Rome, is proved in the following words of Benedict Fitzpatrick: "In the lands, formerly included in the Western Roman Empire, where

---

[29] Stokes, *Celtic Church in Ireland,* page 165.

Latin was the medium of Christianity and education, there hardly existed a school in the full meaning of the term, save such as had already been established, directly or indirectly, by Irish hands."[30] This Roman Catholic author further says: "Pope Eugenius II for the first time in history issued in A. D. 826 bulls enjoining throughout Gaul and the rest of Christendom schools of the kind that had then been in existence in Ireland for centuries."[31]

Columbanus and Dinooth of Wales had expressed Christian courtesy to the Catholic leaders, but they had refused to be brought into subjection.[32] They sought, without any surrender of their own historic past which reached back to the apostles, to cultivate a fraternal atmosphere as far as possible.

As was noted in the controversy between Roman Catholic Queen Margaret of Scotland and the successors of the great Columba, one serious difference between the Celtic Church and the Roman Catholic Church was the observance of Saturday as the sacred day of rest. Pope Gregory I, who in the days of Columbanus opposed classical learning, was so incensed because many Christians in the city of Rome observed Saturday as the Sabbath that in 602 he issued a bull declaring that when antichrist should come, he would keep Saturday for the Sabbath. This act is a matter of common record.[33] Was the severe opposition of many popes to the wonderful work of the Irish missions in Europe due in large measure to the fact that it was the practice of the Celtic Church to observe Saturday as the day of rest and worship?

Denouncing the Celtic Church on the Continent as heretical in many aspects, particularly because of the seventh-day Sabbath observance, Rome charged it with Judaizing. Thus, Epistle 45 of Pope Gregory III to the bishops of German Bavaria exhorts them to cling to Rome's doctrines and beware of Britons coming among them with false and heretical priests.[34] Those missionaries who labored without papal authority were denounced by Boniface, the pope's legate, as seducers of the people, idolaters, and (because they were married)

---

[30] Fitzpatrick, *Ireland and the Making of Britain,* page 5.
[31] *Ibid.,* page 80.
[32] Edgar, *The Variations of Popery,* pages 181, 182.
[33] *Epistles,* of Pope Gregory I, coll. 13, ep. 1, found in *Nicene and Post-Nicene Fathers,* 2d Series, vol. 13.
[34] Neander, *General History of the Christian Religion and Church,* vol. 3, p. 49, note.

adulterers. In all of this the Roman Catholic Church took good care that only vague and indefinite accounts of all the points at issue remain to the present day.

As to the charge that certain churches were Judaizing, the minutes of the synod at Liftinae (the modern Estinnes), Belgium, 743, give more particular information. Dr. Karl J. von Hefele writes: "The third allocution of this council warns against the observance of the Sabbath, referring to the decree of the Council of Laodicea."[35] As early as the Council of Laodicea, held about the close of the fourth century, it was decreed that all who would rest from their labors on Saturday were Judaizers, and should be excommunicated.

Luxeuil, St. Gaul, and Bobbio

Among the multiplied centers which were created by Columbanus and his associates, it has been observed that Luxeuil was the leading center in France, St. Gaul the leading center in Germany and Switzerland, while Bobbio held the position for Italy. There were, however, a multitude of other centers. Of Luxeuil, Benedict Fitzpatrick writes: "Luxeuil proved to be the greatest and most influential of the monasteries and schools established by Columbanus. It became the recognized spiritual capital of all the countries under Frankish government. . . . In the seventh century Luxeuil was the most celebrated school in Christendom outside of Ireland."[36] Of St. Gaul and Bobbio, he writes: "St. Gaul itself became known as 'the intellectual center of the German world,' as Bobbio, founded by Columbanus, was long 'the light of northern Italy.' "[37]

Any attempt to evaluate the work of Columbanus must be feeble indeed. It is not within the power of man to give adequate praise to that which God hath wrought in making His truth triumphant. This pioneer built his spiritual foundations upon the ruins of the Roman Empire. His missionary centers became the nursery of civilization, the campus and pulpit of evangelism. The noble character of this man, his multiplied talents, his high executive ability, and above all his entire surrender to God make him a type of the amazing work done by the Celtic Church.

---

[35] Hefele, *Conciliengeschicte,* vol. 3, p. 512, sec. 362.
[36] Fitzpatrick, *Ireland and the Foundations of Europe,* page 68.
[37] Fitzpatrick, *Ireland and the Making of Britain,* page 21.

CHAPTER XIV

The Church in Europe
After the Time of Columbanus

The real work of the early Irish missionaries in converting the pagans of Britain and central Europe, and sowing the seeds of culture there, has been overlooked when not willfully misrepresented. Thus, while the real work of the conversion of the pagan Germans was the work of Irishmen, Winfried or, as he is better known, St. Boniface, a man of great political ability, reaped the field they had sown, and is called the apostle of Germany, though it is very doubtful if he ever preached to the heathen.[1]

THE sun of Columbanus had shone brilliantly upon the cold hearts of Europe. He and his followers brought light to the lands overspread with darkness since the advent of the Franks.[2] Three revolutions immediately succeeded one another, which tell the story of Europe after his death during the medieval period of the Church in the Wilderness. These were: first, the development of civilization on the Continent through the efforts of the Celtic Church leaders who succeeded Columbanus and through the early Waldensian heroes; secondly, the organized opposition of the papacy to this work; and lastly, the disastrous centuries which followed the crowning of Charlemagne by the pope as the founder of the Carolingian line of kings and the first emperor of the Holy Roman Empire.

The Celtic missionaries who came from Ireland in the seventh and eighth centuries found Europe in ignorance and disorganization. Their training centers raised the intellectual level of the territories in which they labored. By evangelizing and manifesting the spirit of sacrifice, they lifted the courage and hope of the populace toward truth triumphant. They impressed upon the people the love of reverence for sacred and noble themes. The dignity of labor was not neglected. Farms arose in territories which once looked slovenly. They were stocked with cattle and other necessary domestic animals. Bright flowers bloomed where formerly was a desert. Again the eyes

---

[1] *The Historians' History of the World*, vol. 21, p. 342.
[2] Smith and Wace, *A Dictionary of Christian Biography*, art. "Columbanus."

looked upon the fields of waving grain, and the smile of prosperity beamed upon the land.

What became of the manifold centers of civilization in Europe planted by Columbanus and his followers? Clarence W. Bispham says: "Columban introduced into Gaul such a durable monument of the religious spirit of Ireland, that during his life no less than one thousand abbots recognized the laws of a single superior."[3] Columbanus arrived on the Continent less than a half a century after the beginning of the 1260-year period, which began in 538. The Merovingian kings, descendants of Clovis, were the founders of the Frankish realm. The story is well known of how the enfeebled progeny of Clovis, known as the "Do-Nothing Kings," introduced into the administration the Major Domus (the mayor of the palace), a sort of prime minister. These became powerful, and in time displaced the weakling king to found the Carolingian dynasty, so named from Charles the Great (Charlemagne). The predecessors of Charlemagne gained power with the assistance of the clergy from Rome, and then harassed the successors of Columbanus.[4]

Attention is called to the companions of Columbanus, who appear to have left Ireland with him and who like himself became the founders not merely of training centers, but of schools, towns, and cities. These men were diligent in evangelism and in the study of literature.

> Early Irish manuscripts still extant in Continental libraries testify both to the culture and to the widespread missionary activity of these Irish monks. What writings have come down to us in Old Irish are exclusively religious. These Irish monks also surpass the rest of western Europe at this time in illuminating manuscripts; that is, in decorating them with colored initials, border designs, and illustrations.[5]

Mention has already been made of Gallus, also called St. Gall. Benedict Fitzpatrick gives attention to Eurcinus, who after creating a miniature Christendom on the shores of the Lake of Bienne, Switzerland, founded the town of St. Ursanne; Sigsbert who, taking leave of Columbanus at the foot of the Alps which separate Italy from Switzerland, crossed the perilous glaciers and high in the region of perpetual snow established the valuable community of Dissentis; and Dicuil,

---

[3] Bispham, *Columban—Saint, Monk, Missionary*, page 44.
[4] Newman, *A Manual of Church History*, vol. 1, pp. 411, 413.
[5] Thorndike, *History of Medieval Europe*, pages 165, 166.

brother apparently of St. Gall, who laid out the foundations of the town and mission center of Lure.[6] These and many other training centers of Celtic culture endured through the centuries of crises. They continued from their eminences to educate the rude population of Europe and to produce new generations of scholars and teachers.

The Holy Scriptures must have been greatly multiplied when one considers the vast stretch of territory in which were located the foci of the Celtic Church on the Continent. Some of these seminaries were thronged with students. Reckoning only one copy of the Bible to every three or four students, and that would be little enough, there must have been a widespread dissemination of the Old and New Testaments throughout the countries we now call France, Belgium, Germany, Switzerland, Austria, and Italy. Momentous political changes, brought about by the papacy's entering into alliance with the rulers of these different sections to advance her church, pushed the Scotch-Irish establishments into the background.

There are writers who have tried to indict the Celtic Church on the false ground that it was poorly organized and without central control. The probabilities and the facts of the case both are against this conclusion. The Irish colonizers studied and obeyed the Bible admonition, "Let all things be done decently and in order."[7] It is true that they were not driven under the lash of a church united with the state nor forced to obey under threat of the sword. Rather, they were kept together by the invincible bonds of truth, blessed by the inspiration of the Holy Spirit. They sought to avoid the hierarchical gradation, and so they employed other names than those used by Rome. On the other hand, the Church of the East, all the way from Assyria to China, which was the counterpart of the Celtic Church in the West, recognized as supreme pastor, the catholicos sitting at Seleucia in southern Mesopotamia, the headquarters of that church.[8] Surely this was organization. After the conquest of Persia by the Moslems, the organization continued; but the patriarchal seat was removed to Bagdad, and five hundred years later to Mosul (near Nineveh) on the Tigris River in northwestern Mesopotamia.[9]

---

[6] Fitzpatrick, *Ireland and the Foundations of Europe,* pages 69, 70.
[7] 1 Corinthians 14:40.
[8] Rae, *The Syrian Church in India,* pages 35-38.
[9] Purchas, *His Pilgrimes,* vol. 1, page 359.

Papal Hostility to the Celtic Church on the Continent

One power, however, viewed with fear and alarm the scope of the work being built up by the Celtic Church. Pope Zachary in a letter to his chief agent in this section of Europe recognized that the pastors of this church were more numerous than those of his own church.[10] Neander quotes Epistle 45 from Pope Gregory III to the bishops of Germany admonishing them to be steadfast in the doctrines and practices of the Roman Catholic Church, and to beware of the doctrine of the Britons and of false and heretical priests, coming among them.[11] This same historian quotes from other epistles of the same pope addressed to bishops and dukes, informing them that one of the reasons he had sent Boniface among them was to win back those who had become the victims of "heresy through diabolical craft."

This leads to the consideration of Boniface (originally Winfried), so often presented to us as the apostle and founder of Christianity in Germany. The quotation at the beginning of this chapter notes, what any fair-minded reader of history would find, that Columbanus and his successors should be given the credit for the founding of Christianity in the countries in which the credit is usually given to Boniface. Unless one pays particular notice, it will escape his attention that Boniface was an Englishman brought up in scornful hatred of the Celtic Church. Wilfrid, another Englishman, must not be confounded with Winfried. The first led the bitter opposition to Celtic Christianity in England; the second, under the name of Boniface, did the same in Germany.

As to the objectives of Boniface, Dr. A. Ebrard writes:

> His life's goal and his life's work was the subjection of the Christian churches of Austrasia as of Neustria to the papal decrees of canon law, especially the enslavement and destruction of that Christianity denomination, which refused to recognize the primacy of the Roman seat but held firmly to its own constitutions and to its own ordinances.[12]

Benedict Fitzpatrick, a Roman Catholic scholar of wide research, pictures how greatly Boniface was aroused against the Irish mission-

---

[10] Monastier, *A History of the Vaudois Church*, pages 11, 12.
[11] Neander, *General History of the Christian Religion and Church*, vol. 3, p. 49, note 1.
[12] Ebrard, *Bonifatius, der Zerstörer des Columbanischen Kirchentums auf dem Festlande*, page 213.

aries because of their teachings.[13] The papal agent brought them before councils and secured their condemnation as if they were heretics.

The pope greatly feared that Boniface himself might fall under the superb influence of the missionaries whose work he was delegated to destroy. Therefore, he bound Boniface, at the beginning of his labors, to the papacy by a solemn oath. At the supposed tomb of the apostle Peter at Rome, he took this oath:

> "I promise thee, the first of the Apostles, and thy representative Pope Gregory, and his successors, that, with God's help, I will abide in the unity of the Catholic faith, that I will in no manner agree with anything contrary to the unity of the Catholic church, but will in every way maintain my faith pure and my co-operation constantly for thee, and for the benefit of thy church, on which was bestowed, by God, the power to bind and to loose, and for thy representative aforesaid, and his successors. And whenever I find that the conduct of the presiding officers of churches contradicts the ancient decrees and ordinances of the fathers, I will have no fellowship or connection with them; but, on the contrary, if I can hinder them, I will hinder them; and if not, report them faithfully to the pope."[14]

Neander goes on to say that although the missionaries whom Boniface had sworn to oppose were his superiors in learning and in soul winning, his oath to the pope meant that German Christianity was to be incorporated into the old system of the Roman hierarchy, creating a reaction against free Christian development by suppressing the British and Irish missionaries.[15] This shocking oath not only required Boniface to hinder all who did not agree with the papacy; but also bound him to stifle his own convictions and concur in all things with Rome. It is the first oath of its kind; but it has since been demanded of every Roman Catholic bishop. Of it the historian Archibald Bower writes:

> When Boniface had taken this oath (and it is the first instance that occurs in history, of an oath of obedience, or, as we may call it, of allegiance, taken to the pope), he laid it, written with his own hand, on the pretended body of St. Peter, saying, This is the oath, which I have taken, and which I promise to keep. And indeed how strictly he kept it, what pains he took to establish, not in Germany only, but in France, the sover-

---

[13] Fitzpatrick, *Ireland and the Foundations of Europe,* pages 18, 162-164.
[14] Neander, *General History of the Christian Religion and Church,* vol. 3, page 48.
[15] *Ibid.,* vol. 3, p. 49.

eign power of his lord the pope, and bring all other bishops to the abject state of dependence and slavery, to which he himself had so meanly submitted, will appear in the sequel.[16]

Heinrich Zimmer writes that when the Anglo-Saxon Boniface (Winfried) appeared in the kingdom of France as papal legate in 723 to Romanize the churches already there, not one of the German tribes, i. e., Franks, Thuringians, Alamanni, or the Bavarians, could be considered pagan. What the Irish missionaries and their foreign pupils had implanted, quite independently of Rome, for more than a century, Boniface organized and established under Roman authority, partly by the force of arms.[17]

From this we learn that when Boniface started out on the subjection and Romanizing of the Columban missions, the Bavarian provinces practically belonged to the Columban church system.[18] When Boniface arrived there, he at once condemned Ehrenwolf, who was an outstanding Columban clergyman.[19] After Charles Martel had won his victory over the Moslems in the well-known Battle of Tours (A. D. 732), the duke of Thuringia who had previously been pressed to drive out from his territory the Scotch-Irish clergy, did not dare disregard this command from the victorious Charles. So in 733-734 the Celtic clergy were exiled.[20] However, the lack of pastors was so great that Boniface, terrified as he recognized the danger that whole stretches of land would swing back into heathenism, obtained a permit to reinstate a certain number of the Columban clergy.[21] In 743 Boniface threw two Scotch-Irish clergymen into prison on the grounds that they forbade any church to consecrate apostles or saints for veneration; that they declared pilgrimages to Rome useless; and that they rejected canonical law as well as the writings of Jerome, Augustine, and Gregory.[22] However, there was such an uproar among the people that even the mayor of the palace, Pepin, thought it wise to set both of the men free.

---

[16] Bower, *The History of the Popes*, vol. 2, pp. 23, 24.
[17] Zimmer, *The Irish Element in Medieval Culture*, page 35.
[18] Ebrard, *Bonifatius, der Zerstörer des Columbanischen Kirchentums auf dem Festlande*, page 127
[19] *Ibid.*, pages 127, 128.
[20] *Ibid.*, page 130.
[21] *Ibid.*, pages 130-133.
[22] *Ibid.*, pages 197, 199.

Charles Martel

Like Boniface, Charles Martel has been overrated. There are writers who recognize that his victory over the Mohammedans has been overplayed. Walter F. Adeney tells us that all that Charles Martel did was to check a Moorish raid in the west that had nearly spent its force—a raid that could never have resulted in the permanent subjection of Europe.[23] Many do not know how weak this Moslem invasion was which Martel blocked, because of the great extent to which history has been written to glorify papal heroes.

Alban Butler reveals the further influence of the oath of Boniface in its relation to Charles Martel. "Pope Gregory gave him [Boniface] a book of select canons of the church, to serve him for a rule in his conduct, and by letters, recommended him to Charles Martel."[24]

Charles Martel continued after his overrated victory to build up the papacy. Italy was still under the Eastern Roman emperor at Constantinople. The day of the Holy Roman Empire in the West was about to dawn. John Dowling presents an accurate picture of conditions at that time as he writes:

> In the year 740, in consequence of the pope refusing to deliver up two rebellious dukes, the subjects of Luitprand, king of the Lombards, that warlike monarch invaded and laid waste the territories of Rome. In their distress, their fear of the resentment of the emperor forbidding them to apply to him for the assistance they urgently needed, they resolved to apply to the celebrated Charles Martel. . . .
>
> It is certain that he turned a deaf ear to these pathetic appeals of the pope; till the latter, despairing of gaining his help by appealing to his piety or superstition, attacked him in a more vulnerable part, by appealing to his ambition. This Gregory did by proposing to Charles, that he and the Romans would renounce all allegiance to the emperor, as an avowed heretic, and acknowledging him for their protector, confer upon him the consular dignity of Rome, upon condition that he should protect the pope, the church, and the Roman people against the Lombards; and, if necessity should arise, against the vengeance of their ancient master, the emperor. These proposals were more suited to the warlike and ambitious disposition of Martel, and he immediately dispatched his ambassadors to Rome to take the pope under his protection, intending, doubtless, at an early period, to consummate the agreement.[25]

---

[23] Adeney, *The Greek and Eastern Churches,* pages 188, 189.
[24] Butler, *Lives of the Saints,* vol. 6, p. 77.
[25] Dowling, *The History of Romanism,* pages 166, 167.

In the meantime Charles Martel died and was succeeded by his son Pepin. The new Major Domus conceived the design of dethroning his feeble monarch, the descendant of Clovis. He resolved to obtain the spiritual recognition of the people for his project by arguing that since he possessed the power without the title, he had a right to obtain the title. Pope Zachary, who at that time had strained relations with the imperial ruler at Constantinople on the one hand, and was exposed to the warlike Lombards in northern Italy on the other, was obliged, he felt, to secure the favor and protection of the powerful Pepin and his Franks. An agreement was consummated. The feeble king was deposed. Pepin was crowned and knighted shortly after this by Boniface, who acted as the pope's legate. This conspiracy is an example of how the papacy built itself up by alliances with the kings of the earth.

The papacy had aided Pepin to become a king. It was now the turn of Pepin to aid the papacy. The king of the Lombards had laid siege to the city of Ravenna and threatened to march on Rome unless his rightful authority was recognized. The pope immediately appealed for deliverance to the emperor at Constantinople, who was nominally the sovereign of Rome. When, however, he was unable to secure that succor, the pope considered that the power of the eastern emperor in Italy was at an end; and he appeared in person before King Pepin of France to request deliverance. After a short delay Pepin and the pope at the head of a victorious army recrossed the Alps and defeated the Lombards. The king then fulfilled a promise made to the pontiff by delivering up to him all the cities, castles, and territories formerly belonging to the emperor in the West to be held and possessed forever by the pope and his successors.[26]

Charlemagne and the Holy Roman Empire

The colorful scene of Christmas Day at Rome (A. D. 800) when the pope placed an imperial crown on the head of Charlemagne, Pepin's son, and named him the head of the whole Roman Empire, signified a vast European revolution. It meant the removal of the emperor at Constantinople from further power in European affairs. It meant the passing of many princes, dukes, and duchies, and the subduing of Aquitaine, Alamannia, Saxony, and Bavaria, because

---

[26] Dowling, *The History of Romanism*, pages 168, 169.

Charlemagne was now too strong with the sword to permit rivals in power. It meant the union of church and state; the union of the papacy with the empire for more than a thousand years. It meant that Charlemagne as a crushing warrior would wield his mighty battle-ax to spread throughout Europe the rule of the papal church. Henry Hart Milman writes:

> The Saxon wars of Charlemagne, which added almost the whole of Germany to his dominions, were avowedly religious wars. If Boniface was the Christian, Charlemagne was the Mohammedan, apostle of the gospel. The declared object of his invasions, according to his biographer, was the extinction of heathenism; subjection to the Christian faith or extermination.[27]
>
> Throughout the war Charlemagne endeavored to subdue the tribes as he went on by the terror of his arms; and terrible indeed were those arms! On one occasion at Verdun-on-the-Aller, he massacred four thousand brave warriors who had surrendered, in cold blood.[28]

Such actions of Charlemagne were eloquently praised by leading papists as the pious acts of an orthodox member of the church. Among the barbarians who were supposed to be newly converted, the church instilled its superstitions and its hatred of heretics and unbelievers. The polygamy of Charlemagne was more like an Oriental sultan. The notorious licentiousness of his court was unchecked, and indeed unreproved by the religion of which he was at least the temporal head. The spiritual sovereign of this same religion had placed on his brow the crown of the Holy Roman Empire. The Mohammedans, in their fury against idols and images, claimed that God had raised them up to destroy idolatry; but the papacy allowed its leaders to erect images in the churches.

It is a well-known fact that it was because of the fierceness with which Charlemagne drove the inhabitants of Europe into the papal faith that the Danes left their native home in great masses and sailed away, swearing that they would destroy Christians and Christian churches wherever they could find them. They soon afterward conquered England and Ireland, having invaded these countries with great forces. They wreaked their vengeance on Christianity in both these kingdoms. Two centuries passed by before Ireland, under the

---

[27] Milman, *History of Latin Christianity,* vol. 2, pp. 215, 216.
[28] *Ibid.,* vol. 2, p. 220.

famous Brian Boru,[29] overthrew the Danish kingdom and re-established an Irish rule. And so far as England is concerned, it was not until the Norman conquest that the present line of kings displaced the Danes and gained the throne of Great Britain. From the date of the founding of the Holy Roman Empire we can hardly say that the leadership of the Church in the Wilderness in Europe was limited to the spiritual successors of Columbanus. Events occurred which brought forth the strength of all evangelical bodies. Visible unity of evangelical faith throughout the different persecuting kingdoms of the empire was impossible. But leaders arose in different sections of the Continent, and the groups of the Church in the Wilderness were united in essential doctrines though visibly separated.

The decree of Pope Gregory IX (A. D. 1236), mentioning these different bodies by the names they had acquired, recognized the unity of their evangelical teachings. It reads thus: "We excommunicate and anathematize all the heretics, the Puritans, Paterines, the poor of Lyons, Pasagines, Josephines, Arnoldists, Speronists, and all others of whatever name: their faces might differ, but their tails are entangled in one knot."[30] By the expression, "their tails are entangled in one knot," the papacy recognized how deep was the unity among the evangelical bodies. Earlier (A. D. 1183) Pope Lucius had published a bull against heresies and heretics to be found in different states of Europe and who bore different names, declaring, "all Cathari, Paterini, and those who called themselves the humble or poor men of Lyons, and Passagini . . . to lie under a perpetual anathema."[31]

The Dark Ages, as many authorities state, settled deep upon the masses of the Continent. John Dowling says:

> The period upon which we are now to enter, comprising the ninth and tenth centuries, with the greater part of the eleventh, is the darkest in the annals of Christianity. It was a long night of almost universal darkness, ignorance, and superstition, with scarcely a ray of light to illuminate the gloom. This period has been appropriately designated by various historians as the "dark ages," the "iron age," the "leaden age," and the "midnight of the world." . . . During these centuries, it was rare for a layman of whatever rank to know how to sign his name.[32]

---

[29] See the author's discussion in Chapter VII, entitled, "Patrick, Organizer of the Church in the Wilderness in Ireland."

[30] Mansi, *Sacrorum Conciliorum Nova et Amplissima Collectio,* vol. 23, p. 73.

[31] Gilly, *Waldensian Researches,* pages 95, 96.

[32] Dowling, *The History of Romanism,* page 181.

Also, J. L. Mosheim writes: "It is universally admitted, that the ignorance of this century was extreme, and that learning was entirely neglected. . . . The Latin nations never saw an age more dark and cheerless."[33]

Ignorance and poverty left the people an easy prey to superstition. The number and order of monks and nuns, the religious soldiers of the Vatican, greatly increased. The papacy on several occasions had sworn emperors, princes, and local rulers to hunt out those who refused to follow the imperial church and to condemn them as heretics. The masses had been so cowed by the political sword and by superstitious terrors that as time went on, if even the emperor refused to bend to the demands of the papacy, the church declared his subjects absolved from their oath of allegiance to him. So the pope's power vastly increased. Peoples of simple evangelical faith who truly loved the Scriptures and were willing to die for them were to undergo imprisonment, confiscation of property, and slaughter.

The Albigenses and the Paulicians

About the time of the establishment of the Holy Roman Empire, if not considerably before, a large body of evangelical Christians entered Europe from Asia Minor. These were the Paulicians, for centuries misrepresented and falsely accused but lately exonerated. It was because of their earnest desire to live according to the Epistles of Paul that they were called Paulicians. They soon spread over Europe, and although no chronicle records their dispersion, the fact is attested to by the appearance of their teachings in many countries of the West. They joined themselves to migrating groups, and as J. A. Wylie says, "From this time a new life is seen to animate the efforts of the Waldenses of Piedmont, the Albigenses of southern France, and of others who, in other parts of Europe, revolted by the growing superstitions, had begun to retrace their steps towards the primeval fountains of truth."[34]

The noble work which had been done formerly by Vigilantius in northern Italy was to be augmented by the coming of the Paulicians, and the New Testament doctrines which had been impressed upon Western Europe by Columbanus, and the liberty-loving Christianity

---

[33] Mosheim, *Institutes of Ecclesiastical History,* b. 3, cent. 10, pt. 2, ch. 1, pars. 1, 4.
[34] Wylie, *The History of Protestantism,* vol. 1, p. 34.

that characterized the Visigothic Christians, were to be re-emphasized.
Historians maintain that although the Paulicians have been the most
wantonly libeled of all gospel sects, it has been clearly proved that
they represent the survival of a more primitive type of Christianity.
Nevertheless, men who should have known better have endeavored to
brand them as Manichaeans. W. F. Adeney writes of them:

> Mariolatry and the intercession of saints are rejected; image worship,
> the use of crosses, relics, incense, candles, and resorting to sacred springs
> are all repudiated as idolatrous practices. The idea of purgatory is rejected.
> The holy year begins with the feast of John the Baptist. January sixth is
> observed as the festival of the baptism and spiritual rebirth of Jesus.
> Zatik, or Easter, is kept on the fourteenth Nisan. We meet with no special
> Sunday observances, and possibly the Saturday Sabbath was maintained.
> There is no feast of Christmas or of the Annunciation. When we come to
> consider the question of doctrine, we note that the word "Trinity" never
> appears on the book.[35]

Edward Gibbon, who writes a whole chapter on the Paulicians,
has vindicated them of the charge of Manichaeism.[36] Likewise the
scholar, George Faber, in his volume dedicated to the vindication of
the Albigenses and Waldenses, in writing of Constantine, the founder
of the Paulicians, says: "It is true, indeed, that Constantine, deeply
imbued with the discourses of Christ and with the writings of Paul,
openly rejected the books of the ancient Manichaeans." Faber further
speaks of the purity of their Scriptures, "Now this single circumstance alone, independently of all other evidence, is amply sufficient
to demonstrate the impossibility of their pretended Manichaeism."[37]

Thus, the greatly increased supremacy of the papacy faced the
growing triumph of pure Bible truth in the hearts of evangelical
bodies. A struggle began which would never cease until the Reformation had broken the power of darkness. Though much research has
been given to the relation of the Paulicians and Albigenses to each
other, only this much is clear—their beliefs and history are similar, if
not identical. The Albigenses were numerous in southern France
where they gained myriads of converts. Here they maintained an
independence of the papacy, and rejected transubstantiation.[38]

---

[35]Adeney, *The Greek and Eastern Churches,* page 218.
[36]Gibbon, *Decline and Fall of the Roman Empire,* ch. 54, pars. 2, 7.
[37]Faber, *The Ancient Vallenses and Albigenses,* pages 37, 56.
[38]*Ibid.,* page 65.

The papacy became alarmed over the growth in dissent, and acted. First, there were persecutions on a minor scale. In 1198 Rome dispatched legates to the south of France, and a large number of Albigenses were committed to the flames. When these measures failed to secure the desired results, Raymond, the reigning count of Toulouse, was ordered to engage in a war of extermination against his unoffending subjects. Raymond hesitated. Later events increased the bitterness, and the pope proclaimed a crusade against southern France. Ample forgiveness of sins committed through a lifetime was promised to all who would join. Without entering into detail concerning the numerous adventurers, soldiers, and aspiring fighters who composed the invading army, we may say that hideous massacres and widespread slaughter upon these numerous, simple-hearted believers in the New Testament ensued.

The assembled host of the invaders were encamped around the fortified city of Beziers in July, 1209. When the citizens of the beleaguered place, the majority of whom were good Catholics, refused to surrender, the crusaders demanded of the pope's legate how they should distinguish the Catholics from the heretics. He replied, "Kill them all; God will know His own."[39] A terrible massacre followed. For several years the revolting slaughter went on from city to city until a cry of horror arose not only in Roman Catholic nations, but throughout Europe. The moral prestige of the papacy suffered.

The Franciscans and Dominicans

There is another bit of history connected with this exterminating crusade that will come as a surprise to many. In the track of these hysterical religionists who had slaughtering weapons in their hands, followed the Franciscan and Dominican monks inflaming the fanatics with their mystic fury.[40] It was largely in order to exterminate the widespread dissent throughout the Continent, and particularly in southern France, against the unacceptable doctrines of Rome that these two orders of monks came into existence. The Franciscans were formally approved in 1223 by the pope; the Dominicans shortly before. About the year 1200, Pope Innocent III established the Inquisition. Bishops and their vicars being, in the opinion of the pope, neither fit

---

[39] Green, *A Handbook of Church History*, page 508.
[40] Mosheim, *Institutes of Ecclesiastical History*, b. 3, cent. 13, p. 2, ch. 2, par. 26.

nor sufficiently diligent for the extirpation of heretics, two new orders, those of St. Dominic and St. Francis were duly instituted.[41]

It is astonishing to read the vast amount of literature put forth lately by modern authors glorifying St. Francis, the founder of the Franciscans, for what they call his holy, gentle life and powerful preaching. He has been surrounded with a halo of so-called miracles and experiences as well as being made participant in events which never happened. The real facts of the case indicate that his only claim to a place on the pages of history is that he brought the unoffending believers in the New Testament to prison, to the stake, and to exile for no other crime than refusing to believe the doctrines of the papacy. However, there is more to be said about the active work of the Dominicans in connection with the Inquisition than the Franciscans. Also there are good authorities who, writing without any reference whatever to the heresy-hunting policy of the Franciscans and Dominicans, claim that their mystic teachings and beliefs were similar to Manichaeism and other pantheistic Oriental teachings.[42]

The Power of the Reformation

Swiftly the years rolled by. The fundamental teachings of the Church in the Wilderness, which according to Revelation 12 was the successor of the apostolic church, gained an increasing number of adherents throughout Great Britain and on the Continent. About the time efforts were made to turn the homeland of the Albigenses into an Aceldama, the papacy, through the successors of William the Conqueror, sent armies marching into Ireland to complete the subjection of early Celtic Christianity.

Nevertheless new and vigorous spiritual leaders were arising who, though of different names and organizations, took up the banner of truth as it was struck from the hands of the Celts and the Albigenses. Wycliffe, "the Morning Star of the Reformation," during the fourteenth century filled all England with his opposition to Rome and with his championship of the Bible. In Bohemia he was followed by Huss and Jerome, both of whom were burned at the stake. Before the epochal Reformation led by Luther had broken forth in Germany,

---

[41] Jones, *The History of the Christian Church,* vol. 2, p. 93.
[42] Neander, *General History of the Christian Religion and Church,* vol. 4, pp. 275, 276.

the papacy had slaughtered the Waldenses of northern Italy as it had previously persecuted the Albigenses. John Calvin, the successful leader against the papacy in France and Scotland, is recognized as a direct descendant of the Waldenses.[43] The Lollards, as the followers of Wycliffe are often called, were indoctrinated by the Albigenses and the Waldenses.[44]

In previous chapters we have noted the rage of Rome against those who continued to believe that Saturday, the seventh day of the week, was the Sabbath of the fourth commandment. It is recalled that the historian A. C. Flick and other authorities claim that the Celtic Church observed Saturday as their sacred day of rest, and that reputable scholarship has asserted that the Welsh sanctified it as such until the twelfth century. The same day was observed by the Petrobrusians and Henricians, and Adeney, with others, attributes to the Paulicians the observance of Saturday. There are reliable historians who say that the Waldenses and the Albigenses fundamentally were Sabbath-keepers.

The Reformation came, and within a third of a century from its inception powerful nations of Europe had been wrenched away from the papacy. Would one now be tempted to say that this was the time that the church came up out of the wilderness? Hardly. The Reformation forms part of the history covered by the Church in the Wilderness. It falls inside the 1260-year period. The twelfth chapter of Revelation, however, does not present the Reformation church as the successor of the Church in the Wilderness. The Remnant Church, or the last church, is to proclaim the soon-coming of Jesus Christ and the keeping of "the commandments of God, and the faith of Jesus." Revelation 14:12. The Remnant Church is the true and final successor to the Church in the Wilderness.

The End of the Holy Roman Empire

What the Reformation did in restoring the Bible to western lands, the armies of the French Revolution were to do in releasing the nations of the Continent from the grip of the old regime. The human race was to have one more chance in perfect freedom and with unprecedented advantages in learning and science to demonstrate to the

---

[43] Leger, *Historie Generale des Eglises Vaudoises*, bk. 1, p. 167.
[44] McCabe, *Cross and Crown*, page 32.

universe whether or not it would believe and live according to the revealed will of God in the light of fulfilling prophecy. The United States of America was the first nation to write complete religious liberty into its Constitution. The British Empire and some other governments manifest a tolerance which in practice amounts to religious liberty, but they still maintain a state church and do not, as a legal right, grant full liberty of conscience to their citizens.

The effect of the American Revolution was electrifying on France. The common people arose and broke the tyrannical rule of the nobles and the clergy; and, copying the American Bill of Rights, not only proclaimed religious liberty to France, but also to all peoples wherever the armies of the French Revolution went. The crowning act occurred in May, 1798, when the armies of France entered Rome, took the pope prisoner, dispersed the college of cardinals, and proclaimed religious liberty upon Capitoline Hill, the most famous of Rome's seven mountains. At this point in history one is most nearly justified in saying that the 1260-year prophecy terminated.

The crushing of the old regime continued. That military genius, Napoleon, placed himself at the head of France's revolutionary armies, and disposed of what was left of the order established by the illegitimate union between Charlemagne and the pope throughout the Continent. The Holy Roman Empire is usually said by historians to have breathed its last by the fatal strokes of Napoleon in 1804. It is true Napoleon made a concordat for France with the pope in 1801, but in it the victorious general refused to accord the papacy its old standing under the former kings; he would recognize no more than that the Catholic faith was the religion of the majority of Frenchmen. Though Napoleon accorded other recognitions to the papacy, they were nothing more than the usual gains sought through diplomacy.

To whom shall be ascribed praise for having liberated the oppressed Western world from this awful tyranny?—not to the sword of any great conqueror, but to the Church in the Wilderness, which suffered and bled and died throughout centuries for freedom, truth, and the Holy Scriptures. The example of these martyrs put into the hearts of the people the spirit to resist tyranny until liberty became the law of the land.

Thus the spirit and power of Columbanus and his successors, mingled with the spirit of freedom, dwelt in the descendants of the

Celts, the Goths, and the Lombards, and arose to a crescendo in the hearts of kings who determined to do the will of God. The story of Europe is not complete, however, without knowing how richly the Waldenses contributed to dispelling the Stygian shades of the Dark Ages and to restoring Biblical Christianity; and there is much to be told of the Church in the Wilderness in the Near East, in India, in central Asia and China.

CHAPTER XV

Early Waldensian Heroes

Whenever, therefore, in the following sketches, the terms Berengarians, Petrobrusians, Henricians, Arnoldists, Waldenses, Albigenses, Leonists, or the poor men of Lyons, Lollards, Cathari, etc., occur, it must be understood that they intend a people, who agreed in certain leading principles, however they might differ in some smaller matters, and that all of them were by the Catholicks comprehended under the general name of Waldenses.[1]

TO NORTHWESTERN Italy, southeastern France, and northern Spain one must look for that spiritual fortress which for centuries was invincible to the fierce onslaughts of the medieval hierarchy. There the giant Alps had been piled high as a mighty wall between France and Italy. In the peaceful valleys and dales of the Alps lived the noble and heroic Waldenses. The charm of those verdant fields was rendered more charming by the presence of a people who were ever loyal to the gospel.

The Waldenses, while covering many lands with their Bible teachings, did not spread into all the countries in which are found other branches of the Church in the Wilderness. They may not have counted their members by the millions as did other churches during the Dark Ages. Their first mention is due to the fact that they remained the longest of any Christian group in the struggle to preserve the Bible and primitive Christianity. When the Reformation came, they were still protesting against ecclesiastical tyranny. Among them truth triumphed.

It is not difficult to discern in the lines of influence emanating from the Waldenses a force which aided the spiritual upheavals led by Martin Luther and John Calvin. The ensign of the gospel was passed from their battle-scarred hands to those of the Reformers, and was carried with victorious acclaim to the Teutonic nations of northern Europe and on to the young republic in North America.

To the Waldenses was given the task of passing the light on to the Protestants of modern times and of penetrating the darkness of the

---

[1] Benedict, *A General History of the Baptist Denomination,* vol. 1, pp. 112, 113.

world with the glory of true Bible doctrine. Through the Dark Ages the Waldensian heroes kept the faith which they had received from their fathers, even from the days of the apostles. Of them Sir James Mackintosh writes:

> With the dawn of history, we discover some simple Christians in the valleys of the Alps, where they still exist under the ancient name of Vaudois, who by the light of the New Testament saw the extraordinary contrast between the purity of primitive times and the vices of the gorgeous and imperial hierarchy which surrounded them.[2]

Shut up in mountain valleys, they held fast to the doctrines and practices of the primitive church while the inhabitants of the plains of Italy were daily casting aside the truth.[3] When one gazes upon their magnificent mountain bulwarks, he cannot but admit that here God had provided for His people safe and secure retreats as foretold by John in the Apocalypse.

After Emperor Constantine had declared (A. D. 325) which of the Christian churches he recognized, and had decreed that the Roman world must conform to his decision, there came a struggle between the Christians who refused to compromise the teachings of the New Testament and those who were ready to accept traditions of men. Mosheim declares:

> The ancient Britons and Scots could not be moved, for a long time, either by the threats or the promises of the papal legates, to subject themselves to the Roman decrees and laws; as is abundantly testified by Beda. The Gauls and the Spaniards, as no one can deny, attributed only so much authority to the pontiff, as they supposed would be for their own advantage. Nor in Italy itself, could he make the bishop of Ravenna and others bow obsequiously to his will. And of private individuals, there were many who expressed openly their detestation of his vices and his greediness of power. Nor are those destitute of arguments who assert, that the Waldenses, even in this age [seventh century], had fixed their residence in the valleys of Piedmont, and inveighed freely against Roman domination.[4]

Robert Oliveton, a native of the Waldensian valleys, who translated the Vaudois Bible into French in 1535 wrote thus of the Scriptures in the Preface:

---

[2] Mackintosh, *History of England,* vol. 1, p. 321, found in Lardner's *Cabinet Encyclopedia.*
[3] Bompiani, *A Short History of the Italian Waldenses,* page 9.
[4] Mosheim, *Institutes of Ecclesiastical History,* b. 2, cent. 7, pt. 2, ch. 2, par. 2.

It is Thee alone [the French Reformation Church] to whom I present this precious Treasure . . . in the name of a certain poor People thy Friends and Brethren in Jesus Christ, who ever since they were blessed and enriched therewith by the Apostles and Ambassadours of Christ, have still enjoyed and possessed the same.[5]

Waldenses Date Back to the Apostles

The connection between the Waldenses, the Albigenses, and other believers in the New Testament and the primitive Christians of Western Europe is explained by Voltaire thus:

> Auricular confession was not received so late as the eighth and ninth centuries in the countries beyond the Loire, in Languedoc and the Alps—Alcuin complains of this in his letters. The inhabitants of those countries appear to have always had an inclination to abide by the customs of the primitive church, and to reject the tenets and customs which the church in its more flourishing state judged convenient to adopt.
>
> Those who were called Manichaeans, and those who were afterward named Albigenses, Vaudois, Lollards, and who appeared so often under different names, were remnants of the first Gaulish Christians, who were attached to several ancient customs, which the Church of Rome thought proper to alter afterward.[6]

For nearly two hundred years following the death of the apostles, the process of separation went on between these two classes of church members until the open rupture came. In the year 325 the first world council of the church was held at Nicaea, and at that time Sylvester was given great recognition as bishop of Rome. It is from the time of this Roman bishop that the Waldenses date their exclusion of the papal party from their communion. As the church historian Neander says:

> But it was not without some foundation of truth that the Waldenses of this period asserted the high antiquity of their sect, and maintained that from the time of the secularization of the church—that is, as they believed, from the time of Constantine's gift to the Roman bishop Silvester [A. D. 314-336]—such an opposition as finally broke forth in them, had been existing all along.[7]

---

[5] Morland, *The Church of the Piedmont,* pages 16, 17.
[6] Voltaire, *Additions to Ancient and Modern History,* vol. 29, pp. 227, 242.
[7] Neander, *General History of the Christian Religion and Church,* 5th Period, sec. 4, p. 605.

These Christians of the Alps and Pyrenees have been called Waldenses from the Italian word for "valleys," and where they spread over into France, they have been called Vaudois, a French word meaning "inhabitants of the valleys" in a certain province. Many writers constantly call them Vaudois. The enemies of this branch of the Church in the Wilderness have endeavored to confuse their history by tracing to a wrong source the origin of the name, Waldenses. They seek to connect its beginnings with Peter Waldo, an opulent merchant of Lyons, France, who came into notice about 1175. The story of this remarkable man commands a worthy niche in the temple of events. However, there is nothing in the original or the earliest documents of the Waldenses—their histories, poems, and confessions of faith—which can be traced to him or which make any mention of him.

Waldo, being converted in middle life to truths similar to those held by the Vaudois, distributed his fortune to the poor and labored extensively to spread evangelical teachings. He and his followers soon met with cruel opposition. Finally, in desperation they fled for refuge to those Waldenses who had crossed the Alps and had formed a considerable body in eastern France.

The great antiquity of the Waldensian vernacular preserved through the centuries witnesses to their line of descent independent of Rome, and to the purity of their original Latin. Alexis Muston says:

> The patois of the Vaudois valleys has a radical structure far more regular than the Piedmontese idiom. The origin of this patois was anterior to the growth of Italian and French—antecedent even to the Romance language, whose earliest documents exhibit still more analogy with the present language of the Vaudois mountaineers, than with that of the troubadours of the thirteenth and fourteenth centuries. The existence of this patois is of itself a proof of the high antiquity of these mountaineers, and of their constant preservation from foreign intermixture and changes. Their popular idiom is a precious monument.[8]

Turning back the pages of history six hundred years before Peter Waldo, there is even a more famous name connected with the Waldenses. This leader was Vigilantius (or, Vigilantius Leo). He could be looked upon as a Spaniard, since the people of his regions were one in practically all points with those of northern Spain. Vigilantius took his stand against the new relapses into paganism. From these

---

[8] Muston, *The Israel of the Alps,* vol. 2, p. 406.

apostatizing tendencies the Christians of northern Italy, northern Spain, and southern France held aloof. The story of Vigilantius and how he came to identify himself with this region is told in another chapter.[9] From connections with him, this people were for centuries called Leonists, as well as Waldenses and Vaudois.

Reinerius Saccho, an officer of the Inquisition (c. A. D. 1250), wrote a treatise against the Waldenses which explains their early origin. He had formerly been a pastor among them, but had apostatized and afterward had become a papal persecutor. He must have known as much about them as any enemy could. After declaring on his own personal testimony that all the ancient heretical sects, of which there were more than seventy, had been destroyed except four—the Arians, Manichaeans, Runearians, and Leonists—he wrote, "Among all these sects, which still are or have been, there is not any more pernicious to the church than that of the Leonists."

He gave three reasons why they were dangerous to the papacy:

> "First, because it is of longer duration; for some say that it hath endured from the time of Pope Sylvester; others from the time of the apostles; second, because it is more geheral. For there is scarcely any country wherein this sect is not. Third, because when all other sects beget horror in the hearers by the outrageousness of their blaphemies against God, this of the Leonists hath a great appearance of piety: because they live justly before men and believe all things rightly concerning God and all the articles which are contained in the creed; only they blaspheme the Church of Rome and the clergy."[10]

Thus Saccho showed that the Leonists, or Waldenses, were older than the Arians; yes, even older than the Manichaeans.

Their Territory Was Not Roman

A distinction has long been recognized between the northern Italian peninsula and the central part, so that for more than one thousand years the bishoprics in northern Italy were called Italic, while those in central Italy were named Roman. Or, as Frederick Nolan says, in speaking of an early Latin Bible in this territory: "The

---

[9] See the author's discussion in Chapter VI, entitled, "Vigilantius, Leader of the Waldenses."
[10] Saccho, *Contra Waldenses*, found in *Maxima Bibliotheca Veterum Patrum*, vol. 25, p. 264.

author perceived, without any labor of inquiry, that it [Italic Bible] derived its name from that diocese which has been termed the Italick, as contradistinguished from the Roman."[11]

The city of Milan in the northern part of the Italian peninsula has always been one of the most famous cities of history. At times it has been a rival to Rome. Several Roman emperors, abandoning the city on the banks of the Tiber, fixed their capital here. It was a famous meeting place for the East and the West. One author states that the religious influence of Milan was regarded with respect, and that its authority was especially felt in Gaul and in Spain.[12] It was the chief center of the Celts who lived on the Italian side of the Alps.[13] Before it could come under the dominant influence of the Roman bishop, the Gothic armies had completed their conquest of Italy as well as France. These newcomers, who had been converted to Christ more than one hundred years previously, held fast to the usages and customs of the primitive church and did no harm to Milan.[14]

Since the Goths granted religious freedom to their subjects, Milan profited by it. When from all parts of Europe newly chosen bishops came to Rome to be consecrated, none appeared from the Italic dioceses of Milan and Turin. They did not join the procession. In fact, for many years after 553 there was a widespread schism in northern Italy and adjacent lands between Rome and the bishops of nine provinces under the leadership of the bishop of Milan who renounced fellowship with Rome to become autonomous. They had been alienated by the famous decree of the "Three Chapters," passed in 553 by the Council of Constantinople condemning three great leaders of the Church of the East.[15] The people of this region knew the straight truth. They did not believe in the infallibility of the pope and did not consider that being out of communion with him was to be out of fellowship with the church.[16] They held that their own ordination was as efficacious as the pretended apostolic succession of the bishop of Rome.

---

[11] Nolan, *The Integrity of the Greek Vulgate,* Preface, page xvii.
[12] Gordon, *"World Healers,"* pages 237, 238.
[13] *The Catholic Encyclopedia,* art. "Milan."
[14] See the author's discussion in Chapter x, entitled, "How the Church Was Driven Into the Wilderness."
[15] Ayer, *A Source Book for Ancient Church History,* pages 596, 597.
[16] Allix, *The Ancient Churches of Piedmont,* page 33.

While the papacy was bringing much of Europe under her control, the two dioceses of Milan and Turin continued independent. It was unbearable to the papacy that, in the very land in which was her throne, there should be a Mordecai in the gate. Two powerful forces nullified all her efforts to annex the Milan territory. First, the presence of the Lombard kings, unconquered until about 800, assured religious tolerance there. Moreover, the Lombards, like the Goths before them, rejected so many innovations brought in by Rome that they never admitted the papal bishops of Italy to a seat in their legislative councils.[17] Therefore, they were promptly called Arians, the name given by Rome to her opponents.

Early Waldensian Heroes

Because of the desperate attempt of papal writers to date the rise of the Waldenses from Peter Waldo, all Waldensian heroes before the time of the crusades which largely destroyed the Albigenses, will be called "early." This term refers to those evangelical leaders that kept continental Europe true to primitive Christianity between the days of the apostles and the Albigensian crusades. Such believers did not separate from the papacy, for they had never belonged to it. In fact, many times they called the Roman Catholic Church "the newcomer."

To relate the godly exploits of early Alpine heroes from the days of Vigilantius to Waldo is to answer the thesis of the papists that the Waldenses did not begin until about 1160. The most noted papal antagonist of the Waldenses who has endeavored to brand them as originating at that date is Bishop Jacques Bénigne Bossuet. Bossuet, the brilliant French papist, is reckoned by some to be one of the seven greatest orators of history. With almost undetectable shrewdness he analyzed every item of history which he thought might give the Waldenses an early origin, and then drew his false conclusions. Of him Mosheim says: "This writer certainly did not go to the sources, and being influenced by party zeal, he was willing to make mistakes."[18] A casual reader, or one partially informed, could easily be misled by Bossuet. Full acquaintance with the records, however, exposes this bishop to the charge of a scandalous misuse of information.

---

[17] Gibbon, *Decline and Fall of the Roman Empire*, ch. 45, par. 18.
[18] Mosheim, *Institutes of Ecclesiastical History*, b. 3, cent. 9, pt. 2, ch. 5, par. 4, note 5.

To those who lay too much stress upon Peter Waldo as being the founder of the Waldenses, it can be said that there were many by the name of Waldo. Particular attention has been called by a papal author to a Peter Waldo, an opponent of the papacy, who arose in the seventh century.[19]

Certain papal writers have grouped all religious bodies in Europe hostile to Rome since the year 1000 or earlier, under the title of Waldenses.[20] Their reason for doing this can be seen when one contemplates the record of the growth of the churches refusing to go along with Rome's innovations. Consider to what extent the Waldenses were leaders in this policy. The teachings and organizing ability of Vigilantius gave leadership to the evangelical descendants of the apostles in northern Italy, southern France, and northern Spain.[21] In those days evangelical churches were unable to effect visible unity in these sections of Europe. As those who preserved primitive Christianity multiplied on the Continent and as they contacted the Celts of the British Isles and the Church of the East, they discovered that they were one in their essential beliefs. Then they realized more fully the fulfillment of our Saviour's prediction that His church would be of all nations. Though great efforts were made to fix various names on these different evangelical groups, even their enemies, at times, were obliged to recognize that they were "men of the valleys," or Waldenses.

The masses of the heathen naturally became a mission field for the efforts of the two rival communions—Rome and the Church in the Wilderness. Outwardly, the papacy seemed dominant because of her apparent victories by law, by the sword, and by political alliances. The evangelical churches, however, increased in power.

The eighth century opens with strong leadership appearing in both of these communions. The successors of Columbanus, as well as the powerful evangelists of northern Italy and of the Celts, were making irresistible appeals to the masses. The Council of Frankfort (A. D. 794) attended by bishops from France, Germany, and Lombardy at-

---

[19] Pilchdorffius, *Contra Pauperes de Lugduno,* found in *Maxima Bibliotheca Veterum Patrum,* vol. 25, p. 300; also, Robinson, *Ecclesiastical Researches,* page 303.

[20] Bossuet, *Variations of the Protestant Churches,* vol. 2, p. 67. "The fact is, in Gretser's time, the general name of Vaudois was given to all sects separate from Rome ever since the eleventh or twelfth century down to Luther's days." See also Robinson, *Ecclesiastical Researches,* page 56.

[21] See the author's discussion in Chapter VI, entitled, "Vigilantius, Leader of the Waldenses."

tests the independence shown by national clergy to the will of Rome. In the presence of papal legates they rejected the second Council of Nicaea (A. D. 787) which had decreed for the worship of images.[22] In the Orient, in this same century, the independent Church of the East had just erected in the capital of China that famous monument, still standing, which tells of the wide conquests won by consecrated missionaries in central and farther Asia.[23]

Claude of Turin

One cannot be rightly acquainted with the ninth century without recognizing a famous apostle of that time—Claude, the light of northern Italy. Although a Spaniard by birth, his eminent talents and learning attracted the attention of the reigning Western emperor. Claude was first called by this prince to his capital in northern Europe, and was afterward promoted by him to be bishop of Turin, Italy, an influential city nestled in the midst of the Waldensian regions. When he arrived at his new post, he found the state church in a deplorable condition. Vice, superstition, simony, image worship, and other demoralizing practices were rampant. There is an almost unanimous testimony of historians on this point. The papacy was slipping back into paganism. Claude at once undertook the almost impossible task of stemming the tide. He found that even the evangelical churches had been obliged to struggle hard against the prevailing influences. Claude boldly hurled defiance at the papacy and called the people back to New Testament faith and practice.

Evidently Claude, while maintaining that Christ was divine by nature, did not accept the extreme speculations concerning the Godhead voted by the first Council of Nicaea. This was true of most of the evangelical bodies which differed from the Church of Rome.[24] Nothing in the writings of the famous reformer has ever been brought forth to inculpate him of any heresy, although a well-known antagonist accused him after his death of heresy.[25] On the contrary, his

---

[22] Mézeray, *Abregé Chronologique de L'Histoire de France*, vol. 1, p. 244; also Mosheim, *Institutes of Ecclesiastical History*, b. 3, cent. 8, pt. 2, ch. 3, par. 14; also note 29.

[23] See the author's discussion in Chapter XXI, entitled, "Adam and the Church in China."

[24] Robinson, *Ecclesiastical Researches*, pages 99, 106, 440, 441, 445, 446; Adeney, *The Greek and Eastern Churches*, page 218.

[25] This accuser was Jonas, bishop of Orleans.

Biblical commentaries and his other works plainly reveal him to be a New Testament Christian. In one of his epistles Claude vehemently denies that he had been raising up some new sect, and points to Jesus who was also denounced as a sectarian and a demoniac. He claims that he found all the churches of Turin stuffed full of vile and accursed images, and he at once began to destroy what was being worshiped.[26]

From another opponent to this reformer can be learned the interesting fact that Claude's diocese was divided into two parts: on the one hand, those who followed the superstitions of the time and who were bitterly opposed to him; on the other hand, those who agreed with him in doctrine and practice. These evidently were the Vallenses of the Cottian Alps. This opponent, Dungal by name, exalted by modern papal writers as a brilliant churchman, constantly accused Claude of perpetuating the heresies of Vigilantius. The fact that such opponents never ceased to hurl the accusation against Claude and his Vallenses that they believed and taught the same doctrine as Vigilantius, the eminent reformer who lived four hundred years earlier, proves the continuous chain of truth among the inhabitants of northern Italy during the lapse of those four centuries.[27]

Claude cried out thus against image worship: " 'If a man ought not to worship the works of God, much less should he worship and reverence the works of men. Whoever expects salvation which comes only from God, to come from pictures, must be classed with those mentioned Romans 1, who serve the creature more than the Creator.' " Against the worshiping of the cross he taught: " 'God has commanded us to bear the cross; not to pray to it. Those are willing to pray to it, who are unwilling to bear it, either in the spiritual or in the literal sense. To worship God in this manner, is in fact to depart from Him.' " When accused of not holding to the authority of the pope, he wrote: " 'He is not to be called the Apostolical, . . . who sits in the apostle's chair; but he who performs the duties of an apostle. For of those who hold that place, yet do not fulfill its duties, the Lord says, They sit in Moses' seat.' "[28] Claude wanted to know why they should

---

[26] Claude, *Epistle to Abbot Theodimir*, found in *Maxima Bibliotheca Veterum Patrum*, vol. 14, p. 197.

[27] Dungali *Responsa*, found in *Maxima Bibliotheca Veterum Patrum*, vol. 14, pp. 201-216.

[28] Mosheim, *Institutes of Ecclesiastical History*, b. 3, cent. 9, pt. 2, ch. 3, par. 17, note 24.

adore the cross and not also worship many other things—as mangers, fishing boats, trees, thorns, and lances—with which Jesus came in contact. He also defended himself against those who reviled him because he denounced pilgrimages.

The Rise of a New Controversy

Thus the gulf was widening between those congregations descended from the apostles and those attached to the papacy. About this time (A. D. 831) a book was written which widened the breach.[29] It dealt in a revolutionary manner with the subject of the bread and wine of the Lord's Supper. Perhaps this bold venture was made because the writer knew himself to be supported in his novel doctrine by the papacy. The bishop of Rome had just succeeded with the help of Charlemagne in organizing the Holy Roman Empire, and thus he had gained powerful influence. The author, therefore, supported by the theocracy, boldly put into print a doctrine which had been considered for some time. There had already appeared advocates of the papal thesis that the priest had power to change the bread and wine into the actual body and blood of Jesus Christ, but now this startling theory was presented to the public.

Simple scriptural believers concluded that this teaching belittled the sacrifice of Christ on the cross. Christians who were under apostolic influence took the stand that salvation was obtained by the one and only death of the Redeemer. If this new doctrine prevailed, they saw it would logically follow that the Decalogue, which the Redeemer had died on the cross to uphold, would occupy an inferior status. From that time on, strong evangelical leaders never ceased to oppose these innovations. This revolutionary book on transubstantiation was printed about six years before the death of the noble Claude in 839. There is no record that this reformer was acquainted enough with this latest lapse into paganism to assail it.

Whenever from the midst of the Church in the Wilderness a new standard-bearer appeared, the papacy promptly stigmatized him and his followers as "a new sect." This produced a twofold result. First, it made these people appear as never having existed before, whereas they really belonged among the many Bible followers who from the

---

[29] This book was *De Corpore et Sanguine Domini (On the Body and Blood of Christ)*, by Paschasius Radbertus.

days of the early church existed in Europe and Asia. Secondly, it apparently detached the evangelical bodies from one another, whereas they were one in essential doctrines. The different groups taken together constituted the Church in the Wilderness. It is as if one wrote of the Washingtonians, the Jeffersonites, the Lincolnites, and the Americans; or, as if one would describe the Matthewites, the Thomasites, the Peterites, the Paulites, and the Christians. The grouping was not of their own originating; instead, it was a device of their antagonist.

As Philippus Limborch writes: "And because they dwelt in different cities, and had their particular instructors, the papists, to render them the more odious, have represented them as different sects, and ascribed to them as different opinions, though others affirm they all held the same opinions, and were entirely of the same sect." [30]

About this time John Scot, a famous Irish scholar, was called to the court of Charles the Bald, grandson of Charlemagne. He is usually called Joannes Scotus Erigena. In those days, the word "Scotus" definitely designated an Irishman. "Erigena" is the Greek equivalent of Scotus. This man, the head of the royal school at Paris, was the author of many celebrated works, and ranks as a leading scholar of his time. He was shocked at the awful import of the treatise advocating that the bread and wine of the Lord's Supper is changed into the actual body of Christ by the ritual of the mass. He took up his pen and produced a book which successfully met the new enemy of evangelism and profoundly stirred believers in primitive Christianity. Two centuries later a papal council condemned this work because the participants recognized the powerful influence it long had possessed over the people.

Glaring Papal Forgeries

This century also witnessed certain other new and disastrous claims issuing from the ranks of the papacy. The Dark Ages were already beginning to overshadow the masses of Europe. Religious thought was poisoned by the work of one who compiled and issued a series of falsified documents. [31] The collection, usually called the Pseudo-Isidorian Decretals, purported to produce early authentic

---

[30] Limborch, *The History of the Inquisition*, vol. 1, page 42.
[31] Usually attributed to Isidore Mercator, a fictitious person formerly erroneously identified with Isidore of Seville, Spain.

records verifying the claims of the popes to spiritual and temporal world power. These documents were employed with powerful effect throughout the subsequent eight centuries (A. D. 800-1520) to mislead both rulers and the ruled. Although about seven hundred years later their perfidy was exposed, the tyranny and dominion obtained by the papacy through them was not surrendered. In a dull and declining age, such fabricated decrees, clothed with an authoritative antiquity, were used against the Church in the Wilderness. If it had not been for its innate virility, born of the Spirit of God, the apostolic religion would surely have gone down before the baneful influence of such falsifications. Rome itself centuries later was compelled to drop this forgery.

Eleventh-Century Waldensian Heroes

In discussing the churches of south central Europe which preserved primitive Christianity, the greatest credit is usually given to those peoples who lived along both sides of the Alps and in the Pyrenees. In these deep, beautiful, secluded valleys they were often called by names which indicated their location. Thus Ebrard of Bethune, a papal author (c. A. D. 1200) in attempting to explain the name "Vallenses," wrote, "They are some who are called Vallenses, because they dwell in the Valley of Tears."[32] Pilchdorffius, a writer recognized by Rome, wrote this about 1250: "The Waldenses . . . are those who claim to have thus existed from the time of Pope Sylvester."[33] Since Sylvester was bishop of Rome in the early part of the fourth century, here is another witness to the claim that the men of the valleys existed as early as 325.

Cardinal Peter Damian, one of the able builders of the papal edifice, in his campaign (A. D. 1059) against these primitive Christians in northern Italy, called them Subalpini.[34] The word in common parlance to designate these borderers of the Alps was "Vallenses," from which in time the V was changed into W; one of the l's into d, and they have since the twelfth century generally been called Waldenses.

---

[32] Bethuensis, *Liber Antihaeresis*, found in *Maxima Bibliotheca Veterum Patrum*, vol. 24, p. 1572.
[33] Pilchdorffius, *Contra Haeresin Waldensium Tractatus*, ch. 1, found in *Maxima Bibliotheca Veterum Patrum*, vol. 25, p. 278.
[34] Damian, *Opuscula*, Opusculum 18, found in Migne, *Patrologia Latina*, vol. 145, p. 416.

Primitive Christianity, enlarging its influences, became such a threat to the papal hierarchy that many synods and councils were summoned to combat it. Evangelical dissent from the growing paganism of the papacy was so strong that even Rome's champions were forced to call it "inveterate."[35] The papacy decided to challenge this new power with ruthless measures. At one synod or council after another, either the evangelicals were brought to trial or actions were passed against them. An example of the injustice enacted in such courts took place in the case of the Canons of Orléans, France, in 1017. The so-called heresy must have affected numerous provinces, because the judges claimed that it was brought into Gaul from Italy through a missionary "by whom many in many parts were corrupted." Papal authorities were horrified to learn that Stephen, formerly chaplain of the queen; Heribert, who had been one of the realm's ambassadors; and Lisoye—all famous for learning and holiness—were members of the hated church. As prisoners, indicted for heresy, they were arraigned before the prelates.

Four conflicting accounts come down to us of the Council of Orléans.[36] Papal writers, such as Bossuet, take out of these accounts the material that they wish, thinking thus to justify their unfounded charge of Manichaeism against the evangelicals. Writers studying these reports cannot refrain from noticing that the charge was not proved, and that the facts were garbled in a ridiculous manner.[37] Three things happened in connection with the Council of Orléans which revealed the spirit of the papal judges who condemned thirteen

---

[35] Such as Bishop Otto (d'Achery, *Spicilegium,* vol. 1, pp. 434, 435, 1723 ed.) of Vercelli of northern Italy, who in 945 complained of Separatists in his own province; also Bishop Rudolphus (*Spicilegium,* vol. 2, p. 702) of Trom, Belgium, about 1125, who called the Dissenters "inveterate." *"Inveterata haeresi de corpore et sanguine Deo."*

[36] (a) Adolphus Glaber; (b) John of Fleury; (c) The Acts of the Council; (d) *An History of Aquitaine.*

[37] Says George S. Faber: "Through a space of eight hours the examination was prolonged. And the *same* men, we are assured, in the course of the *same* scrutiny, confessed: that *They believed in one God,* that *They believed in two Gods,* and yet that *They believed in no God;* that *They asserted one God in heaven to be the Creator of all things,* that *They asserted the material world and the spiritual world to have been severally created by two Gods,* and yet that *They asserted the entire world both material and spiritual to have never been created at all but to have existed without any Creator from all eternity:* that *They totally denied a future state of rewards and punishments,* and yet that *Their assured confidence in an everlasting state of future glory and joy celestial was such as to make them face without shrinking the most terrible of all deaths!"—The Ancient Vallenses and Albigenses,* page 146.

primitive Christians to be burned at the stake. First, Queen Constantia was stationed at the door, and as the condemned martyrs filed out, she thrust a stick into the eye of Stephen, who formerly had been her private chaplain and had evidently rebuked her for her loose conduct. For this act, her praises have been voluminously sung by the ultramontanes. Secondly, it is known that one of the Frankish nobility, in order to secure evidence, pretended to join the primitive Christians as a member of their church. By means of this double dealing, he obtained catch phrases which could be falsely turned at the trial against the accused. Thirdly, after these martyrs were burned at the stake, it was discovered that a certain nobleman had been a member of the hated church for three years and had died before the trial. In anger, his body was dug up and publicly dishonored.

The faith of those condemned at this court of injustice may be understood from the words that they addressed to the judges at the close of eight hours of grilling. They said:

> You may narrate these doctrines to others, who are wise in worldly wisdom, and who believe the figments of carnal men written upon animal parchment. But to us who have the law written in the inner man by the Holy Ghost, and who know nothing else save what we have learned from God the Creator of all things, you vainly propound matters which are superfluous and altogether alien from sound divinity. Put therefore an end to words: and do with us what you list. We clearly behold our King reigning in heavenly places, who with His own right hand, is raising us to an immortal triumph; and He is raising us to the fullness of joy celestial.[38]

Can this be the testimony of profligates or erratic religionists?

Eight years later (A. D. 1025) at Arras in northern France another farcical trial was held. The defendants were accused of Manichaeism, the usual false accusation of the papacy against evangelicals. If the trial resulted in anything, it revealed that these devoted missionaries were guilty of no such demeanors.[39] It made clear that the doctrine unacceptable to that unjust court came from northern Italy. The martyrs were not called Waldenses in the report. Their beliefs, however, were those of the martyrs of Orléans and were similar to the teachings of the Waldenses. From the testimony obtained in these

---

[38]d'Achery, *Spicilegium,* vol. 1, pp. 604-606.
[39]*Ibid.,* vol. 1, pp. 607, 608.

trials of the primitive Christians, we are enabled to conclude that their churches were numerous, with some scholars and eminent persons. The renowned city of Toulouse in southern France is an example of how certain communities held fast to the doctrines of the apostles from the early days of Christianity until they aroused the fury of an exterminating crusade. Toulouse is blamed not only as the breeding place of so-called heresy, but is also said to have successfully housed rejecters of Rome throughout the centuries, first in the days of Gothic Christianity, and later in times of the Albigenses and Waldenses.[40] None of these dissenters can be called "reformed," because they never diverged far enough from the early church either in beliefs or practices to necessitate a movement of reform.

As to the remote antiquity of the hated evangelicals in the city and kingdom of Toulouse, there is a remarkable statement from the chaplain who accompanied the bloody crusade of 1208-1218, which destroyed the beautiful Albigensian civilization. "This Toulouse," he said, "the completely wretched, has, it is asserted, from its very foundation, rarely or never been free from the miasma or detestable pestilence of condemned heresy, handing down, and successively diffusing throughout generations from father to son, its poison of superstitious infidelity."[41]

Berengarius

The cruel use of fraud and force against the inoffensive and persecuted followers of Jesus Christ only confirmed them in the conviction that their cause was of God. The common people sympathized with the oppressed Bible believers and prayed for deliverers. Noble and scholarly leaders arose to oppose the oppressors. However, they were cut down before they were permitted to go far enough in their sacrificing efforts to turn the tide of persecution and intolerance. Among those whose protest went home with force was Berengarius of France, who comes in to claim special attention. His followers were called the Berengarians or earlier Waldenses.[42]

More church councils were probably held against Berengarius than against anyone else. The papists hated him alive and dead. He

---

[40] *The Catholic Encyclopedia*, art. "Toulouse."
[41] De Vaux Cernay, *Historia Albigensium*, ch. 1, found in Migne, *Patrologia Latina*, vol. 213, pp. 545, 546.
[42] Benedict, *A General History of the Baptist Denomination*, vol. 1, pp. 112, 121.

was the second prominent witness in whose mouth the truth was established. Joannes Scotus Erigena, a world figure two hundred years previous, had been the first. There is a tradition to the effect that Scotus came from one of the schools established by Columba. Both had truly analyzed the doctrine of transubstantiation. To Berengarius it was not simply an error of the church; it was the height of seducing delusions. Other errors were tradition, allegorizing, abolition of the Decalogue, disregard of the Sabbath, and obscuration of the one and sufficient sacrifice of Jesus Christ. Apostasy had strengthened since the days of Vigilantius and Claude, and Berengarius was obliged to oppose all that they had denounced and more. He was therefore branded as the "purveyor of many heresies." He gathered disciples around him and committed to many groups of trained young men the task of spreading the light everywhere. Thousands in whose hearts lingered the love of primitive Christianity received his disciples gladly.

Matthew of Westminster (A. D. 1087) complains that the Berengarians and Waldenses had corrupted all of France, England, and Italy.[43] This was a full century before Peter Waldo. Many authorities acknowledge that the resistance of the Berengarians to the papacy was the same as the resistance shown by the Waldenses. Others, as Ussher and Benedict, see in Berengarius a leader of the Waldenses.

Archbishop Lanfranc was counselor and ecclesiastical peer to William of Normandy when he set out to conquer England. After William had added the English kingdom to his French possessions, he offered Lanfranc the primacy of the newly conquered lands. Lanfranc was anxious to overthrow Berengarius, whom he considered an enemy in doctrine. He set out to destroy him by the use of his pen, because Berengarius was too prominent and too greatly beloved to be burned at the stake, although in the fifty years previous many believers in the doctrines issuing from northern Italy had expired in flames. Repeatedly condemned by many councils, Berengarius was driven into exile. Though nominally a Roman Catholic prelate, he had doctrinally gone over to the Waldenses. From Lanfranc it is learned that the Berengarians called the Church of Rome "The Congregation of the Wicked and the Seat of Satan," which also the Waldenses did. The papacy promptly branded the thousands who rejoiced in his bright and shin-

---

[43] Matthew of Westminster, *The Flowers of History*, vol. 2, p. 15.

ing light as Berengarians. Actually they were a part of the increasing numbers who had refused to follow Rome in departing from the teachings of the apostles.

Separation Between Greek and Latin Churches

In the midst of its attempt to overthrow the spiritual leadership of Berengarius and its military victory in the conquest of England, the papacy reached its final break with the Greek Church. During these eventful years the Roman pontiff possessed three ecclesiastical fields marshals of outstanding shrewdness. They were Lanfranc, Damian, and Humbert. The papacy had used Lanfranc against Berengarius. Cardinal Humbert was sent to Constantinople (A. D. 1054) to demand that the Greek Church recognize completely the world leadership of the pontiff in the Vatican. Cardinal Damian was sent into northern Italy (A. D. 1059), the region of the Waldenses, to bring into subjection the diocese of Milan which had ever remained independent of the Roman see. Since the scholarly rejection which this haughty priest met at Constantinople took place before the mission to Milan, it greatly strengthened the Waldenses in their resistance.

Both the Greek and the Latin churches had lost much of the spiritual power maintained by the Waldenses. Dean Stanley reveals how much deeper the Latin apostasy was than the Greek as late as the twelfth century: " 'At certain periods of their course, there can be no doubt that the civilization of the Eastern Church was far higher than that of the Western.' "[44] Rome's discontent at the lagging Eastern Church was first manifest when the king of Bulgaria and his nation were converted to Christianity by Greek missionaries in 864. The pope noted that these missionaries had followed the example of Eastern evangelism by translating the Bible not from the Latin Vulgate, but from the original Greek. They also had given the Bulgarians a liturgy, or order of church services, which was not pliable to the unscriptural Roman liturgy. The papacy was as determined to achieve spiritual supremacy over Bulgaria as over Lombardy and England.

Again the Sabbath question became prominent. The churches of the East from earliest days had sanctified Saturday as the Sabbath,

---

[44] Quoted in Gordon, *"World Healers,"* page 470.

and wherever Sunday had crept in, religious services were observed on both days.[45] Bulgaria in the early season of its evangelization had been taught that no work should be performed on the Sabbath.[46] Long before this time, migrations from the Paulician church had reached Bulgaria. These Paulicians observed the seventh-day Sabbath of the fourth commandment. Consequently, they were a strong reinforcement to the Greek attitude on this question.

Pope Nicholas I, in the ninth century, sent the ruling prince of Bulgaria a long document elucidating political, territorial, and ecclesiastical questions, and saying in it that one is to cease from work on Sunday, but not on the Sabbath. The head of the Greek Church, offended at the interference of the papacy, declared the pope excommunicated. The Greek patriarch also sent a circulatory letter to some leading bishops of the East, censuring the Roman Catholic Church for several erroneous doctrines, especially emphasizing its rebellion against past church councils in compelling its members to fast on the seventh-day Sabbath. This fast was commanded in order that they might unfavorably compare the austerity of the seventh day with the pleasures of the first day. The letter rebuked the papacy for seeking to impose this yoke on the Bulgarians. A complete break between the churches, however, did not occur at that time. The heat of the controversy continued, only to break out anew later.

Events conspired to drive the Greek and Latin branches of the church more and more apart. Two hundred years later (A. D. 1054) the controversy again arose. The Greek patriarch, Michael Cerulaius, and a learned Greek monk, both attacked the Roman Catholic Church on a number of points, including fasting on the Sabbath. Now the haughty Cardinal Humbert comes into the picture. While Lanfranc was assailing Berengarius, and Cardinal Damian was preparing to gather Waldensian territory into the fold, the pope sent three legates to Constantinople with countercharges. Amongst others, the following charge was made by the pope against the Greek Church: "Because you observe the Sabbath with the Jews and the Lord's Day with us, you seem to imitate with such observances the sect of Nazarenes who

---

[45] Bower, *The History of the Popes,* vol. 2, p. 258; also, note 2, 1845 ed.

[46] *Responsa Nicolai Papae I ad Consulta Bulgarorum,* Responsum 10, found in Mansi, *Sacrorum Conciliorum Nova et Amplissima Collectio,* vol. 15, p. 406; also to be found in Hefele, *Conciliengeschicte,* vol. 4, sec. 478.

in this manner accept Christianity in order that they be not obliged to leave Judaism."[47] Enraged at his failure to bring the Greek Church under subjection, Humbert declared it excommunicated. He found that the leading bishops of the East sided with the Greek patriarch. The gulf between these two communions was final.

The following quotation from John Mason Neale will reveal the difference in attitude toward the Sabbath between the Greek and the Latin Church: "The observance of Saturday is, as everyone knows, the subject of a bitter dispute between the Greeks and Latins."[48]

The Revolution in Northern Italy

The pope immediately turned his attention to the Waldenses. Having shaken himself loose from the Greek Church, he had now become the titular spiritual head of Europe. He resolved to tolerate the independence of the diocese of Milan no longer. He saw, as a new enemy, the rising tide throughout the Continent of evangelical churches whose nerve center was northern Italy. He resented their claim to be the only true church directly descended from the apostles, and he detested their preaching that the papacy was the mystical Babylon predicted by the Apocalypse.

It never occurred to the pope that, instead of crushing the northern Italian diocese, he might create a small but well-organized minority with dangerous possibilities. He relied for support upon the infiltration into that diocese of those who sided with Rome. These latter were determined to eliminate the opponents of Vatican policies. Therefore, the shrewd Cardinal Damian was sent to Milan in 1059 to work with the malcontents and to bring into subjection that diocese.

Clergy and people alike were greatly stirred. They demanded to know by what authority one diocese could invade the rights and prerogatives of another.[49] They were deeply incensed when Damian assembled a synod of the clergy of Milan and seated himself above their archbishop, Guido. Using deceptive documents, he cajoled, threatened, and promised. He followed the Jesuit motto, "Where we cannot convince, we will confuse." He proposed among other things

---

[47] Migne, *Patrologia Latina*, vol. 145, p. 506; also, Hergenroether, *Photius*, vol. 3, p. 746. The Nazarenes were a Christian denomination.

[48] Neale, *A History of the Holy Eastern Church*, General Introduction, vol. 1, p. 731.

[49] Damian, *Opuscula*, Opusculum 5, found in Migne, *Patrologia Latina*, vol. 145, p. 90.

that they adopt several doctrinal articles rejected by the Greeks, including celibacy of the priesthood. The result was that as soon as his legation left the city, the loyal clergy and the nobility called a council which asserted the right of the clergy to marry. On the other hand, the papal party had succeeded so far in their efforts that they had induced the prefect of the city to use public threats against the Milanese. With the city torn by strife and contest, those in favor of a married clergy concluded that the only thing for them to do was to retire for their devotions to a separate place called Patara, whereupon they were reproachfully called Patarines.[50] "They have given this nickname of Patarines to the Waldenses, because the Waldenses were those Subalpini in Peter Damian, who at the same time maintain'd the same doctrines in the Archbishoprick of Turin."[51]

The maneuvering of the cardinal not only destroyed the agelong independence of the Milan diocese, but it also transformed the Patarines into a permanent organization of opposition. Thus, he produced a revolution. By Lanfranc's opposition, the papacy had publicized the preachings of Berengarius; through Humbert's hostility, it had left on the pages of history a mighty opponent in the Greek Church; through the work of Damian, it had transformed Milanese dissent into the organized Patarines. Thus the imperious work of these three papal legates not only alienated the public, but also caused large additions to Christian congregations clinging to primitive Christianity. Three new names were now given to the men of the valleys; namely, Berengarians, Subalpini, and Patarines.

Gregory VII, the Imperious Innovator

While the incompatibilities between tradition and the Bible, and between apostolic and medieval Christianity, were growing in intensity, Pope Gregory VII (A. D. 1073-1085) assumed the tiara. When chosen as supreme pontiff, he began immediately to subject the Roman Catholic clergy more completely to the bishop of Rome. He changed the simpler liturgies, or services of worship, existing since primitive days to suit later corruptions; he rigidly enforced celibacy upon the priesthood; and he brought the princes of Europe under his iron heel.[52]

---

[50] M'Clintock and Strong, *Cyclopedia*, art. "Patarenes."
[51] Allix, *The Ancient Churches of Piedmont*, pages 121, 122.
[52] "Nearly the whole form of the Latin church therefore, was changed by this pontiff; and the most valuable rights of councils, of bishops, and of religious societies,

He is the pope who made the western emperor, Henry IV, stand barefooted and bareheaded in the outer court of the castle at Canossa for three days in winter imploring the forgiveness and support of the offended pontiff. Gregory's harsh and cruel measures to make the married clergy put away their wives finally fastened celibacy upon the Roman Catholic Church. It produced such an opposite effect upon the evangelical groups that it hastened the coming of the Reformation.

That primitive Christianity was growing strong enough to worry the pontiff of Rome may be seen in the decree of Urban II, the pope who attempted to carry on the reforms of Gregory VII. This Vatican ruler issued a bull in 1096 (nearly a century before Peter Waldo) against one of the Waldensian valleys on the French side of the Alps for being infested with "heresy."[53]

In the following one hundred years, three other names were bestowed upon the people known as the Waldenses; namely, Petrobrusians, Henricians, and Arnoldists. But these were more than mere names. Behind each appellation stood the record of a powerful leader in evangelism. As each new apostle arose, Rome at first was content to treat him and his followers as a "new sect," for by so doing she aimed to cover up the fact that the renewed evangelical wave sweeping over Europe was another manifestation of the Church in the Wilderness. Later, however, when primitive Christianity made devastating inroads upon her flock, she began to persecute, and the inquisition, the stake, and the torture chamber followed.

Three important events occurred in the eleventh century which formed a background for the reactions which produced famous spiritual leaders among the primitive Christians. The first event was the conquest of England. The second consisted in the power of Archbishop Lanfranc as spiritual overlord of England whereby he instituted the policy designed to crush the Celtic Church in Scotland and

---

were subverted, and transferred over to the Roman pontiff. The evil however was not equally grievous in all the countries of Europe; for in several of them, through the influence of different causes, some shadow of pristine liberty and customs was preserved. As Hildebrand introduced a new code of ecclesiastical law, he would have introduced also a new code of civil law, if he could have accomplished fully his designs. For he wished to reduce all kingdoms into fiefs of St. Peter, i. e., of the Roman pontiffs; and to subject all causes of kings and princes, and the interests of the whole world, to the arbitrament of an assembly of bishops, who should meet annually at Rome."—Mosheim, *Institutes of Ecclesiastical History,* b. 3, cent. 11, pt. 2, ch. 2, par. 10.

[53]Muston, *The Israel of the Alps,* vol. 1, pp. 3, 14, note 1.

Ireland. The third, the Crusades which followed the conquest of England, made Europe overnight into one vast armed confederacy, with Rome at the head of the armies moving out of Europe into Asia to rescue Palestine from the Mohammedans.

Pope Urban II, author of the bull denouncing the "heresy" of the men of the valleys, summoned all kings, princes, bishops, and abbots to seize the sword and start for Palestine in 1096. The hour was propitious, for he had filled the Continent with tradition instead of Bible teachings. Then too, the masses were brooding over a wrong interpretation of the Apocalypse. A millennium having passed since the writing of the book, the hour was at hand, they thought, for the chaining of Satan, for the descent of the Holy City, and for the final judgment. When pilgrims, returning from Jerusalem and the scenes of our Saviour's journeyings, told the pitiful stories of Moslem cruelties upon Christians, more fuel was added to the fire. The Vatican sent its agents up and down the land to inflame them to crush the Mohammedans and magnify the leadership of the Roman Catholic Church.

In less than a century and a half there was the crushing defeat of four Crusades. In the midst of these, Rome aroused the mob and rabble under bloodthirsty swashbucklers to destroy the beautiful civilization of the Albigenses in southern France. The eyes of Europe opened. They became satiated in seeing lands rent with civil feuds and drenched in fraternal blood. Reform movements grew. Justice depended less upon the caprice of one man. Nationalism grew. Commerce expanded. The claims of the Roman pontiff grew weaker and weaker, and the teachings of the Church in the Wilderness grew stronger and stronger.

Peter de Bruys

The Crusades had a different effect upon the masses than the papacy had anticipated. The Cross was not victorious over the Crescent. The downtrodden and defeated armies, returning from the East, exposed the folly of papal policies. They demonstrated to the people that the teachings of Christ should be lived in a different way. They realized that Christian victories in this life are not gained by the sword. This drove many to a re-examination of the Holy Scriptures, and they turned to the Waldenses, Albigenses, and Paulicians— different names for the same primitive Christians—who had always circulated translations of the Bible in their native language and who had adopted a simple church service. Men of profound devotion and great learning were stirred by the needs of the masses. The twelfth century saw the emergence of three outstanding evangelical heroes. First among these in point of time was Peter de Bruys. He was born in the Waldensian valley on the French side of the Alps which Urban II had declared to be infested with "heresy." This youth's blood ran warm with evangelical fervor. The decrees proclaiming that no church council could be assembled without the consent of the pope had aroused the indignation of southern France. Peter de Bruys began his work about 1104. One must read the writings of an abbot, a contemporary and an enemy, to secure much of what can be learned concerning this evangelical preacher.[54]

For twenty years Peter de Bruys stirred southern France. There was a deep spiritual movement among the masses. He brought them back to the Bible and to apostolic Christianity. His message had the power to transform characters. He especially emphasized a day of worship that was recognized at that time among the Celtic churches of the British Isles, among the Paulicians, and in the great Church of the East; namely, that seventh day of the fourth commandment, the weekly sacred day of Jehovah. Five centuries later, during heated debates on the Sabbath, a learned bishop of the Church of England referred to the Sabbathkeeping of the Petrobrusians.[55] For centuries evangelical bodies, especially the Waldenses, were called Insabbati or Ensavates, that is, Insabbatati, because of Sabbathkeeping.[56] "Many took this position," says Ussher.[57] The learned Jesuit, Jacob Gretzer, about 1600, recognized that the Waldenses, the Albigenses, and the Insabbatati were different names for the same people.[58] The

[54] See Peter of Cluny, *Tractatus Contra Petrobrussianos,* found in Migne, *Patrologia Latina,* vol. 189, pp. 720-850.

[55] White, Bishop of Eli, *A Treatise on the Sabbath Day,* page 8, found in Fisher, *Tracts on the Sabbath.*

[56] Gui, *Manuel d' Inquisiteur,* vol. 1, p. 37. Pope Innocent III was the inspiring force in legalizing the Inquisition; Dominic became its founder; Francis dragged the unoffending evangelicals to its prisons; but Bernard Gui drew up the processes of condemning and of afflicting the victims.

[57] "Dicti sunt et Insabbatati: non 'quod nullum festum colerent' ut opinatus est Johannes Massonus, nec quod in Sabbato Colendo Judaizarent, ut multi putabant," wrote Ussher, *Gravissimae Quaestionis de Christianarum Ecclesiarum Successione,* ch. 8, par. 4.

[58] Gretzer, *Praeloquia in Triadem Scriptorum Contra Valdensium Sectam,* found in *Maxima Bibliotheca Veterum Patrum,* vol. 24, pp. 1521, 1522.

thesis that they were called Insabbatati because of their footwear is indignantly rejected by the learned Robert Robinson.[59] To show how widespread this term, Insabbatati, was applied to the Waldenses, the following oath is quoted which the monks directing the Inquisition would exact from prisoners suspected of holding different religious views from those of the Church of Rome:

> The oath by which a person suspected of heresy was to clear himself was this, to be taken in publick. "I, Sancho, swear, by Almighty God and by these holy gospels of God, which I hold in my hand, before you lord Garcia archbishop, and before others your assistants, that I am not, nor ever have been, an Inzabbatate Waldense, or poor person of Lyons, or an heretick of any sect of heresy condemned by the church; nor do I believe, nor have I ever believed, their errours, nor will I believe them in any future time of my life: moreover I profess and protest that I do believe, and that I will always hereafter believe, the catholick faith, which the holy apostolical church of Rome publickly holds, teaches and preaches, and you my lord archbishop, and other prelates of the catholick church publickly hold, preach and teach."[60]

The worst criticism against the work of Peter de Bruys was the branding of it as a revival of Manichaeism. This has been repeatedly proved to be false. Nevertheless, many modern historians whose thinking has been distorted by papal documents, repeat the charge. A century or more before Peter de Bruys, Manichaeism had ceased to be a force in the world. All churches detested its wild teachings and its idolatrous practices. To make this accusation against innocent followers of primitive Christians was to say all manner of evil against the Petrobrusians. Peter de Bruys was hounded and harassed by his enemies, and he was finally apprehended and burned at the stake about 1124. The name, Petrobrusians, was added by papists to the other names already given the evangelical bodies.

Henry of Lausanne

Another great hero of this age is Henry of Lausanne. While the papacy was wasting the man power of Europe in the Crusades, Henry of Lausanne, generally accepted as a disciple of Peter de Bruys, was changing the characters of men. Henry was no visionary crusader; he wielded the sword of the Spirit, not the sword of steel.

---

[59] Robinson, *Ecclesiastical Researches,* page 304.
[60] *Ibid.,* pages 322, 323.

As in the case of Peter de Bruys, much that is known of his teachings is found in a treatise written against him by an abbot.[61] To let it be seen how little information the adversary of Henry possessed in order to write his treatise, it is only necessary to quote his own words:

> After the immolation of Peter deBruis at St. Giles, through which, the zeal of the faithful, in burning him, was repaid, and that impious man has passed from temporal to eternal fire, Henry, the heir of wickedness, with, I know not what others, had not so much amended as altered his Satanic teaching; so that he lately published in a volume, said to have been dictated by him, not merely five but many articles. Against which the spirit is stirred again, to oppose Satanic words with holy speeches. But because I am not yet fully confident that he so believes and preaches, I will postpone my reply to such a time when I am fully confident concerning the things reported concerning him.[62]

This writer confesses that his knowledge comes from hearsay. He discourses generously about the doctrines of the followers of Peter de Bruys and of Henry, and at the same time admits that his information is inadequate. This book of Henry, mentioned by Peter of Cluny, could hardly have failed to influence both Arnold of Brescia and Peter Waldo, two reformers who followed after him.

As Henry traveled, labored, prayed, and preached to raise the masses to triumphant truth, he was assailed by the most commanding figure in the papal world. Bernard, abbot of Clairvaux, was the only man with force enough to whip superstitious Europe into the frenzy of a second crusade. The first crusade had flickered out so disastrously that the papacy was compelled to subpoena the services of Bernard. The word of this champion was powerful enough to decide even the choice of popes. A number of his poetical compositions, having had the good fortune to be set to charming music, have been placed by his admirers in Protestant hymnbooks. He entertained and directed the Irish bishop who did more than any other man to betray the Celtic Church in Ireland. He trained the Irish monks who returned home to overthrow the followers of Patrick. He is called "the oracle of those times." It was this Bernard who poured forth his biting invectives against Henry. Though he could determine the choice of popes, though he could throw crusading armies of Europe

---

[61] Peter of Cluny, *Tractatus Contra Petrobrussianos*, found in Migne, *Patrologia Latina*, vol. 189, pp. 720-850.
[62] *Ibid.*, vol. 189, p. 723.

into Asia, though he could help to direct the Normanizing and the Romanizing of the Celtic Church in the British Isles, he could not cower the indefatigable Henry. Bernard summoned the count of St. Giles to stop Henry by imprisonment and death. He said:

> How great are the evils which I have heard and known that the heretic Henry has done and is daily doing in the churches of God! A ravening wolf in sheep's clothing is busy in your land, but by our Lord's direction I know him by his fruits. The churches are without congregations, congregations without priests, priests without their due reverence, and, worst of all, Christians without Christ. Churches are regarded as synagogues, the sanctuary of God is said to have no sanctity, the sacraments are not thought to be sacred, feast days are deprived of their wonted solemnities. . . . This man, who says and does things contrary to God is not from God. Yet, O sad to say, he is listened to by many, and he has a following which believes in him. . . . The voice of one heretic has put to silence all the prophets and apostles.[63]

Bernard was a relentless persecutor of Peter de Bruys, Henry of Lausanne, and Arnold of Brescia. Besides assailing them in particular writings, he took occasion to launch forth his diatribes against the whole evangelical movement of his day. A letter from a neighboring clergyman in Germany, namely, Evervinus, bishop of Cologne, asked Bernard to explain why these so-called heretics went to the stake rejoicing in God. When Bernard wrote an answer to this question, he called these heretics Apostolicals, giving as his reason for so naming them that no one could trace them back to the name of any particular founder. He admitted that the Arians had Arius for a founder; that the Manichaeans had Mani (or Manes); and the Sabellians had Sabellius; the Eunomians had Eunomius; and the Nestorians had Nestorius.[64] He recognized that all the foregoing bodies bore the name of their leaders, but he could find no such founder under whom he might tabulate the hated churches he was fighting, unless, as he concluded, they were the offspring of demons. The fact that Bernard declared the name of these Christians to be Apostolicals and that they called themselves after no human founder, singles them out as descendants of the early primitive church.

---

[63] Bernard of Clairvaux, Epistle 241 (A. D. 1147) to Hildefonsus, Count of St. Eloy, found in Eales, *The Works of St. Bernard,* vol. 2, pp. 707, 708.

[64] Bernard of Clairvaux, Sermon 66, on the Canticles, found in Eales, *The Works of St. Bernard,* vol. 4, pp. 388, 400-403.

The unity of these believers in essential doctrines and the fact that they were the forerunners of Luther and Calvin has been recognized by eminent authorities. Thus, François Mézeray indicates that there were two sorts of "heretics:" the one ignorant and loose, somewhat of the nature of the Manichees; the other, more learned and less disorderly, maintaining much the same doctrines as the Calvinists, and called Henricians and Waldenses.[65] Allowance must be made for the papal attitude of this writer. He did not clearly bring out the fact that the followers of Peter de Bruys and Henry were probably confounded with the Manichaeans by the bishop and clergy.

There is also the remarkable statement by Gilbert Genebrard who states definitely that the spiritual fathers of the Calvinists were the Petrobrusians, the Henricians, and the Albigenses.[66]

The numerous disciples raised up by Peter de Bruys and Henry of Lausanne occasioned the calling of ecclesiastical councils to combat the rising tide of evangelism. In 1119 Pope Calixtus assembled a council at Toulouse, France, in which, "the sentence of excommunication was thundered out against a sect of heretics in those parts, condemning the eucharist, the baptism of infants, the priesthood, all ecclesiastical orders, and lawful marriages."[67] By lawful marriages the papists referred to the opposition of the evangelicals to calling marriage a sacrament, and requiring it to be performed only by a priest.

When Pope Innocent II held a council at Pisa, Italy, in 1134, "the doctrines taught by a hermit named Henry, were declared heresies and condemned with their author and all who taught or held them."[68] This same pope convened a general council in Rome five years later to which all the princes of the West were summoned, and it was a large council. "By the twenty-third canon of the present council the opinions of Arnold of Brescia were declared repugnant to the doctrine received by the Catholic Church, and condemned as such."[69] Naturally, such a council would not be held unless it was to deal with large propositions. As all of these councils were held many years before

---

[65] Mézeray, *Abregé Chronologique de L'Histoire de France,* vol. 2, pp. 654-657.
[66] Genebrard, *Sacred Chronology.* See Allix, *Remarks Upon the Ecclesiastical History of the Ancient Church of the Albigenses,* page 172.
[67] Bower, *The History of the Popes,* vol. 2, p. 456.
[68] *Ibid.,* vol. 2, page 468.
[69] *Ibid.,* vol. 2, pp. 470, 471.

Peter Waldo appeared on the scene, the reader can see that evangelism had grown to be a mighty force before Waldo's time.

Arnold of Brescia

To Arnold of Brescia belongs the glory of openly denouncing the overgrown empire of ecclesiastical tyranny. In his soul were the spirit of both the evangelist and the general. Arnold was from Brescia, a city with an independent spirit like Milan and Turin. From there comes the beautiful Brixianus manuscript, exemplar of the beloved Itala, the first translation of the New Testament from Greek into Latin, three centuries before Jerome's Vulgate. Born amid such traditions, Arnold needed only to sit at the feet of the renowned Abelard to receive the full flame of freedom which was already glowing within him. From his studies under Abelard he returned to Brescia where his voice was with power. His words were heard in Switzerland, southern Italy, Germany, and France. In this latter land, the sensitive ears of Bernard detected an ominous note in his teachings.

Arnold was far ahead of his age. In fact, he did what the reformers failed to do. He attacked the union of church and state. Arnold's idealism and eloquence aroused the people to a high pitch of enthusiasm. Papal bishops and clergy combined against him. A church synod—ever a potential enemy of progress—was called, and in 1139 Arnold was condemned to silence and to expulsion from Brescia.

He fled to Zurich, Switzerland, and again took the field against the wealth, luxury, and the temporal power of the clergy. He called for a democratic type of ministry, and he mightily stirred those regions. Even the papal legate, a future pope, came over to his side. Bernard of Clairvaux promptly reduced that prospective pope into submission. The bishop of Constance came out for Arnold, but Bernard frightened him out of any further participation in Arnoldism. The lordly Cistercian monk demanded that all of Arnold's books and writings be burned. This was done.

But in spite of this bitter opposition, Arnold labored on. The soil was good, and the reformer scattered the seeds far and wide. Who knows but that the future strength of Switzerland in her stand for freedom and religious liberty was due in some measure to the sowing of Arnold. The papists could not forgive his opposition to certain doctrines. He preached against transubstantiation, infant baptism, and prayers for the dead.[70] Because of this, Bernard of Clairvaux continually pressed for the execution of Arnold.

Meanwhile events were taking place in Rome. That city had come out for civil government. The pope fled, but as he went out, Arnold came in. The people welcomed him in a frenzy of enthusiasm. Here is where Arnold compromised his truly evangelical lead by sanctioning, if not directing, the masses in using force. Here is where a flaw affected his vision. Possessing unopposed leadership, however, he divorced religion from the civil government in the city. He restored the Roman senate. The old glories of Italy returned. His opposition to tradition, to unacceptable ceremonies, and to unscriptural doctrines encouraged the believers in the New Testament. Primitive Christians lifted up their heads, and their followers multiplied everywhere. Papal writers promptly declared that a new sect had been founded, whom they called the Arnoldists.

Then the pope and the emperor leagued against Arnold. He soon learned that they who take the sword shall perish by the sword. The fickle crowd deserted him and his political friends took to cover. After the pope at the head of an army had driven Arnold out of Rome, he was taken by the armed forces of the emperor. His body was burned and his ashes were thrown into the Tiber River.

Thus perished a fearless leader who, singlehanded, dared to denounce the unholy union of church and state. He had no visible support upon which to rely except the vigorous assent of the human mind to the greatness of his message. His effect upon future generations was far-reaching. "The Waldenses look up to Arnold as to one of the spiritual founders of their churches; and his religious and political opinions probably fostered the spirit of republican independence which throughout Switzerland and the whole Alpine district was awaiting its time." [71]

That the provinces of southern France were crowded with the followers of Peter de Bruys and Henry long before Waldo or his followers began to labor there is seen in the letter written about 1150 by the archbishop of Narbonne to King Louis VII: "My Lord the King, we are extremely pressed with many calamities, amongst which there is one that most of all affects us, which is, that the Catholic faith

---

[70] Bower, *The History of the Popes,* vol. 2, p. 471.
[71] Milman, *History of Latin Christianity,* vol. 3, p. 281.

is extremely shaken in this our diocese, and St. Peter's boat is so violently tossed by the waves, that it is in great danger of sinking."[72]

Still further testimony is given by Pope Leo, as is recorded in *The Annals of Roger de Hoveden* in the year 1178 as follows:

> Wherefore, inasmuch as, in Gascony, the Albigeois, and other places inhabited by the heretics whom some style "Catarri," others "Publicani" and others "Paterini," and others, call by other names, their damnable perverseness has waxed so strong that they practice their wickedness no longer in secret as elsewhere, but publicly expose their errors, and draw the simple and weak to be their accomplices, we do decree them and their protectors and harborers to be excommunicated.[73]

The Nobla Lecon

If no spiritual movement among men is great unless it has produced a glorious literature, then the message of the Waldenses can be called great. Among other products remaining from the writings of this martyred and wonderful people mention should be made of the *Nobla Leçon* (Noble Lesson) written in the Romaunt tongue, the common language of the south of Europe from the eighth to the fourteenth century. Its opening words claim that the date of the composition was 1100. On it the people to whom the treatise belongs is definitely called the Vaudois, and this is nearly a century before Peter Waldo. Much study has been made to determine whether the statement regarding 1100 is from the author or authors of the *Nobla Leçon,* or is from another hand. There has also been considerable thought given to the commencement of the 1100 years.

The *Nobla Leçon* begins, "Hear, oh brothers, a Noble Lesson." Then there appears before the reader a sublime presentation of the origin and the story of the plan of redemption. The *Nobla Leçon* stands for the eternal moral obligation of the Ten Commandments, and in that light it presents the great expiation on the cross. One is led along step by step in considering what manner of love the Father has bestowed upon man in such divine provisions for his ransom from the fall. Its soft and glowing terms stir the soul. No one can read the chapter by Peter Allix in which he analyzes and presents the message

---

[72]Allix, *Remarks Upon the Ecclesiastical History of the Ancient Church of the Albigenses,* page 117.

[73]*The Annals of Roger de Hoveden,* translated from the Latin by Riley, vol. 1, p. 502.

of the *Nobla Leçon* without feeling that a great contribution has been made to the world's literature.

Peter Waldo

Mention is now made of that famous individual, Peter Waldo. Some authorities claim that the name Waldo was derived from the Waldenses because of his prominent work among them. Whether this is true or not, we do know that from his time on the name Waldenses was more generally used to indicate those large reforming bodies which had previously been called "men of the valleys," or Vallenses, Albigenses, Insabbatati, Berengarians, Subalpini, Patarines, Petrobrusians, Henricians, Arnoldists, and other names.

Peter Waldo of Lyons, France, began his work somewhere between 1160 and 1170. He was a wealthy merchant who gave away all his goods and began to preach the genuine doctrines of the New Testament. He claimed the papacy to be the "man of sin," and the beast of the Apocalypse. He devoted much time to translating and distributing the Bible.

CHAPTER XVI

The Church of the Waldenses

The Vaudois (Waldenses) are in fact descended from those refugees from Italy, who, after St. Paul had there preached the gospel, abandoned their beautiful country and fled like the woman mentioned in the Apocalypse, to these wild mountains, where they have to this day handed down the gospel from father to son in the same purity and simplicity as it was preached by St. Paul.[1]

THE preceding chapter brought the story of the Waldenses up to the work of Peter Waldo. He gave a new impetus to this church, and forged a new weapon for evangelicals who refused to walk with Rome, in that he provided popular editions of the word of God in the vernacular. As is always the case when the Bible is circulated among the laity, the believers became imbued with the spirit of evangelism. Thus Peter Waldo can be credited with contributing to the increase in numbers and influence of the Waldenses throughout the world.

However, it was not long before he felt the wrath of the papacy. When persecuted, he withdrew to the north of France. Pursued, he fled to Bohemia. When the anger of persecution turned from him to his converts, great numbers then hastened to the Waldensian valleys in Italy.

The passing of Waldo into east central Europe and the migration of large numbers of his followers into surrounding mountainous terrain were in the providence of God. The seeds of truth sown in previous centuries were beginning to grow into a large harvest. In the twelfth century there was a longing throughout Europe to return to that type of religion which Jesus pointed out when He said, "All ye are brethren." Churches with pomp and ceremonies, which had put so great a gulf between priest and people and which had graded the clergy into ascending ranks with titles of honor, were growing in disfavor. Enforcement of doctrines by law had brought rebellion. The Scriptures were now more largely circulated. Bible principles were contrasted with hierarchical canons. Multitudes, becoming aware of a more excellent Christianity shorn of ecclesiastical accretions,

---

[1]Arnaud, *The Glorious Recovery by the Vaudois*, Preface by the author, page xiv.

(246)

drew together to form large bodies. They had been called such names as Albigenses, Cathari, and Passagians. But the former multiplicity of names bestowed upon them began to disappear as they took the general name of Waldenses.[2]

On the other hand, the priests who had allied themselves with kings, generals, and world officials were determined to hold what temporal power they had acquired and to possess the seat of absolute authority. Their aggressions were so plainly visible and their harsh, domineering spirit so keenly resented that the masses could no longer link heresy with vice. The attempt to dub people as criminals for freedom of belief, brought growing resentment. Therefore, the name Waldenses was found more on the people's lips, a title that was to be synonymous in Europe with the Christianity set forth by Christ and the apostles in the New Testament.

How dreadfully the Waldenses suffered under persecution is a well-known story in all histories. Their steadfastness and their victory was nothing short of miraculous. Much of the liberty, enlightenment, and advance of civilization today can be attributed to the faithfulness of the Church in the Wilderness, and especially to the courageous Waldenses because of their valiant and truimphant efforts to maintain the principles of democracy.

Their Records Destroyed

Persecution was not the only way of waging war against the evangelicals. Their records were systematically destroyed. In the empires of antiquity a new conqueror often followed up his purging of the preceding dynasty by the destruction of all writings telling of its past, even to the extent of chiseling annals from stone monuments. In like manner the noble and voluminous literature of the Waldenses, whether of the Italian, French, or Spanish branches, was almost completely obliterated by the rage of the papacy.[3] Only fragments remain. For the rest, one must use the tirades written to vilify them, the accounts of papal inquisitors, the reports of investigators to their prelates, and the decrees and sentences pronounced by emperors, papal councils, and the Inquisition against them to aid in reconstructing their history.

---

[2] Benedict, *A General History of the Baptist Denomination*, vol. 1, p. 112.
[3] Gilly, *Waldensian Researches*, page 39; Jones, *The History of the Christian Church*, vol. 2, p. 6; Robinson, *Ecclesiastical Researches*, page 178.

Learning of the Waldenses

The Waldensian pastors and teachers were well trained. To refute the reproach sometimes cast on them, the following quotations are given. Alexis Muston writes:

> Gilles says, "This Vaudois people have had pastors of great learning . . . versed in the languages of the Holy Scriptures . . . and very laborious . . . especially in transcribing to the utmost of their ability, the books of Holy Scripture, for the use of their disciples."[4]

S. V. Bompiani states:

> Unfortunately many of these books were lost during the persecutions of the seventeenth century, and only those books and ancient documents sent to the libraries of Cambridge and Geneva by Pastor Leger were preserved. The papists took care after every persecution to destroy as much of the Waldensian literature as possible. Many of the barbes were learned men and well versed in the languages and science of the Scriptures. A knowledge of the Bible was the distinctive feature of the ancient, and is now of the modern Vaudois. . . . Deprived for centuries of a visible church, and forced to worship in caves and dens, this intimate knowledge of God's word was their only light. Their school was in the almost inaccessible solitude of a deep mountain gorge called Pra del Tor, and their studies were severe and long-continued, embracing the Latin, Romaunt, and Italian languages.[5]

Alexis Muston also writes:

> Superstition, obscuring the moral and religious perceptions, casts its shadows equally over all the regions of human intelligence; as, on the other hand, also, the light of the gospel . . . elevates, augments, and purifies all the powers of the mind. Of this, the Vaudois themselves are a proof, for they had taken their place, . . . at the head of modern literature, having been the first to write in the vulgar tongue. That which they then used was the Romance language, for all the early remains of which we are indebted to the Vaudois. It was from this language that the French and Italian were formed. The religious poems of the Vaudois still continue to be the most perfect compositions belonging to that period; and they are also those in which the rays of the gospel shine with the greatest brightness.[6]

The idea engendered and fostered by Rome that the Waldenses were few in number, without much organization or learning, and de-

[4] Muston, *The Israel of the Alps*, vol. 2, p. 448.
[5] Bompiani, *A Short History of the Italian Waldenses*, pages 56, 57.
[6] Muston, *The Israel of the Alps*, vol. 1, p. 36.

pendent upon Rome for their Bible and culture is dispelled by abundant trustworthy and scholarly testimony. Much proof can be produced to show that in some places the nobility were members of the Waldensian churches; that among them were the greatest scholars and theologians of the age; that among them were leaders in language, literature, music, and oratory.

Their missionary endeavors were widespread. How powerful their influence was upon the Reformation is well expressed in the following quotation:

> Seemingly they took no share in the great struggle which was going on around them in all parts of Europe, but in reality they were exercising a powerful influence upon the world. Their missionaries were everywhere, proclaiming the simple truths of Christianity, and stirring the hearts of men to their very depths. In Hungary, in Bohemia, in France, in England, in Scotland, as well as in Italy, they were working with tremendous, though silent power. Lollard, who paved the way for Wycliffe in England, was a missionary from these Valleys. . . . In Germany and Bohemia the Vaudois teachings heralded, if they did not hasten, the Reformation, and Huss and Jerome, Luther and Calvin did little more than carry on the work begun by the Vaudois missionaries.[7]

The extent to which the doctrines of the Waldenses or Albigenses had been accepted by the nobility may be seen by the following quotation from Philip Mornay:

> Many great and noble men joined unto them as namely, Raymund Earle of Toulouse and of S. Giles, the king's cousin, Raymund Roger Vicount of Besiers and of Carcarsonne, Peter Roger Lord of Cabaret, Raymund, Earle of Foix, near kinsman to the king of Arragon, Gasto Prince of Bearn, the Earle of Bigorre, the Lady of the Vaur, the Earle of Carman, Raymund de Termes, Americ de Montreuil, William de Menerbe, and infinite others, both Lords and Gentlemen, men truly of that rank, that no man of sound judgment will think, they would have exposed to manifest danger their life fortunes and honor for the defense of vices and errors so execrable as they were charged with all.[8]

After early schooling it was not uncommon for the Waldensian youth to proceed to the seminaries in the great cities of Lombardy or to the University of Paris.[9]

---

[7] McCabe, *Cross and Crown*, page 32; also Perrin, *History of the Ancient Christians,* pages 47, 48.
[8] Mornay, *The Mysterie of Iniquitie,* page 354.
[9] Wylie, *The History of Protestantism,* vol. 1, pp. 29, 30.

A People of the Bible

It is indeed gratifying that this branch of the Church in the Wilderness was a Bible people. No subsequent Protestant church reverenced the Holy Scriptures more than did they. Their obedience to the Book of God was at once the cause of their incomparable success, as it was also the offense which they gave to their enemies. Through the long night of the Dark Ages these people were a sanctuary for the Holy Scriptures. They were the ark in Europe which safely carried the Bible across the stormy waters of medieval persecution.

Since the Waldenses existed from the early Christian centuries, it would naturally be expected that their first Bible in their own tongue would be in Latin. Diligent research has proved that this is so. They early possessed that beautiful Latin version of the Bible called the Itala, which was translated from Greek manuscripts.[10] This is proved by comparing the Itala version with the liturgy, or fixed form of divine service, used in the diocese of Milan for centuries, which contains many texts of Scripture from this Itala.[11] H. J. Warner says: "The version current amongst the Western heretics can be shown to be based upon the Greek and not upon the Vulgate."[12] When the fall of the Roman Empire came because of the inrush of the Teutonic peoples, the Romaunt, that beautiful speech which for centuries bridged the transition from Latin to modern Italian, had become the mother tongue of the Waldenses. They multiplied copies of the Holy Scriptures in that language for the people.[13] In those days the Bible was, of course, copied by hand.[14]

The Bible formed the basis of their congregational worship, and the children were taught to commit large portions of it to memory.[15] Societies of young people were formed with a view of committing the Bible to memory. Each member of these pious associations was entrusted with the duty of carefully preserving in his recollections a certain number of chapters; and when the assembly gathered round their minister, these young people could together recite all the chap-

---

[10] Nolan, *The Integrity of the Greek Vulgate,* pages 88, 89.
[11] Allix, *The Ancient Churches of Piedmont,* page 37.
[12] Warner, *The Albigensian Heresy,* vol. 1, p. 12.
[13] Henderson, *The Vaudois,* pages 248, 249.
[14] In a famous library in Dublin, Ireland, the writer saw one of the four extant copies of this Waldensian Bible.
[15] Bompiani, *A Short History of the Italian Waldenses,* pages 2, 3.

ters of the Book assigned by the pastor.[16] It thus can be seen how naturally their pastors, called "barbes," were a learned class.[17] They were not only proficient in the knowledge of the Bible in Latin and in the vernacular, but they were also well schooled in the original Hebrew and Greek, and they taught the youth to be missionaries in the languages which then were being used by other European peoples.

Thus through these people has been handed down to the present generation the Bible of the primitive church, which found a permanent influence in the translation of the Authorized Version.

Persecutions of the Waldenses

There were persecutions before the thirteenth century against those considered as Waldenses, who perhaps went under other names. For hundreds of years, wars of extermination were waged in order to destroy every vestige of the writings of these different bodies. No artifice, no exertion, no expense, was spared by their enemies to efface all the records of the ancient Waldenses from the face of the earth.

There was no village of the Vaudois valleys but had its martyrs. The Waldenses were burned; they were cast into damp and horrid dungeons; they were smothered in crowds in mountain caverns, mothers and babes and old men and women together; they were sent out into exile in a winter night, unclothed and unfed, to climb the snowy mountains; they were hurled over the rocks; their houses and lands were taken from them; their children were stolen to be indoctrinated with the religion that they abhorred. Rapacious individuals were sent among them to strip them of their property, to persecute, and to exterminate them. "Thousands of heretics, old men, women, and children, were hung, quartered, broken upon the wheel, or burned alive, and their property confiscated for the benefit of the king and Holy See."[18]

So many books have been written relating these circumstances and picturing these heart-rending scenes that further enumeration is unnecessary. It is sufficient to say that the Waldenses remained true to the truth. When the Reformation dawned, under Luther, Zwingle, Calvin, and others, they were ready to receive a delegation from the

---

[16] Muston, *The Israel of the Alps,* vol. 1, p. 52.
[17] *Ibid.,* vol. 2, p. 448.
[18] Thompson, *The Papacy and the Civil Power,* page 416.

new movement of Reformers who came to inquire of their beliefs. There were enough of them left in 1550, according to W. S. Gilly, so that eight hundred thousand souls in the Alpine provinces continued to refuse to accept the beliefs and practices of the papacy.[19]

Truth Planted in Many Lands

Urged on by the power of truth triumphant, the Waldenses went forth to Europe. How widespread was the work of this noble people may be seen in the words of Samuel Edgar:

> The Waldenses, as they were ancient, were also numerous. Vignier, from other historians, gives a high idea of their populousness. The Waldenses, says this author, multiplied wonderfully in France, as well as in other countries of Christendom. They had many patrons in Germany, France, Italy, and especially in Lombardy, notwithstanding the papal exertions for their extirpation.
>
> This sect, says Nangis, were infinite in number; appeared, says Rainerus, in nearly every country; multiplied, says Sanderus, through all lands; infected, says Caesarius, a thousand cities; and spread their contagion, says Ciaconius, through almost the whole Latin world. Scarcely any region, says Gretzer, remained free and untainted from this pestilence. The Waldensians, says Popliner, spread, not only through France, but also through nearly all the European coasts, and appear in Gaul, Spain, England, Scotland, Italy, Germany, Bohemia, Saxony, Poland, and Lithuania. Matthew Paris represents this people as spread through.Bulgaria, Croatia, Dalmatia, Spain, and Germany. Their number, according to Benedict, was prodigious in France, England, Piedmont, Sicily, Calabria, Poland, Bohemia, Saxony, Pomerania, Germany, Livonia, Sarmatia, Constantinople, Philadelphia, and Bulgaria.[20]

Some have claimed that the Albigenses were different from the Waldenses. However, the truth is that they did not differ in belief. They are called Albigenses only because of Albi, the French city which was their headquarters. But the decrees of the popes have condemned them as Waldenses; papal "legates made war against them as professing the beliefe of the Waldenses; the monks Inquisitors, have formed their Proces and Indictments as against the Waldenses: the people have persecuted them as being such. . . . Many historiographers call them Waldenses."[21]

---

[19] Gilly, *Waldensian Researches,* page 76.
[20] Edgar, *The Variations of Popery,* pages 51, 52.
[21] Perrin, *Luther's Forerunners,* pt. 2, pp. 1, 2.

How the Waldenses or Albigenses made converts among Bulgarians the following quotation from Philip Mornay will show:

> Matthew Paris saith further, That they spread themselves so far as into Bulgaria, Croatia, and Dalmatia, and there took such root, that they drew unto them many bishops: and thither came one Bartholomew from Carcassone in the country of Narbon in France, unto whom they all flocked, . . . and he created bishops, and ordained churches.[22]

Protestantism a Glorious Fruit of Waldensianism

In 1517, the dawn of the Protestant Reformation came to Europe. Protestantism was not so much a separation from the Church of Rome as it was a revival of apostolic doctrines so long held by the Waldenses. Protestantism was a spiritual expansion of the Church in the Wilderness. Of the remaining evangelical churches which had come down from the days of the apostles, the Waldenses were the purest and the most prominent. James D. McCabe writes concerning the delegates of early Reformers sent to a synodal assembly of the Waldenses:

> Thus the time passed on until the Reformation dawned upon the world. The Vaudois were well pleased at this general awakening of the human mind. They entered into correspondence with the Reformers in various parts of Europe, and sent several of their Barbas to them to instruct them. The Reformers on their part, admitted the antiquity of the Vaudois rites and the purity of their faith, and treated the mountain church with the greatest respect. On the twelfth of September, 1532, a Synodal Assembly was held at Angrogna. It was attended by a number of deputies from the Reformed Churches in France and Switzerland. Among them was William Farrel of France. . . . He manifested the greatest interest in the manuscript copies of the Bible which the Vaudois had preserved from the earliest times, and at his instance the entire Bible was translated into French, and sent as a free gift from the Vaudois to the French Church.[23]

The simplicity and purity of their lives was the result of the simplicity and purity of their doctrines. They followed the command of the apostle John that no man should add to, nor take from, the word of God. This attitude was a great defense against error, and constituted the divine rule for success in missionary enterprises. Even their enemies admitted that their beliefs were like those of the early Christians. An enumeration of these beliefs sounds like the preachings of

---

[22] Mornay, *The Mysterie of Iniquitie*, page 392.
[23] McCabe, *Cross and Crown*, page 37.

Vigilantius in the fourth century and of Claude in the eighth. Antoine Monastier shows in the following words some of the errors that they rejected:

> The ancient Vaudois constantly rejected doctrines that were based on authority and human tradition; they repelled, with holy indignation and honor, images, crosses, and relics, as objects of veneration or worship; the adoration and intercession of the blessed Virgin Mary and the saints; they consequently rejected the feasts consecrated to these same saints, the prayers addressed to them, the incense and tapers that were burned in their honor; they likewise rejected the mass, auricular confession, purgatory, extreme unction, and prayers for the dead, holy water, Lent, abstinence from meat at certain times and on certain days, imposed fasts and penances, processions, pilgrimages, the celibacy of the clergy, monkery, etc., etc. Their declaration on these points is as explicit as it is strong.[24]

Reinerius, their enemy, was obliged to admit that they were a commandment-keeping people:

> Concerning their manners, he [Reinerius] writes, they were modest, simple, meddling little with bargains or contracts. . . . That the first rules and instructions which for rudiments they gave unto their children was the Decalogue of the law, the Ten Commandments.[25]

It was to be expected that persecutions, isolation, and desperate circumstances would tear away many of the people from some of their beliefs; and that at times there would be a certain amount of conformity to papal practices. Furthermore, when the Reformation, manifesting extreme liberalism in many things, swept over Europe, it had a great influence upon the ancient churches which had long suffered for many of the doctrines to which the Reformers turned. These ancient churches possessed in many points identical beliefs with those announced by the Reformation. Unfortunately, in their joy over the Reformation they conformed to certain shortcomings of the Reformers. The Reformation was a mighty influence for good as far as it went; but it is widely recognized that it did not go far enough.[26] Others than the pioneer Reformers were obliged to labor for the further restoration of primitive Christian beliefs and practices in the churches that were sincerely following the Master's precepts.

---

[24] Monastier, *A History of the Vaudois Church,* pages 83, 84.
[25] Mornay, *The Mysterie of Iniquitie,* page 449.
[26] Muir, *The Arrested Reformation,* page 3.

Did the Early Waldenses Keep the Sabbath?

Before taking up the specific cases of the observance of the Sabbath by the ancient Waldenses, it would be profitable to glance at the status of Sunday observance at the end of what is usually reckoned to be the first period of church history, terminating in the Council of Nicaea (A. D. 325).

Constantine, who was the first Christian ruler of the Roman Empire at the time when the church and the state were coming together in perfect union, issued his now-famous Sunday law (A. D. 321). A comment upon this by a leading Roman Catholic journal states the case clearly:

> The emperor Constantine after his conversion to Christianity, made the observance of Sunday a civil duty, and the law which commanded it is found in the Roman code. "Let all judges and people of the town rest, and the trades of various kinds be suspended on the venerable day of the sun. Those who live in the country may, however, freely and without fault apply to agriculture, because it often happens that this day is the most favorable for sowing wheat ·and planting the vine, lest an opportunity offered by divine liberality be lost with the favorable moment." Now we can scarcely conceive that Constantine would have excepted agricultural labor, if the church had from time immemorial strictly forbidden among Christians that kind of work which it prohibited at a later period. . . . Hence it has been the unanimous doctrine of divines, from time immemorial, that cessation from servile work is not only a point of discipline liable to change but it can be dispensed with by the ecclesiastical authority whenever a reasonable cause presents itself.[27]

There is ample evidence to show that the above quotation does not reveal any incidental condition or anything unusual in the observance of Sunday in the fourth century. This was not only the custom of the state church in general, but it can be proved that the same church claimed that she had power enough to institute Sunday in the beginning, and also to say how much work should or should not be done on that day. As evidence, another quotation from the same journal is given:

> To place the subject in a clearer light, we may state that, according to many learned writers it was not strictly commanded to abstain from work on Sunday during the first ages of the church. This day was undoubtedly viewed by Christians as a day of joy, of triumph, and of gratitude

---

[27] *The United States Catholic Magazine*, Index to vol. 4, 1845, pp. 233, 234.

to God; and they convened in the church to offer their homage to the Almighty; but there is no evidence to show that cessation from work was considered obligatory; probably because there might have been some danger of Judaism in this cessation from work, and perhaps also because practice, in the time of persecution, would have greatly exposed the professors of Christianity. It was deemed sufficient to substitute public prayer for the Jewish Sabbath, particularly as the latter was observed by many of the faithful.[28]

Thus it can be seen that Sunday in the early Christian centuries was not a holy day of divine appointment; but was, rather, appointed by man, and physical labor was carried on. From the quotations of church historians which follow, it will be seen that in the churches of the East as well as in all the churches of the West, except Rome, the Sabbath was publicly observed by those who were courageous enough to withstand the rising tide of those endeavoring to appease a sun-worshiping heathen world which gave special prominence to Sunday.

In contrast to the questionable beginnings of Sunday, consider the seventh-day Sabbath at the same time. The following two quotations have been given before, but are worthy of repetition. Socrates, a church historian of the fourth century, wrote thus: "For although almost all the churches throughout the world celebrate the sacred mysteries on the Sabbath of every week, yet the Christians of Alexandria and at Rome, on account of some ancient tradition, have ceased to do this."[29]

Another quotation from the church historian, Sozomen, who was a contemporary of Socrates, declares: "The people of Constantinople, and almost everywhere, assemble together on the Sabbath, as well as on the first day of the week, which custom is never observed at Rome or at Alexandria."[30]

The substance of these two quotations reveals that the Christianity of the Greek Church was a Sabbathkeeping Christianity; and that the Christianity of the West, with the exception of the city of Rome and possibly Alexandria, was also a Sabbathkeeping Christianity.

---

[28]*The United States Catholic Magazine*, Index to vol. 4, 1845, p. 233.
[29]Socrates, *Ecclesiastical History*, b. 5, ch. 22, found in *Nicene and Post-Nicene Fathers*, 2nd Series, vol. 2.
[30]Sozomen, *Ecclesiastical History*, b. 7, ch. 19, found in *Nicene and Post-Nicene Fathers*, 2d Series, vol. 2.

However, there is more specific information regarding the observance of the Sabbath before 325 when one considers the history of Spain. Spain had the good fortune to escape for centuries any marked influence of the church at Rome. Its church history is divided into two periods: first, that which covered the time up to 325; and secondly, the period between 325 and 1200. For the first four centuries it is more than fortunate that the eighty-one church resolutions or canons passed by the council held at Elvira, Spain (c. A. D. 305), still exist.

The records of the Council of Elvira reveal three things: first, up until the time of that council, the Church of Spain had adopted no creed, and certainly not the creed later adopted at Nicaea;[31] secondly, punishment of faulty members by the church did not go farther than dismissal, for there was no appeal to civil law; thirdly, up to the time of the Council of Elvira, movements toward a union of the church and the state had made no progress, but it was evident that attempts were being made along that line.

When it is a matter of inquiry as to what was the attitude of Christians in Spain on Sabbath observance, the evidence is clear. Canon 26 of the Council of Elvira reveals that the Church of Spain at that time kept Saturday, the seventh day. "As to fasting every Sabbath: Resolved, that the error be corrected of fasting every Sabbath."[32] This resolution of the council is in direct opposition to the policy the church at Rome had inaugurated, that of commanding Sabbath as a fast day in order to humiliate it and make it repugnant to the people.[33]

What connection is there between these facts and the early Waldenses? It is this: that while for centuries Christianity in Spain was one, yet when the encroachments by Rome on these primitive Christians in Spain began, the people of the Pyrenees separated themselves from the errors that crept in upon them. Robert Robinson writes that the people living in the valleys in different countries became known as the "valley dwellers," or Vallenses. In fact, this author

---

[31] Robinson, *Ecclesiastical Researches,* page 180. It should be noted that some church historians place the date of the Council of Elvira at A. D. 324; among these is Michael Geddes, an eminent authority on Spanish church history.

[32] "Errorem placuit corrigi, ut omni Sabbati die superpositiones celebremus."— Mansi, *Sacrorum Conciliorum Nova et Amplissima Collectio,* vol, 2. p. 10.

[33] See the author's discussion in Chapter xx, entitled, "The Great Struggle in India," pages 324-326.

states his belief that the inhabitants of the Pyrenees were the true original Waldenses.[34] The original word is the Latin, *vallis*. From it came "valleys" in English, Valdesi in Italian, Vaudois in French, and Valdenses in Spanish.[35] Resolution 26 of the Council of Elvira having revealed that the early church of Spain kept the Sabbath, and history having proved that the Waldenses of north Spain existed at that time, these connections prove the keeping of the seventh-day Sabbath by the early Waldenses in Spain.

It is a point of further interest to note that in northeastern Spain near the city of Barcelona is a city called Sabadell, in a district originally inhabited, in all probability, by a people called both "Valdenses" and "Sabbatati."[36] Could not this name, Sabadell, have originated from the expression, "dell of the Sabbathkeepers"? It is also shown that the name Sabbatati comes from the fact of their keeping the Sabbath. There are still in the vicinity of Sabadell archaeological remains of these ancient peoples.[37]

Many centuries later when the papacy rose to dominion in Spain, and persecution fell upon these dwellers in the valley, they often would go over to northern Italy where they were welcomed and given a home among the Waldenses of the Alps.[38]

The Waldenses, a Bible People

The stronger the church at Rome grew, the greater was the emphasis placed upon Sunday. On the other hand, the churches which continued in apostolic Christianity clung as long as possible to the day which Jesus Christ and the apostles sanctified.

The Waldenses were so thoroughly a Bible people that they kept the seventh-day Sabbath as the sacred rest day for centuries. Two centuries after Pope Gregory I (A. D. 602) had issued the bull against the community of Sabbathkeepers in the city of Rome, a church council which disclosed the extent of Sabbathkeeping in that peninsula was held at Friaul, northern Italy (c. A. D. 791). Friaul was one of the three large duchies into which the Lombard kingdom had been

---

[34] Robinson, *Ecclesiastical Researches,* page 299.
[35] *Ibid.,* page 302.
[36] *Ibid.,* page 310.
[37] The writer had the privilege of visiting Sabadell many years ago and assisting in the baptism of Christian converts.
[38] Robinson, *Ecclesiastical Researches,* pages 319-321.

originally organized. This council, in its command to all Christians to observe the Lord's Day, testified to the wide observance of Saturday as follows: "Further when speaking of that Sabbath which the Jews observe, the last day of the week, which also all peasants observe.[39] About one hundred years later (A. D. 865-867), when the sharp contest between the Church of Rome and the Greek Church over the newly converted Bulgarians and their observance of the Sabbath came to the front, the question again entered into the controversy, as can be seen in the reply of Pope Nicolas I to the one hundred six questions propounded to him by the Bulgarian king.[40]

Peter Allix, speaking of an author who was discussing the doctrines of the Waldenses, writes: "He lays it down also as one of their opinions; that the Law of Moses is to be kept according to the letter, and that the keeping of the Sabbath, circumcision, and other legal observances, ought to take place."[41] However, the accusation that they practiced circumcision has been repeatedly proved to be false. Writing of the Passagians, who are taken to be a branch of the Waldenses, David Benedict says:

"The account of their practicing circumcision is undoubtedly a slanderous story forged by their enemies, and probably arose in this way. Because they observed the seventh day, they were called, by way of derision, Jews, as the Sabbatarians are frequently at this day; and if they were Jews, it followed of course, that they either did or ought to circumcise their followers. This was probably the reasoning of their enemies; but that they actually practiced the bloody rite, is altogether improbable."[42]

Adam Blair says:

Among the documents we have by the same peoples, an explanation of the Ten Commandments, dated by Boyer 1120. It contains a compend of Christian morality. Supreme love to God is enforced, and recourse to the influence of the planets and to sorcerers, is condemned. The evil of worshiping God by images and idols is pointed out. A solemn oath to confirm anything doubtful is admitted, but profane swearing is forbidden. Observation of the Sabbath, by ceasing from worldly labors and from sin, by good works, and by promoting the edification of the soul through prayer and hearing the word, is enjoined.[43]

---

[39] Mansi, *Sacrorum Conciliorum Nova et Amplissima Collectio,* vol. 13, p. 852.
[40] *Responsa Nicolai Papae I ad Consulta Bulgarorum,* Responsum 10, found in Mansi, *Sacrorum Conciliorum Nova et Amplissima Collectio,* vol. 15, p. 406.
[41] Allix, *The Ancient Churches of Piedmont,* page 154.
[42] Benedict, *A General History of the Baptist Denomination,* vol. 2, p. 414.
[43] Blair, *History of the Waldenses,* vol. 1, p. 220.

In spite of the fury of the oppressors, the protecting hand of Christ was on His commandment-keeping people. They grew in numbers. But it was not until the twelfth century that the bishop of Rome became terrified over the growth of the Waldenses. The so-called heretics in southern France were in reality the western portion of the Waldenses, and were usually referred to as Albigenses because of their great numbers in the large city of Albi. The province in which Albi attracted attention was in alliance with the king of France, though not incorporated legally into that realm. The papacy was allied with the French kings. A synod of "heretics" was held in 1167 in the district of Toulouse at which were present Cathari from Lombardy and Italy, as well as from France. Nicetas, the Paulician leader or bishop at Constantinople, attended by request and presided.[44] Yet the Paulicians, as Adeney indicates, disregarded Sunday and sanctified Saturday.[45]

In order to meet the new economic conditions in which the Roman Church found itself and to combat the threat of heresy, two orders of monks were formed—the Franciscans and the Dominicans. As one author writes: "It has been affirmed that the orders of the Franciscans and Dominicans were instituted to silence the Waldenses."[46]

As to the persecutions suffered by the Waldenses for Sabbath-keeping, the following is found in the decree of Alphonso, published about 1194:

> Alphonse, king of Aragon etc., to all archbishops, bishops, and to all others: . . . "We command you in imitation of our ancestors and in obedience to the ordinances of the church, that heretics, to wit, Waldenses, Insabbathi and those who call themselves the poor of Lyons and all other heretics should be expelled away from the face of God and from all Catholics and ordered to depart from our kingdom."[47]

The use of the term "Insabbathi" in the previous quotation, designating those who should be expelled from Spain, leads to a consideration of Spanish Sabbathkeepers in medieval times. That the Insabbatati were Waldenses is proved by the statement of Bernard Gui, famous program builder of the Inquisition, that "Ensavatés [Insab-

---

[44] Warner, *The Albigensian Heresy*, vol. 1, p. 15.
[45] Adeney, *The Greek and Eastern Churches*, page 218.
[46] Gilly, *Waldensian Researches*, page 98, note 2.
[47] Marianae, *Praefatio in Lucam Tudensem*, found in *Maxima Bibliotheca Veterum Patrum*, vol. 25, p. 190.

batati] was the name given to the Vaudois."[48] Abundance of evidence can be produced to show that these Sabbathkeepers were interchangeably called Waldenses and Insabbatati.[49]

There are two items of interest which throw light upon the term "Insabbathi" used in the decree of King Alphonso (A. D. 1194) as given above. The first item is that there was a Gothic Spanish liturgy.[50] It was very different from that of Rome, and was not abolished until 1088.[51] The following quotation from Michael Geddes will help to show the interrelationship of the facts: "The papal supremacy was a thing not known in the ancient Gothick Catholic Church: So that the popish doctrines of transubstantiation, and of purgatory, and of praying to angels and saints, and of adoring images, and of auricular confessions, etc. were as little known in her; may, I conceive, easily be proved from her records, which are extant."[52] Then the author goes on to say in the same paragraph that the faith in the ancient Spanish Gothic Church was the same as that of the ancient British Church. The reader needs only to refer to former chapters in this book to be able to rehearse the evidences there given that the ancient British or Celtic Church sanctified the seventh day as the Sabbath of the fourth commandment. This constitutes another link in the chain of evidence that the term Insabbatati refers to the keeping of the seventh day as the Sabbath.

The second item of interest is worthy of special note. The decree of King Alphonso of Aragon was given in the year 1194. This indicates how late in the Middle Ages the Waldenses were keeping the Sabbath in Spain. That papal authors in Germany, Italy, and France about the same time as the above decree were putting forth their writings against the Sabbatati, or Insabbatati, discloses how many and widespread were these people. There is an abundance of reference to "heretics" under the name of Sabbatati, or Insabbatati, in the records of the Inquisition. Explanations of their belief, however, are scarce because, as Robert Robinson writes: "It was a maxim with the catholicks to avoid the mention of heresy in their synods, lest it should

---

[48] Gui, *Manuel d' Inquisiteur,* vol. 2, p. 158.
[49] Du Cange, *Glossarium Mediae et Infimae Latinitatis,* art. "Sabatati."
[50] Geddes, *Miscellaneous Tracts,* vol. 2, p. 26.
[51] Whishaw, *Arabic Spain,* pages 19, 20; also Mosheim, *Institutes of Ecclesiastical History,* b. 3, cent. 11, pt. 2, ch. 4, par. 1.
[52] Geddes, *Miscellaneous Tracts,* vol. 2, p. 71.

create a desire in any to inquire what it was. They forbad preachers to quote even their good arguments lest the people should entertain a favorable opinion of the authors."[53]

These terms Sabbati, Sabbata, Insabbatati refer to keeping the seventh day as the Sabbath. The historian Goldast says of those who were called Insabbatati, "They were called Insabbatti, not because they were circumcised, but because they kept the Sabbath according to the Jewish law."[54]

Shortly after the decree of King Alphonso against the Insabbatati there flourished a fervent papal writer in Spain who has subsequently obtained considerable notoriety. This was Lucas of the city of Tuy, generally known as Lucas Tudensis. His writings make it clear how strong and how numerous were the Insabbatati in Spain about 1260. Lucas died about seventy-five years before the appearance of Wycliffe, "Morning Star of the Reformation." A splendid summary of his writings is given as follows:

> Those, who will take the trouble to read this work, and observe how fondly Lucas dwells upon the presumed opinions of Isidore, the Spanish saint, how he laments that Spanish enthusiasm should be cooled, and should not burst out in arms against the enemies of the Catholic faith—how he declaims against heretical conventicles—the public disputations of heretics—their profanation of the parish churches—the arrival of Arnald in Spain and the transactions at Leon,—will perceive that the mind of Lucas was occupied by the consideration of Spanish, and not of Albigensian, or foreign nonconformity.[55]

The following testimony concerning the Sabbath was given by a Waldensian prisoner before the Inquisition (probably in Freiburg, Germany):

> Barbara Von Thies testified . . . That on the last Saint Michael's day concerning confession as it is administered by the priests she has nothing to do with it. As to that which has to do with the Virgin Mary, on that she has nothing to answer. Concerning Sunday and feast days she says: "The Lord God commanded us to rest on the seventh day and with that I let it be; with God's help and His grace, we all would stand by and die in the faith, for it is the right faith and the right way in Christ."[56]

---

[53] Robinson, *Ecclesiastical Researches,* pages 271, 272.
[54] Quoted by Dr. Jacob Gretzer, *Opera Omnia,* vol. 12, pt. 2, p. 11.
[55] Gilly, *Waldensian Researches,* pages 102, 103.
[56] *Der Blutige Schau-Platz, Oder Martyrer Spiegel der Taufs Gesinnten,* b. 2, pp. 30, 31.

The blessing of Christ upon these, His persecuted children, was so great that they entered into many lands. Mosheim declares that, prior to the age of Luther, there lay concealed in almost every country of Europe—especially in Bohemia, Moravia, Switzerland, and Germany—many persons in whose minds were deeply rooted the principles of the Waldenses, the Wycliffites, and the Hussites.[57]

The Sabbath of of the fourth commandment was observed among these peoples in obedience to the moral law. How high was the standing of Sabbatarians among lords and princes may be seen from the following quotation of Lamy:

> All the counsellors and great lords of the court, who were already fallen in with the doctrines of Wittenburg, of Ausburg, Geneva, and Zurich, as Petrowitz, Jasper Cornis, Christopher Famigali, John Gerendi, head of the *Sabbatarians,* a people who did not keep Sunday, but Saturday, and whose disciples took the names of Genoldists. All these, and others, declared 'for the opinions of Blandrat.[58]

There is an abundance of testimony to show the harmonious chain of doctrine extending from the days of the apostles down to the Reformation and later, including the beliefs held by the believers of northern Italy, the Albigenses, the Wycliffites, and the Hussites. Andre Favyn, a well-known Roman Catholic historian, who wrote in French, traces the teachings of Luther back through Vigilantius to Jovinianus, claiming that Vigilantius gave his doctrines to "the Albigenses, who otherwise were called the Waldenses," and that they in turn passed them on to the Wycliffites and the followers of Huss and Jerome in Bohemia.[59]

Inspired by their Redeemer, the Waldenses were always going forth in missionary labors. Because of this, they were in some places at certain times called Passaginians. Thus Gilly writes (in *Waldensian Researches,* page 61, note 2): "Passagii and Passagini, or the inhabitants of the passes, from the Latin word *passagium,* is one of the names given by ancient authors to the Waldenses."

A large proportion of the Waldenses, whether called by that name or by other names, believed the observance of the fourth commandment to be obligatory upon the human race. Because of this they were

---

[57] Mosheim, *Institutes of Ecclesiastical History,* b. 4, cent. 16, sec. 3, pt. 2, ch. 3, par. 2.
[58] Lamy, *The History of Socinianism,* page 60.
[59] Favyn, *Histoire de Navarre,* pages 713-715.

designated by the significant title of Insabbati, or Insabbatati. Farmers or townsmen going on Saturday about their work were so impressed by the sight of groups of Christians assembling for worship on that day that they called them Insabbatati. The term "Sabbath" was almost never applied to Sunday. Speaking of Constantine's Sunday law of 321, Robert Cox writes: "No evidence has been adduced, that before the enactment of this law there was Sabbatical observance of the Lord's Day in any part of Christendom." [60]

That the Waldenses would be committed to Saturday as the Sabbath can be seen in these words: "They hold that none of the ordinances of the church that have been introduced since Christ's ascension ought to be observed, being of no worth; the feasts, fasts, orders, blessings, offices of the church and the like, they utterly reject." [61] This is said of them in Bohemia. Erasmus testifies that even as late as about 1500 these Bohemians not only kept the seventh day scrupulously, but also were called Sabbatarians. [62]

Thus, from direct historical statements, from unquestioned historical evidence that under various names and designations the Waldenses kept the Sabbath, as well as from their being called Sabbatati, Insabbatati, and other forms of this name, it is plain that one of the fundamental teachings and practices of the larger part of the Waldenses was that of observing the seventh day as the sacred day of the fourth commandment.

The Waldenses and the Reformation

Although the reformed churches transformed the face of Europe, they failed to reject certain Latin practices which arose later to plague them. Pastor Robinson, in his farewell address to the Pilgrims departing from the shores of Holland to seek a new world, said that it was impossible for churches (referring to the Reformers) which had lately come out of such thick anti-Christian darkness to have received all the light.

Perhaps, if the churches of the Piedmont, in their joy and boundless feelings of fraternity toward the new army of Protestants, had been able to continue to hold to their ancient purity, the question concern-

---

[60] Cox, *The Literature of the Sabbath Question,* vol. 1, p. 257.
[61] See Lewis, *A Critical History of Sabbath and Sunday,* pages 211, 212.
[62] Cox, *The Literature of the Sabbath Question,* vol. 2, pp. 201, 202.

ing the modern Waldenses' tallying with the accounts of their primitive and medieval brethren would not now be raised. The answer is found in the events of 1630.

> The descendants of the Waldenses who lived shut up in the valleys of Piedmont, were led by their proximity to the French and Genevans to embrace their doctrines and worship. Yet they retained not a few of their ancient rules of discipline, so late as the year 1630. But in this year the greatest part of the Waldenses were swept off by pestilence; and their new teachers, whom they obtained from France, regulated all their affairs according to the pattern of the French Reformed Church.[63]

Although the Waldenses were one in essential doctrines with the churches of the Reformation, they did not lose their separate organization. The reformed churches grew in power to such an extent that in countries like Germany and England, they were free from Rome's persecutions. This, however, was not the case of the Waldenses, still under the rule of Italy.

After a synod when a delegation of Reformers met with them, they vowed to witness publicly more boldly than ever before. January 21, 1561, the day after delegates from their churches had sworn eternal friendship upon the snowy summits of the Alps, a decree from their enemies was published ordering all Waldenses to attend mass. After warlike attempts to drag them to the galleys, the stake, the prison, and the gallows, they developed such resistance and endurance that the duke of Savoy, influenced by his Protestant wife, granted them amnesty.

The persecution which raged from 1655 to 1689 was most terrible. It all but extinguished this evangelical people. Horrible massacres, incredible acts of perfidy, burning of villages, children torn from their mothers to be dashed against the rocks, hosts of fugitives driven across the borders—such revolting acts as these followed one another. Half of the Waldenses were driven into exile for three and half years. Concerning the persecutions of this period, one authority states: "In 1655 the persecution raged again, and if all the Protestant powers of Europe had not interposed, a complete annihilation of the Waldenses would have been the result."[64] In 1689, their pastor and hero, Henri

---

[63]Mosheim, *Institutes of Ecclesiastical History*, b. 4, cent. 16, sec. 3, pt. 2, ch. 2, par. 25.
[64]M'Clintock and Strong, *Cyclopedia*, art. "Waldenses."

Arnaud, led nine hundred of their warriors from Switzerland to the border town of Balsille. All winter they resisted an army of ten thousand. When all seemed lost the duke of Savoy joined the Protestant prince of Holland, and they were permitted to return in peace to their valleys. This great exploit is called the "Glorious Return." By the time the 1260-year period had run out, this faithful branch of the Church in the Wilderness had secured religious toleration.

The persecution of the Waldenses led John Milton to write his famous sonnet, "On the Late Massacre in Piedmont."

> Avenge, O Lord, Thy slaughtered saints, whose bones
> Lie scattered on the Alpine mountains cold,
> Ev'n them who kept Thy truth so pure of old
> When all our fathers worshiped stocks and stones.
> Forget not: in Thy book record their groans
> Who were Thy sheep and in their ancient fold
> Slain by the bloody Piedmontese that rolled
> Mother with infant down the rocks. Their moans
> The vales redoubled to the hills, and they
> To heaven. Their martyred blood and ashes sow
> O'er all the Italian fields where still doth sway
> The triple tyrant: that from these may grow
> A hundredfold, who have learned Thy way,
> Early may fly the Babylonian woe.

A World-Wide Awakening to Bible Prophecies

Protestantism was largely an abundant fruitage of the Church in the Wilderness. Protestantism rejected the development theory, an important and essential doctrine of Romanism. Through this theory the papacy claims innate power to go on developing the teachings of the apostles. Through it Rome went on in its development of doctrine until it brought forth teachings contrary to the Bible. Cardinal Gibbons writes, "The Scriptures alone do not contain all the truths which a Christian is bound to believe."[65]

Protestantism was a return to the Bible. It emphasized a more and more conscientious and enlightened application of scriptural truths. Protestantism grew mightily, and as it went on in expanding Bible study, its churches awoke in the eighteenth century to the urgent necessity of heeding the warnings wrapped up in Bible prophecies. Intensive study was applied to the great prophetic time periods.

---

[65] Gibbons, *The Faith of Our Fathers*, p. 111, 63d ed.; p. 86, 76th ed.

Thus John Wesley cried out in 1756 concerning the two-horned beast of Revelation 13 : "He has not yet come, though he cannot be far off; for he is to appear at the end of the forty-two months of the first beast."[66]

The 1260-year period of prophecy had become the concern of all. This led to a closer study of the seventy weeks of Daniel 9 in which the date of Christ's crucifixion was a determining factor. The time was near for the church to come up out of the wilderness. This led to prayerful and learned consideration of the longer 2300-day period of Daniel 8. Bible societies sprang into existence; missionary associations were formed. Missionaries departed into all lands to announce that "the time of the end" had come. The centuries of faithfulness seen in the history of the Church in the Wilderness were succeeded by the period of the Remnant Church who would "keep the commandments of God, and the faith of Jesus."[67]

---

[66] Notes on Revelation 14.
[67] Revelation 14:12.

CHAPTER XVII

Aba and the Church in Persia

In the sixth century, according to the report of a Nestorian traveler, Christianity was successfully preached to the Bactrians, the Huns, the Persians, the Indians, the Persarmenians, the Medes, and the Elamites: the barbaric churches, from the Gulf of Persia to the Caspian Sea, were almost infinite. . . . The zeal of the Nestorians overleaped the limit which had confined the ambition and curiosity both of the Greeks and Persians. The missionaries of Balch and Samarcand pursued without fear the footsteps of the roving Tartar. . . . In their progress by sea and land the Nestorians entered China by the port of Canton.[1]

PROMINENT among the dauntless leaders who spread the faith from the Tigris eastward is Aba (c. A. D. 500-575). He is identified with that great church which has been called the Waldenses of the East. For centuries the followers of Jesus in Asia generally were called Messiahans, or Messiah people. Many renowned Messiahans who withstood the fierce opposition of the Persian state religion, or Mithraism, carried primitive Christianity to India, central Asia, China, and Japan. Outstanding among them was Aba. If the victory of Christianity over Mithraism in the Roman Empire was a European triumph, the victory of the Church in the Wilderness over this counterfeit in Persia was still more outstanding. Mithraism was proud not only of her sway in Persia, but also of having adapted Zoroastrianism to the western world; thus having paved the way for this form of sun worship to become a universal religion in the Roman world.[2]

The two centuries and a half which spanned the time between Papas (A. D. 285), the first catholicos, or supreme head over the Church of the East, to Catholicos Aba (A. D. 538), were alternating years of peace and persecution. One must recall that the supreme head of the Church of the East was called "catholicos" and his incumbency, a "catholicate." A former chapter related how in this same year the papacy was securely seated in the city of Rome. During the intervening decades there were many bright luminaries over the Assyrian

---

[1] Gibbon, *Decline and Fall of the Roman Empire*, ch. 47, par. 30.
[2] Foakes-Jackson, *The History of the Christian Church*, page 184.

Church to guide the faithful. Some of these sealed their witnessing with their blood. Persia at war with Rome naturally spelled persecution. The Persian commanders in chief did not distinguish between the papal Christianity of the Roman Empire and the Church of the Messiah. All Christians were alike to them whether the believers were of Persia or of Rome. The Iranian lords feared collusion between Persian evangelicals and Rome, and also suspected the existence of spies. Moreover, Mithraism sought to secure any occasion to attack the simple but ever-expanding Church in the Wilderness.

The sun was sacred to Mithraism. Persecutions fell upon the believers who lived and worked in the presence of the sun worshipers, and the Christians dared not say that the sun was not a living being. Mithraists imitated Bible ceremonies.[3] The Church of Rome which, according to some authorities, had imbibed much of the lure and philosophy of Mithraism, was very near to it in spirit.[4] The Christians in Persia refused the sublimated idolatry of the Iranians and suffered because they did so.

The first persecution of magnitude after the union of all districts of the Church of the East under Papas was launched by the Persian king, Shapur II. It began during the catholicate of Shimun (Simeon) and continued through forty years (A. D. 335-375). King Shapur was ambitious to recover all the territories ruled over by King Xerxes of the early Persian Empire. He launched his attack as soon as he deemed the time favorable. But church members refused to serve in the army, and the exasperation of the king knew no bounds. He was enraged not only at the defeat of his campaign, but also because the courageous defenders in the great fortress of Nisibis had withstood his attacks and had been kept alive by James, the resident bishop appointed by the church at Rome. On his return to Seleucia, the capital, the king determined to exact retribution from the Persian Christians.

The mobeds, the priests of Magianism, were at hand to arouse the wrath of the king. The first firman of persecution laid a double tax upon the Messiahans to defray the expenses of the war. Shimun, the catholicos, was ordered to collect it. He refused on the grounds of religious scruples and because of the poverty of his people. Though

---

[3] Foakes-Jackson, *The History of the Christian Church,* pages 184, 185.
[4] Newman, *A Manual of Church History,* vol. 1, p. 296.

Shimun was a personal friend of the king, nothing now was to stand in the way of teaching the Christians a lesson. The destruction of church buildings throughout the empire was commanded, and the catholicos was arrested. He was offered freedom for himself and his people if he would adore the sun but once. Upon his refusal, he, with five associates over districts and one hundred other clergy, was put to death.

Forty years of trial by fire now descended upon the children of God. Provincial governors had the power to condemn or acquit. In the case of a kind and just governor, the church fared well; but such was not usually the situation. The popular complaints sufficient to keep alive resentment against the Christians would run something like this: "They despise our sun-god. Did not Zoroaster, the sainted founder of our divine beliefs, institute Sunday one thousand years ago in honor of the sun and supplant the Sabbath of the Old Testament which the Jews in our land then sanctified? Yet these Christians have divine services on Saturday. They desecrate the sacred earth by burying their dead in it and pollute the water by their ablutions. They refuse to go to war for the shah-in-shah; and they preach that snakes, scorpions, and creeping things were created by a good God."

The intention of Shapur II to deal effectively with the followers of the New Testament did not stop with the death of Shimun. The next catholicos, elected as his successor, followed him to a martyr's grave. And when another head of the church was chosen and was also put to death, the office remained vacant for twenty years. Naturally the main objects of attack were the clergy, but the bitterest feelings were displayed against converts from Magianism. While it was true that the Church in the East did not have monasteries in the sense of the celibate life which had spread over Egypt and Europe, nevertheless there were those who believed that they could work more effectively by remaining single. Those who have lived for many generations in nations of liberty and light can little appreciate the desperate opposition which the heralds of the cross met in different lands throughout the early centuries. In the East, Christianity encountered Buddhism, a religion carried on largely by monks and nuns. To cope with such powerful antagonists as Buddhism and Zoroastrianism, there were those who naturally felt that they could do it more effectively by not marrying.

Advocacy of an unmarried clergy never had the ascendancy in the Church of the East. Such houses of celibate life would not have been able to endure in Persia. The persecution was bitter enough against the eastern theological training centers, and it was furious against unmarried clergy. The Mithraic faith was strong in advocating marriage and the presenting of children to the state who could serve in the army and be of other service.

After the death of Shapur II there was a lull for a time in the sufferings of the church. Finally, the believers gathered up strength to elect another head. Then the catholicos and leading clergy took advantage of the time of peace to reorganize the church. There was now a greater demand for stronger organization, for persecution had fired the zeal of the believers. Many of the oppressed had fled eastward to other lands, there to found new churches. It was not long, however, until in the subsequent reigns of Yazdegerd I, Bahram V, and Yazdegerd II, waves of death and destruction swept over the Persian believers. These were not as long as under Shapur II, but they were much more severe. The facts concerning the outbreak of persecution under Yazdegerd I, the first of these kings, are given by DeLacy O'Leary.

The Persian bishop of Susa, who was given to impetuosity, destroyed one of the fire temples of the Zoroastrians. Complaint being made to the king, the bishop was ordered to restore the building and to make good all damage that had been done. When the bishop refused, Yazdegerd I threatened to destroy every church in his dominion. Such orders were issued and were carried out eagerly by the Zoroastrians inflamed with jealousy against the believers. Before long the destruction of the churches developed into a general persecution. Yazdegerd I died in 420, and his son, Bahram V, increased the afflictions of the church.[5]

Clergy and laity alike were subjected to the most horrible tortures. Their feet were bored with sharp irons, and some experienced what is called the "nine deaths," where bit by bit their bodies were cut to pieces. It was quite common under the different monarchs to confiscate the wealth of the well to do and to pillage their homes.

Had there been no state Christianity in the Roman Empire, prob-

---

[5] O'Leary, *The Syriac Church and Fathers,* pages 83, 84.

ably in Persia there would not have been persecutions of Christianity. Zeno, the Roman emperor, closed the Assyrian church college at Edessa because it did not agree with the theological views then prevailing in the state religion. A powerful leader in the Church of the East moved the school to Nisibis, a strong fortress city in which the college developed into one of the intellectual centers of the world.

The phenomenal work and influence of the new college at Nisibis opened by Barsumas, reached to Oxford, Cambridge, and Paris. Thus W. A. Wigram writes:

> When we remember how much of the culture of medieval Europe was to come to her through the Saracens, and that the "Nestorians" were the teachers of the Saracens, one is set asking whether Oxford, Cambridge and Paris do not owe an unsuspected debt to Bar-soma, though the road from Nisibis to those centers may run through Bagdad and Salamanca.[6]

Persia later became tolerant of Christianity; liberty was increased there while it was vanishing in Europe. If Mohammedanism had not conquered Persia, the Christians would probably have gained complete religious liberty.

Persian Christians Escape Theology of Rome

The Christianity of Persia existed not only as a challenge to Mithraism, but it also differed widely from the ruling church in the Roman Empire. The forty years of persecution by Shapur II made impossible any contact between the believers in the two dominions. The revolutionary events which centered in the Council of Nicaea and in the angry controversies which followed that gathering were unknown to the churches beyond the Euphrates. They had no part in the fierce disputes concerning the Godhead. They had grown in strength and had performed miracles in spreading the gospel eastward before the contest arose over Nestorius. Nestorianism, according to Samuel Edgar, is a dispute about words.[7] It is a misnomer to call the Church of the East, Nestorian. Even to this day communions so labeled resent the name.[8] The Church of the East in India also

---

[6] Wigram, *Introduction to the History of the Assyrian Church*, page 167.
[7] Edgar, *The Variations of Popery*, page 62.
[8] Before the writer visited the bishop of the cathedral in Trichur, India, he had been informed that it was a Nestorian church. When, however, he sat at the table with the bishop, this official declared that not only he but all the directors belonging to his denomination rejected the name Nestorian.

was free from the controversies of imperial Christianity. This fact reveals the separation between the Church of India and the Western hierarchy.

To note some points of difference between the Church of the East and the papacy, it may be observed that the first rejected the use of images, and interposed no mediator like the Virgin Mary between God and man. The Church of the East also dispensed with candles, incense, relics, and many other usages of imperial Christianity. They had a different Bible than that of Rome; for their Bible they used the Peshitta, evidently the work of the school of Lucian.[9] Assyrian Christians (the name often given to the Church of the East) rejected the supremacy of the bishop of Rome. At this time Seleucia, the church headquarters, was full of Jews,[10] and many Christians throughout the East were of Jewish blood.

Of the Persian Christians, W. F. Adeney writes:

> They have no doctrine of transubstantiation, no purgatory; they do not sanction Mariolatry or image worship; nor will they even allow icons to be exhibited in their churches. Men and women take the communion in both kinds. All five orders of clergy below the bishops are permitted to marry.[11]

Missionary Expansion From Papas to Aba

"In the early Christian centuries there was a system of roads and posts between the cities of central Asian plains (as lately shown by the recovery of documents in some of the unearthed cities), and there was no pass unknown to the Chinese pilgrims—not only the direct routes but all the ways which linked up the Buddhist centers."[12]

"When the Persian king, Kawad (A. D. 498), because of rebellions in his kingdom, twice took refuge with the Huns and Turks, he found Christians there who helped him to reconquer his land."[13] When he had regained his throne, he killed some Mithraists, incarcerated others, but was benevolent toward the Christians because a company of them rendered service to him on his way to the king of the Turks.[14]

---

[9] O'Leary, *The Syriac Church and Fathers,* page 46.
[10] Milman, *The History of Christianity,* vol. 2, pp. 248, 249.
[11] Adeney, *The Greek and Eastern Churches,* pages 496, 497.
[12] Gordon, *"World Healers,"* pages 231, 232.
[13] Mingana, "Early Spread of Christianity," *Bulletin of John Ryland's Library,* vol. 9, p. 302.
[14] *Ibid.,* vol. 9, p. 303.

About this same time the Assyrian Christians were credited with having taught the Turks the art of writing in their own language. In commenting upon their expansion eastward, Wigram indicates their influence over Tibet: "The seventh century was the period of missions to China; and the strangely Christianlike ceremonial of modern lamas was quite possibly borrowed from Assyrian sources."[15]

The scholar, Alexander von Humboldt, reveals how thorough were education and organization in the Church of the East before Aba. He also shows how this same church taught arts and sciences to the Arabs:

> It was ordained in the wonderful decrees by which the course of events is regulated, that the Christian sects of Nestorians, which exercised a very marked influence on the geographical diffusion of knowledge, should prove of use to the Arabs even before they advanced to the erudite and contentious city of Alexandria, and that, protected by the armed followers of the creed of Islam, these Nestorian doctrines of Christianity were enabled to penetrate far into Eastern Asia. The Arabs were first made acquainted with Greek literature through the Syrians, a kindred Semitic race, who had themselves acquired a knowledge of it only about a hundred and fifty years earlier through the heretical Nestorians. Physicians, who had been educated in the scholastic establishments of the Greeks, and in the celebrated school of medicine founded by the Nestorian Christians at Edessa in Mesopotamia, were settled at Mecca as early as Mohammed's time, and there lived on a footing of friendly intercourse with the Prophet and Abu-Bekr.[16]

In 549 the White Huns, inhabiting the regions of Bactria, and the Huns on both the north and south banks of the Oxus River sent a request to Persia to Catholicos Aba that he would ordain for them a director. The Persian king was astonished to see these representatives of the thousands of Christians in that distant land coming to him; and being amazed at the power of Jesus, he concurred. The spiritual director was ordained, and he returned with the mission.[17] A. Mingana gives a list of twenty-one towns and provinces west of the Oxus River which had spiritual leaders ordained to rule the churches in them

---

[15] Wigram, *Introduction to the History of the Assyrian Church,* page 227.

[16] Humboldt, *Cosmos: A Sketch of a Physical Description of the Universe,* vol. 2, p. 208.

[17] Mingana, "Early Spread of Christianity," *Bulletin of John Ryland's Library,* vol. 9, pp. 304, 305.

and mentions especially those leaders of the fifth and sixth centuries. He also maintains that the majority of the two powerful divisions of the eastern Turks, the Uigurs and the Keraits, were Christians, and that the gospel of Christ had penetrated into the mighty confederacy of Naimans comprised of nine powerful clans.[18] These missionaries had also converted a fourth conglomeration of tribes of the Turkish stock with an infusion of Mongolian blood, called the Merkits.[19] All these vigorous peoples lived far away to the northeast in Asia. As to supplementary records of this expansion, Mrs. E. A. Gordon says: "Dr. Aurel Stein recently discovered in the loess in Chinese Turkestan, thousands of rolls of precious MSS."[20]

Claudius Buchanan, who has left a thrilling account of his own experiences and life in India about 1812, declares that he saw in that land a Syrian version of the Bible which according to popular belief would date probably as far back as 325, the year of the Council of Nicaea.[21] There is no doubt that the fierce forty-year persecution of King Shapur II of Persia hurried many Christians away into India. One supreme head of the church wrote that the book of Romans was translated into Syrian (c. A. D. 425) with the help of pastor Daniel from India.[22] The Syrians in the fifth century in India as elsewhere were well trained not only in church services, but also in learning, and India was under the catholicos of Seleucia. Marco Polo, the famous Venetian traveler, speaks of the large island of Socotra in the Arabian Sea near the Gulf of Aden, possessing many baptized Christians who had nothing to do with the pope at Rome, but were subject to the catholicos at Bagdad. Some writers find a connection between that island's Christianity and the Abyssinian Church.[23] Of this widespread missionary endeavor, P. Y. Saeki writes: "The famous Bar Somas, bishop of Nisibis from 435 to 489 A. D., did much to spread Nestorian teaching in the East—in central Asia, and then in China."[24]

Mingana reveals the civilizing influences of these missions: "We

---

[18] Mingana, "Early Spread of Christianity," *Bulletin of John Ryland's Library*, vol. 9, p. 316.
[19] *Ibid.*, vol. 9, p. 317.
[20] Gordon, *"World Healers,"* page 146.
[21] Buchanan, *Christian Researches in Asia*, pages 141, 142.
[22] Mingana, "Early Spread of Christianity," *Bulletin of John Ryland's Library*, vol. 10, p. 459.
[23] Yule, *Travels of Marco Polo*, vol. 2, pp. 407-409, with notes.
[24] Saeki, *The Nestorian Monument in China*, page 105.

need not dwell here on the well-known fact that the Syriac characters as used by the Nestorians gave rise to many central Asian and Far Eastern alphabets such as the Mongolian, the Manchu, and the Soghdian."[25]

These facts reveal that the missionaries of the church in Asia were the makers of alphabets as well as the creators of a Far Eastern literature. In fact, there still exists a voluminous Syrian Church literature which, with research, yields thrilling facts of the past.

All directors of ecclesiastical districts were expected to report to headquarters annually. Those from distant Oriental lands were required to report to the catholicos not less than once in six years. It must have been an astonishing sight to the Persian king to see the representatives from so many different countries arriving at Seleucia upon official missions.

There are in the writings of Cosmas, the traveled geographer of about 530, some thrilling descriptions of Assyrian churches in lands eastward from Persia. Cosmas was of the same church and of the same land as were Papas and Aba. He lived at the same time as Aba and was a personal friend of the catholicos. His explorations being in many Asian lands, he has been called "Indicopluestes," or India traveler, because of his voyages in the Indian Seas early in the sixth century. He believed that the earth was shaped like Moses' Tabernacle, and he engaged in research far and wide in studying his thesis. His book, entitled *Topographia Christiana (Christian Topography),* contains an omnibus collection of remarkable facts, many of which are of real value. From it can be learned how widely extended were the worshipers in the Church of the East.

> In the sixth century, according to the report of a Nestorian traveler, Christianity was successfully preached to the Bactrians, the Huns, the Persians, the Indians, the Persarmenians, the Medes, and the Elamites: the barbaric churches, from the Gulf of Persia to the Caspian Sea, were almost infinite; and their recent faith was conspicuous in the number and sanctity of their monks and martyrs. The pepper coast of Malabar and the isles of the ocean, Socotora and Ceylon, were peopled with an increasing multitude of Christians; and the bishops and clergy of those sequestered regions derived their ordination from the catholicos of Babylon.[26]

---

[25] Mingana, "Early Spread of Christianity," *Bulletin of John Ryland's Library,* vol. 9, p. 341.
[26] Gibbon, *Decline and Fall of the Roman Empire,* ch. 47, par. 30.

Aba Comes to the Catholicate

Aba came to the catholicate after years of confusion caused by the quarrels and laxness due to rival claimants for the position. He was a convert from Zoroastrianism. While still a worshiper of the sun, his learning and ability had advanced him until he was a teacher of the Magi. After his conversion he studied for a while in the celebrated college of the Assyrian Church at Nisibis. Later he took a voyage farther west to observe the state of Christianity in Syria and at Constantinople. Upon his return he was called to be a teacher in the Christian college at Nisibis. For further incidents of his life the following excerpts from the splendid work of W. A. Wigram are given:

> The work of organization and reform had not been accomplished too soon; for not many weeks can have elapsed after the patriarch's return from his tour when his persecution at the hands of the Magi began—a trial that was to continue until his death.[27]

> Naturally it was not long before an "apostate" so conspicuous as the patriarch was attacked; he being accused to the king by the mobed mobedan in person, and charged with despising the national "din," and with proselytizing. . . .

> The patriarch was arrested, and tumultuously accused as an apostate and a proselytizer, both of which charges he fully admitted, and was threatened with death.[28]

> Aba was given no opportunity of defending himself, but was declared guilty and worthy of death. On this he appealed to the king, who had by this time (for the proceedings took time) returned from the war to Seleucia.

> Chosroes heard the case, the mobeds demanding the death of the enemy of "the religion," and called on the patriarch for his answer. "I am a Christian," he said; "I preach my own faith, and I want every man to join it; but of his own free will, and not of compulsion. I use force on no man; but I warn those who are Christians to keep the laws of their religion." "And if you would but hear him, sire, you would join us, and we would welcome you," cried a voice from the crowd. It was one Abrudaq, a Christian in the king's service, and the words, of course, infuriated the mobeds, who demanded the death of the blasphemer.[29]

> Still a false accuser was found and produced in court—where he broke down utterly and ignominiously, confessing himself that all his accusations were false. Such an end to such a charge against a man who had

---

[27] Wigram, *Introduction to the History of the Assyrian Church,* page 199.
[28] *Ibid.,* page 200.
[29] *Ibid.,* page 201.

done Aba's reforming work is as high a testimony to the character of that work as could well be given.[30]

Shortly afterwards Chosroes met Aba in the street (the patriarch was apparently allowed a measure of personal liberty), and to the horror and rage of the Magi returned his salute with marked friendliness, and summoned him to an audience. Here he told him frankly that, as a renegade, he was legally liable to death. . . . "But you shall go free and continue to act as catholicos if you will stop receiving converts, admit those married by Magian law to communion, and allow your people to eat Magian sacrifices." Obviously the mobeds had been influencing the king; but the royal offer sheds an instructive light on the rapid growth of the Church, and on the position of the patriarch as recognized head of his *melet.* To the terms, however, Aba could only return his steadfast *non possumus,* and the king, annoyed at the attitude, ordered him to prison under the care of the Magi. This was equivalent to a sentence of death, though it was probably not so intended; for when he was in prison it would be easy to dispatch him by the hand of some underling, and represent that an act of possibly mistimed zeal towards a notorious apostate ought not to be judged severely.[31]

Amid the passionate grief of all Christians he departed, and reached the appointed province; but the local rad, Dardin (a man selected for his notoriously hard character), soon showed such respect and regard for the patriarch that he was removed thence, and sent to "Sirsh," the very center and stronghold of Magianism. . . . Here his confinement was purposely made very severe at first, in the undisguised hope that his death would be caused by it; and the hard winters of the high Persian plateau must have been a further trial to one bred in the land of Radan, which is practically the Babylonian plain. Later, however (perhaps in response to a hint from court), he was allowed to live in a house of his own, where he furnished a room as a church, and his friends were allowed to visit him. Here for seven years he continued in a captivity which may without irreverence be compared to that of St. Paul; and acted as patriarch from his prison in the Magian stronghold. He consecrated bishops, reconciled penitents, governed by interviews and correspondence. Men came in numbers to see him, and "the mountains of Azerbaijan were worn by the feet of saints" who came either on Church business, or on what tended to become a pilgrimage to a living saint.[32]

Finally his persecutors, disappointed no doubt at the failure of their double plan, to deprive him of his power or to compass his death, determined to be done with him forever. An assassin was hired, one Peter of Gurgan, an apostate Christian priest; and a plot formed for the murder of Aba, who, it was to be explained, had been cut down in attempting to

---

[30] Wigram, *Introduction to the History of the Assyrian Church,* page 202.
[31] *Ibid.,* pages 202, 203.
[32] *Ibid.,* pages 203, 204.

make his escape. The plot failed, and was discovered, and the wretched instrument fled. Aba, however, recognized that the attempt would be repeated, perhaps with better fortune, and took a bold resolution. He left his place of exile with one or two companions, but went, not to any place of concealment, but straight to Seleucia and the king, before whose astonished gaze he presented himself. The Magians, were of course, delighted, thinking that their enemy was at last delivered into their hands. The patriarch was, of course, arrested; and the amazed Chosroes asked what he expected, after thus flying in the face of the royal command. Fearlessly Mar Aba replied that he was the king's servant, ready to die if that was his will; but though willing to be executed at the king's order, he was not willing to be murdered contrary to his order. Let the king of kings do justice! No appeal so goes home to an oriental as a cry to "the justice of the king." . . .

Now he heard the stream of accusations that the Magians poured out, and then addressed the patriarch. "You stand charged with apostasy, with proselytizing, with forcing your *melet* to abstain from marriages that the state accepts, with acting as patriarch in exile against the king's order, and with breaking prison—and you admit the offences. All the offences against the state I pardon freely; as a renegade from Magianism, however, you must answer that charge before the mobeds. Now, as you have come of your own accord to the king's justice, go freely to your house, and come to answer the accusation when called upon." The decision shows at once the strength and weakness of the king: he could pardon offences against himself, and he could respect a noble character; but he dared not defy the Magian hierarchy. . . .

Still fear of the mobeds prevailed with the king, and he allowed them to arrest the patriarch and convey him to prison secretly, for fear of riot; though it must be owned that he gave strict orders that he was on no account to be killed. For months Aba remained in prison and in chains; though, as is usual in Oriental prisons, his friends were allowed to visit him (probably by grace of the great power Bakhshish), and he was allowed even to consecrate bishops while in confinement. Still a captive, he was obliged to accompany the king on the whole of his "summer progress;" though at every halting place Christians crowded to see him and receive his blessing, and to petition the king for his release. Even mobeds respected him, and promised to intercede for his pardon if he would but promise to make no more converts.

Finally, soon after the royal return to Seleucia, his patient constancy was victorious. Chosroes sent for him, and released him, absolutely and unconditionally. It is true that when the king left the city, soon after, the mobeds pounced on their prey, and the patriarch found himself in prison once more; but though Chosroes might hesitate long, he was not the tool the mobeds imagined him to be, and this open contempt of the royal decree roused him. A sharply worded order for the instant release of the prisoner came back; and Mar Aba, worn in body and broken in health, but victorious, came out once more, and finally, from his prison. Nine years of persecution and danger had been his portion, but he had endured to the end, and he was saved.[33]

Shortly after this Aba passed away. He is presented as a type of those patriarchs who ruled the Church of the East during the eventful days when the religion of Mithra dominated the throne of Persia. Aba was called to his heavy task in an hour when the cause needed the hand of a strong leader.

From Aba to the Moslem Conquest

The individual history of the successors of Aba in the two centuries which elapsed between his catholicate and the overthrow of the Zoroastrian government by the Mohammedans are full of interest. The people who followed the Bible lived on. The hills of Persia and the valleys of the Tigris and Euphrates re-echoed their songs of praise. They reaped their harvests and paid their tithes.[34] Not burdened with the superfluity of observances which obtained with the hierarchy of the West, they concentrated their attention on the words of Holy Writ. They repaired to their churches on the Sabbath day for the worship of God.[35] In their foreign missionary societies the youth of the faith offered themselves as ready to go to Turkestan, Scythia, Mongolia, Tibet, Manchuria, China, or wherever God would call. These people with their simplicity of faith and worship and deep reverence for the Scriptures; with their opposition to images, icons, the confessional, purgatory, and the adoration of the host, were the Protestants of Asia.[36] Reformers before the Reformation, they sent gifts and messages of truth and light to the submerged believers of Europe, who during the Dark Ages were praying and dying for the triumph of Bible Christianity. Concerning their missions to central Asia, India, China, and Japan during the supremacy of the Moslems, the recitation of these eventful hours is reserved for following chapters.

Jacob, the organizer of another eastern church protesting against

---

[33] Wigram, *Introduction to the History of the Assyrian Church*, pages 204-207.
[34] Yule, *Travels of Marco Polo*, vol. 2, b. 3, p. 409, note 2; also Gordon, *"World Healers,"* page 466.
[35] *Realencyclopedie für Protestantische Theologie und Kirche*, art. "Nestorianer;" also, Bower, *The History of the Popes*, vol. 2, p. 258, note 2.
[36] Couling, *The Luminous Religion*, page 44.

the innovations of Rome, was called to be the leader of the Jacobites the same year that Aba was made catholicos of the Assyrian Christians.[37]

The Jacobites constitute a large sector of the dissenting Eastern millions who recoiled from Rome's speculative analysis of the divine nature. Because of the doctrines passed on by the Council of Chalcedon (A. D. 451), the Ethiopian Church, the Coptic Church of Egypt, the Jacobite Church of Syria, and the Church of Armenia broke off all connection with Rome. It is remarkable how these bodies through the centuries were kept free from the accumulating beliefs and practices of Rome which later were rejected by the Reformation. It is true that in spite of the comparative purity of the apostolic faith which they maintained during the supremacy of the papacy, they gave way at times to some papal or heathen practice.

Sir E. A. Wallis Budge, on commenting on the controversy over the two natures of Christ, writes: "It is very difficult to find out exactly what Nestorius thought and said about them, because we have only the statement of his enemies to judge by."[38] The interference of the state in religion had put things on a tension among the Jacobites. Great masses of believers were bitter over the situation into which state-dictated religion had forced them. They were ready for a leader when Jacob Baradai appeared, and he imparted to them an enthusiastic organization which has persisted to this day. The cause of the Jacobites, and even that of dissenters in other lands, was made strong by the hands of Jacob Baradai.

Edward Gibbon, showing the preference of the Eastern Church for Turkish rule rather than papal rule even under dire conditions, wrote: "After a period of thirteen hundred and sixty years . . . the hostile communions still maintain the faith and discipline of their founders. In the most abject state of ignorance, poverty, and servitude, the Nestorians and Monophysites [another name for the Jacobites] reject the spiritual supremacy of Rome, and cherish the toleration of their Turkish masters."[39]

---

[37] When the writer was in Beyrouth, Syria, he visited the Jacobite bishop. A series of questions were asked the church leader regarding his people and their history. The last remark of the bishop was that his church had anathematized Nestorius. He admitted that the papacy had anathematized the Jacobites.

[38] Budge, *The Monks of Kublai Khan, Emperor of China*, page 37.

[39] Gibbon, *Decline and Fall of the Roman Empire*, ch. 47, par. 28.

While it would be incorrect to say that the Jacobites and the Church of the East agreed in doctrines, organization, and practices, nevertheless their differences fundamentally were not great. The Church of the East, growing up in an entirely Oriental environment, never was under Rome. The Monophysites, in all their branches—Abyssinians, Copts of Egypt, Jacobites, and Armenians—though citizens of the empire until their break with Rome, early refused to go along with the religion of the Caesars. The believers located in the valleys of the Tigris and Euphrates escaped many of the beliefs and practices which the papacy later adopted.[40] When, from about 650, both bodies passed more or less under Mohammedan rulers, their afflictions were less severe than those experienced by evangelicals in the Gothic ten kingdoms of western Europe when brought under papal rule. Assyrian Christians and Jacobites suffered comparatively little at the hands of the Moslems, but later much more so at the hands of the Jesuits. These later afflictions had a tendency to draw them together. As an illustration, witness the Assyrian Christians of India, when the devastating persecutions of the Jesuits had laid them low, accepting the leadership of a Monophysite bishop who happened at the moment to arrive on the Malabar Coast. There have been already noticed in detail many fundamental differences between these two bodies on the one hand and the church of the empire on the other. In the further history of the expansion of the Assyrian Church during the Moslem rule in Persia, authorities will be cited as evidence that the Sabbath of the fourth commandment was observed by both Monophysitism and the Church of the East in their separate areas in near and far Asia.

Rise and Conquests of the Mohammedans

Like the smoke out of the bottomless pit,[41] darkening the sun and the air, the new religion of Mohammed suddenly issued from Arabia. Like a whirlwind from the desert, it swept furiously over rivers and plains until all of western Asia, northern Africa, and the southern extremities of Europe had been conquered. Three factors contributed to the sudden and amazing conquests of the Arabians. The first was the new national awakening among the Arabs. The second was the

---

[40] Edgar, *The Variations of Popery,* pages 60-67.
[41] Revelation 9:1-3.

exhaustion of the Roman and Persian Empires caused by four centuries of constant warfare between themselves plus the gigantic invasions of the Goths which had overrun the western provinces of Rome. The third was Mohammed himself.

In the days of Aba and his successors new movements were stirring the Arabians. They were throwing off their old idolatry and longing for a monotheistic religion like the Jews and other powerful neighbors. They had a strong urge toward national unity. Several forays accompanied by success had convinced them of the weakness of both the Roman and Persian Empires. All they needed was a leader, and that leader was Mohammed.

Of course, it took some time for this obscure camel driver to convince his fellow countrymen of his pretended revelation from heaven that there is but one God and Mohammed is His prophet. Born about A. D. 570 at Mecca, he rose from an ordinary laborer until he married a wealthy widow in whose employ he was. With deepening religious fervor he began to see visions and to dream dreams, but for some time his success was limited to converting his immediate relatives and servants. His growing progress excited the hostility of Mecca. So when, about the year 622, he fled with his most trusted companion to the city of Medina, where he was received as a prophet, this flight, the Hegira, was chosen as the first year of the Mohammedan era.

The new prophet and his belligerent disciples began by attacking rich caravans. Strengthened by the riches and arms of their plunder, they began the subjugation of Arabia, which was accomplished by the time of the death of Mohammed. Under the impetuosity of his immediate successors, abu-Bekr, Omar, and Othman, it was not long before Syria, Egypt, and Persia were subdued. When the Arabian empire was fully established, it built up Bagdad, its magnificent new capital. The Church of the East, still recognizing the importance of having its headquarters at the center of the secular government, removed its spiritual capital from Seleucia to Bagdad, where it remained for approximately the next five hundred years.

Nevertheless, great conquests for God were accomplished by the Church of the East while Mohammedanism reigned in all lands stretching toward the Pacific. This will be the theme in succeeding chapters.

CHAPTER XVIII

Timothy of Bagdad; The Church Under Mohammedan Rule

It was not from Nestorius, but from Thomas, Bartholomew, Thaddeus, and others that this people first received the knowledge of a Saviour, as will be seen in the sequel.[1]

They were a strong, and prosperous people before the Mohammedans overran Asia, living on the plains of Assyria, sustaining schools and colleges, whose students carried to China, and throughout India, probably, the first message telling that the Messiah had come.[2]

TIMOTHY is an outstanding leader of the Church of the East in connection with its great expansion throughout Asia. He belongs to the period when the Mohammedans dominated not only Persia, but also the Near East after having overthrown the Zoroastrian dominion. He is a representative of that line of patriarchs who guided the church through centuries of Moslem power.

From the time of Timothy, and even from a short while before, the Church of the East took its place in gospel and prophetic history when it was driven into the wilderness. This is not because the Arabian rulers persecuted Christians but rather because of the attitude of the papal church in the West. When the Moslem power struck low the Mithraic kings of Persia, Mohammedanism was not yet strong enough to completely oppose other religions. In many general ways Mohammed himself felt kindly toward Christianity, especially toward the more simple believers in Jesus, such as the Assyrian Christians.[3] When the victorious Moslem general conquered Zoroastrian Persia, the Church of the East was in the hands of a wise and able head, who secured in the following way a charter of privileges for Christians.

Ishoyabh (sometimes called Jesus-Jabus), as catholicos, succeeded in obtaining a pledge granting protection and freedom of worship on

---

[1] Grant, *The Nestorians, or the Lost Tribes,* page 72.
[2] Wishard, *Twenty Years in Persia,* page 18.
[3] Saeki, *The Nestorian Monument in China,* pages 50, 51.

condition that the Christians paid certain tribute. Of this Sir E. A. Wallis Budge says:

> The patriarch Isho-yahbh II, who sat from 628-44, seeing that the downfall of the Persian Empire was imminent came to terms with Muhammad, or Abu Bakr. . . . The patriarch stipulated that the Christians should be protected from the attacks of their foes; that the Arabs should not make them go to war with them; that they should not compel them to change their manners and laws; that they should help them to repair their old churches; that the tax on the poor should not exceed four zuze; that the tax on the merchants and wealthy men should be ten zuze per man; that a Christian woman servant should not be compelled to change her faith, nor to neglect fasting and prayer.[4]

These immunities extended by abu-Bekr were not only confirmed by Omar, his successor, but even the taxes were remitted. It remained for the renowned warrior Caleb to confirm and extend the high rights and privileges which were allowed the church. The Arabs, like the Persians, were very partial to the Assyrian Christians because they found it necessary in the early days of their power to lean upon the splendid schools which this church had developed. Medicine made great progress in the hands of the Church of the East.[5] The Arabian court and its extended administrations employed its members as secretaries and imperial representatives.

Justinian's grievous laws against the leaders in Asia Minor and Persia afflicted the Church of the East. He destroyed any possibility of reconciliation with the Assyrian Church when he issued the imperial condemnation of the three church leaders usually called the Three Chapters. By this decree he bitterly alienated the millions of believers in Asia without winning the malcontents. Never again would there be any general movement among the Asiatic Christians toward the religion of Rome. The year of this decree is 553.

Catholicos Moves to New Capital of Moslem Empire

The Mohammedans used the conquered Persian Empire as a steppingstone to further and more rapid conquests. They looked with greedy eyes upon the rich and cultured kingdoms of central Asia. It is difficult for travelers of today who behold the sandy expanses of Palestine to visualize the once mighty kingdoms of Israel and Judah

---

[4] Budge, *The Monks of Kublai Khan, Emperor of China,* pages 30, 31.
[5] Schaff, *History of the Christian Church,* vol. 3, pp. 731, 732, note 2.

that occupied those wastes. With whirling advances into those gardens of Eden, the intrepid warriors of Mohammed secured decisive victories; then returned to display to astonished eyes the dazzling riches of Transoxiana. Extension of the dominion brought weakness of control. The rapid and unexpected victories of Islam's western armies stretching along the southern Mediterranean to the Atlantic Ocean and extending northeast to Turkestan broke the unity of the empire.

Strife for pre-eminence came in between different branches of Mohammed's progeny. Instead of one, there arose three caliphates. The name Ommiads was given to the dynasty of the prophet's family which seized the power reaching from the Mediterranean Sea to the borders of China. The birth of this new caliphate was the signal for the creation of a new capital. An excellent site on the Tigris River was chosen, and the city of Bagdad, which still stands today, arose in all its splendor.

In 762 with their usual foresight the leaders of the Church of the East removed the central administration of their widely extending work to the new capital at Bagdad. They had received recognition from the caliph as a *melet,* the term usually given to subject religions under Oriental monarchs. Abraham Yohannan writes that an Arabian history of India records for the year 1000 that the bulk of population in Syria, Iraq, and Khurasan was Christian.[6] He further states that Assyrian Christians held high offices under the caliphs. The historian Arminius Vambery notes that by 1000 the Church of the East had made greater progress in central Asia than Mohammedan historians are willing to allow.[7]

The Catholicate of Timothy

Timothy I (A. D. 780-824) was elected as catholicos at a time when Charlemagne was wielding his heavy sword to advance the interests of the papacy in Europe. His election took place twelve years before the founding of Kyoto, the most famous of Japan's ancient cities. It was during the early years of his catholicate that Japan sent Kobo Daishi, of whom more shall be said later, to visit China and bring

---

[6] Yohannan, *The Death of a Nation,* page 102.
[7] Vambery, *History of Bokhara,* page 32; also page 89, note 2.

about a reconciliation in Japan between Buddhism and the old indigenous religion of the mikado's realm, called Shintoism.

In the days of Timothy a wave of inquiry was sweeping over the minds of men in eastern and northeastern Asia. Literature and learning were in the hands of the Church of the East. Practically all the subjects offered in similar institutions today were taught in their colleges.[8] Some of the lines of instruction given were science, philosophy, materia medica, medicine, astronomy, law, Bible, theology, geometry, music, arithmetic, dialectics, grammar, rhetoric, Greek literature, and the Greek, Syrian, Chaldean, and Egyptian languages. Claudius Buchanan writes:

> They have preserved the manuscripts of the Holy Scriptures incorrupt, during a long series of ages, and have now committed them into our own hands. By their long and energetic defence of pure doctrine against anti-Christian error, they are entitled to the gratitude and thanks of the rest of the Christian world.[9]

Timothy grasped the situation with a master's hand. This unwearied worker was ever busy receiving reports from distant lands, at the same time stimulating training centers to graduate more and still more missionaries. He watched over the purity of the doctrine. He was continually consecrating devoted young men that had the spirit of sacrifice, missionaries who would bring mercy into cruel hearts, who would instill culture into repulsive peoples, and who would gather the galloping tribes of the desert around them to study the messages of the Sacred Word. Timothy must have been thrilled by the news from China, even though delayed because of the immense distances, that in the day of the preceding catholicos a stone monument had been erected with imperial co-operation in Changan, the capital of the nation, to the triumphs of Christianity amid the yellow race. Moreover, China was then the greatest empire in the world, and its imperial center was the most thrilling city on the globe.[10]

---

[8] Neander, *General History of the Christian Religion and Church*, vol. 2, p. 183, note; Saeki, *The Nestorian Monument in China*, pages 116-118; Schaff, *History of the Christian Church*, vol. 3, pp. 731, 732, note; Draper, *History of the Intellectual Development of Europe*, pp. 290, 291.

[9] Buchanan, *Christian Researches in Asia*, pages 146, 147.

[10] Among all the memorials which still remain to revive the glorious centuries of the Church of the East, this stone, which it was the privilege of the writer to study and to photograph, attracts the greatest attention.

There is a record of a letter that Timothy wrote, exulting in the news of the conversion of a king of the Turks. He states that these people have turned from idolatry, have become Christians, and have asked that a metropolitan be consecrated and sent to guide their nation in the new faith. Their demand for a metropolitan would indicate the existence of many leaders of provincial clergy among the Turks. The request, Timothy declares, has already been granted.[11] Or, as the letter recites, "In these days the Holy Spirit has anointed a metropolitan for the Turks, and we are preparing to consecrate another one for the Tibetans."[12] The making of this provision for Tibet portrays the success achieved by the Church of the East in that tableland nation.

In other letters to a certain Rabban Sergius, the patriarch not only records the fact that he was preparing to consecrate a metropolitan for the inhabitants of Tibet, but also that in his time many missionaries "crossed the sea and went to the Indians and the Chinese with only a rod and a script." In one of these epistles he apprises his correspondents of the death of the metropolitan of China.[13] Thus while Charlemagne by the strokes of his battle-ax was destroying the beautiful centers of Celtic Christianity in northwestern Europe, and while agents from Rome were laboring to resist the onward march of Scottish and Irish Christianity into England, the Church of the Wilderness in the East was consecrating metropolitans to superintend spiritual leaders in Tibet, China, India, and among the nations of the Turks.

Thomas of Marga, writing concerning the indefatigable labors of Timothy, tells of the appointment of eighty missionaries sent to convert the heathen of the Far East:

> These were the bishops who preached the teaching of Christ in those countries of the Dailamites and Gilanians, and the rest of the savage peoples beyond them, and planted in them the light of the truth of the gospel of our Lord. . . . They evangelized them and they baptized them, worked miracles and showed prodigies, and the news of their exploits reached the fartherest points of the East. You may learn all these clearly from the

---

[11] Mingana, "Early Spread of Christianity," *Bulletin of John Ryland's Library,* vol. 9, p. 306.

[12] *Ibid.,* vol. 9, p. 306.

[13] *Ibid.,* vol. 9, p. 306.

letter which some merchants and secretaries of the kings, who had penetrated as far as there for the sake of commerce and of affairs of state, wrote to [the patriarch] Mar Timothy.[14]

In another place the same historian relates that about this time Shubbalisho was ordained by Timothy to evangelize the primitive peoples inhabiting the country beyond central Asia. The patriarch declared that the one newly ordained for this task was fitted for it because he was versed not only in Syriac, but also in Arabic and Persian. In this letter it is to be noted that the Church of the East not only brought heathen into their faith, but also overcame a difficult task in converting heretics like the Marcionites and Manichaeans. Thus he continues:

> He taught and baptized many towns and numerous villages, and brought them to the teaching of the divine life. He built churches, and set up in them priests and deacons, and singled out some brethren who were missionaries with him to teach them psalms and canticles of the Spirit. And he himself went deep inland to the farthest end of the East, in the work of the great evangelization that he was doing among pagans, Marcionites, Manichaeans, and other kinds of beliefs and abominations, and he sowed the sublime light of the teaching of the gospel, the source of life and peace.[15]

By these facts, which have been well authenticated, one can get a glimpse of the tremendous activity going on in the bosom of the Assyrian Church. This work was to go on for many centuries after Timothy. Timothy may be taken as a type of the intelligent, devoted, and industrious leaders who, for decade after decade throughout Asia, turned many to righteousness.

In the midst of these labors India was not forgotten. It has already been noted how Timothy sent many missionaries to India at the same time he was sending them to China. The patriarch Ishoyabh, who consummated the contract with the Moslem caliph for the protection of his people more than one hundred years previous to Timothy, censured for misconduct the metropolitan of southeastern Persia, who was located near the borders of northwestern India. His written rebuke bemoaned the disastrous effect of this leader's irregularities, because he says that, "Episcopal succession had been interrupted in India,"

---

[14] Mingana, "Early Spread of Christianity," *Bulletin of John Ryland's Library*, vol. 9, p. 307.
[15] *Ibid.*, vol. 9, pp. 307, 308.

and that "divine teaching by means of rightful bishops" had been withheld from India. In other words, the rebuke infers that throughout the whole of the Hindu peninsula, clergy, provincial directors, organized churches, and companies of Christian communities could be found.

Of Timothy himself it is recorded that while writing to the monks of Mar Maron regarding the disputed words, "who was crucified for us," adds: "In all the countries of the sunrise, that is to say,—among the Indians, the Chinese, the Tibetans, the Turks, and in all the provinces under the jurisdiction of this patriarchal see, there is no addition of the words 'crucified for us.' "[16]

Conquests of the Mongols

Mingana quotes a letter purporting to have been written by Philoxenus. He was a famous writer attached to the smaller Eastern church (Monophysite).[17] The document is in two parts. The second part, which is evidently the work of a later writer, outlines the introduction of Christianity among the Turks. The scope and analysis of its treatment dealing with the nations of farther Asia, as well as the freshness of its descriptions, sheds unusual light on a region that is little known. It presents the Turks as dwelling in tents and having no towns, villages, or houses. Well organized, they live as the children of Israel did during their forty years of wandering in the wilderness. These Turks had their premises well kept, while the people themselves were clean and neat in their habits. They accepted both the Old and New Testaments in Syriac, although evidence indicates that they had the Scriptures also in their own script. When the divine writings were used in public services, they were translated by officiating pastors into the vernacular in order that the people might understand what was read.

It is a most illuminating statement concerning these Turks to read that they were ruled over by four great and powerful kings who evidently lived at quite a distance from each other. The letter applied the name Tartar to all the divisions, and designated their country as Sericon. This is the name (as Mingana points out) which was given

---

[16] Mingana, "Early Spread of Christianity," *Bulletin of John Ryland's Library,* vol. 10, p. 466.
[17] O'Leary, *The Syriac Church and Fathers,* page 113.

to China in the days of Christ. Each of these kings ruled over four hundred thousand families who accepted and obeyed the teachings and gospel of Christ. If each family was composed of an average of five persons, it would mean that the four kingdoms had a population of about eight million, and they all were Christians. From the twenty-seven grand divisions of the church administration covering the Orient, communications were sent in not only concerning new religious developments, but also about events of international importance. Thus in the year 1009, Abdisho, metropolitan of Merv, the church director in the powerful province of Khurasan, northeast Persia, wrote to the patriarch John informing him that two hundred thousand Turks and Mongolians had embraced Christianity. He pointed out that the conversion occurred because the king of the Keraits, which people spread over the region around Lake Baikal, Siberia, had been found wandering in a high mountain where he had been overtaken by a violent snowstorm. In his hopelessness he considered himself lost, and dreamed or thought he saw a giant appear to him in vision, saying, "If you will accept Christ, I will lead you to safety." Having promised to become a Christian and having returned safely to his kingdom, he sought out Christian merchants who were traveling among his tribes, and learned from them the way of salvation.

Mention should be made here of the name of Prester John, stories of whom stirred medieval Europe. Reports came through to the West of a powerful Christian king who, in the depths of Scythia, ruled over a mighty people. He is known variously by the names, Prester John, Presbyter John, and Priest John. Some think he was king of the Keraits, and others believe that, in addition to being a great king himself, he was also son-in-law to the king of the powerful Karakitai. The picture of these nations with their dreaded kings, all, or nearly all, of whom had been brought to Christ, confirms the opinion expressed by Mingana that the Church of the East "was by far the greatest missionary church the Christian cause has produced."[18] In following its evangelical conquests, one ranges through Turkestan, Siberia, Mongolia, Manchuria, and Tibet. One is introduced to stretches of territory more vast than would be possible to visualize in any other

---

[18]Mingana, "Early Spread of Christianity," *Bulletin of John Ryland's Library,* vol. 10, p. 113.

quarter of the globe. One becomes interested in, and familiarized with, peoples and portions of the earth's nations which previously had no claim upon man's attention. Truly, the Church in the Wilderness was a wonderful missionary church.

Conquests of Genghis Khan

Twelve centuries of ever-widening spiritual conquests were not accomplished any too soon by the Church of the East. The fierce energy of the countless tribes of Mongolia and Siberia, stirred by the new ideas heard from the lips of missionaries, was beginning to display itself as a world menace. These hordes needed only a leader possessing the caliber of a Julius Caesar to go forth on conquests never halting until Germany, France, and England trembled before the next blow. In the beginning of the thirteenth century, that leader appeared. His name was Genghis, a chief of the Mongols. After his first victories over surrounding tribes in Siberia, he took the title of khan, or king. How Genghis Khan conquered all Asia, how he and his son, Ogotai, devastated eastern Europe, and how the pope started up in alarm at the report of this news and sought to utilize the influence of the Church of the East to save Catholic nations in the West is a story of great significance.

The name Mongol, for two centuries after Genghis Khan, was the terror of central Asia. Yet the origin of the tribe is in obscurity. Numerically it was not the largest of the Tartary kingdoms. Genghis came of a warlike father and mother, but was left fatherless when he was only thirteen years of age. His mother resolutely assumed the reins of the kingdom, and regained supremacy over half of the revolting chiefs. Later, Genghis brought all the rebels back into subjection and began successful conquest of the near-by kingdoms of the Keraits, Merkits, Uigurs, and Naimans.

The immense victories won by Genghis in China were the results as much of strategy as of prowess. He possessed skillful ability in co-ordinating massive bodies of troops spread over wide areas, aiming at separate points of conquest. He was tolerant of religion. He treated Christianity, Buddhism, Mohammedanism, and other faiths with impartiality; some authorities say he killed them all alike if they were in the way of his conquests or were in the cities doomed to destruction. Abul Faraj writes of him that he "commanded the scribes of the Uigurs and they taught the children of the Tatars their books."[19] He was a lawgiver of high order, creating for the people over whom he ruled, a code of regulations which later conquerors were glad to adopt. Fortified by his victories in Siberia, Mongolia, and China, he turned his attention to new successes in western Asia and eastern Europe.

Of the ruin wrought by Genghis Khan, Arminius Vambery writes:

> Though already seventy years old, Djenghiz once more took the field against Tanghut, which had rebelled against him; but he died during this campaign in the year 624 (1226), leaving behind him traces throughout all Asia of the fire and sword with which his love of war had devasted the whole continent; but nowhere so deeply marked as in Transoxania, where the civilization of centuries had been destroyed, and the people plunged into a depth of barbarism in which the remembrance of their former greatness and their whole future were alike engulfed. No part of all Asia suffered so severely from the incursions of the Mongolian hordes as the countries bordering on the Oxus and the Yaxartes. . . .
>
> No wonder, then, that within five short years, the great high roads of central Asia, by which the products of China and India were conveyed to western Asia and to Europe, were deserted; that the oases, well known for their fertility, lay barren and neglected; or, finally, that the trade in arms and jewelry, in silks and enamels, so celebrated throughout Islam, decayed forever. The towns were in ruins, the peasants either murdered or compulsorily enrolled in the Mongolian army, and the artisans sent off by thousands to the farthest East to adorn and beautify the home of the conqueror. . . .
>
> Bokhara and Samarkand never regained their former mental activity, and their intellectual labors were henceforth entirely devoted to casuistry, mysticism, and false religion.[20]

At the time Russia was conquered it consisted of many small independent states constantly at war with one another and nominally under the common suzerainty of a grand prince or czar.[21] All the cities ravaged by the armies of Genghis were so completely obliterated from the sight of man that the Mongol chieftain could say, as he said many times to his fallen foe, that he was "the scourge of God." Thus, while his armies were subduing the northern Chinese empire in the east and other armies of the Mongols were conquering the northwestern part of India, Genghis Khan was also laying waste a part of Russia and

---

[19]Abul Faraj, *Chronography*, vol. 1, p. 354.
[20]Vambery, *History of Bokhara*, pages 137, 138.
[21]Pott, *A Sketch of Chinese History*, page 81.

attacking on the upper Volga. Death overtook him while in this warfare.

He was not a persecutor of Christianity. It is stated that one of his wives, a Kerait by birth and a near relative of Prester John, was a Christian.[22] He bequeathed his vast empire, reaching from China all the way to Hungary and Poland, to his three sons. One of the three, Ogotai, was chosen as the king of kings to succeed his father.

Kuyuk Spares Europe

It was the terrible wars waged by Ogotai which brought home to the nations of Europe the threat of subjection to the Mongols. Batu, the intrepid and invincible general of Ogotai, suddenly appeared on the eastern flanks of Poland and Hungary. Hungary had been relied upon to check the Mongols, but unexpectedly it offered comparatively feeble resistance; and for a number of years the forces of the Tartars passed and repassed over her lands, pillaging, ravaging, and devastating. Only the Holy Roman Empire now lay between the conquerors on the east and France and England on the west.

Ogotai died in the year 1241. The princes were recalled from war to elect a new khan. While they were coming together, the queen mother labored earnestly for the election of her favorite son, Kuyuk, and her work resulted in his election. Kuyuk was a true Christian, and in his days the prestige of the numerous Christians in his dominions was very high.[23] Mingana relates that his camp was full of church leaders, clergy, and scholars, and that a Christian by the name of Kaddak was his grand vizier. Under Kuyuk the massacres and devastations which had characterized the rule of Genghis and Ogotai seem to have come to an immediate end. It is a question if Europe was not spared further Mongolian wrath because a Christian, such as Kuyuk, was elected to supreme command.

After the death of Kuyuk in 1251 the succession passed to Mangu. Tule, a brother of Ogotai, was a mighty general. Of Sarkuti Bagi, the wife of Tule, Mingana shows that she was another Christian queen, a true believer and the wisest of all.[24] She was the mother of three sons who in turn became vested with imperial dignity, and all of them

---

[22] Huc, *Christianity in China, Tartary, and Thibet,* vol. 1, p. 129.
[23] Mingana, "Early Spread of Christianity," *Bulletin of John Ryland's Library,* vol. 9, p. 312.
[24] Abul Faraj, *Chronography,* vol. 1, p. 398.

were professed Christians or possessed of Christian wives. Their names were Mangu, Hulagu, and Kublai. The thrilling story of their contributions to the Church of the East belongs to the history of China in a later chapter.

When the sword of destruction hung over Germany, Italy, France, and England through the menacing attitude of Ogotai's skillful generals, the pope decided to send an envoy to the relentless Batu, leader of the Tartar armies. Friar John of Plano Carpini was chosen for this task. He journeyed to the banks of the Dnieper where the Tartar legions were encamped, encountering many difficulties on the way. Receiving scant attention, he was hurried on to the Volga, the headquarters of Batu. But Batu was unwilling to handle the proposition, and the wiry friar had to proceed by forced marches to the central camp farther east. He arrived after the death of Ogotai and before the election of the new emperor. Some years after the journey of Friar John, King Louis IX of France commissioned Friar William of Rubruck to proceed to the central camp of the Mongolians, hoping that he might convert the emperor to the Roman faith. Friar William reports many items about the Assyrian Christians.[25] What interests one most is what Friar William of Rubruck said of the Assyrian Christians (called by him, Nestorians) whom he encountered in his visits to those realms. He found them in nearly all the countries which he traversed; he met with them in the country of Karakhata, where he noticed that the Turkish people, called Mayman, had as king a Nestorian.[26]

The Nestorians, he said, were in those parts inhabited by the Tucomans. They conducted their services in the latter's language and wrote books in their alphabet; in all their towns was found a mixture of Nestorians.[27] He relates that in fifteen cities of Cathay there were Nestorians possessing an episcopal see. The grand secretary of the emperor Mangu, Bulgai by name, was a Nestorian, whose advice was nearly always followed and who was the imperial interpreter.[28]

---

[25] Mingana, "Early Spread of Christianity," *Bulletin of John Ryland's Library*, vol. 9, p. 315.
[26] Rockhill, *The Journey of William of Rubruck*, pages 109, 110.
[27] *Ibid.*, pages 141, 142.
[28] *Ibid.*, page 168.

The Doctrines of the Christian Mongols

The long and predominating favor with which the Mongol rulers treated the Church of the East indicates that the doctrines of the Christian Mongols were those of the Assyrian Church. This will appear to be more the case when the later histories of this remarkable people are considered. The beginning of their power, however, is connected with a significant fact from which conclusions can be drawn respecting the type of Christianity that they fell in with during the first years of their dominion.

Again we consider that celebrated personage, Prester John. The name Prester John is connected with a great revolution which took place in Asiatic Tartary about 1000. Many writers of sincerity who are worthy of credit relate that a king of the Keraits had been converted to Christ. He had taken the name of John, and he with thousands of his people was baptized by the Church of the East. His empire grew; each successive ruler was also called John. After about two centuries, Genghis Khan conquered the last king. Since the victorious Mongol chieftain married the daughter of the slain priest-king, the doctrine of the Church of the East rose to great influence among the Mongols.[29] Mosheim says that Europe was deeply stirred at the report concerning the wealth, strength, and happiness of this Christian realm. The king of Portugal sent an embassy to Abyssinia because he concluded that the doctrines of Prester John were those of the Abyssinians.[30] The legation discovered many things among the Abyssinians that were analogous to those reported of Prester John.

The Church of the East in Its Wide Extent of Missions

The organization of the Oriental believers is equally as interesting as the stirring events in the midst of which they labored. From the days of Timothy the believers in all Asia had been divided by the church into from twenty-six to thirty grand divisions. Over each of these there was the metropolitan or presiding officer. From time to time, possibly annually, these clergy assembled under their sub-province president to report the condition of the faithful in their parishes and to consider with one another the problems with which

---

[29] See Neander, *General History of the Christian Religion and Church,* vol. 4, pp. 46-50.

[30] Mosheim, *Institutes of Ecclesiastical History,* b. 3, cent. 12, pt. 1, ch. 1, par. 7, note 12.

they were similarly confronted. Then occasionally there would be a large convention under the chairmanship of the metropolitan with delegates from the different provinces. When the distances were too great to communicate easily with the catholicos, the head at Bagdad, then the metropolitan was expected to hand in a report at least once every six years.

An account has already been given of the purity of doctrine and practice of the Church of the East, which is often wrongly styled Nestorian after Nestorius. M'Clintock and Strong regards them as the Protestants of Eastern Christianity. "The Christians of Saint Thomas, in East India, are a branch of the Nestorians. They are named after the apostle Thomas, who is supposed to have preached the gospel in that country."[31]

They were entirely separated from the church at Rome. Edward Gibbon shows that the St. Thomas Christians as well as the Syrian Christians were not connected with Rome in any way. He says that when the Portuguese in their first discoveries of India presented the image of the Virgin Mary to the St. Thomas Christians in the sixteenth century, they said, "We are Christians, not idolaters."[32]

Here is a list of the doctrines of that branch of the Assyrian Christians in India which is called the St. Thomas Christians. Those believers—

1. Condemned the pope's supremacy,
2. Affirmed that the Roman Church had departed from the faith,
3 Denied transubstantiation,
4. Condemned the worship of images,
5. Made no use of oils,
6. Denied purgatory,
7. Would not admit of spiritual affinity,
8. Knew nothing of auricular confessions,
9. Never heard of extreme unction,
10. Permitted the clergy to marry,
11. Denied that matrimony and consecration were sacraments,
12. Celebrated with leavened bread and consecrated with prayer.[33]

---

[31] M'Clintock and Strong, *Cyclopedia*, art. "Nestorians."
[32] Gibbon, *Decline and Fall of the Roman Empire*, ch. 47, par. 31.
[33] D'Orsey, *Portuguese Discoveries, Dependencies, and Missions in Asia and Africa*, pages 232, 233.

The remarkable fact is that in the face of titanic difficulties the Church of the East was able to maintain through ages such wonderful unity of belief and soundness of Biblical living. "In the first place," says Etheridge, speaking of one branch of the Church of the East, "the Nestorian church has always cherished a remarkable veneration for the Holy Scriptures. Their Rule of Faith has been, and is, the written word of God."[34]

Widespread and enduring was the observance of the seventh-day Sabbath among the believers of the Church of the East and the St. Thomas Christians of India who never were connected with Rome. It also was maintained among those bodies which broke off from Rome after the Council of Chalcedon; namely, the Abyssinians, the Jacobites, the Maronites, and the Armenians. The numbers sanctifying the Sabbath varied in these bodies; some endured longer than others. Noted church historians, writing of the Nestorians in Kurdistan, say, "The Nestorian fasts are very numerous, meat being forbidden on 152 days. They eat no pork, and keep both the Sabbath and Sunday. They believe in neither auricular confession nor purgatory, and permit their priests to marry."[35]

Sabbathkeeping among the Abyssinians is especially worthy of notice. Of them the historian Gibbon fittingly remarks, "Encompassed on all sides by the enemies of their religion, the Ethiopians slept near a thousand years, forgetful of the world, by whom they were forgotten."[36] When in the sixteenth century Europe again came into contact with the Abyssinians, the seventh day was found to be their weekly rest day; Sunday was only an assembly day. Sorely pressed by Mohammedanism, they made the same mistake which was made by the St. Thomas Christians of India in that they appealed for help in 1534 to the Portuguese, the greatest naval power of Europe in that day. The following argument was presented to Portugal by the Abyssinian ambassador when asked why Ethiopia sanctified the seventh day:

On the Sabbath day, because God, after he had finished the Creation of the World, rested thereon; Which Day, as God would have it called

---

[34] Etheridge, *The Syrian Churches,* page 89.
[35] Schaff-Herzog, *The New Encyclopedia of Religious Knowledge,* art. "Nestorians;" also, *Realencyclopaedie für Protestantische Theologie und Kirche,* art. "Nestorianer."
[36] Gibbon, *Decline and Fall of the Roman Empire,* ch. 47, par. 38.

the Holy of Holies, so the not celebrating thereof with great honour and devotion, seems to be plainly contrary to God's Will and Precept, who will suffer Heaven and Earth to pass away sooner than his Word; and that especially, since Christ came not to dissolve the Law, but to fulfil it. It is not therefore in imitation of the Jews, but in obedience to Christ and his holy Apostles, that we observe that Day. . . . We do observe the Lord's day after the manner of all other Christians, in memory of Christ's Resurrection.[37]

When the Portuguese made a gesture of sending help to the Abyssinians, a number of Jesuits were included in the mission, and they immediately began to win the Abyssinian Church to Roman Catholicism. In 1604 they influenced the king to submit to the papacy. One of their first efforts was to have a proclamation issued by the king prohibiting all his subjects upon severe penalties to observe the seventh day any longer.[38] Civil war followed. The Jesuits were expelled and their laws were rescinded.

With respect to the Jacobites, there is the statement of that well-known and learned Samuel Purchas, who, having visited them in the beginning of the seventeenth century, writes: "They keepe Saturday holy, nor esteeme Saturday Fast lawfull but on Easter Even. They have Solemne Service on Saturdayes."[39]

Another authority, Josephus Abudacnus, writing in the eighteenth century in his history of the Jacobites, stated that they assembled every Sabbath in their temples, to which statement the later editor, J. Nicholai, adds the following footnote:

Our author states that the Jacobites assembled on the Sabbath day, before the Dommical day, in the temple, and kept that day, as do also the Abyssinians as we have seen from the confession of their faith by the Ethiopia king Claudius. . . . From this it appears that the Jacobites have kept the Sabbath as well as the Dommical day, and still continue to keep it.[40]

Alexander Ross writes that the Maronites likewise observed the Sabbath as well as Sunday.[41] Thus, we see how these four Eastern communions, three of which never walked with the papacy, continued to honor the Sabbath.

---

[37] Geddes, *The Church History of Ethiopia*, pages 87, 88.
[38] *Ibid.*, pages 311, 312.
[39] Purchas, *His Pilgrimes*, vol. 8, p. 73.
[40] Abudacnus, *Historia Jacobitarum*, pages 118, 119.
[41] Ross, *Religions in the World*, page 493.

As one looks upon the approximately five centuries of Mohammedan rule in Asia, three things are worthy of notice. In the first place, the comparatively tolerant attitude of the rulers is comforting. This is not to say that at times there were not periods of persecution and fierce opposition. However, one does not witness a persistent, determined purpose to root out Christians by cruel, bloody wantonness. The supreme motive of the Moslem conqueror was the lust of power rather than a fanatical passion to kill and to ruin other faiths. The leaders of Islam were so continuously occupied by war among themselves that they had neither time nor desire to frame within their own ranks an organization of the clergy tied firmly to absolute obedience, as was seen in the papal hierarchy. Dynasties rose and fell, but the Church of the East grew and extended its missions over all the lands of Asia.

Secondly, one is surprised by the splendidly balanced organization which energized the Church of the East. Rejecting the polygamy of the Moslems, it was not distracted by domestic broils. This same church refused to emphasize an unmarried life for its clergy, the rule which prevailed in Buddhism and in Western Romanism. As marriage was designed of God not only to increase love, but to purify love, the Church of the East was safeguarded against such degradation of standards as was seen in the Buddhist priests and nuns. Their thoughts ever turned toward their Sabbath home, dearer to them than any palace halls. In other words, they obeyed the four divine policies laid down in the first chapter of Genesis; namely, the worship of the Creator, Sabbath observance, family life, and proper diet and temperance.

Lastly, the members of the Church of the East were not only a church of evangelical activities, but also a people of sound doctrines. It is difficult to say which is the more dangerous—sound doctrines without evangelism, or evangelism without sound doctrine. The first leads to coldness in religion; the second produces vaudeville in preaching. Both these extremes were avoided by the Church of the East. It was able to give a reason for the faith, and at the same time, it displayed a life of missionary zeal and sacrifice which has seldom been surpassed.

CHAPTER XIX

The St. Thomas Christians of India

With all its intolerance and its terrors, the Inquisition was set up at Goa (India) in the sixteenth century; and when it was resolved to subjugate the Syrian Church to papal jurisdiction, this relentless institution was used to overawe it, and to prevent the arrival of bishops from Babylon. The subjugation was consummated by the Synod of Diamper in 1599, and for nearly two generations Rome's tyranny endured, until the splendid rebellion of the Assyrian Church at Coonen Cross.[1]

IN INDIA, the land of color and romance, the gospel was proclaimed as early as it had been in Italy. Christ had told His disciples that they should be witnesses for Him unto the uttermost parts of the earth,[2] and the apostles were ready to go anywhere. With a faith great enough to remove mountains, they did not hesitate to evangelize any tribe or nation regardless of how terrifying the situation to be encountered.

An early ecclesiastical writer states that when the world was portioned off for evangelization, Thomas was assigned to Parthia.[3] There is evidence enough that Thomas worked in Parthia. Libraries are full of literature telling of his founding churches in India.[4]

The accounts that tell how Thomas raised up and established Christianity in India form an interesting link in the lives of the apostles. The Master chose young men as His disciples, who were able to carry on the work for many years after His crucifixion in A. D. 31. Paul was beheaded about thirty-five years later. Thomas was killed, some authorities state, in 72 on the west coast of India by the lance of Brahman.[5] Evidence shows that the apostle John, living to the

---

[1] Rae, *The Syrian Church in India*, pages 196, 197.
[2] Acts 1:8.
[3] Eusebius, *Ecclesiastical History*, b. 3, ch. 1, found in *Nicene and Post-Nicene Fathers*, 2d Series, vol. 1.
[4] When the writer visited Miramon in the kingdom of Travancore in southern India, where the largest camp meeting in the world is annually held, the St. Thomas Christians enthusiastically pointed out the place where the apostle Thomas had built a church. "See," said they, "that farm over there? That farm is located on the spot where he secured his first converts."
[5] Neale, *A History of the Holy Eastern Church*, vol. 1, General Introduction, p. 145.

ripe old age of one hundred (according to Jerome), must have heard all about the spiritual victories in India before he wrote his Gospel and the book of Revelation.

Thomas and the Gospel in India

The question of whether Thomas ever labored in India or not has been discussed by many authors, and immense research has been done in the hope of arriving at an irrefutable conclusion. It is well known that if the Church in the Wilderness ever suffered in any country, it certainly suffered in India. All are desirous of knowing who was the founder of that church. A. Mingana writes:

> It is the constant tradition of the Eastern Church that the apostle Thomas evangelized India, and there is no historian, no poet, no breviary, no liturgy, and no writer of any kind who, having the opportunity of speaking of Thomas, does not associate his name with India.[6]

J. M. Neale testifies:

> There is a constant tradition of the church, that the gospel was first preached in India by the apostle St. Thomas. Having evangelized Arabia the Happy, and the Island of Zocotra, he arrived at Cranganor, a town situated a little to the north of Cochin, and where the most powerful among the princes who ruled in Malabar then resided. Having here wrought many miracles, and established a church, he journeyed southward to the city of Coulan. Here his labors were attended with equal success, and after traversing the peninsula he arrived at Meliapour, a town close to the more celebrated city of Madras. Sailing from this port he preached Christianity in China, and returning again to Meliapour, extended the knowledge of the faith so widely as to excite the envy and hatred of the Brahmins. Two of them watching an opportunity, stirred up the people against him; they fell on him and stoned him. One of the Brahmins remarking some signs of life in the holy apostle, pierced him with a lance, and thus completed his martyrdom.[7]

M. L'Abbé Huc, the brilliant Jesuit traveler and writer, says:

> The circumstance of St. Thomas having preached at all in India has been frequently called in question by writers deserving of attention; but we find it supported by so much evidence, that it seems difficult for an unprejudiced mind to refuse credit to a fact guaranteed by such excellent historical authorities. All the Greek, Latin, and Syriac monuments pro-

---

[6] Mingana, "Early Spread of Christianity," *Bulletin of John Ryland's Library,* vol. 10, pp. 447, 448.

[7] Neale, *A History of the Holy Eastern Church,* vol. 1, General Introduction, p. 145.

claim that St. Thomas was the apostle of the Indies, who carried the torch of faith into the remote regions where he suffered martyrdom. Some writers have affirmed that he prosecuted his apostolical labors as far even as China; and the mission and the martyrdom of Saint Thomas in the Indies have been alluded to in all the martyrologies, and in the ancient liturgies, which form the most pure and authentic source of Christian tradition.[8]

W. F. Adeney, citing the origins of the Armenian, the Abyssinian, and the Georgian Churches, says:

> The Syrian Church in India, which claims St. Thomas as its founder— all of them independent churches in regions outside the Roman Empire— will claim our attention later on; because as they have remained in independent existence on to our own day we shall want to know something about the course of their history right down the centuries.[9]

The testimony of J. D. D'Orsey is this:

> Amidst the clouds which cover the traditions of the Christians of St. Thomas, the following account seems to possess the greatest amount of probability, and the nearest approach to truth. After having established Christianity in Arabia Felix, and in the island of Dioscorides (now called Socotora), the holy apostle landed at Cranganor, at that time the residence of the most powerful king on the Malabar Coast. We know, from the historians of the Christian people, from Josephus and from the Sacred Books themselves, in the account of the miracle of Pentecost that before the birth of Jesus Christ, there went forth from Judea a great number of its inhabitants, and that they were scattered throughout Egypt, Greece, and several countries of Asia. St. Thomas learnt that one of these little colonies had settled in a country adjacent to Cranganor. Love for his nation inflamed his zeal; and faithful to the command of Jesus Christ who had enjoined His apostles to proclaim the faith to the Jews, before turning to the Gentiles, he repaired to the country which his compatriots had chosen for their asylum; he preached to them the gospel, converted them, and changed their synagogue into a Christian church. *This was the cradle of Christianity in India.*[10]

Entrance of Christianity Into India

In the days of Thomas the apostle, one authority states, "One hundred twenty great ships sailed for India from Egypt every year."[11]

---

[8] Huc, *Christianity in China, Tartary, and Thibet,* vol. 1, pp. 17, 18.
[9] Adeney, *The Greek and Eastern Churches,* page 297.
[10] D'Orsey, *Portuguese Discoveries, Dependencies, and Missions in Asia and Africa,* pages 63, 64.
[11] Mingana, "Early Spread of Christianity," *Bulletin of John Ryland's Library,* vol. 10, p. 90.

As witnesses to the vast trade carried on between Rome and those eastern countries before and after Christ, large quantities of Roman coins have been found in south India lands. Theodor Mommsen evaluated the Roman coinage sent annually to India as being worth five hundred thousand pounds sterling.[12] There is, therefore, nothing to render improbable the pioneer evangelization of Parthia and India by the apostle Thomas.

"Their sound went into all the earth, and their words unto the ends of the world," the apostle Paul could say in his day of those who had spread the gospel.[13] Consider how many nations were represented at Jerusalem on the eventful Day of Pentecost, and the character of their representatives. "Devout men, out of every nation under heaven," is the record. Who were they? "Parthians, and Medes, and Elamites, and the dwellers in Mesopotamia, . . . Cretes and Arabians."[14] The story of Pentecost spread as if on the wings of the wind when these visitors enthusiastically returned to their homes and hearths. Tradition claims that Thomas reached India soon after Pentecost.[15]

Another situation which favored the rapid expansion of the gospel to the East was the dispersion of the Jews throughout Asia. The progeny of Abraham covered the East; there was hardly a land or city where they had not gone. These descendants celebrated their holy days in a way which recalled their Jewish associations.[16] The beginnings of Christianity in Edessa (modern Urfa in Asia Minor), the first intellectual center for the spread of Christianity to the East, was among the Jews.[17] In fact, the Jews for a long time formed the major portion of the infant church.[18]

Another medium for the diffusion of the gospel to the Orient was the Aramaic language. The Hebrew, Syriac, and Aramaic—the latter, Christ's native speech—were cognate languages. History tells that Josephus, the famous Jewish author in the days of the apostles, wrote his *Wars of the Jews* first in Aramaic and later in Greek because of

---

[12] Mingana, "Early Spread of Christianity," *Bulletin of John Ryland's Library,* vol. 10, p. 94.
[13] Romans 10:18.
[14] Acts 2:5, 9-11.
[15] *The Catholic Encyclopedia,* art. "Thomas."
[16] Couling, *The Luminous Religion,* pages 7-10.
[17] Burkitt, *Early Eastern Christianity,* page 34.
[18] *The Catholic Encyclopedia,* art. "Calendar."

the large Aramaic reading constituency in the East. The Aramaic had widely penetrated the Parthian Empire, including Seleucia-Ctesiphon, the brilliant twin-city capital of that empire.[19]

Christianity's Early Growth in India

Naturally, the Church of the East looking back to Thomas as its founder, placed no value on the claim that Peter was the "rock" upon which Christ would build His church and that He would give the "keys" to Peter only. The difference between the Church of India in dating its origins from the apostle Thomas and the Church of Rome in dating its origins from the apostle Peter, is a difference of doctrines and practices. This contrast appears in the account given by the historian Gibbon of the first meeting between the Jesuits when they arrived on the coast of India, and the St. Thomas Christians. He writes:

> When the Portuguese first opened the navigation of India, the Christians of St. Thomas had been seated for ages on the coast of Malabar. . . . The title of Mother of God was offensive to their ear; and they measured with scrupulous avarice the honors of the Virgin Mary, whom the superstition of the Latins had *almost* exalted to the rank of a goddess. When her image was first presented to the disciples of St. Thomas they indignantly exclaimed, "We are Christians, not idolaters!"[20]

How much the world owes to the brave stand made by Christianity in India, man will never know until the judgment. For the first six hundred years the churches of southern India grappled successfully with dominant Buddhism; then for the succeeding one thousand years they contended with a degraded and wily Hinduism. But the real struggle began in the seventeenth century when the Jesuits, supported by the guns of Portugal, entered their parishes. It was not the missionaries from Rome, therefore, who first entered India. The type of New Testament faith first planted on the Malabar Coast nineteen hundred years ago is still there and is similar to that of the rest of the Protestant world.

For sixteen hundred years the St. Thomas Christians refused to put the church above the Bible. They found their starting point in the Sacred Scriptures, rather than in the catch phrase that the church

---

[19] Rae, *The Syrian Church in India,* pages 70-72.
[20] Gibbon, *Decline and Fall of the Roman Empire,* ch. 47, par. 31.

was "instinct with heavenly life." They refused to accept the teaching that the clergy only and not the laity were capable of interpreting the Bible. Accordingly, they clung to the Sacred Writings as the only channel through which the saving and transforming influence of the Holy Spirit could work. They refused to choose salvation through the sacraments rather than through the Scriptures. "The words that I speak unto you, they are spirit, and they are life," said Jesus,[21] and they cherished His admonition.

"Any attempt," Mingana writes, "to speak of early Christianity in India as different from the East Syrian Church, is, in our judgment, bound to fail. Christianity in India constituted an integral part of the church that began to develop vigorously towards the end of the first century in the Tigris valley."[22]

About this time three great revolutions of significance took place —one in the bosom of Christianity, one in the Parthian Empire, and the third in the Roman Empire. The first revolution occurred when the Church of the East definitely broke with the West by electing Papas of Seleucia as its independent supreme head (A. D. 285), thus recognizing the importance of a regular autonomous organization of its own. Why did this new catholicos ten years after his election make India into one of the grand ecclesiastical divisions of the world field and ordain David of Basra, famous for his learning, as the first supervising director of the new division?[23] The answer is not far to seek. The Persians, led on by fanatical Zoroastrianism, organized themselves with new strength, attacked, and overthrew the Parthians. Here was a new situation for the believers. As the victorious Persian Empire was intolerantly Zoroastrian, or Mithraistic, it was necessary for the Church of the East to meet the changed situation by a new setup of its own. This it did by electing Papas as catholicos.

The third revolution was the compromise of Christianity with paganism. The emperor, Constantine, saw it to his advantage to straddle the issue. The last pagan persecution of New Testament believers was raging furiously when Constantine assumed the imperial purple and decreed the termination of religious hostilities. His Sunday

---

[21] John 6:63.
[22] Mingana, "Early Spread of Christianity," *Bulletin of John Ryland's Library,* vol. 10, p. 440.
[23] Keay, *A History of the Syrian Church in India,* page 17.

law of 321 was a bait thrown to compromising Christians and an appeasement for those Romans who glorified the day exalted by the sun-worshiping Zoroastrians.

But Constantine did not stop there. Persecution began anew. This time it was not against all Christians, but against those churches who were determined to defend the faith once delivered to the saints. They fled. The hatred of the Romans by the Persians meant hatred of the new Roman Christianity and sympathy for the gospel believers. Therefore, refugees, some of the best church members in Europe, followed in the steps of their brethren who were persecuted by pagan Rome one hundred years previous, and joined the Church of the East. Following this growth of the Assyrian Church, a new migration of believers, composed of skilled mechanics, merchants, artisans, and clergy, left for India in 345.

It is amazing to learn how quickly blindness settled over the hierarchy of the West after the Council of Nicaea. The Dark Ages, destined to overshadow papal lands for a thousand years, drew on. In the East there was a light. The Church in the Wilderness was the ark which carried the Sacred Writings over from the apostolic age to the dawn of modern liberty. Claudius Buchanan in his researches in 1812 found among the St. Thomas Christians of the Malabar Coast a copy of the Bible which he believes has been among them from the days before the Council of Nicaea. Thus he wrote: "In every church, and in many of the private houses, here are manuscripts in the Syriac language: and I have been successful in procuring some old and valuable copies of the Scriptures and other books, written in different ages and in different characters."[24] He wrote of another city in Travancore, "In this place I have found a good many valuable manuscripts."[25]

Christianity in India During the Dark Ages

Upon report from India on the condition of the Malabar Christians, the catholicos sent Thomas, a merchant, with clergymen, deacons, artisans, and skilled workmen (a company of three thousand persons) to settle among the brethren in Travancore (c. A. D. 345). The king of Malabar received them kindly and gave them social and commercial privileges of great value. Some believe that these privileges granted

---

[24] Buchanan, *Christian Researches in Asia,* pages 126, 127.
[25] *Ibid.,* page 140.

by King Perumal ranked these Christians and their disciples among the nobility.

For more than one hundred years fresh bands of believers kept arriving from Persia. The reign of Shapur II, who was ruling Persia after the adoption of Christianity in the Roman Empire by Constantine, lasted for more than sixty years. When Persia was at peace, primitive believers coming from the West were well treated; but in war it was different. The two empires being in conflict following the death of Constantine, it was natural that the Zoroastrians would be suspicious of all Christians and claim that they were spies in the pay of the Roman Empire. How India would be likely to become a haven of refuge to the persecuted is thus easily understood.

That the existence of Christians in India appealed to the imagination of believers in Europe may be seen from the many references to the fact found in the writings of the second, third, and fourth centuries.

The evangelical and simple spirit shown by the high reverence of these Christians for the Holy Scriptures characterized them as neither papal nor Jewish. Mingana writes: "The fifth century opens with an Indian Christianity which is in such a state of development that she is able to send her priests to be educated in the best schools of the East Syrian Church and to assist the doctors of that Church in their revision of the ancient Syriac translations of the Pauline Epistles."[26]

Thus the opening of the year A. D. 500 discloses communities of Assyrian Christians throughout India. Faithful in their evangelical missionary life, they assembled for worship on the Sabbath day.[27] When priests from Rome entered India a thousand years later, papal hatred stigmatized the persecuted church as Judaizers. These St. Thomas Christians watched carefully over the spiritual training of

---

[26] Mingana, "Early Spread of Christianity," *Bulletin of John Ryland's Library,* vol. 10, p. 459.

[27] Mingana proves that as early as A. D., 225 there existed large bishoprics or conferences of the Church of the East stretching from Palestine to, and surrounding, India. In 370 Abyssinian Christianity (a Sabbathkeeping church) was so popular that its famous director, Musaeus, traveled extensively in the East promoting the church in Arabia, Persia, India, and China. In 410 Isaac, supreme director of the Church of the East, held a world council,—stimulated, some think, by the trip of Musaeus,—attended by eastern delegates from forty grand metropolitan divisions. In 411 he appointed a metropolitan director for China. These churches were sanctifying the seventh day, as can be seen by the famous testimonies of Socrates and Sozomen, Roman Catholic historians (c. A. D. 450), that all the churches throughout the world sanctified Saturday except Rome and Alexandria, which two alone exalted Sunday. A century later (c. A. D. 540) Cosmas, the celebrated world traveler, a

their children, having no higher purpose in life for them than to be ministers or missionaries. Their schools were on a level with the best in the world and were far above those in many lands. The speedy and commodious passage by sea direct from Egypt to southern India, as well as from the Persian Gulf to the same destination, kept them in touch with thought and scholarship elsewhere. They did not ignorantly arrive at the doctrines they held, but founded their faith first on the fact of its transmission direct from the apostles and, secondly, on prayer and devout study. "This union of the Church of India with that of Mesopotamia and Persia is rendered more evident by another scholar of the school of Edessa, Mana, bishop of Riwardashir, who wrote in Persian (i. e., Pahlavi) religious discourses, canticles, and hymns, and translated from Greek into Syriac the works of Diodorus and Theodore of Mopsuestia and sent them all to India."[28]

The Assyrian Christians were not only scholars, translators, and clergymen, but they were also travelers. Cosmas, who resided near Babylon, widely read for his explorations in the first half of the sixth century, sailed the Indian Seas so frequently that he has been called Indicopluestes (India traveler). Cosmas was personally in touch with the patriarch of the Assyrian Church. In his famous passages revealing how far-flung was the Church of the East, of which he was a member, he says that there was an infinite number of churches with their clergy and a vast number of Christian people among the Bactrians, Huns, Persians, Greeks, Elamites, and the rest of the Indians.[29]

In relating his explorations in Ceylon, Cosmas tells that the island

---

member of the great Church of the East, testified to the multiplied number of churches of his faith he had seen in India and central Asia and to those he had learned about in Scythia and China. We wrote in previous pages of the Sabbathkeeping Irish, Scottish, Welsh, and English Churches in the British Isles during these same centuries and down to 1200. We dwelt upon the Paulicians, Petrobrusians, Passagians, Waldenses, Insabbatati, as great Sabbathkeeping bodies of Europe down to 1250. We wrote of the Sabbatarians in Bohemia, Transylvania, England, and Holland between 1250 and 1600, as authenticated by Cox, Jones, Allix, and William of Neuburg. We have mentioned the innumerable Sabbathkeeping churches among the Greeks, Abyssinians, Armenians, Marionites, Jacobites, Scythians, and the great Church of the East (also from A. D. 1250 to 1600) with supporting evidence from competent authorities. The doctrines of all these Sabbathkeeping bodies throughout the centuries were comparatively pure, and the lives of their members were simple and holy. They were free from the unscriptural ceremonies which arose from the following of tradition. They received the Old Testament, and the whole Bible was their authority.

[28] Mingana, "Early Spread of Christianity," *Bulletin of John Ryland's Library,* vol. 10, p. 460.

[29] *Ibid.,* vol. 10, p. 462.

has a church of Persian Christians settled there with a presbyter appointed from Persia and a deacon well furnished with all necessary articles for public worship. Commenting on these facts, Mingana writes: "The above quotations from Cosmas prove not only the existence of numerous Christian communities among many central Asian people, in India, and in the surrounding districts, but also the subordination of all of them to the Nestorian patriarchate of Seleucia and Ctesiphon." [30]

What Cosmas wrote about the island of Socotra in the Indian Ocean, lying directly in the path of sea travel from Egypt to southern India, is significant. He said that all the inhabitants were Assyrian Christians. What his successor in travels, the famous Italian voyager Marco Polo, who belonged to the papal church, wrote concerning Socotra in 1295—long enough after Cosmas to see the headquarters of the church removed from Seleucia to Bagdad—is also revealing:

> Their religion is Christianity, and they are duly baptized, and are under the government, as well temporal as spiritual, of an archbishop, who is not in subjection to the pope of Rome, but to a patriarch who resides in the city of Baghdad, by whom he is appointed. Or sometimes he is elected by the people themselves, and their choice is confirmed. [31]

Of the same place Nicolo de Conti, another renowned traveler, wrote about 1440: "This island produces Socotrine aloes, is six hundred miles in circumference, and is for the most part inhabited by Nestorian Christians." [32]

About the year 774 reinforcements arrived from the West. This event evidently raised the standing of the Malabar Christians in the eyes of the reigning king. He issued one of those copperplate charters, so familiar in the history of India, to Iravi Corttan, evidently the head of the Christian community. This recognized him as a sovereign merchant of the kingdom of Kerala, and evidently promoted the Christians considerably above the level of their pagan surroundings. [33]

About fifty years after the contingent of 774 had arrived, in the providence of God more reinforcements came. They evidently were

---

[30] Mingana, "Early Spread of Christianity," *Bulletin of John Ryland's Library*, vol. 10, p. 462.
[31] Komroff, *The Travels of Marco Polo*, page 311.
[32] Major, *India in the Fifteenth Century*, Travels of Nicolo Conti, page 20.
[33] Rae, *The Syrian Church in India*, page 155.

an overflow of the Christians in Persia who by this time had grown to be a large proportion of the population there. They declined to settle down selfishly in the midst of their homeland affluence. A contingent of outstanding men with their families left for Travancore. Though Mohammedanism by this time had become all-powerful in Iran, it had not yet made a dent on the greater part of India. Led by the prayer of faith, two prominent leaders in the Church of the East conducted this Christian colony to the kingdom of Kerala.[34]

The date of these new arrivals was 822. They were received with honors, and a future status of power and privileges was accorded them in a charter of five copperplates.[35] Into a kingdom of India, then, still sufficiently strong to repel foreign invaders, came the new Christian recruits. The privileges granted at the time on the copperplates politically raised the native church to a position of independence in their pagan surroundings; socially placed them next to the Brahmans; and spiritually gave them freedom in religious life. All this reveals the strength of the church on the Malabar Coast in the ninth century.

Concerning their status seven centuries later, William W. Hunter writes: "The Portuguese found them firmly organized under their spiritual leaders, bishops, archdeacons, and priests, who acted as their representatives in dealing with the Indian princes. For long they had Christian kings, and at a later period chiefs, of their own."[36] Spreading all over the land, they possessed an organization simple and workable as well as strong. Every community that was under a supreme spiritual director endeavored to maintain a college of advanced grades. From these institutions of learning graduates went to the scholarly theological seminaries in Assyria.

The Portuguese arrived about 1500. The Jesuits soon followed. Care was taken to burn all the records of these "heretical" communities; otherwise, more details of the date and place could be given.[37] Nevertheless, enough has come down from secular and church

---

[34] Adeney, *The Greek and Eastern Churches,* pages 520, 521.

[35] Two of these plates were shown to the author by Mar Thomas (the word "Mar" is their title for clergy of official rank), supreme head of the St. Thomas Christians, in his church headquarters at Tiruvalla, Travancore. The other three plates, now in possession of the leader of the Jacobites at Kottayam, could not be seen as he was absent from the church at the time of my visit.

[36] Hunter, *The Indian Empire,* page 240.

[37] Neale, *A History of the Holy Eastern Church,* vol. 1, General Introduction, p. 148.

historians to give a real picture of their activities. There are also the observations made by the European and Moslem travelers.[38] Marco Polo related that there were six great kings and kingdoms in the heart of India, three of which were Christian, the other three being Mohammedan. "The greatest of all the six," he said, "is a Christian."[39]

The Church in the Wilderness in India continued to grow throughout the thirteenth, fourteenth, and fifteenth centuries. After that it entered into its fatal struggle with the Jesuits. Mingana presents the important testimony of Marignolli, who in his *Recollections of Eastern Travel,* speaks of Indian Christians as being the masters of the steelyards and the proprietors of the spices of south India.[40] Nicolo de Conti, another traveler in India in the same century, tells us that the Nestorians "were scattered over all India in like manner as are the Jews among us."[41] As indicative of the carefulness of the life they lived, Conti further reports that though they are spread all over India, they are the only exceptions in the matter of polygamy. He recounts that he met a man from north India who told him that there was a kingdom twenty days' journey distant from Cathay (north China) where the king and all the inhabitants were Nestorians, and that he had come to India to find out about these same Christians. Conti observes that the churches of the Christians in this kingdom which he had described were larger and more powerful than those in India.[42]

Louis of Varthema has written a most interesting book on his itinerary in southern Asia in the fifteenth century. He tells of the St. Thomas Christians which he met on the Malabar Coast in 1505, and also describes the reputed tomb of St. Thomas, a short distance from Madras on the Coromandel Coast.[43]

He recounts a curious story of the merchants of the St. Thomas Christians whom he met in Bengal, as follows:

> They said that they were from a city called Sarnau (in Siam) and had brought for sale silken stuffs, and aloes wood, and benzoin, and musk. Which

---

[38] Smith, *The Oxford History of India,* page 300.
[39] Yule, *Travels of Marco Polo,* vol. 2, p. 427.
[40] Mingana, "Early Spread of Christianity," *Bulletin of John Ryland's Library,* vol. 10, p. 487.
[41] Major, *India in the Fifteenth Century,* Travels of Nicolo Conti, page 7.
[42] *Ibid.,* page 33.
[43] Temple, *The Itinerary of Ludovico di Varthema of Bologna From 1502 to 1508,* pages 59, 60.

Christians said that in their country there were many lords also Christians, but they are subject to the great khan (of) Cathai (China). As to the dress of these Christians, they were clothed in a *kebec* (jerkin) made with folds, and the sleeves were quilted with cotton. And on their heads they wore a cap a palm and a half long, made of red cloth. These same men are as white as we are, and confess they are Christians. . . . We departed thence with the said Christians, and went towards a city which is called Pego (in Burma), distant from Banghella (Bengal) about a thousand miles. On which voyage we passed a gulf (of Martaban) towards the south, and so arrived at the city of Pego.[44]

Varthema was of the papal faith, and he recognized that the religion of the region of Pego was different. He says that the king "has with him more than a thousand Christians of the country which has been above mentioned to you, that is, Nestorians from Sarnau."[45] He and his traveling companions struck a bargain with the Christians that they should act as guides while they visited the islands of Sumatra, Java, Borneo, and Maluko. It is characteristic of this outstanding missionary church that its members were not content with having planted the seeds of their faith in Persia, India, and China, but that they also extended their work down the Malacca Strait over into Sumatra, Java, Borneo, and the Spice Islands. It is written that the catholicos, Elijah V, in 1503 ordained three metropolitans and sent one to India, one to China, and one to Java.

These churches held fast throughout the years to the simple faith which no doubt came down to them from the apostle Thomas. Having won great victories over heathenism, they were now to sustain their greatest trial as the Jesuits began arriving in the sixteenth century.

---

[44] Temple, *The Itinerary of Ludovico di Varthema of Bologna From 1502 to 1508,* pages 79, 80.
[45] *Ibid.,* Preliminary Discourse, page lxix.

CHAPTER XX

The Great Struggle in India

Besides hunting down heretics, Jews, new Christians, and all who were accused of Judaizing (that is, conforming to the ceremonies of the Mosiac law, such as not eating pork, attending the solemnization of the Sabbath, partaking of the paschal lamb, and so forth), the Goanese Inquisitors also replenished their dungeons with persons accused of magic and sorcery.[1]

WHILE the Church of the East was expanding in India and the Orient, events in the West were hastening to the crisis which lifted the gloom of the Dark Ages. The conflict between established systems and the word of God had been precipitated. In 1517 Luther had taken his stand for the Holy Scriptures, and they were being reinstated in their proper place. The Dark Ages were passing.

At this time a new Catholic order of monasticism was formed, called the Society of Jesus, generally known as the Jesuits. It was distinctly brought into existence for the purpose of recovering, if possible, what was lost, to repair what was injured, to fortify and guard what remained, and to advance the revival of the papacy.[2] Before Spain and Portugal had been reached by the reforming power of a newly born Protestantism, the order of the Jesuits had made a secure alliance with the monarchies of those countries. It was a dark night for the St. Thomas Christians when the Jesuits, supported by the guns of Portugal, arrived in India.

It was the lot of Portugal to erect an astonishing empire in the East. It is amazing how little the public remembers of those seven areas seized by the Portuguese men-of-war and completely claimed by the crown as imperial domain, an act to which the pope gave his sanction.[3] Omitting the settlements on the west coast of Africa, this vast colonial dominion may be divided into the following parts: (1) the east coast of Africa with adjacent islands, (2) the south coasts of Arabia and Persia, (3) the coasts of Baluchistan and northwest India, (4)

---

[1] Rae, *The Syrian Church in India*, page 200.
[2] Mosheim, *Institutes of Ecclesiastical History*, b. 4, cent. 16, sec. 3, pt. 1, ch. 1, pars. 10-12.
[3] Hunter, *A Brief History of the Indian People*, page 151.

the west coast of India, in which was located, as the Portuguese called it, the "most noble city of Goa," (5) the east coast of India, (6) the west coast of what is today Burma and the Malay States, (7) the coast from Singapore around to Siam, Indo-China, and China, as far north as the island of Macao. While one is astonished at the thrilling exploits of the Portuguese cavaliers who subdued these overseas kingdoms, he is obliged to deplore their fanaticism and cruelty. As J. D. D'Orsey says: "Religion, or rather religious fanaticism, was the inspiring principle, the very mainspring of every movement, of every heroic exploit. Their wars were rather crusades than patriotic struggles."[4]

One incident illustrating the cruelty which ultimately caused the downfall of the invaders may be recited. On the third expedition from Portugal (A. D. 1502), commanded by Vasco da Gama, a fleet of twenty vessels sailed for Calicut. On the previous expedition the zamorin (ruler) of the Hindu kingdom of Calicut had been induced by Arabian merchantmen of wealth to fall upon the Portuguese, at which time Gasper Correa, a dear friend of Vasco's, was murdered. Vasco da Gama's motives in this new expedition were to punish the Moslems for this death, as well as for their insults to Catholicism. While on his way, he encountered an ocean vessel filled with Moslem pilgrims returning from Mecca. The Arabs, knowing the superiority of the Portuguese, offered a large ransom, which was accepted. Nevertheless, command was given to fire the boat. The desperate people succeeded in extinguishing the flames, but Da Gama ordered them relighted. It is related that mothers held their children up toward Da Gama, pleading for mercy. The conflagration was so terrible that one writer has likened it to the fires of inferno.[5] Nevertheless, the Jesuits were cold to the awfulness of the deed, claiming that it was simply a prelude to further successes.

One expedition followed another, until the Portuguese supremacy was established. As the result of several wars, Goa, at the wide mouth of the Mandavi River, was seized, strongly fortified, and made the capital of the new empire. The mind visualizes the wide harbor teeming with the shipping of the world, the brilliant military caval-

---

[4] D'Orsey, *Portuguese Discoveries, Dependencies, and Missions in Asia and Africa,* page 5.
[5] *Ibid.,* pages 30, 31.

cades, the pomp of state, the coming and going of the ambassadors of the nations, the great warehouses bursting with merchandise to be exchanged between the West and the East, and the magnificent estates of the Latin nobility. Probably the most glamorous of all the spectacles of those brilliant days were the ecclesiastical processions and functions of the church. At Goa one can still gaze upon the splendid cathedral where the bell was tolled as the victims were led out to their execution. Such was the splendor, power, and wealth of Goa. When one visits Goa today, he finds that the Portuguese territory has dwindled to a small section of the country on the west central coast, so badly desolated that it is but a sickly shadow of its former greatness. However, many vestiges still remain of Goa's past grandeur and fame.

As the Jesuits were already in control of Spain and Portugal, they accompanied the conquerors principally for the purpose of converting the St. Thomas Christians.[6] It was the unhappy lot of India to experience the crushing weight of these haughty monks. These men were skilled in sublimated treachery and trained for years in the art of rapid debate in which they could trap an opponent by the cunning use of ambiguous terms; consequently, the simple, trusting St. Thomas Christians were no match for them. The Jesuits proposed to dominate all schools and colleges. This they sought to accomplish in non-Catholic schools by occupying the pulpits and the professorial chairs, not as Jesuits, but as professed adherents of the Protestant churches to which these schools belonged. As an example of their success by 1582, only forty-eight years after the order was founded, they controlled two hundred eighty-seven colleges and universities in Europe, some of which were of their own founding.

It was their studied aim to gain entrance, under the guise of friendship, into services of the state and to climb up as advisers to the highest officers, where they could so influence affairs as to bring them into the orbit of Rome. They were past masters of the ways of deception. They were adept in the policy of secretly bringing on a public disaster, simultaneously providing for salvation from the last terrors of that disaster; thus they would be credited with salvation from the extremity of the calamity, while others were blamed for its cause.

---

[6] Kaye, *Christianity in India*, reviewed in *Dublin University Magazine*, vol. 54, p. 340.

The Jesuits Capture the Council of Trent

This Society of Jesus proposed to subordinate the Holy Scriptures and in their place substitute the interpretations of the Bible by the ecclesiastical writers of the first centuries whom they called the "fathers." All the errors and vagaries of the allegorizers who confused and darkened the first three centuries were selected. The first great papal council which assembled after the Reformation, the Council of Trent (A. D. 1545-1563), was dominated by the Jesuits. This assembly laid down the law, and no papal authority has dared since to dispute it.

In assembling this church council, Emperor Charles V gave the order that only the abuses in the church, not doctrine, should be considered. He was distracted to behold his realm divided between two contending churches, and it mattered little to him which creed prevailed. He only wished some general assembly to remedy conditions. The emperor desired Lutherans and Catholics to sit together in a general council, and he fondly believed Europe again would be united.

The influence of the Jesuits was immediately seen when the pope ignored the imperial command to notify the Reformers. Weeks passed, and finally the council organized itself and accepted the following as its first four decrees: (1) The Vulgate was the true Bible and not the Received Text which the Reformers followed and which had been the Bible of the Greek Church, the Church of the East, and the true churches of the West through the centuries; (2) tradition was of equal authority with the Sacred Scriptures; (3) the five disputed books found in the Catholic Bible, but rejected by Protestant scholars, were declared canonical; (4) the priests only, and not the laity, were capable of rightly interpreting the Scriptures.[7]

When the emperor learned that the Protestants had not been called to the council, he was enraged. Uttering severe threats, he demanded that his original plan be executed. Though the pope reluctantly and with long delay obeyed, the decrees already passed irrevocably compromised the situation. The Lutherans refused to accept the insulting notifications. In the meantime the pope had died and his successor advocated Jesuit policies. The deliberations pro-

---

[7] Froude, *The Council of Trent,* pp. 174, 175; Muir, *The Arrested Reformation,* pages 152, 153; also, M'Clintock and Strong, *Cyclopedia,* art. "The Council of Trent."

ceeded as they had begun. Decree after decree was proclaimed; doctrine after doctrine was settled. Repeatedly the emperor was misled until he expressed his anger strongly to the Roman pontiff over the deceitful maneuvering.

How were the church prelates to defend these doctrines which had no scriptural authority?

Hours, weeks, and months; yes, many sessions went by with this anxious question in their hearts. Then, one morning, January 18, 1562, the archbishop of Rheggio hurried from his room and appeared before his confreres to proclaim that he had the answer. Protestants, he urgently reasoned, never could defend Sunday sacredness.[8] If they continued to offer as their authority "the Bible and the Bible only," it was clear that they had no Bible command for the first day of the week. According to Pallavicini, papal champion of the council, the archbishop said, "It is then evident that the church has power to change the commandments," because by its power alone and not by the preaching of Jesus it had transferred the Sabbath from Saturday to Sunday.[9] Tradition, they concluded, was not antiquity, but continuous inspiration. None could continue to fight the acceptance of tradition when the only authority for Sunday sacredness in the church was tradition. This discovery nerved the council to go forward with its work.

All the doctrines against which the Reformers had protested were thus again formulated and strengthened by Rome. All the rites and practices which the Church in the Wilderness had struggled to escape were incorporated more strongly than ever into papal tradition by the twenty-five sessions of the council between 1545 and 1563.

Henceforth, the papacy was to have only one mission in the world, namely, to command nations and men everywhere to submit to the Council of Trent. The new slogan now invented, which must go reverberating throughout the earth, was, "The Council of Trent, the Council of Trent, the Council of Trent." How poor India was made to tremble and bend beneath this cry!

With the Jesuits the Inquisition came into India. "A still more decided form of compulsion was the Inquisition established at Goa,

---

[8] Holtzmann, *Kanon und Tradition,* page 263.
[9] Pallavicini, *Histoire du Concile de Trente,* vol. 2, pp. 1031, 1032.

in the year 1560, which soon made itself felt by its terrible and mysterious punishments."[10] This was a European, not an Asiatic, engine of torment imposed upon the St. Thomas Christians of India. In it could be found torture by fire, by water, by the rack, and by burning at the stake.

The supreme punishment, of course, was burning at the stake. If the unhappy believer in New Testament Christianity failed to renounce his simple faith and accept all the innovations, rites, and mysteries of the Roman Catholic Church, the day would come when, with a black gown and a cowl over his head, he would be led to the public square to make the supreme sacrifice. Arriving at their Golgotha, those condemned to the flames would be chained to a high stake many feet above the piles of fagots. Then two Jesuits would wail out an exhortation to repent. When finally the nod of the inquisitor was given, blazing torches on long poles were dashed into the faces of the agonizing martyrs; and this continued until their faces were burned to cinder. The flames were then applied below; and as the roaring fire mounted higher and higher, it consumed the sufferers who died for their faith.

About the year 1674, Dr. M. G. Dellon, a French physician, was traveling in India. Suddenly he was seized and put into the prison of the Inquisition at Goa on the charge that he did not honor certain papal doctrines and that he had spoken contemptuously of the Inquisition. The real reason, he suspected, was that he had been sociable with a young lady to whom the Portuguese governor had been paying attention, although the traveler had no serious intentions.[11] He was confined in a dungeon ten feet square, where he remained nearly two years without seeing any person but the one who brought him his meals and those who brought him to trial. When arraigned before the court, he was obliged to walk barefoot with other prisoners over the sharp stones of the streets; this wounded his feet and caused the blood to flow. He says that his joy was inexpressible when he heard that he was not to be burned, but was to be sentenced to work as a galley slave for five years.[12]

---

[10] D'Orsey, *Portuguese Discoveries, Dependencies, and Missions in Asia and Africa,* page 163.

[11] Dellon, *Account of the Inquisition at Goa,* page 8; page 23, 1815 ed.

[12] Buchanan, *Christian Researches in Asia,* pages 169-172.

In his book written upon these experiences in the Inquisition, Dr. Dellon has revealed to the world the horrors of the place. He states that the buildings had two stories and contained about two hundred chambers; that the stench was so excessive that when night approached, he did not dare lie down for fear of the swarms of vermin and the filth which abounded everywhere.[13] Repeatedly he heard the cries of his fellow prisoners as they writhed in torture. He did not suffer this form of affliction; but, having undergone many prolonged examinations, he attempted suicide on several occasions. He was sent to serve out his sentence on a ship, but in voyaging he encountered a friend of influence who was able to obtain a commutation of his condemnation.

Recording the burning at the stake which was inflicted upon many of the St. Thomas Christians, the following statements are from the account by Dr. Dellon, reproduced by George M. Rae:

> But perhaps the blackest acts of this unholy assembly have yet to be recorded. The cases of such as were doomed to be burnt had yet to be disposed of, and they were accordingly ordered to be brought forward separately. They were a man and a woman, and the images of four men deceased, with the chests in which their bones were deposited. . . . Two of the four statues also represented persons convicted of magic, who were said to have *Judaized*. One of these had died in the prison of the Holy Office; the other expired in his own house, and his body had been long since interred in his own family burying ground, but, having been accused of Judaism after his decease, as he had left considerable wealth, his tomb was opened, and his remains disinterred to be burnt at the auto-da-fé. . . . We may well throw a veil over the smoky spectacle on the banks of the river which seems to have attracted the viceroy of Goa and his heartless retinue.[14]

How much the wrath of the Jesuits was directed against the St. Thomas Christians because they observed Saturday, the seventh day of the week, as the Sabbath may be seen in this further quotation from Rae: "In the remote parts of the diocese, as well as towards the south as towards the north, the Christians that dwell in the heaths are guilty of working and merchandizing on Sundays and holy days, especially in the evenings."[15]

---

[13] Dellon, *Account of the Inquisition at Goa*, pages 41, 42.
[14] Rae, *The Syrian Church in India*, pages 217, 218.
[15] *Ibid.*, page 238.

The Jesuits now proceeded methodically to obliterate the St. Thomas Christians. They depended upon their usual weapons: (1) the founding of a Jesuit college in which the youth won over from the Assyrian communities, or the St. Thomas Christians, were trained as papal clergymen in the Syrian tongue; (2) the power of the selecting of the Assyrian leaders; (3) the calling of a synod which they were assured beforehand they could dominate. The Jesuit college founded at Vaipicotta near Cochin introduced the Syrian language. It allowed the youth of the St. Thomas Christians to use Syrian dress. These youth were indoctrinated in the traditional beliefs and practices of the papacy. But when the teachers had finished the training of a number of Syrian Christian young people, these youth found that, as they went among their people, the Assyrian Church would not recognize them as clergymen. This church also refused to allow the Portuguese priests to enter into their places of worship.

Failing in this school venture, the Jesuits moved upon the heads of the church. One after another they singled out the leaders, Mar Joseph, Mar Abraham, and Mar Simeon. Not having bishops in the accepted usage of the term, the Church of the East called their provincial directors by the title, "mar," meaning "spiritual lord;" while the title "catholicos," or "patriarch," was given to the supreme head, the father of fathers at Bagdad (formerly at Seleucia). The Jesuits surrounded the leaders in India with spies. They threatened them with the terrors of the Inquisition at Goa.

During this time there came to Goa a papal prelate, Alexis de Menezes, the agent of Rome who succeeded in crushing the Assyrian Church. He was a man of invincible tenacity and consummate craft. The Vatican had elevated him to be archbishop of Goa and had commanded him to bring to an end the heresies of the St. Thomas Christians. At the death of Mar Abraham, Menezes turned with all his fury upon Archdeacon George, whom Abraham had appointed to act until the arrival from Bagdad of a new head of the church.

Menezes immediately undertook the difficult and unusual journey of approximately four hundred miles from Goa to the Malabar Coast. Archdeacon George was pressed to subscribe to the doctrines of Rome. He refused, saying that the St. Thomas Christians had always been, and always would be, independent of Rome. Of the immediate results, D'Orsey writes as follows:

21

Popular excitement was now at its height. The poor mountaineers, who had at first welcomed their Roman fellow Christians so warmly, were thoroughly excited against their oppressors. They looked upon the Portuguese as the relentless enemies of their ancient faith, and as the barbarous persecutors of their beloved bishops and priests. They therefore rose in arms, expelled the Jesuits from their country, and in two instances, were barely restrained from putting them to death.[16]

But the worst was yet to come. When the archbishop arrived at Cochin, January, 1599, he was received with an uproarious welcome. He had previously obtained an alliance with the Hindu raja, in whose territory the St. Thomas Christians dwelt, because he had used Portuguese fleets to wipe out a nest of pirates. "The grandest preparation had been made for his reception, richly carpeted stairs had been expressly constructed; the governor and a brilliant staff were at the landing place, and the prince of the church disembarked amid the waving of flags, the clang of martial music, the shouts of the people, and the thunder of artillery."[17]

Having soon disposed of military and political matters, the Roman Catholic primate turned his attention to the main project of his life. He summoned before him the perplexed and terrified archdeacon George. The latter decided to play a double game. He reasoned that if he could only temporize until Archbishop Menezes returned to Goa, time might work in his favor. He and his armed escort went to Cochin to welcome the powerful ecclesiastic. They kissed his hand, and gave him permission to preach and to sing mass in the Syrian churches. But when the archbishop learned that the patriarch of Babylon was mentioned in the prayers of the St. Thomas Christians as the universal pastor of the church, his anger knew no bounds. He summoned their professors, students, archdeacons, and clergy to appear before him, asserting with rage that the pope alone was supreme and that the Assyrian catholicos was a heretic. He produced a written document, excommunicating any person who should in the future pray for the patriarchs of Babylon or Bagdad. "Sign it," he ordered the archdeacon. The war galleys of the Portuguese lay in the harbor. In Menezes were united military power and church authority. To the scandal of Christianity, he forced the evangelical shepherd to sur-

---

[16] D'Orsey, *Portuguese Discoveries, Dependencies, and Missions in Asia and Africa*, page 190.
[17] *Ibid.*, page 193.

render the rights of his people. Quailing before the Jesuit archbishop, Archdeacon George signed.

Having struck down the head of the system, the papal prelate now proceeded to make a large number of St. Thomas Christian leaders sign away the remainder of their fifteen-hundred-year-old heritage. Having been given permission to visit the Syrian worshipers on condition that he would teach no papal doctrine, the archbishop broke his promise. He openly preached against the beliefs and practices of the Malabar Church. He even ordained young men to the ministry who promised to renounce the patriarch of Babylon and to recognize the pope. These youth gave up the distinctive teachings of the Church of the East for papal doctrines and rites. This he continued to do until he was assured of enough votes in the approaching synod. The archdeacon appealed to the raja for protection; but Menezes saw to it that by threats and favors all the rajas were restrained. One more act, and he had delivered the final blow.

He ordered Archdeacon George to submit to the pope and ratify the papal decrees authorizing the calling of a synod. The archdeacon hesitated. Then Menezes brought out the most terrible weapon of all which he had kept in reserve. He threatened the tormented leader of the helpless people with excommunication, and the Inquisition at Goa. Visions of the gibbet, the rack, and the fagot rose up before the lonely official. Overcome with terror, he signed the ten articles laid before him, which paved the way for the Synod of Diamper.

The Disastrous Synod of Diamper

The morning of June 20, 1599, was the day when a great church gave up its independence. Eleven days previous, Archbishop Menezes had arrived with his supporters and certain subservient Assyrian Church leaders in order to give final touches to the decrees which he proposed the synod should pass. He planned that this assembly should preserve all the appearances of a deliberative delegation, while in reality it was a subjected body.

It had been decided to hold the synod in the Church of All Saints at Diamper, a community which lies about fourteen miles east of Cochin. The crowds began to gather early. The government administration officers at Cochin, with a large staff of officers richly costumed in silk, velvet, and lace, blending in dazzling colors with polished mail and plumed helmets, had arrived the evening before.[18]

The papal church was represented by the dean, pastor, and choir. Along with them came the town council accompanied by merchants and captains of ships. In fact, all within traveling distance forsook their ordinary avocations in order to be present on the opening day. Archdeacon George, as leader of the St. Thomas Christians, came robed in splendid vestments of dark red silk, a large golden cross hanging from his neck, and his beard reaching below his girdle. One hundred fifty-three of their clergymen accompanied him, clad in their long white vestments and wearing their peculiar headdress of red silk. There were six hundred delegates from various Malabar churches, besides numerous deacons, which increased the body of Syrian representatives to nearly a thousand men.

Menezes delivered an opening address in which he thanked God for the large assembly crowding the little cathedral. His next act was to celebrate a solemn mass using the form designated by the Roman Catholic Church for the removal of the schism. He ignored completely the claims of the Syrian archdeacon to any part in the religious service. Then he mounted the pulpit to set forth vigorously the claims of the Roman pontiff to obedience, because he, as Christ's vicar upon earth, had been commanded to see to it that no Syrian successor should be permitted to land in India after the death of Mar Abraham. After this discourse he brought forth Rome's decrees and demanded that the delegates should pass by and sign them.

The first decree touching the differences between the two churches was like the first decree of the Council of Trent, and was directed against the Protestant Bible. This decree set up the Latin Vulgate as the Bible to be followed in contrast to the Syrian Bible. Other decrees were presented, aimed at the acknowledgment of the seven Roman sacraments, whereas the Syrians had recognized only three; they demanded that communion should be celebrated according to the papal rite, and that the Syrians should recognize in the eucharist, or Lord's Supper, the claim of transubstantiation. Then followed the decrees to bring the Syrian Church into line with the papal doctrines of penance, auricular confession, extreme unction, adoration of images, reverence for relics, purgatory, eternal punishment, the worship of

---

[18] D'Orsey, *Portuguese Discoveries, Dependencies, and Missions in Asia and Africa,* pages 215, 216.

saints, the doctrine of indulgence, papal supremacy, and above all, the worship of the Virgin Mary. All who taught anything contrary to the Council of Trent were to be accursed. Nine decrees were passed respecting the eucharist and fifteen regarding the mass, all pointing to the extirpation of Syrian practices and the introduction of Roman doctrine and ritual without the slightest concession.[19]

In addition to eliminating the Syrian Bible, it was demanded that all Syrian books were to be delivered up, altered, or destroyed; that every trace relating to the patriarch of Babylon or to the doctrines of the St. Thomas Christians was to be condemned; and that all St. Thomas Christians were to be subject to the Inquisition at Goa. Forty-one decrees were passed with reference to fasts and festivals, organization, and order in church affairs. In all there were nine sessions lasting a week and promulgating two hundred sixty-seven decrees.

The submission demanded of the archdeacon and his associated clergy is presented in the following words of the learned Geddes who gives an abbreviated translation of the actions of the synod, handed down by a scribe recognized as official by Portuguese authorities:

> The most reverend metropolitan after having made this protestation and confession of faith, rose up, and seating himself in his chair, with his miter on his head, and the holy Gospels, with a cross upon them in his hands; the Reverend George, archdeacon of the said bishopric of the Serra, kneeling down before him, made the same profession of faith, with a loud and intelligible voice, in the Malabar tongue, taking an oath in the hands of the lord metropolitan, and after him all the priests, deacons, subdeacons, and other ecclesiastics that were present, being upon their knees, Jacob, curate of Pallarty, and interpreter to the synod, read the said profession in Malabar, all of them saying it along with him; which being ended, they all took the oath in the hands of the lord metropolitan, who asked them one by one in particular, whether they did firmly believe all that was contained in the profession."[20]

Three of the demands passed by this crushing assembly stand out above all others for their cruelty. First, there was the decree demanding the celibacy of the clergy. If the synod had passed this regulation as of force from then on, it would have been a great enough

---

[19] D'Orsey, *Portuguese Discoveries, Dependencies, and Missions in Asia and Africa,* page 228.
[20] Geddes, *The Church History of Malabar,* pages 116, 117.

revolution; but the decree was made retroactive. All the Syrian priests were immediately to put away their wives. Since it had been the practice of the St. Thomas Christians to permit the wife of the priest to draw some little financial pay from the revenues of the church, this also was cut off, leaving the poor woman and her children without support.

Another of the cruel regulations was to single out for burning at the stake those Christians whom the Roman Catholic Church chose to designate as apostate.[21] As has been noted before, the Christians whom they designated as apostate were generally called Judaizers, or those who observed the seventh day as the Sabbath. Decree 15 of Action VIII, as recorded by Geddes, reads, "The synod doth command all the members thereof upon pain of mortal sin, not to eat flesh upon Saturdays."[22] Decree 16, which will not be rendered verbatim, demands that all feast and fast days shall commence and cease at midnight, because the practice of beginning and ending the day at sundown is Jewish.[23] This decree is in direct opposition to the Scriptures which command that the day begin at sunset.

The effort of the papacy to disgrace the Sabbath by turning it into a fast day is attested by many authors. The historian Neander has stated that the early opposition to the honoring of the seventh-day Sabbath by Christians led to the special observance of Sunday in its place.[24] Bishop Victorinus, about 290, betrays the real motive of the papacy in the introduction of the Sabbath fasting as follows: "Let the parasceve become a rigorous fast, lest we should appear to observe any Sabbath with the Jews."[25] Neander also wrote: "While in the Western, and especially in the Roman Church, where the opposition against Judaism predominated, the custom, on the other hand, grew out of this opposition, of observing the Sabbath also as a fast day."[26] Archbishop Menezes, therefore, in harmony with the usual practice of imperial Christianity forced the decree which turned Saturday into a fast day through the Synod of Diamper. This put those St. Thomas

---

[21] Rae, *The Syrian Church in India,* page 201.
[22] Geddes, *The Church History of Malabar,* page 357.
[23] *Ibid.,* pages 357, 358.
[24] Neander, *General History of the Christian Religion and Church,* vol. 1, p. 295.
[25] Victorinus, *On the Creation of the World,* found in *Ante-Nicene Fathers,* vol. 7, p. 342.
[26] Neander, *General History of the Christian Religion and Church,* vol. 1, p. 296.

Christians who in the future would observe the Sabbath as a festival, into the category of apostate Christians, and destined them for the stake at Goa. Thomas Yeates, who traveled largely in the Orient, writing of the St. Thomas Christians and other Christians of the East, said that Saturday "amongst them is a festival day agreeable to the ancient practice of the Church."[27]

Samuel Purchas, in enumerating the doctrines of the Syrian Church, said that they believed "that the Holy Ghost proceedeth only from the Father; that they celebrate Divine Service as solemnly on the Sabbath, as on the Lord's Day; that they keepe that day festivall, eating therein flesh, and fast no Saturday in the yeere but Easter Eve, . . . that they acknowledge not purgatory."[28]

In an earlier chapter it was noted how the papacy stigmatized as Arians those who disagreed with her in general, and in particular how she branded those as Judaizers who were convinced that "the Sabbath" of the fourth commandment was the seventh day. Writings are extant of irregular Gnostic or semi-Gnostic writers of the first three centuries who attempted to prove that God had abolished the Ten Commandments and that all the conscience needed was the guidance of the Holy Spirit. This no-law strain was strongly accentuated in ecclesiastical Christianity. Pope Gregory I, in 602, issued his famous bull in which he branded those Christians who conscientiously believed the seventh day to be the holy Sabbath of the fourth commandment as Judaizers and antichrist.[29] Consequently, down through the centuries the papacy has allowed no standing room whatever for sincere Christians who were convinced that the seventh day of the week was still binding upon the followers of Christ.

As an evidence that the St. Thomas Christians came under this unjust and reviling opprobrium of Judaizers because they solemnized the Sabbath, the reader's attention is called to the quotation at the head of this chapter. Moreover, as further testimony that other Christian bodies in India also sanctified Saturday, there is the authority of trustworthy historians that the Armenians kept Saturday as the Sabbath: "The Armenians in Hindustan . . . have preserved the Bible

---

[27] Yeates, *East Indian Church History*, page 72.
[28] Purchas, *His Pilgrimes*, vol. 1, pp. 351-353.
[29] *Epistles* of Gregory I, coll. 13, ep. 1, found in *Nicene and Post-Nicene Fathers*, 2d Series, vol. 13.

in its purity, and their doctrines are, as far as the author knows, the doctrines of the Bible. Besides they maintain the solemn observance of Christian worship, throughout our empire, on the seventh day."[30]

Another act of the Synod of Diamper which historians consider unforgivable was the decree to destroy, or alter beyond recognition, all the writings of the St. Thomas Christians. Having crushed the distinctive theological values of this church, the assembly reached out to obliterate all the cultural ties which bound her to the past. Manuals of church activities were torn to pieces, records of districts and documents relating the manifold contacts of this wonderful people were burned. What a wealth of evangelical literature was ruined in a moment!

Who can tell how much of the literature destroyed went back even to apostolic days, and would have thrown great light upon the work of the apostle Thomas and upon the early years of the Church of the East? Many difficult problems which face zealous missionary endeavors today in the Far East might have found their solution in this literature so wantonly obliterated. It has been noticed before that certain celebrated writers of the Assyrian Church in Persia and in other parts of the East not only translated their own productions to be sent to fellow believers in India, but also translated productions of other authors of great value and had them carried to the Malabar Coast. One would naturally have expected the Mohammedans to burn and destroy Christian literature when they overran central and farther Asia, but who would ever have expected this attempt to destroy such priceless treasure by a church which calls itself Christian?

Jesuit Seapower Destroyed by the English

While the Jesuits were destroying the Church of the East in India, events were moving toward a world revolution in Europe. In 1582 the Jesuits had launched their new translation of the Latin Vulgate in English in order to counteract the powerful effects of Tyndale's epoch-making Bible translated into English in 1525 from the Received Text in Greek. The 1582 Jesuit New Testament in English declares in its preface its opposition to the Waldensian New Testament.

Spain marshaled all the power and wealth which she had gained from her possessions in the New World to send forth the greatest

---

[30] Buchanan, *Christian Researches in Asia*, page 266.

navy man had yet seen. She had just conquered Portugal, possessing through this conquest the navies of two countries. A fleet of about 130 Spanish ships, great and small, some armed with fifty cannon, sailed up the English Channel to accomplish by force the ruin of English Protestantism.

John Richard Green gives this information about the Spanish Armada:

> Within the Armada itself, however, all hope was gone. Huddled to-gether by the wind and the deadly English fire, their sails torn, their masts shot away, the crowded galleons had become mere slaughterhouses. Four thousand men had fallen, and bravely as the seamen fought, they were cowed by the terrible butchery. Medina himself was in despair. "We are lost, Señor Oquenda," he cried to his bravest captain: "what are we to do?" "Let others talk of being lost," replied Oquenda, "Your Excellency has only to order up fresh cartridge." But Oquenda stood alone, and a council of war resolved on retreat to Spain.[31]

Glorious Revolt of the St. Thomas Christians

The victory of the English over Spain paved the way for the Jesuit defeat on the Malabar Coast. It was several years before the full meaning of the conquest over the Spanish Armada worked its way to the Orient. A ray of light was seen by the suffering St. Thomas Christians. They groaned beneath what they called their Babylonian captivity. They loathed the worship of images, the adoration of relics, processions, incense, confessional, and all the ceremonies their fathers knew not. They longed for the crystal streams of the Scriptures. They yearned for the literature which the church had fostered since the days of the apostles. As they meditated on the "city which hath foundations, whose builder and maker is God," their spirit burned within them.

Then an event occurred which caused a revolution among the people. The successive victories of the Dutch and English over the papal armies in India had opened the way for the patriarch at Babylon to ordain and send a new head to the church in India, Ahatalla. He was seized when he landed at Mailapore near Madras, shipped to Goa, and burned at the stake. Immediately a cry of horror ran through the Malabar churches. At the summons of protest, they came from town and village. Before a huge cross at a place near Cochin they

---

[31] Green, *A Short History of the English People*, b. 6, pt. 2, ch. 6, par. 26.

assembled by the thousands to take their stand against the papacy. Since all were not able to touch the sacred symbol, long ropes were extended from it which they firmly grasped while they took the oath renouncing their allegiance to Rome. This happened in 1653, and the incident is known as Coonen Cross.

When the papal leaders beheld nearly 400,000 Christians lost to their church, they immediately dispatched monks to go in among them and, if possible, to remedy the disaster. "The result," says Adeney, "was a split of the Syrian Church, one party adhering to the papal church as Romo-Syrians, while the more daring spirits reverted to the Syrian usages. It is estimated that the former, known as Puthencoor, or the new community, now number about 110,000, while the latter, the Palayacoor, or old community, amount to about 330,000."[32]

Divisions along these lines still exist there, and a large field presents itself for evangelization by those who give the Bible first place in advancing the kingdom of heaven.

---

[32]Adeney, *The Greek and Eastern Churches,* page 530.

CHAPTER XXI

Adam and the Church in China

The return from the captivity, which Cyrus authorized almost immediately after the capture of Babylon, is the starting point from which we may trace a gradual enlightenment of the heathen world by the dissemination of Jewish beliefs and practices.[1]

THE name of Adam singles out an unusual leader whose history is connected with the Church of the East in China. When he was director of the Assyrian Church in China, a memorial in marble was erected in that land in 781 to the praise of God for the glorious success of the apostolic church. From the time that it was excavated in 1625 it has stood as one of the most celebrated monuments of history. The events which led to its erection and the story told by its inscription reveal the early missionary endeavors which carried the gospel to the Far East.

When the Spirit of God moved upon the heart of Adam, director of the Assyrian Church in China, and his associates to erect this revealing witness, New Testament Christianity had for some time been shining brightly there. The fact that these missionaries possessed sufficient freedom to plant this remarkable memorial in the heart of the empire, when in Europe the father of Charlemagne was destroying the Celtic Church, shows a remarkable existence of religious liberty in the Orient. It furthermore discloses that the Church of the East was large and influential enough to execute so striking a project.

To indicate how great a statesman Adam was and how strong he was in 781 in the circles of influence in the Chinese, Japanese, and Arabian Empires, let the following facts testify: He was a friend of the Chinese emperor who ordered the erection of the famous stone monument; of Duke Kuo-Tzu, mighty general and secretary of state, who defeated the dangerous Tibetan attack; of Dr. Issu, Assyrian clergyman, loaded with state honors for his brilliant work; of Kobo Daisha, greatest intellect in Japanese history; of Prajna, renowned

---

[1] Rawlinson, *The Seven Great Monarchies of the Ancient Eastern World,* vol. 2, p. 444.

Buddhist leader and Chinese teacher of Kobo Daisha; of Lü Yen, celebrated founder of the powerful Chinese religious sect known as the
Pill of Immortality; of the Arabian court where Harun-al-Rashid,
most mighty of the Arabian emperors, had just secured the services
of an eminent Assyrian church educator to supervise Harun's new
imperial school system.[2]

In 1625 this remarkable stone was unearthed in or near the city
of Changan, long known as Sian or Sianfu, but now recently called
again by its ancient name, Changan. It was the most cosmopolitan
city among all nations when the memorial was erected. It is located
about fifteen hundred miles inland from the coast. The imperial
Tang Dynasty (A. D. 618-907) was on the throne. It is generally con-
ceded among historians that the period of the Tang emperors was the
most brilliant, liberal, and progressive era of all the Chinese dynasties.
Changan was already well known two thousand years before Christ,
being called "the well-watered city."[3] Its history is the history of the
Chinese race. Its civilization influenced all the surrounding nations.
For example, Kyoto, the ancient capital of Japan, is laid out on lines
following the plan of Sianfu (Changan).

G. B. Sansom, in his learned work on the Nipponese, has given a
splendid description of Changan in these years. Recognizing the debt
of Japan to China, many authors point out that it was the civilization
of the Tang period which influenced Japan, a civilization built on the
splendid contribution made by the Church of the East.

> Politically China was at this moment perhaps the most powerful, the
> most advanced, and the best-administered country in the world. Certainly
> in every material aspect of the life of a state she was overwhelmingly
> superior to Japan. The frontiers of her empire stretched to the borders
> of Persia, to the Caspian Sea, and to the Altai Mountains. She was in
> relations with the peoples of Annam, Cochin China, Tibet, the Tarim
> basin, and India; with the Turks, the Persians, and the Arabs. Men of
> many nations appeared at the court of China, bringing tribute and mer-
> chandise and new ideas that influenced her thought and her art. Persian
> and, more remotely, Greek influence is apparent in much of the sculpture
> and painting of the T'ang period. There had since the days of the Wei
> emperors been friendly intercourse between China and Persia, a Zoroas-
> trian temple was erected in Chang-an in 621. . . .

---

[2] See Saeki, *The Nestorian Monument in China,* pages 54, 171, 231, 265; also, Gordon, *"World Healers,"* pages 134, 181-183, 285, 476.

[3] Sansom, *Japan,* pages 80, 81; Saeki, *The Nestorian Monument in China,* page 3.

It would be too much of a digression to go on to speak of the paintings, the bronzes, the pottery, the colored silks, the poems and the fine calligraphies. It is enough to say that all these arts were blossoming in profusion when the first Japanese missions found themselves in the T'ang capital. And what perhaps impressed them more than the quality of Chinese culture was its heroic dimensions. Nothing but was on a grand, a stupendous scale. When the Sui emperor builds a capital, two million men are set to work. His fleet of pleasure boats on the Yellow River is towed by eighty thousand men. His caravan when he makes an Imperial Progress is three hundred miles long. His concubines number three thousand. And when he orders the compilation of an anthology, it must have seventeen thousand chapters. Even making allowance for the courtly arithmetic of official historians, these are enormous undertakings; and though the first T'ang emperors were rather less immoderate, they did nothing that was not huge or magnificent. To the Japanese it must have been staggering.[4]

The famous monumental stone now stands in the Pei Lin (forest of tablets) in the western suburb of Changan.[5] It was set up by imperial direction to commemorate the bringing of Christianity to China. Dug out of the ground by accident in 1625, where it evidently had lain buried for nearly a thousand years, this marble monument ranks in importance with the Rosetta stone of Egypt or the Behistun inscription in Persia. It has engraved upon it 1,900 Chinese characters reinforced by fifty Syriac words and seventy names in Syriac. The mother tongue of the Christian newcomers and the official tongue of the Assyrian Church was Syriac.[6] The unearthing of this corroborating evidence to the greatness of early Christianity in China created a profound impression upon scholars in all countries.[7] Many works have been written about it. The revealing facts embedded in the chiseled letters never cease to grip the attention of anyone interested in the history of the true church.

How great was the degree of civilization in these days throughout central Asia and the East may be seen in the following quotation from a recognized author:

With unexampled honors, Kao-Tsung and his empress received back to China, in 645, *The Prince of Pilgrims*, Hüen T'sang, after his sixteen years'

---

[4] Sansom, *Japan*, pages 81-84.

[5] It was the writer's privilege to examine the stone firsthand, having made an airplane trip there for that purpose. We took particular pains to take pictures of this renowned memorial and to study the city with its surrounding country.

[6] Saeki, *The Nestorian Monument in China*, pages 14, 15.

[7] Huc, *Christianity in China, Tartary, and Thibet*, vol. 1, pp. 45, 46.

pilgrimage of over 100,000 miles to Fo-de-fang, the Holy Land of India, in search of precious sûtras and "the true, good law," finding everywhere, among the tribes of central Asia, the highest degree of civilization and religious devotion.[8]

Hsüan Tsang was beginning his research journey just after Columbanus had finished his glorious labors. The Celtic Columbanus, however, carried his Bible with him as he journeyed east, while Hsüan Tsang traveled west from his native China to obtain the scriptures of Buddha in India.

Many who have written about this great stone mistakenly call it the Nestorian monument. The word "Nestorian" is nowhere found on it. In fact, the inscription has no reference whatever to either Nestorius or Nestorians. Moreover, it does explicitly recognize the head of the Church of the East by giving the name and the date of the patriarch of Bagdad, Persia, who at that time was ruler of the church in its vast extent. These are the words as translated from the Syriac: "In the day of our Father of Fathers, My Lord Hanan-isho, Catholicos, Patriarch. . . . In the year one thousand and ninety-two of the Greeks. (1092-311= A. D. 781)"[9] The title at the head of the monument, engraved in nine Chinese characters, as translated in Saeki's book is, "A Monument Commemorating the Propagation of the Ta-Chin Luminous Religion in the Middle Kingdom." Ta-Chin, this author asserts, was the Chinese name of Judea, and the "luminous religion" was the term they then used for Christianity.

In the period in which this monumental witness was erected in China, three great empires ruled the world. In the West, the pope crowned Charlemagne on Christmas Day, 800, as head of the newly created Holy Roman Empire. In the Far East the Chinese world, considered by some at that time, the strongest of all states, was ruled by the Tang dynasty. Between these lay the mighty Arabian Empire. The most famous emperor in the history of this Arabian Imperium was Harun-al-Rashid.

There was much to facilitate contact between Persia and China at this time. Most of the nations lying between them were well populated. Travel was frequent, the highways were well cared for, and an abundance of vehicles and inns to facilitate merchants and tourists

---

[8] Gordon, "World Healers," page 147.
[9] Saeki, The Nestorian Monument in China, page 175.

was at hand.[10] It would yet be many a century before the devastations of the Mongols and the ravages of Tamerlane would lay these countries desolate. The population was large enough to keep back the encroaching sands which later buried many a fine city. The Buddhists of China were constantly traveling west, especially to India, to obtain ancient writings of the faith.[11] Much evidence goes to prove, moreover, that the rulers of China were tolerant of, or indifferent to, all faiths, so that the door was open to the arrival of new religions.

Did Confucius Counterfeit Daniel's Religion?

About five hundred years before the commencement of the Christian Era a great stir seems to have taken place in Indo-Aryan, as in Grecian minds, and indeed in thinking minds everywhere throughout the then-civilized world. Thus when Buddha arose in India, Greece had her thinker in Pythagoras, Persia, in Zoroaster, and China in Confucius.[12]

In a former chapter it was stated that within a hundred years after the death of the prophet Daniel, Zoroastrianism flourished in Persia, Buddhism rose in India, and Confucianism began in China.[13] From Pythagoras, possibly a pupil of Zoroaster, philosophy had obtained its grip upon Greece. According to the dates generally assigned to Daniel and Confucius, the founder of Confucianism was about fourteen years of age when the great prophet died. There is a striking similarity between parts of the philosophy of Pythagoras and that of Confucius. A quotation from a well-known author will show the close relationship between Buddhism and Confucianism:

It is related that a celebrated Chinese sage, known as "the noble-minded Fu," when asked whether he was a Buddhist priest, pointed to his Taoist cap, when asked whether he was a Taoist, pointed to his Confucianist shoes; and finally, being asked whether he was a Confucianist, pointed to his Buddhist scarf.[14]

As the Jews had been dispersed throughout all nations, the stirring prophecies of Daniel were disseminated everywhere. These led all peoples to look with hope for the coming of the great Restorer. The

---

[10] Yule, *Travels of Marco Polo,* vol. 1, p. 191, note 1.
[11] *Ibid.,* vol. 1, p. 191; also Beal, *Buddhists' Records of the Western World.*
[12] Monier-Williams, *Indian Wisdom,* page 49.
[13] See the author's discussion in Chapter II, entitled, "The Church in the Wilderness in Prophecy."
[14] Sansom, *Japan,* page 133.

three Magi who came from the East to worship at the Saviour's manger are but an example of those who were stirred by the promise of the Coming One. Suetonius and Tacitus, Roman historians of the first century A. D., bear witness to the universal expectation of a coming Messiah.

The prophecy of Buddha concerning the predicted Prophet is another example. Buddha said: "Five hundred years after my death, a Prophet will arise who will found His teaching upon the fountain of all the Buddhas. When that One comes, believe in Him, and you shall receive incalculable blessings!"[15]

Also it is reported that Confucius, the famous founder of China's national religion in the sixth century B. C., said that "a saint should be born in the West who would restore to China the lost knowledge of the sacred tripod."[16]

It must not be concluded that the Chinese emperor, surrounded by the greatest scholars of his realm, took the astonishing decision to permit Adam to build the celebrated stone monument solely because he was influenced by the teachings which he heard from the Christian missionaries of that date. He and his scholars were well aware of the remarkable events which crowded the history touching the Church of the East. The Chinese were not ignorant of the expansion of Christianity among the nations of central Asia.

Furthermore, it is not without solid basis that commentators claim that China is contemplated in the well-known prophecy of Isaiah which foresees converts to the gospel as coming from the land of Sinim. There are scholars of research who conclude that the original Chinese colonists who settled on the western branch of the Yellow River came from the plains of the Euphrates.[17] It must be true that the great facts of early Bible history were known in some form in the Orient from early days, there being much travel back and forth from Persia to China. As Moses led the Israelites out of Egypt, so the Separatists from the Tigris and Euphrates valleys are considered by some to have taken their long trek through Turkestan to the Wei

---

[15] Gordon, *"World Healers,"* pages 31, 32, 229.
[16] *Ibid.,* page 27.
[17] Geikie, *Hours With the Bible,* vol. 6, p. 383, note 1; Old Testament Series on Isaiah 49:12; *Encyclopedia Britannica,* 9th and 11th eds., art. "China;" M'Clatchie, "The Chinese in the Plain of Shinar," *Journal of the Royal Asiatic Society,* vol. 16, pp. 368-435.

River of northwestern China carrying many elements of Chaldean civilization to that region.[18] From the Babylonian plains they are reckoned to have brought many religious and astronomical observances which they practiced in China, among which was the honor bestowed upon a weekly period of seven days.[19]

How early and how influential the Jews (being repeatedly carried as captives to the East) were in China before the Christian Era, may be seen in the following quotations:

> Many of those Israelites whom God dispersed among the nations, by means of the Assyrian and Babylonian captivities, found their way to China, and were employed (says the celebrated chronicler Père Gaubil) in important military posts, some becoming provincial governors, ministers of state, and learned professors. Père Gaubil states positively that there were Jews in China during the fighting states period, i. e., 481-221 B. C.[20]

Thus, we know that China in Daniel's day was in contact with the Old Testament religion.

According to *Spring and Autumn,* a book compiled by Confucius himself in 481 B. C., notice is taken of the frequent arrival of "the white foreigners." Saeki thinks that these could be from the plains of Mesopotamia. The vigorous earlier Han dynasty (206 B. C. to A. D. 9) carried its conquests far to the west and to the Babylonian plains.[21] Study in a previous chapter touching the work of the apostle Thomas in India cites the old tradition that after he had founded Christianity in the Hindu peninsula, he then brought the gospel to the country of the Yellow River.[22] The apostle Paul in his day said that the gospel had been carried "to the ends of the world." How strong was the gospel in China is seen in the statement of the Ante-Nicene Father Arnobius, written about 300, which enumerated that nation as one of the Oriental peoples among whom the church was established.[23] Also it is to be noticed that Isaac, the patriarch of the Assyrian Church, ordained a metropolitan for China in 411. As metropolitans usually were directors of from six to eight supervisors of church provinces,

---

[18] Pott, *A Sketch of Chinese History,* 3d ed., p. 2.
[19] Lacouperie, *Western Origin of Early Chinese Civilisation,* pages 9, 12.
[20] Gordon, *"World Healers,"* page 54.
[21] Saeki, *The Nestorian Monument in China,* pages 39, 40.
[22] The attendant at the "forest of tablets" in Changan showed the writer a stone slab with a face carved upon it which, he claimed, was believed to be the face of the apostle Thomas.
[23] Arnobius, *Against the Heathen,* found in *Ante-Nicene Fathers,* vol. 6, p. 438.

22

each of which in turn was the presiding officer over many clergy, it can readily be understood that Christianity, in order to have had such a large growth, must early have been planted in the Middle Kingdom, or China.

Returning to the discussion of Old Testament teachings in China long before Christ, it may be seen that the teachings of the Old Testament came to China not only by way of India, but also by way of Turkestan. During the period in which the counterfeiting of the Old Testament by heathen religions began, King Darius, the able Persian organizer, effected the conquest of Bactria. That rich and prosperous kingdom lying between the northeast of Persia proper and the Oxus River is said to have contained a thousand towns.[24] Darius pushed his conquests on to the famous city of Khotan in Turkestan.[25] This was a pivotal city in the commerce and travel between China and Bactria. Between Khotan and China unnumbered cities, since buried by the moving sands, covered the territory of eastern Turkestan. "Where anciently were the seats of flourishing cities and prosperous communities," says a Chinese chronicler speaking of this region, "is nothing now to be seen but a vast desert; all has been buried in the sands."[26] It was centuries after the Christian Era before these cities began to disappear.[27]

In Turkestan the road to China was flanked by many cities; consequently, the roads had so many travelers that no one had need to search out companions for his journey. The roads, moreover, were then in such splendid condition that the journey from Khotan to China could be completed in fourteen days.[28] Thus, the bewitching story of the new and aggressive religion in the west could spread eastward quickly on the lips of travelers.

If the revolution brought about by Confucius is considered in the light of the generations influenced and the length of its duration, it can be reckoned as one of the greatest revolutions in history. For two thousand years Confucianism held undisputed sway over the Chinese people. Being a man of the highest literary ability and one that was conversant with current events of his time by means of travelers,

[24] Smith, *The Oxford History of India,* page 122.
[25] Forsythe, *Journal of the Royal Geographical Society,* vol. 47, p. 2.
[26] Yule, *Travels of Marco Polo,* vol. 1, p. 192, note.
[27] Johnson, *Journal of the Royal Geographical Society,* vol. 37, p. 5.
[28] Quatremere, *Notices des Manuscrits,* vol. 14, pp. 476, 477.

Confucius could not have been without foresight enough to make his system of religion escape too great competition with Buddhism, Zoroastrianism, and Judaism. He found China politically and religiously in chaos. He gave to his native land a religion and a code of social ethics which stood for centuries. It is believed that he understood and profited by the great reformation which had just taken place in Judaism, and that he incorporated in the new system he was premeditating, ideas from not only Judaism, but also from Zoroastrianism and Buddhism. It seems most logical to believe that Confucius beheld the great movements just mentioned, and by his superior ability saw his opportunity to do the same for China.

Consider how great was the reform which came to Judaism in the days of Daniel, and how the heathen received much of their wisdom from the Old Testament. George Rawlinson, historian of the ancient civilizations, writes:

> Parallel with the decline of the old Semitic idolatry was the advance of its direct antithesis, pure spiritual monotheism. The same blow which laid the Babylonian religion in the dust struck off the fetters from Judaism. . . . The return from the captivity, which Cyrus authorized almost immediately after the capture of Babylon, is the starting point from which we may trace a gradual enlightenment of the heathen world by the dissemination of Jewish beliefs and practices.[29]

While these three founders of new religions—Zoroaster, Buddha, and Confucius—were willing to borrow from a cult earlier than their own, it is evident that in order to escape the charge of copying, they would want their own system not to be a duplication of the one from which they borrowed. There is sufficient basis in the teachings of Confucius to conclude that he, like Buddha and Zoroaster, was stimulated enough by the new light shining in the west to launch a religious system of his own.

The fundamental truth of the Supreme Being was impressed so powerfully upon Zoroastrianism, Buddhism, and Confucianism that in the establishing of their schemes of religion, they maintained one chief deity. The elimination of lesser divinities in favor of one God over all, such as the Old Testament had taught for centuries, won immediate favor with the masses.

---

[29] Rawlinson, *The Seven Great Monarchies of the Ancient Eastern World*, vol. 2, p. 444.

One more point will be presented as an outstanding evidence that the teachings of the Old Testament were known and imitated throughout the Far East. The knowledge of creation's seven days had been so deeply impressed upon Oriental peoples that it wove itself into all religious life and customs of the Orient. Speaking of the widespread influence of the Old Testament system of worship, Thomas M'Clatchie writes:

> According to the Zend-Avesta, the God Ormuzd (Adam or Noah deified), created the world at six different intervals, amounting in all to a whole year; man, in almost exact conformity with the Mosaic account, being created in the sixth period. The Etrurians state that God (Adam or Noah) created the world in six thousand years; man alone being created in the sixth millenary. Eusebius mentions several of the ancient poets who attached a superior degree of sanctity to the seventh day. Hesiod and Homer do so, and also Callimachus and Linus. Porphyry says that the Phenicians dedicated one day in seven to their god Cronus (Adam appearing in Noah). Aulus Gellius states that some of the heathen philosophers were accustomed to teach only on the seventh day; Alexander Severus used to frequent the temples on the seventh day; Lucian mentions the seventh day as a holiday. The ancient Arabians observed a Sabbath before the era of Mohammed. The mode of reckoning by "seven days," prevailed alike amongst the Indians, the Egyptians, the Celts, the Sclavonians, the Greeks and the Romans. Josephus then makes no groundless statement when he says, "there is not any city of the Grecians, nor any of the barbarians, nor any nation whatsoever, whither our custom of resting on the seventh day hath not come!" Dion Cassius deduces this universal practice of computing by weeks from the Egyptians, but he should have said from *the primitive ancestors* of the Egyptians, who were equally the ancestors of all mankind. Theophilus of Antioch states as a palpable fact, that the seventh day was everywhere considered sacred; and Philo (apud Grot. et Gale) declares the seventh day to be a festival, not of this or of that city, but of the universe.[30]

Especially to be noted in the above citation is the reckoning by seven days not only in India, but also among the Celts, Slavs, Greeks, and Romans. Homer and Hesiod, who lived about the ninth and eighth centuries before Christ, are included in those believing in the sacredness of the seventh day. Such was the powerful influence of the Old Testament in not only European, but also Oriental lands, even to the determining of their division of time.

---

[30] M'Clatchie, *Notes and Queries on China and Japan* (edited by Dennys), vol. 4, nos. 7, 8, pp. 99, 100.

Already mention has been made of the large number of Jews who dwelt in China after 400 B. C. Throughout the centuries they observed the seventh day for the Sabbath, and one author, writing in recent years of his investigations touching the small remnant of these Jews still remaining in China, says, "They keep the Sabbath quite as strictly as do the Jews in Europe."[31]

If honoring the seventh day was true among the ancient inhabitants of the land of Chaldea, from which it is asserted that the ancestors of the Chinese came, it was also prominently true in ancient China. A passage from one of the classical works of Confucius, written about 500 B. C., is as follows: "The ancient kings on this culminating day (i. e., the seventh) closed their gates, the merchants did not travel and the princes did not inspect their domains."[32] Charles de Harlez adds, "It was a sort of a day of rest."[33] All the evidences therefore would seem to support the conclusion that Confucius was influenced either directly or indirectly by the teachings of the Old Testament in general and by the visions of Daniel in particular.

Christianity's Early Growth in China

At the time of the erection of the celebrated stone monument, missionaries of Adam's faith had penetrated everywhere throughout central Asia, and already possessed multiplied churches in China. How far these evangelists had spread the knowledge of Adam's mother tongue, the Syriac, may be gathered in the following words of Ernest Renan:

> It will be seen what an important part the Syriac language played in Asia from the third to the ninth century of our era, after it had become the instrument of Christian preaching. Like the Greek for the Hellenistic East, the Latin for the West, Syrian became the Christian and ecclesiastical language of Upper Asia.[34]

---

[31] Finn, *The Jews in China*, page 23.

[32] M'Clatchie, *A Translation of the Confucian Classic of Change*, page 118.

[33] Harlez, *Le Yih-King: A French Translation of the Confucian Classic on Change*, page 72. Translated by this author from a French version (using the important footnote of M. de Harlez). Many translators of the Chinese render the "culminating day" differently. Most all agree, some at length, that this section of the Yih-King, the oldest Chinese book, is a glorification of the seventh day as the symbol of returning or success. The influence of this glorification determined the customs of kings, merchants, and landed possessors.

[34] Renan, *Histoire General et Systéme Comparé des Langues Semitiques*, page 291.

Even today there are in other countries many thousands of believers who derive their church past from the Assyrian communion and who use the Syriac in their divine services.

Political, social, and commercial relations between China and the western nations were carried on many centuries before the population of its capital dedicated the memorial monument. About one hundred twenty years before Christ an official embassy of exploration was sent out by the Chinese emperor to study the kingdoms of the west and to bring greetings to their peoples and rulers. This exploration party returned to relate that they had gone through Bactria, Parthia, Persia, and Ta-Chin (that is, Palestine, the country of Adam's religion according to the monument). Two hundred years later—or, in the days of the apostles—a Chinese general led the victorious regiments of his emperor across Persia to the shores of the Caspian Sea.[35] The Chinese Chronicles report an embassy from the emperor of Rome to the imperial court of China about A. D. 168, and one or two similar embassies about one hundred years later. They also record that about two hundred years later (A. D. 381) more than sixty-two countries of the "western regions" sent ambassadors or tribute to the Middle Kingdom.[36]

If the Chinese traveled so extensively to the west, it is no wonder that Saeki exclaims: "It would be very strange if the energetic Syrian Christians, full of true missionary zeal, did not proceed to China after reaching Persia about the middle or end of the second century!"[37] Another authority sees them well settled in China in 508.[38] Thus, there is ample justification to conclude that many true believers were in Asia several centuries before Adam and his associates erected the monument to their church.

Beliefs of Early Christianity in China

Many documents and historical references tell of the faith held by the Church of the East in China in Adam's day. Already notice has been made of the prophecy which Isaiah uttered predicting converts in that far-distant land. Testimony has also been used to show that in 481-222 B. C., Jews held important military posts, some becom-

---

[35] Smith, *The Oxford History of India,* page 129.
[36] Saeki, *The Nestorian Monument in China,* pages 41, 42.
[37] *Ibid.,* page 43.
[38] Lloyd, *The Creed of Half Japan,* page 194, note.

ing provincial governors, ministers of state, and learned professors.[39] These Old Testament church members would teach the Chinese the truths of the law and the prophets.

It is astonishing to see how the Assyrian Church preserved the unity of its faith throughout its far-flung spiritual domain whether it was in India, Tibet, Turkestan, Persia, or China. The church members who worshiped according to the teachings laid down by the Church of the East were not only in harmony with one another in these different countries, but also with the headquarters in Persia. It is known first of all that it was strictly an evangelical church. Many writers of note have commented upon the apostolic nature of its missionary activities and also upon the New Testament simplicity of its beliefs and practices. These believers constantly claimed that they accepted only that which was taught by Christ, the prophets, and the apostles. In quiet simplicity, accompanied by the minimum of ceremonies, they accomplished an unusual amount of missionary work.

The position held by Adam substantiates the splendid organization of the Church of the East, also the strength of its position in China. On the monument Adam is called Pastor, Vice-Metropolitan, and Metropolitan of China.[40] This official title would indicate that the churches he directed must have had many members and were of considerable strength. The inscription further reveals that Adam recognized the father of fathers, or catholicos, at Bagdad.

In China, Adam and his associates were obliged to battle against polygamy. The custom of binding the feet of Chinese girls was a distressing problem to the Christian missionaries. The belief of the Chinese in the spirits of the dead, glorified by ancestor worship, arrayed against the missionaries the forces of spiritism, magic, and astrology.

The two languages composing the inscriptions upon the monument —the Syriac and the Chinese—might raise the hope that the cumbersome system of the sign language of the Chinese would give way before the better alphabetical method represented by the Syriac. The prevalence of the sign orthography even to the present time indicates the stubborn resistance to any endeavor to simplify Chinese. How-

[39] Gordon, *"World Healers,"* page 54.
[40] Saeki, *The Nestorian Monument in China,* pages 162, 255; see also pages 186, 187.

ever, Adam had at his command a vast Christian literature for use. Saeki gives in detail the titles of thirty-five books which, whole or in fragments, were discovered in 1908 in a cave in northwestern China, all of which were the literature put forth by the Church of the East among the Chinese. He writes:

> They had the Apostles' Creed in Chinese. They had a most beautiful baptismal hymn in Chinese. They had a book on the incarnation of the Messiah. They had a book on the doctrine of the cross. In a word, they had all literature necessary for a living church. Their ancestors in the eighth century were powerful enough to erect a monument in the vicinity of Hsi-an-fu.[41]

From Adam to the Mongol Emperors

The time which elapsed from the Tang dynasty of the days of Adam to the close of the Mongolian conquest was about five hundred years. During that time the nature of the development of the Church of the East in the land of the Yellow River is seen in the character of the clergy, the type of sacred literature used, the life of the believers, the abundant activities of the communities, and the public services rendered by it to the nation.

The clergy who led the Church of the East to victory were men of consecration and scholarship. They found the ancient religions of Confucianism and Taoism in China entrenched in the affections of the people. Confucius himself upheld polygamy.[42] Confucius was also a spiritist; he ever believed that he was accompanied by the spirit of the duke of Chu.[43] The Buddhists were idolaters; they worshiped the image of Buddha.[44] They terrified the people both by their teachings and by the representations upon the walls of their temples of horrible pictures and statues.[45] They also set forth the carnal delights of a Buddhistic paradise. Nevertheless, in the face of such powerful heathen religions, the Assyrian Church grew and prospered.

Buddhism in China was harsh; it provided no saviour, and, until it copied the atoning doctrines of Christianity, it was generally repulsive to the people. In the midst of such darkness as this, Adam and

---

[41] Saeki, *The Nestorian Monument in China,* pages 70, 71.
[42] Li Ung Bing, *Outlines of Chinese History,* pages 50, 51.
[43] Sansom, *Japan,* page 111.
[44] Huc, *Christianity in China, Tartary, and Thibet,* vol. 1, pp. 167, 221.
[45] Cable and French, *Through Jade Gate and Central Asia,* pages 136-138. See Gordon, *"World Healers,"* for a study of the idolatry of Buddhism.

his associates trained a clergy that was the most enlightened of the day. It was this same type of clergy who in Mesopotamia had carried Greek and Roman civilization to the Arabians who in turn passed it on to the West.

Concerning the teachings of these Syriac Christians, this is recorded in Syriac upon the Chinese monument: "In the year 1092 of the Greeks (1092-311 = A. D. 781) my Lord Yesbuzid, Priest (Pastor) and chor-episcopos of Kumdan, the Royal city, son of the departed Milis, Priest (Pastor) from Balkh, a city of Tehuristan, erected this Monument, wherein is written the Law of Him, our Saviour, the Preaching of our forefathers to the Rulers of the Chinese."[46]

It must not be thought, however, that their growth progressed smoothly. Often they met with bitter opposition. Upon the death of one of the great Tang emperors, the throne was occupied during two short reigns by rulers of inferior capacity. One of these favored Buddhism. The Buddhists, seizing this advantage, raised their voices against the Christian religion. In the other reign, inferior scholars of the Taoists, favored by the imperial majesty, ridiculed and slandered Christianity.

A furious religious persecution against all western religions took place in 845. Some think that it was in this hour of trial that the believers buried the celebrated stone in the ground to preserve it. The time of trial was due to influence maliciously exercised over the emperor by the Confucianists and Taoists. "Christianity, however, did not seem to have been much affected by it," Mingana observes, "because in an early and important statement the contemporary patriarch Theodose (A. D. 852-858) still mentions the archbishops of Samarkand, India, and China."[47]

It is noteworthy that this last persecution was commanded by one of the last Tang emperors. The dynasty was tottering to its fall. Then followed years of anarchy and confusion in which seven different dynasties succeeded one another.

Through the favoring smile of the government not only were several splendid churches erected during the early years of Christianity in the capital city itself, but orders were given to aid in the erecting

---

[46] Saeki, *The Nestorian Monument in China,* page 175.
[47] Mingana, "Early Spread of Christianity," *Bulletin of John Ryland's Library,* vol. 9, pp. 325, 338.

of the same throughout the ten provinces. By this it is not understood that there was a union of church and state. For example, George Washington could be a member of a certain church and use his influence to favor the erection of churches of his own denomination, without its indicating that the clergy were paid officials of the state. Such was the situation in China.

From the year 1020 and onward, stirring tales were widespread throughout Europe concerning a great king over Tartar tribes who was a Christian and who was called Prester John. Coupled with this came the news written about the year 1009 by the metropolitan of the capital city in the northwestern province of Persia to the catholicos of Bagdad concerning two hundred thousand Turks and Mongols who had embraced Christianity.[48] The strength of the Church of the East in the eleventh century may be seen in these records. As Dean Milman says editorially: "The Christianity of China, between the seventh and the thirteenth century, is invincibly proved by the consent of Chinese, Arabian, Syriac, and Latin evidence."[49]

---

[48] Mingana, "Early Spread of Christianity," *Bulletin of John Ryland's Library,* vol. 9, pp. 308-310.

[49] Gibbon, *Decline and Fall of the Roman Empire,* ch. 47, note 118.

CHAPTER XXII

Marcos of Peking

These historical facts suffice to prove the existence of the land bridge between China and the Roman Orient; and that ancient China had overland communication with Mediterranean countries as well as with India. The route may have been by way of Khotan and Turkestan, to northern India, Afganistan, etc. It would be very strange if the energetic Syrian Christians, full of true missionary zeal, did not proceed to China after reaching Persia about the middle or end of the second century![1]

AN OUTSTANDING figure during this period of expansion in China was Marcos. From obscurity this lad in China rose to be supreme administrator over the Church of the East.

During the three centuries of stormy wars and many dynasties between the fall of the Tang emperors and the ascendancy of the Mongol rulers (A. D. 1204), there is little in the way of reports concerning the growth of Christianity in China. For that interim, recourse must be made to the records of the church headquarters at Bagdad, or to histories of central Asia, or of those countries bordering on China.

With the rise of the Tartar supremacy over the yellow race, however, the situation changes. The world revolution which accompanied the Mongol conquests of Asia and eastern Europe brought to light the enormous gains made by the Church of the East in China, central, and farther Asia. Genghis Khan unified the Oriental nations, while at the same time he opened the way for their advance in civilization.[2]

The careers of Genghis Khan and his son, Ogotai, and their friendly relations to the Church of the East, belong more to the history of Asia as a whole. This story has already been told. The story of the three nephews of Ogotai—also emperors and conquerors; namely, Mangu, Kublai, and Hulagu—are prominently connected with the triumphal hours witnessed by the Church in China. Emperor Mangu and his father, Tule, completed the conquest of China. Kublai, succeeding Mangu, removed the capital of the Scythian world from its ancestral

---

[1]Saeki, *The Nestorian Monument in China*, pages 42, 43.
[2]Montgomery, *The History of Yaballaha III*, page 11.

center in Siberia to Peking, called in those days Khanbalig. When Kublai mounted the throne of the Mongolian world, he appointed his brother, Hulagu, to be independent emperor, or viceroy, over territories bordering on Europe, with his palace in Persia. King Frederick of Saxony gave no stronger support to Luther than these three sons of the victorious general Tule gave to the Assyrian catholicos of Bagdad and his far-flung churches in India, Asia, and China. In the writings of an author who lived contemporaneously with Mangu, the Christian convictions of that emperor are clearly set forth in the following words: "a follower and a defender of the religion of Jesus."[3] Mangu treated Christians, Moslems, and Buddhists with kindness; but he was especially anxious to attract the communities of the Church of the East to his country, because he found their medical learning and great business ability to be beneficial to his subjects.[4]

The kings of Germany, France, and England, as well as the pope, feared a return of the conquering armies under the Mongolian rulers. They relied upon the influence which Assyrian Christians exercised in Asiatic realms to give weight to their negotiations. Many embassies went back and forth between England, France, Germany, and the pope and the courts of Mangu, Kublai, and Hulagu. These western powers hoped to wrest Palestine and Jerusalem from the subjection of the hated Mohammedans through the assistance of Emperor Kublai Khan of Peking and his brother Hulagu, viceroy of Persia. In these negotiations the two young pastors who had traveled from Peking to Bagdad were counted of great use because of their standing with Kublai Khan, their knowledge of the Mongolian and Chinese tongues, and their acquaintance with the people and customs of their mother country.

At this point it will be fitting to recount the story of the two young pastors who in 1284 made their famous journey from Peking to Persia on their way to Jerusalem. It was astonishing how many large communities belonging to the Church of the East welcomed them in different cities on their long journey across the mountains, deserts, and plains. It can be noted with interest that, in addition to the fact that both the youth belonged to the Uigur nation, they were subjects of

---

[3]Mingana, "Early Spread of Christianity," *Bulletin of John Ryland's Library*, vol. 9, p. 312, note 1.
[4]Budge, *The Monks of Kublai Khan, Emperor of China*, page 45.

the Mongolian empire of Kublai Khan under whose protection, if not by whose command, they set out from China to go and worship at Jerusalem.[5]

When these two young pastors, Marcos and Sauma, arrived in Persia, they were welcomed not only by the head of the Assyrian Church and all the leading clergy of that realm, but also by the vice-royal court of Hulagu. Naturally, that court, though living in Persia, spoke the Mongolian as well as the Chinese language. They were delighted with these two protégés of Emperor Kublai Khan because they could speak Mongolian, Chinese, and Persian.

Early History of Two Young Clergymen

The manuscript containing the account of the joint travels of Sauma and Marcos was originally written by the latter in Persian, but the Syriac abridgments, in which language the story is accessible, were made by an unknown author. Scholars are indebted to Priest Paul Bedjan of the Roman Catholic Church for the presentation of the Syriac text. Consequently, the rendition of the original into English, wherein general terms are used which can be given a religious slant, may be colored by the point of view of those through whose hands the story passed. This should be kept in mind while meeting such terms as "monk," or "bishop." The early history of these two young men in China throws light upon the growth and standing obtained there by the Church of the East.

Sauma, who was later called Rabban Sauma (the title "rabban" carrying the idea of supervisor), was the son of a well-to-do Assyrian Christian who held an important office in the church at Peking. The boy was carefully educated and well instructed in the history of his church. When he was of age, he was betrothed to a maiden; and his father secured for him the position of keeper of the central church building in Peking. At the age of twenty, however, he refused to marry because he desired to give himself to religious studies. He retired from his parental city to a private domicile of his own about a day's journey west of the capital. This brought about his ordination to the ministry by Mar George, metropolitan of Peking. His fame soon spread abroad, and people came from afar to listen to his sermons.

---

[5] Budge, *The Monks of Kublai Khan, Emperor of China*, page 1.

About this time there was another young man who lived many days' journey away. He was also an Assyrian Christian, whose father held the office of archdeacon in his home city. The name of this young man was Marcos. Renouncing the world and consecrating himself to the advancement of the gospel in those rough and troublesome times, Marcos joined himself to Sauma whose fame had previously reached him. Sauma endeavored to persuade him to return to his parents; but failing in this, he had Marcos ordained to the ministry by Mar Nestorious, who was then the metropolitan of Peking.

These two, in deciding to go to Jerusalem, resisted the entreaties of parents and friends to remain in their native country. They sold all their possessions and set out to join a caravan that plied its commerce between China and the lands to the west. Undoubtedly, the metropolitan of northern China, whose seat was Peking, gave them letters of introduction to the brethren whom they would meet on their journey. When they reached Kawshang, the home of Marcos, they were welcomed with open arms. The Tartar princes of that place heard of their arrival. Failing in their endeavors to have the two missionaries settle down in Marcos's native country, they bestowed upon them horses, rugs, clothing, money, and an abundant supply of provisions for their long journey.[6]

The first place they reached in their westward journey was Tunhuang, famous as the gateway between China proper and Turkestan. This locality is well known for its caves of the thousand Buddhas.[7] It was then an influential city of the kingdom of Tangut, which realm authors today usually claim included the modern China province of Kansu. There were many Assyrian Christians in this kingdom. The brethren in Tun-huang, in which city Marco Polo said there were three large churches, hearing of the arrival of the youth, went out in a reception committee to give them a hearty welcome.

From here, after two months' traveling over the sands of the eastern Turkestan desert, they came to the city of Khotan, famous for the production of jade. Former cities of great renown in this region have been overwhelmed by the shifting sands of the desert which appear to have been advancing for ages.[8]

---

[6] Budge, *The Monks of Kublai Khan, Emperor of China*, pages 45, 46.
[7] Cable and French, *Through Jade Gate and Central Asia*, page 133.
[8] Yule, *Travels of Marco Polo*, vol. 1, p. 192.

However, in the days of Marcos and Sauma this was a region dotted with well-populated and flourishing centers. In the city of Khotan itself dwelt the director over the Assyrian churches in that province, so that one may be well assured that there was a public welcome to the two young men upon their arrival. As war was raging at that time between a chieftain and the great khan against whom he had rebelled, the two travelers were compelled to remain in Khotan for six months.

From Khotan these enterprising missionaries journeyed northwestward to Kashgar. Marco Polo, who had traveled over this route only a few years before, but in the opposite direction, wrote: "There are in the country many Nestorian [Assyrian] Christians, who have churches of their own. The people of the country have a peculiar language, and the territory extends for five days' journey."[9] 'The town was an important center of trade, and formed the terminus of many caravan routes from east to west; the country round about was very fertile, and the merchant and farmer classes were well-to-do.[10]

From Kashgar the adventuresome theological students passed over the high mountains of The Pamirs as they entered into Khurasan, the powerful northeastern province of Persia, where they arrived after the greatest difficulties and in a state of mental and physical exhaustion. But they comforted themselves at this time because God had delivered them from every affliction, and had allowed no calamities to befall them by highway robbers and thieves.[11]

They came to a military camp in a place called Talas. King Kaidu, who had descended from one of the oldest sons of Genghis Khan, never accepted the fact that his own grandfather had not been made supreme in imperial authority. At this time he was waging war with Emperor Kublai Khan because of contentions over matters of inheritance. The travelers went to King Kaidu; and having bestowed upon him their religious blessing, they requested him to give them a written permission to pass through his country.

Then they went to one of the spiritual training centers of the Assyrian Church located in or near the great city of Tus, capital of Khurasan, where they were received with hospitality by the provincial

[9]Yule, *Travels of Marco Polo*, vol. 1, p. 182.
[10]Budge, *The Monks of Kublai Khan, Emperor of China*, page 47.
[11]*Ibid.*, page 139.

director of the churches and his associate clergy. Here, like the apostle Paul when he arrived in Rome, they "thanked God, and took courage."[12]

The Pastors Meet the Catholicos

It was their intention to proceed from Khurasan to the frontier province in the northwest of Persia near the Caucasus, that they might reach the capital city of Bagdad in which was located Mar Denha, the catholicos of the Church in the East. However, they encountered the catholicos in Maragha, the city which Hulagu had made the provincial capital. At the sight of him, their hearts swelled with joy; they fell down on the ground before him and wept as they paid respect to his position as supreme director over the Church of the East. The membership of this great church, plus the Jacobites, surpassed the membership of the Greek and Latin churches.[13] The catholicos was astonished when he learned that they had come from the king of kings, Kublai Khan. They said that they had come to be blessed by the father of fathers, and by the clergy and holy men of this quarter of the world. And if a road were opened to them, they continued, and God had mercy upon them, they would go to Jerusalem.[14] The catholicos was moved to tears and spoke words of comfort to them.

Since they were so well acquainted with the city of the great king and could speak in the Mongolian tongue, the catholicos requested that they repair to the emperor of the west, who may be called the viceroy of the western Mongolian dominion, to request the emperor to ratify the choice of himself, Mar Denha, who had been elected catholicos by the western clergy. In this mission they were successful. In return, the catholicos wrote a letter of introduction for them, since they intended to visit the western religious centers of renown connected with the Assyrian Church. At that time, Abagha, the son and successor of Hulagu, and great-grandson of Genghis Khan, was on the throne of Persia. When they came to his camp and were brought before him, he received them graciously and commanded the nobles of his kingdom to grant their petition in behalf of the catholicos, Mar Denha, and gave them the written orders necessary to ratify that which they were requesting.

---

[12] Acts 28:15.
[13] Gibbon, *Decline and Fall of the Roman Empire*, ch. 47, par. 30.
[14] Budge, *The Monks of Kublai Khan, Emperor of China*, pages 140, 141.

Upon returning to the catholicos, he told them that this was not the time for them to journey to Jerusalem because the roads were in a disturbed state. He passed on the startling news of the death at Peking of the provincial director of the church, and had therefore decided to ordain Marcos in his stead as metropolitan for China and to consecrate his companion, Suama, as visitor-general of the churches in the west. They both endeavored to be freed from his proposed appointments; but when they saw that he was not willing it should be so, they said, "The will of our Father be done."

Marcos was well received and highly honored in different regions even though he was a foreigner, because he held Bible truths in common with the Church of the East. Not least among these doctrines generally held was the seventh-day Sabbath. Since the Christians of China, the homeland of Marcos, observed the seventh-day Sabbath, as pointed out in a previous chapter, here was a bond of union among the medieval church members in Asia.[15]

There was greater responsibility in store for these enterprising pastors. Shortly after their appointment, Mar Denha himself died. The directing clergy of the west easily discerned that Marcos stood high in favor with the viceroy of Persia and the supreme emperor, Kublai Khan. After counseling with one another, they decided that Marcos should be elected catholicos. This was satisfactory to King Abagha, who bestowed upon the new catholicos large gifts, ratified his election, and fostered an increase in church training centers and general facilities for the growth of the work. Shortly after this, King Abagha died.

Ahmad, a brother of Abagha, succeeded him on the throne; and lacking education or knowledge, he persecuted the Christians because of his considerable association in the past with the Mohammedans. However, his reign was short, not lasting more than two years; and he was followed on the throne by the son of Abagha, whose name was Arghun. The name given to Marcos after he had been consecrated to his new position was Yabhalaha. God blessed him with good health, and he lived to see six different kings as viceroys upon the imperial throne of the west in Persia. Passing over the many stirring incidents of his life, it will be sufficient to say that the splendid devotion of the

---

[15] See the author's discussion in Chapter XIX, note 27, and in Chapter XXI.

church, which had done such a marvelous work until the time when Marcos (Yabhalaha) arrived at the patriarchate, still continued. Thus the story of these two young men illustrates the vast extent to which the Church of the East had spread in the Orient, as well as its power and influence.

Marco Polo and the Assyrian Christians

The same century in which Marcos and Sauma traveled from China to Persia witnessed five other journeys which have been recorded. They give us remarkable pictures of the Mongolian world from the Mediterranean Sea to the Pacific Ocean, from Siberia to the Indian Ocean. The most outstanding of these travels were the voyages made by Marco Polo, an Italian from the city of Venice and a devout Roman Catholic. How his education in Catholicism colored his interpretation of the situations he encountered is seen in the following description:

> Mosul is a large province inhabited by various descriptions of people, one class of whom pay reverence to Mahomet, and are called Arabians. The others profess the Christian faith, but not according to the canons of the church, which they depart from in many instances, and are denominated Nestorians, Jacobites, and Armenians. They have a patriarch whom they call Jacolit, and by him archbishops, bishops, and abbots are consecrated and sent to all parts of India, to Baudas (Bagdad), or to Cathay (China), just as the pope of Rome does in the Latin countries.[16]

When John of Plano Carpini and William of Rubruck set out to interview the Tartar emperors, the capital was still at Karakorum in Siberia amid the nomadic tribes of the Asiatic plains. The journey made by Marco Polo, however, brought him to Peking, the new capital of the Mongolians under Emperor Kublai. The following description of Peking at the time of Marco Polo's arrival is given by Manuel Komroff:

> Two outstanding engineering marvels had already been completed before Marco Polo arrived. One was the Great Wall of China and the other the Grand Canal, the last 600 miles of which was finished by Kublai Khan. This canal runs from Peking to Canton and to this day remains the longest waterway constructed by man. Land communications by post-riders were developed to a high degree and are fully described by Marco Polo. In the various arts China was already mature. Painting, engraving,

---

[16] Komroff, *The Travels of Marco Polo*, page 29.

bronze casting, sculpture, and the making of porcelain and architecture were already very highly developed. Literature, too, was greatly respected. The invention of paper came as early as A. D. 105 and books were printed from wood blocks in 932. About fifty years later the large encyclopedia, consisting of a thousand different sections, was ordered printed under the personal supervision of the emperor. Marco Polo could have found books already in circulation dealing with political economy, philosophy, religion, warfare, agriculture, painting, music and other arts. Movable type first made its appearance in China in the form of baked clay blocks at the early date of 1043 and paper money, spoken of with such wonder by Marco Polo, was the currency in many sections of the empire. Mechanical devices were not lacking. Water clocks were found on bridges, astronomical instruments were in constant use, metals and coal were mined and salt extracted from brine. It was in this world of wonders that Marco Polo, an impressionable youth of twenty-one, found himself.[17]

When Marco Polo, a lad of nineteen, journeyed with his father and uncle, he took practically the same route from west to east which Marcos and Sauma had traversed from east to west. He, too, noted how strong the Church of the East was in Yarcan (i. e., Yarkand), which is in the western part of Turkestan, in these words: "Yarcan is a province five days' journey in extent. The people follow the law of Mahommet, but there are also Nestorian and Jacobite Christians."[18]

When he reached Tangut, one of the places mentioned by Sauma, Marco Polo noticed the existence of Assyrian Christians,[19] and also in Tun-huang, a city which he calls by the name of Chingintalas.[20] From there on he brings to view about ten other places where he tarried on his journeys to and fro in the empire. Writing of the city which is known today as Süchow, he says: "At the end of those ten days you come to another province called Sukchur." He indicates that part of the people in this place were Christians and part were idolaters.[21] From there he traveled to the city of Campichu (now, Kanchow) in which place, he says, the Christians have "three very fine churches."[22]

From Campichu he went still farther east to the kingdom of Erguiul with the capital of the same name, which evidently is the

[17] Komroff, *The Travels of Marco Polo,* pages xvi, xvii.
[18] Yule, *Travels of Marco Polo,* vol. 1, p. 187.
[19] *Ibid.,* vol. 1, p. 203.
[20] *Ibid.,* vol. 1, p. 212.
[21] *Ibid.,* vol. 1, p. 217.
[22] *Ibid.,* vol. 1, p. 219.

modern city of Liangchow. Marco Polo says: "It is one of the several kingdoms which make up the great province of Tangut. The people consist of Nestorian Christians, idolaters, and worshipers of Mahommet."[23] At this point Marco Polo mentions another city directly south from Liangchow, evidently the modern city of Ining, which he credits with being the home of Assyrian Christians.

Starting again eastward from Liangchow, Marco Polo came to a province whose capital city was Calachan. He credits this region with containing numerous cities and villages in which there are fine churches belonging to the Assyrian Christians.[24] From there he proceeded eastward until he entered another province whose rule was in the hands of the Christians. To this next province he gives the name of Tenduc, of which he says:

> The rule of the province is in the hands of the Christians, as I have told you. . . . The king of the province is of the lineage of Prester John, George by name, and he holds the land under the Great Kaan; not that he holds anything like the whole of what Prester John possessed. It is a custom, I may tell you, that these kings of the lineage of Prester John always obtain to wife either daughters of the Great Kaan or other princesses of his family.[25]

Shakespeare wrote about Cathay, the next kingdom into which Marco Polo and his company rode. For centuries China was in the west called Cathay. The great emperor soon discovered the abilities of Marco Polo and chose him for an imperial officer. As such, he made many journeys throughout the realm and reported concerning the numerous towns and villages in which he found Nestorian Christians.[26]

As an officer of Emperor Kublai Khan, he went to the southwest part of China and noticed the existence of Assyrian Christians at Yünnanfu, the capital city of the province of Yünnan.[27] Of the city of Yangchow, over which Marco Polo was placed for a time as governor and which had twenty-seven other wealthy cities under its administration, it is related that it had three such church buildings.[28]

Thus, there are famous witnesses who saw with their own eyes the flourishing churches in the empire of China from 600 to 1300. These

---

[23] Yule, *Travels of Marco Polo,* vol. 1, p. 274.
[24] *Ibid.,* vol. 1, p. 281.
[25] *Ibid.,* vol. 1, p. 284.
[26] *Ibid.,* vol. 1, p. 285.
[27] *Ibid.,* vol. 2, p. 66.
[28] *Ibid.,* vol. 2, p. 154, and note 2.

churches are not there now. What has happened since then? Another revolution embracing Asia and Europe in its sweep overthrew the Mongols and made the Turks dominant.

Rise of Tamerlane

The question naturally arises, What became of the widespread Christianity in the Orient, the fruit of labor carried on by the Church of the East? This leads to new scenes involving Tamerlane, the Jesuits, and the ever-changing desert sands.

Tamerlane (c. a. d. 1333-1405) was another world conqueror.[29] Many famous men of military genius look like pygmies compared to Genghis Khan and Tamerlane. With the exception of southern India, Genghis conquered all of Asia and most of eastern Europe. It has been thought that had it not been for the Christian influences exercised by the Church of the East on the successors of Genghis Khan to spare certain Christian nations, all of them today might be speaking the Mongolian tongue. Tamerlane won dominion over all the lands subjected by Genghis, with the exception of China. Genghis was a Mongolian, displaying throughout his empire a religious liberty wonderful for his day.

Tamerlane was a Turk, a fanatical Mohammedan, who slew Christians by the hundreds of thousands, if not by the millions, and destroyed Christian churches and training centers. His violence is one of the reasons for the ruin of Assyrian Christianity in far Asia. The other reason was the coming of the Jesuits, supported by the guns of Spain and Portugal, of which more shall be written later.

Tamerlane has been unrivaled in world history for ferocity and cruelty. Wherever he passed, provinces became deserts and the inhabitants were either slaughtered or enslaved. He came to power about the time the Mongolian Empire had been weakened by being parceled out among the grandsons of Genghis Khan. He possessed abilities of the highest order as a general. In thirty years of constant warfare he subdued central Asia and Persia. At Ispahan alone, seventy thousand heads were made into a pyramid. He marched into Asia Minor and Georgia, then a very powerful country, and struck a terrifying blow at Russia. He sent his armies into Siberia, subduing northward as far as the Irtish River and eastward to the boundary of

---

[29] Variously known as Tamerlane, Timor, or Timour.

China. His conquest of northern India was a notable campaign. Tamerlane was more than sixty years of age when he forced a passage of the Indus River, marching forward to destroy the houses and to massacre the inhabitants.[30] The Tartar army had taken one hundred thousand prisoners before they reached Delhi. An order was issued for their slaughter, and terrible vengeance was denounced against any person who should attempt to evade the bloody mandate; it is believed that not one condemned person escaped.[31]

Tamerlane's victories over the Ottoman Turks after his return from India were rendered notable by the capture of Bagdad, Aleppo, and Damascus, and also by the seizing of the sultan. Tamerlane was attacked by fever in the midst of a gigantic campaign for the extirpation of China.[32]

The onsweep of the savage Tamerlane was the last storm to uproot the stable foundations of Asiatic civilization. All chance was now removed that central or far Asia would ever become a great contributing factor to the upbuilding of a better world. The days of prosperity and energy gave way to ignorance and poverty. As a missionary objective, those lands presented a hard and difficult problem for the success of high standards such as Christianity seeks to implant. The Saviour taught His disciples that when they were persecuted in one city, they were to flee into another. From the days of Tamerlane on, one must seek in other lands for the growth of a dominant and fruitful Christianity. For fifteen centuries the Church in the Wilderness had done a glorious work in the countries eastward from the Mediterranean. It remained now for a continent newly discovered by Columbus to take up the Christian leadership at a time when the Church of the East was laying it down. America would arise in power to give the gospel of Jesus Christ.

The Sahara would be as alluring a prospect for missionary endeavor as would be Siberia, Turkestan, or northern China when inundated by swirling clouds of sand. The laborious years spent in erecting cities came to nought before the encroaching storm. Man with all his weapons of defense was unable to stand before the avalanches of the desert. A glance at the modern *Atlas of China* prepared by

---

[30] *Encyclopedia Britannica*, 9th ed., art "Timur."
[31] Malcolm, *History of Persia*, vol. 1, pp. 471, 472; pp. 301, 302, 1829 ed.
[32] *Ibid.*, vol. 1, p. 478; pp. 306, 307, 1829 ed.

A. Herrmann will reveal a map locating ruined towns near Turfan in eastern Turkestan.[33]

Between Khotan and China the moving sands of the desert have covered uncounted cities in eastern Turkestan which anciently were the seats of flourishing commerce and prosperous communities.[34] W. H. Johnson is authority for the statement that on one occasion three hundred sixty cities were buried in twenty-four hours.[35]

The researches of Sir Aurel Stein amid the ruined cities of Cathay, and the interesting books of Sven Hedin on the ancient remains of Lop-nor give other interesting facts concerning the burial of once flourishing and populous centers in farther Asia.[36] Sven Hedin shows that amid the ruins of Lou-lan in northwestern Turkestan, the finds unearthed, such as strips of paper with writing, tablets of wood, coins, cups, and bowls, and other data, point to a period between the middle of the third century and the beginning of the fourth. One document speaks of a military expedition, another of a government visit in which the city welcomed forty officials from the army of the frontier. There were also indications of numerous farms.[37]

The Coming of the Jesuits to China

There was another factor, more powerful than Tamerlane, more powerful than the shifting sands of the deserts, which contributed to the weakening of the Assyrian Church in China, and to its disappearance from leadership. This factor was the Jesuit organization.

With the arrival of the Jesuits in China, the battle for the faith was transferred to new soil. The devastating effects on the Church in the Wilderness by the newly arrived Jesuits in India, bringing with them the Portuguese Inquisition, have been previously pointed out. "The downfall of the Nestorian Church in India," writes William W. Hunter, "was due, however, neither to such reversions to paganism nor to any persecutions of native princes; but to the pressure of the Portuguese Inquisition, and the proselytizing energy of Rome."[38] The same results were produced in China and Japan by the Jesuits.

---

[33] Herrmann, *Atlas of China*, page 46.
[34] Yule, *Travels of Marco Polo*, vol. 1, pp. 191, 192.
[35] Johnson, *Journal of the Royal Geographical Society*, vol. 37, p. 5.
[36] Hedin, *Central Asia and Tibet*, vol. 2, pp. 112-120.
[37] *Ibid.*, vol. 2, pp. 134, 135.
[38] Hunter, *The Indian Empire*, page 240.

The famous pioneer of the order, Francis Xavier, who introduced the Inquisition into India, sailed for Japan in 1549. He built his first church in 1552 at Yamaguchi. How much he assimilated Buddhist philosophy and paganism in his papal preaching may be seen in the following quotation: "He utilized, also, the altar vessels, lights, incense, and some of the images found in their temples—differing as they do so little from those of the Catholic Church."[39]

His stay in China, however, was short. His successors for a time experienced much opposition from the mandarins. It was not until January, 1601, that Matteo Ricci, a Jesuit priest from Portugal, succeeded in obtaining a foothold in Peking, principally through his skill in mathematics, the building of war engines, and astronomy.[40]

Backed by the power of Portugal and Spain, the Jesuits gained great prestige with the lettered class and the imperial court. So successful were they among the learned that at the time of the death of Father Ricci in 1610, the three most celebrated doctors in the corporation of the lettered (the scholars, Paul, Leon, and Michael) were in the ranks of those converted by the Jesuits.[41] In fact, about 1615, two of the principal magistrates of China petitioned the emperor to have all the best European books translated into Chinese by the Jesuits, with a view to enriching the national literature.[42]

About this time there was great strife among the Jesuits themselves, not only in China but also in Europe, over the manner in which Father Ricci was adopting heathen customs, baptizing converts who still held them, and so claiming that Christ and the Roman Catholic Church were not antagonistic to such practices as ancestral worship and other pagan rites. The Jesuit historian Huc, discussing Father Lombard, co-worker and successor of Father Ricci, says:

> Regarded from this point of view, the customs of China appeared to Lombard and the missionaries who took his side, as an idolatry utterly incompatible with the sanctity of Christianity—criminal acts, the impiety of which must be shown to the Chinese on whom, by the grace of God, the light of the gospel had shone, and which must be absolutely forbidden to all Christians, whatever might be their condition.[43]

---

[39] Gordon, *"World Healers,"* page 481.
[40] Huc, *Christianity in China, Tartary, and Thibet,* vol. 2, chs. 3, 4.
[41] *Ibid.,* vol. 2, pp. 235, 317; p. 292, 1857 ed.
[42] *Ibid.,* vol. 2, pages 265, 266.
[43] *Ibid.,* vol. 2, p. 230.

It will thus be understood how much the Jesuits in China differed from the Church of the East. It will also be seen that they, by offering beliefs and practices which endorsed rather than opposed heathen idolatry, had acquired power sufficient to wreck New Testament Christianity there as they did in India. Moreover, their acceptance of household gods and prayers for the dead would lead them to utilize the opportunity offered by the unearthing of the famous Chinese stone monument. They would be impelled to corrupt the Chinese characters on this famous stone discovered in the former capital of the Chinese Empire some twenty to twenty-five years after their initial successes. To distort the ancient inscription to teach papal doctrine would offer a decorative screen behind which they could work their machinery of propaganda.

The Corrupted Chinese Inscription

The celebrated Chinese stone monument, as was related in the previous chapter, was dug out of the earth in 1625 at Changan, and its immense importance was immediately recognized. This precious find was at once seized upon by the learned Chinese officials and the Jesuits for their own protection. The first step was to chisel out a duplicate stone in order to get rid of the original.[44] In order to do this, the Jesuits were necessary to the mandarins, and those officials were necessary to the Jesuits. Both needed to protect themselves from the damaging testimony of this revolutionary historical find. At the same time the unearthing of the original had occasioned too much widespread excitement to permit of its being destroyed without a substitute.

Dr. Charles W. Wall maintains that the Syriac inscription upon the stone is genuine. He lays down the following three lines of argument to prove that the Chinese letters chiseled upon the marble are a falsification: "(1) by the circumstances under which it was communicated to the public; (2) by the nature of its contents; and (3) by the characters in which it is written."[45]

On the first point, that the original was destroyed by the Chinese government, it can be said that this fact is well authenticated. It is claimed that an exact copy was made. D'Athenese Kircher, a

---

[44] Wall, *Ancient Orthography of the Jews,* vol. 2, p. 160.
[45] *Ibid.,* vol. 2, pages 159, 160.

Jesuit who was living at the time and who took great interest in the matter of the memorial stone, quoted the following from Martin Martini, an erudite Jesuit, leader of missionary work in China:

> The governor was no sooner appraised of the discovery of the monument than by a curiosity natural to the Chinese, he betook himself to the place and as soon as he examined the tokens of its venerable antiquity, he first composed a book in honor of the monument and ordered that a stone of the same size be made, on which he had engraved the contents of the other and had inscribed point-by-point the same characters and the same letters which had been impressed on the original.[46]

Dr. Wall quotes from two other Jesuit priests, Boim and Samedus, also leaders in the same mission field, to prove that the Chinese inscription was wrought upon a second stone of the same dimension as the first, in the wording of which inscription the Jesuit pundits gave their assistance as they were at hand immediately after the stone was disinterred.[47]

What were the motives of both the learned Chinese and the Jesuits in giving to the public a substitute Chinese inscription? The sign language of China had so greatly altered in the centuries during which the stone lay buried that the inscription on the marble was indecipherable. However, the mandarins claim that the strokes and curves of their sign language, as well as the meaning of each sign, have not changed in two thousand years. For this reason the scholars of the Celestial Empire destroy or efface, whenever possible, and as soon as they can, any ancient inscription upon which they may lay their hands.[48] But since the Changan monument had been found near a large and populous city, and had made a great stir, it was necessary to bring back to the public a duplicate in all respects as nearly like the original as possible while destroying the telltale, indecipherable Chinese inscription.

Now, what was the motive of the Jesuits in being accomplices in this imposition? Why was it necessary for the mandarins to depend upon their help? The Jesuits saw quickly that the historic monument proclaimed the early advent into China of the Church of the East,

[46] Kircher, *La Chine*, pages 10, 11; also Wall, *Ancient Orthography of the Jews*, vol. 2, p. 160.
[47] Wall, *Ancient Orthography of the Jews*, vol. 2, p. 163.
[48] *Ibid.*, vol. 2, p. 162.

which had been excommunicated about A. D. 200 by the bishop of Rome.[49] Here was a chance to write the doctrines of the Church of Rome upon this part of the stone, taking care that the other facts did not clash with the part of the marble chiseled in Syriac. As the lettered class were totally ignorant of church history and of Christian doctrines, they were obliged to have recourse to the Jesuits to fabricate a story which would not suffer exposure by conflicting with what was written on the Syriac part of the stone.

Taking up the second point, one can see that the nature of the doctrines presented in the Chinese part of the inscription also proves a Jesuit fraud. These references in the present Chinese text relating to the use of images in Christian worship and to prayers for the dead were declarations of doctrine which had never been taught by the Church of the East. Yet the Jesuits were compelled to recognize from the Syriac part of the inscription, which they could not alter, that the monument was erected to the glory of that great missionary body. As the Chinese characters with their interpretations can be found in any standard work on the subject, the fraudulent passages will not be quoted here. Furthermore, the Chinese characters on the stone do not stress an evangelical program. There is no reference to the miracles of Christ and nothing regarding His death, resurrection, and ascension.

There is, moreover, fulsome praise given to the Chinese emperors and the endorsement of their practice of hanging the portraits on the walls of the churches. Other teachings differing widely from those of the Church of the East which were rejected by that body appear in the Chinese part of the inscription.[50]

As to the third point, Wall produces a masterly argument to claim genuineness for the Syriac writing on the stone and hence for the original find itself, and to prove that the Chinese inscription was a counterfeit. In his books, by presenting plates which compare the characters of both languages on the monument with those used at different eras throughout the centuries, he convinces the reader of the genuineness of the Syriac and the falsity of the Chinese.[51]

---

[49] See the author's discussion in Chapter IX, entitled, "Papas, First Head of the Church in Asia."

[50] Wall, *Ancient Orthography of the Jews,* vol. 2, pp. 185, 186.

[51] *Ibid.,* vol. 2, pp. 200-245.

A full presentation of the inscription in Syriac on the monument would show that it gives definitely the year in which the stone was erected. Secondly, it states clearly and correctly the name of the head over the Church of the East in China. It gives also clearly and correctly the name of the father of fathers, supreme head over the Church of the East throughout the world, allowing no doubt but that the monument was a memorial to that church and to its triumph in China. The Syriac also states definitely that on this stone was the doctrine of Him who was our Redeemer and the teaching that was preached by their forefathers to the kings of China.

Philology has shown clearly how the meaning of Chinese characters change from century to century. Their sign characters, usually employed in writing, do not convey a word; they express an idea or a picture. The official reason given for destroying the original stone and substituting one newly carved was that the Chinese characters were badly damaged upon the unearthed monument. It is therefore to be concluded that the literary class of Changan wished to reproduce more beautiful and acceptable Chinese characters.

The reason why the authenticity of the Syriac characters is acceptable is readily apparent. In the first place, neither the Chinese nor the Jesuits of the seventeenth century in China were acquainted with the Syriac language of the seventh century. When, however, the Syriac characters of the stone were submitted to Syriac scholars, they tallied well with the records of the church headquarters. They tallied also with the history written about the Church of the East, whether by church members or by disinterested historians.

From the statements chiseled centuries ago in the Syrian language upon this remarkable table, the story of the outstanding work accomplished by the Church of the East in China is confirmed. An unnumbered throng who have been converted to Christ in China through the efforts of the Church of the Wilderness will stand victorious on the sea of glass redeemed from the earth.

CHAPTER XXIII

The Church in Japan and the Philippines

The spread of Buddhism did not destroy, though it may have transformed, the ancient beliefs of the Japanese; nor did it prevent them from practicing other forms of religion. The ancient Chinese cult of heaven worship was not neglected, as is clear from the official chronicles.[1]

JAPAN owes much of her civilization to the Church of the East. This may come as a surprise to many. If so, there will be more surprises in store for those who are not informed as to how strong a determining factor Christianity was in the career of the Island Empire.

The religion indigenous to Japan is Shintoism. The meaning of "Shinto" is "the way of the gods." Dr. Nitabe does not hesitate to say that Shintoism is the most polytheistic of polytheisms.[2] It sees a god in everything, whether in the sublime operations of nature or in the humble objects of furniture in the kitchen. Shintoism remained the sole proprietor of the Japanese religious soul until Christian doctrines and Buddhistic organization brought their influences to bear upon it.

The answer to the query as to how Shintoism could maintain its hold upon the Nipponese with its limited offerings, is found in the fact that it makes a strong bond for national unity. Though the records upon which a history of Japan is built are of comparatively recent origin, the traditions of the people go back more than six hundred years before Christ. The veneration in which the emperor is held has always been the leading Japanese tradition. In every period of the nation's life he has been recognized as a true descendant of the sun-goddess. To that extent he has been considered divine. Shintoism is the expression of this cult. All points of national existence center around the supreme figure of the emperor.

Amazing transformations have taken place in the social, political, and religious life of the people; but these two elements—emperor

[1] Sansom, *Japan*, page 225.
[2] Underwood, *Shintoism*, page 18.

worship and Shintoism—have persisted through Japan's history. Developments have affected even these. Japanese scholars have been graduated with highest honors from Western universities only to return home without the slightest change in their religious convictions regarding the imperial family. This is an illustration of the principle that the head can talk to the head, but the head cannot talk to the heart. Education does not necessarily change the heart.

Japan's records of the past are both written and traditional. The earliest written documents relating to history are the *Kojiki*, penned in mingled archaic Japanese and Chinese and the *Nihongi*, written wholly in Chinese. Both date from the eighth century A. D. The historian Underwood writes:

> The Kojiki has sometimes been called the "Bible of the Japanese," but it is difficult to find a religious motive behind its compilation, save in so far as it sets forth the old stories of the "origin of deities and the establishment of men." The predominant aim of the compilation was to demonstrate the divine origin of the ruling family and the remote antiquity of the foundation of the state.[3]

Of the Nihongi, he says that it covers in part the same ground as the other document, with alternate versions of the same myth or event.

For the first twelve centuries of the Christian Era, the inescapable trait of Japan's history was its servile imitation and copying of the ways and life of China. It received the penetration of Chinese thought and language. In this respect, Japan was practically a province of the Celestial Empire. As P. Y. Saeki puts it:

> If the court buildings in Hsianfu were painted red, so were those at Nara. If a temple was built and supported by the Chinese government in each province, so must it be in Japan. If the birthday of the Chinese emperor was observed as a national holiday in China, so was it here. If the nobles and upper class in the Chinese capital played football, it was soon imitated by the Japanese aristocracy in Nara, and Asuka-oka.[4]

Buddhism was among the influences from China deeply affecting Japan. How Buddhism itself was profoundly transformed by Christianity and how this force dominated Japanese history will be related.

The emperor is looked upon as a direct descendant from the sun-goddess, Amaterasu. Shinto priests assert that the temple at Ise, the

---

[3] Underwood, *Shintoism*, pages 14, 15.
[4] Saeki, *The Nestorian Monument in China*, page 145.

national shrine of Amaterasu, was erected by revelation at the very time Christ was born.[5] They claim incarnation for their sun-goddess as Christians do for the Messiah. There are many points of similarity, if not of identity, between Christianity and Shintoism. The Shintoists are, therefore, in a position to contend that their revelation is the original which the apostles counterfeited, or that both religions have a common origin. Ise, as a religious center, is the holy of holies to the Nipponese. Millions daily turn to it in prayer as in other lands religionists do to Mecca or Jerusalem. In solving the problems which are bound to come in the clash between the Orient and the Occident, it is important to study how the national religion of Japan came to approximate Christianity in doctrine and in religious ceremonies. How did Shintoism and Buddhism come to fuse in Japan, and how did this national religion set out to rival Bible revelations?

Counterfeiting Christianity in the Orient

Buddhism, in general, is not today what it was at the time of its founder's death. The original doctrine taught by Buddha lacked the depth, breadth, and force of the messages of the Bible. If it had not obtained in Asoka (emperor of the great Hindu Empire in India about 273 B. c.) a patron and an apostle, it probably would not have survived. Although Buddhism in India enjoyed imperial support from many different emperors, such as the true church of Christ never enjoyed, it was so sterile and so unresponsive to the needs of the human soul that if it had not appropriated the satisfying doctrines and the productive machinery of Christianity, it would be a dead issue today. As it now stands, Buddhism is one of the greatest religions in the world.

Buddhism, the new faith which its founder placed in the midst of a cruel, filthy, primitive Hinduism, was quite an advance over the crude idolatries in his native land. Yet it was a meager and unsatisfying doctrine of man's relation to God and of his hopes in the future. It was, moreover, too weak to stand up against a rejuvenated Hinduism and an advancing Christianity. In its earlier form, it had no trinity.[6] It presented a clearer idea of divinity than had previously come to India through Hinduism, but it left a great gulf between man

---

[5] Gordon, *"World Healers,"* p. 471, note 2; p. 481, note 4.
[6] Saeki, *The Nestorian Monument in China,* page 123.

and God. It had no Saviour. It had no person of the Godhead akin to the Christian's conception of the Holy Ghost. Man was left to find within himself the power to bridge the chasm between himself and his Creator. Vincent Smith writes: "The primitive Buddhism which ignored the divine was known in later times as Hina-yana, or Lesser Vehicle of salvation, while the modified religion which recognized the value of prayer and acknowledged Buddha as the Saviour of mankind was called the Maha-yana, or the Greater Vehicle."[7] The great doctrine of salvation through faith alone, or Mahayana, appeared in Buddhism about a thousand years after the death of its founder.

Buddhism entered China in the year A. D. 67. Six years prior, Emperor Ming Ti had had a dream which produced in his soul a consternation as profound as that which alarmed Nebuchadnezzar.. The Chinese ruler, so the legend goes, beheld a great golden image flying from the heights to pause over the palace in which he slept. At that spot it halted long enough to sway backward and forward. The sun and the moon falling in radiant splendor upon the heavenly visitant made it glow with a light supernal. The emperor called for one of his able ministers, who promptly interpreted the event as a visit from the Indian deity Buddha. Whereupon the monarch commissioned a deputation of eighteen men to travel west for information about this Buddha.

The commission returned, accompanied by white horses laden with writings and relics, to Loyang, capital of China at that time. Thereupon the emperor built to the new faith a temple, and called it the White Horse, on account of the animals which carried back from India the relics and writings of Buddhism.

Karl Reichelt adds, "Thus began the invading stream of Buddhist monks from India to China, which continued for over seven hundred years, and which became of such great significance to the 'Middle Kingdom.' "[8]

While Buddhism was making its way into China, it was undergoing a transformation. Though supported in the beginning by imperial patronage, it found itself too cold and sterile as a doctrine to

---

[7] Smith, *The Oxford History of India*, page 55.
[8] Reichelt, *Truth and Tradition in Chinese Buddhism*, page 12.

compete with Confucianism, the leading indigenous religion in China.[9] Contact with the Church of the East was an opportunity for Buddhism to assimilate the invincible doctrines of a religion whose founder, Christ, had appeared nearly six centuries after Buddha lived. This is exactly what took place. Shan-tao, a prominent Chinese Buddhist priest who died in 681, began to proclaim through China salvation by faith in Buddha under his new name, Amitabha. Shan-tao also taught the doctrine of a trinity so successfully that it was said of him, "when he preached, the three Buddhas appeared in his breath."[10] He promoted the idea of a vicarious savior of an unlimited light or of eternal life by faith in Amitabha. Where did he get this conception? Evidently from Christian missionaries.

To prove that Christian missionaries and the Buddhist leader Shan-tao were both present in the capital of China during the same generation, it is only necessary to notice, in the following quotation, that "Kao-Tsung (A. D. 650-683), who was a great friend of Shan-tao, was the very emperor who most helped the Assyrian Church in China."[11] Buddhism under the direction of the Chinese, a race more creative than the Hindu, was guided by New Testament truths. Thus it raised itself from the cold doctrine of salvation by works to the heights of the good news of salvation by faith. Reichelt says of Amitabha, the new name in Buddhism, "What has been said here of Amitabha will be sufficient to give an impression of the tremendous significance his name acquired in China, and will show how all the threads in the web of Mahayana lead back to him."[12]

"We have thus," writes Arthur Lloyd, "as it were, three different Buddhist trinities . . . all claiming to come from the beginnings of Mahayana, all supposed to have appeared simultaneously in China, just at the time when Christian missions first made their way to that empire, and all three brought over to Japan during the early years of the Nara period. At bottom the three sets meant pretty much the same thing."[13] There is a Chinese Buddhism and a Japanese Buddhism, as well as an Indian Buddhism.

---

[9] See the author's discussion in Chapter xxi, entitled, "Adam and the Church in China."
[10] Saeki, *The Nestorian Monument in China,* page 148.
[11] *Ibid.,* page 153.
[12] Reichelt, *Truth and Tradition in Chinese Buddhism,* page 41.
[13] Lloyd, *The Creed of Half Japan,* pages 203, 204.

Buddhism Adopts the Second Coming of Buddha

The Buddhists, in adding Amitabha to their godhead, had been enabled to preach a redeemer. In order to satisfy the longings of the sinful soul, they went further. They were compelled to prophesy a second coming or a glorious return of their new mediator who had been translated to nirvana, their heaven. After the flight of centuries, he would return, they said, to earth. One Orientalist writes of the second coming of Buddha under this Japanese title, "Meitreya (Miroku) the Loving One who is Returning."[14]

In order to behold the influence of this teaching in Japan as well as in China, let one journey from Changan, the ancient capital of China, to Kyoto, the former capital of Japan, and ascend by the inclined railway to Mt. Koya, the holy mountain of Japan. In the famous cemetery at the top of the mountain he will find a replica of the celebrated stone monument in Changan, China. Concerning the famous cemetery and the Buddhist monastery therein, founded by Kobo Daishi (A. D. 816), Saeki writes:

> It [the stone] stands just within the entrance to the wonderful cemetery of the Okuno-in, where tens of thousands of the Japanese, from emperors to peasants, have been laid to rest in expectation of the coming of Miroku—the expected Messiah of the Buddhists—during the eleven hundred years since their beloved and venerated saint Kobo Daishi returned from Ch'ang-an, where he is supposed to have seen that "Speaking Stone" which the Nestorian monks had erected there only twenty-three years before his arrival.[15]

Where did Buddhism in general and Japanese Buddhism in particular conceive the idea of the second coming of Miroku, the Japanese Buddhist messiah? As they witnessed the amazing grip of Christianity on the human race, they recognized how ethereal and illusive was their picture of an immortal soul without a body watching the years fly by in an endless chain somewhere. They recognized how gripping was the teaching of the believers in the New Testament when they pictured the Lord Jesus Christ returning in the clouds of heaven with power and great glory. It was then that they moved to enrich the body of their teachings with a similar Messiah who would at the end of a limited number of years descend from heaven to usher in a

---

[14] Gordon, *"World Healers,"* page 38.
[15] Saeki, *The Nestorian Monument in China,* page 12.

Buddhist millennium. The deepest and liveliest thoughts of Buddhism were bound up in Miroku, as the Japanese called him, the man of the future.

The Eclipse of Shintoism by a Christianized Buddhism

The profound transformation of Shintoism in Japan by a Christianized Buddhism centers around the figure of Kobo Daishi, Japan's mightiest intellect. It was he who founded on Mt. Koya a monastery which is now the largest and perhaps the most flourishing in Japan.[16] Having evinced in early youth unusual intellectual brilliancy, he was sent by the Japanese emperor to Changan, the capital of China, to make an effort to reconcile Buddhism and Shintoism. Saeki maintains that the Buddhist convent where Kobo Daishi dwelt for two years[17] was only one street from the great Christian training center built by imperial order for the Church of the East in Changan.

Thus, in the capital city of China, when China was the greatest empire in the world, the Christian delegations from their Persian headquarters were placed face to face with the learned delegation from Japan. The question now arises, Did the Christians from Persia learn from Kobo Daishi, or did the Japanese delegation learn from the Christian missionaries? The Chinese civilization had been raised to a higher level by the Church of the East through the arrival of the gospel missionaries from Persia. Therefore, the Christian leaders came to China to give; Kobo Daishi, the heathen leader from Japan, came to China to receive.

What did he get? It is reasonably safe to conclude that this Kobo Daishi, whose name is a household word today throughout Japan, returned to the Sunrise Kingdom with the higher teachings of a civilization which had dawned upon China when Christianity came.

First, he simplified the Japanese style of writing, which up to then had been an obstacle in translating the best works from other lands into Japanese thought and literature. When he was in China he was most impressed with the teaching of Amitabha, or, as the Japanese named him, Amita. Amitabha was the divinity who obtained the supreme position in the Buddhist body of doctrine. Kobo Daishi had been sent by Japan not to reconcile Christianity with Shintoism, but

[16] Sansom, *Japan*, page 223.
[17] Saeki, *The Nestorian Monument in China*, page 214.

to reconcile Buddhism with Shintoism. Nevertheless, he was so powerfully impressed by Christianity that when he returned to his native land he introduced a new body of doctrine which he called Shingon, or true word. In the course of time this Shingon sect was destined to become the largest sect in Japan. Baptism became an important rite in the mysteries of Shingon. Kobo Daishi succeeded in reconciling the native gods of Japan with the Buddhist divinity. Thus, he could identify the Japanese sun-goddess with Amita, the great illuminator.

"Shinto architecture took many hints from Buddhist temples," says Sansom.[18] Many other items might be enumerated to show how Kobo Daishi, mightily influenced by Christianity, brought about such a reconciliation between his native idolatry of Japan and Buddhism that from that day forward Japanese civilization was indebted to Christianity through the medium of China.

The Church of the East Monument in Japan

The church monument in stone on the summit of Mt. Koya, Japan, is a replica of the famous stone unearthed in Changan, China's capital, about 1625; and it is the Oriental key to the halls of the Christian past in the Orient. In these halls the modern world may walk and see again the vast work which the Church of the East did in the Celestial Empire. The stories engraved there present Bible facts touching patriarchs, prophets, Christ, and the apostles. The Chinese Christian leaders, whose names were engraved by the chisel, resided in the spacious Bible training center only a short distance from the Buddhist temple in China in which Kobo Daishi dwelt. Christian evangelists came to China to bring the spiritual light and civilization of the West. Kobo Daishi came to China to bring back from her to Japan the best civilization which she had. M. Anesaki says:

> Here at Koya-san hundreds of people are seen day in and day out, many of whom are pious pilgrims in white robes, chanting their diverse formulas, but there are also many who are curious visitors. . . . This cemetery stretches for more than a mile from the center to the mausoleum of Kobo Daishi, where, according to the legend, he caused himself to be buried alive in his sammai, or posture of meditation.[19]

---

[18] Sansom, *Japan*, page 223.
[19] Anesaki, *Religious Life of the Japanese Peoples*, page 58.

In the centuries immediately preceding and following 804, Japan from a cultural standpoint could reasonably be considered a part of China. The lanes of civilizing culture which ran from the capital to the eastern province of China extended across the water to the Sunrise Kingdom. As before mentioned, the monument of the Church of the East was erected under imperial favor. The echoes of its magnificent dedicatory ceremonies were still reverberating when Kobo Daishi resided in the same city. Like some chapters in the Bible which give much in rapid sentences, this stone discloses the teachings which raised China from the depths of ignorance to its position as a mighty civilization; and which in so doing, raised Japan with it. "It brings to light," writes P. Y. Saeki, speaking of the original monument in Changan, "the background of the Ch'ang-an civilization which influenced the neighboring countries of High Asia. . . . Besides the stone is actually the great torch which reveals the nature of the civilization which the Japanese received from the Asiatic continent as the result of their intercourse with China during the T'ang dynasty."[20]

There are three turning points which changed the history of Japan prior to the nineteenth century. The first is the return of Kobo Daishi from China to give his report to the government and become the author of influential works. By his powerful preaching he brought into existence a new sect which even today is the largest religious association in Japan. Before the arrival of Christianity, China's civilization and religious conceptions had been devoid of the best in scholarship and in the graces of the gospel which the Church in the Wilderness had already brought forth in Persia and in Ireland. Now Japan, as well as China, was feasting on the treasures brought forth by the West and imprinted upon China. China had been going to school to the Church of the East for two hundred years when the Japanese scholar came to spy out Changan's glory. There he encountered the "Pure Land School," the strongest and most influential of the Buddhist sects. It had been brought to perfection by Shan-tao who developed his teachings while the Nestorian mission flourished.[21]

It was Shan-tao who brought the Amitabha doctrine, or the conception of a compassionate savior in the Buddhist godhead, to its fullest presentation. "The holy trinity from the West appears more

[20] Saeki, *The Nestorian Monument in China*, page 2.
[21] *Ibid.*, page 148.

distinctly."[22] Kobo Daishi went a step further. He appropriated all this, and with it amalgamated Shintoism. His new sect, the Shingon-shu, did not destroy the Shinto deities, it only transformed them. Of Kobo Daishi, G. B. Sansom writes:

> His memory lives all over the country, his name is a household word in the remotest places, not only as a saint, but as a preacher, a scholar, a poet, a sculptor, a painter, an inventor, and explorer, and—sure passport to fame—a great calligrapher. Many miraculous legends cluster about his name.[23]

The brilliant ceremonies which accompanied the setting up of the Christian memorial monument in Changan in 781, found their re-duplication in 1911 when the replica stone was erected on Mt. Koya, Japan. Because of the galaxy of circumstances clustering around the sojourn of Kobo Daishi in Changan near to the original stone, an exact copy of it was erected with dedicatory ceremonies near the grave of the great teacher. The duplicate was set up to call to the mind of Japan, and particularly to the Buddhist church, the source from which their brilliant leader drew his inspiration. As an example of how the Church of the East penetrated the thought and life of modern Japan, see how the doctrine of the second coming of Christ in glory was counterfeited by Buddhism. Thus, Sansom writes of Kobo Daishi:

> When he passed out of this life on Koya he did not die, for he lies uncorrupted in his sepulcher, awaiting the coming of Maitreya, the Buddhist Messiah. More authentic, if less wonderful, merits ascribed to him are the introduction of tea into Japan, much useful work like bridge building and path making, and the invention of the kana syllabary. Such traditions of excellence cling only to the memory of truly exceptional men, and we may be sure that in him Japan nourished a genius, probably one of the greatest in her history.[24]

The Crushing Defeat of China by Japan

The second decisive turning point in the history of Japan was her repulse of China's large armada about 1284. More than four hundred years had passed since the transformation in Japan's civilization was accomplished by Kobo Daishi and his associates. During this time

---

[22] Reichelt, *Truth and Tradition in Chinese Buddhism*, page 131.
[23] Sansom, *Japan*, page 223.
[24] *Ibid.*, page 224.

she continued to look up to China as her superior. There was no other worth-while nation whom she could contact, and so possess an opportunity of comparison. During the first twelve hundred years of the Christian Era, China had never taken enough notice of Japan to desire to subdue it territorially. The hour was reached, however, when a Mongolian occupied the throne of the Orient. Kublai Khan, succeeding to the throne of the Mongolian empire, removed his capital to Peking, China.

The first attempt of Kublai Khan against Japan, when his fleet carried thirty thousand troops against that country, was not a success. As the island rang with triumph, the central administration was satisfied that the Chinese monarch would renew his assault with larger forces. Seven years passed by, and during that time the whole empire, whether nobles, farmers, or slaves, responded as one man in preparation. The blow fell June, 1281. Two formidable armies sailed away for Japan composed of more than one hundred thousand Chinese, Mongolians, and Koreans. The second invasion was a crushing defeat for China. It meant more than that; it meant the loss of prestige. Japan henceforth ceased to look with respect and trust upon her big neighbor. It was a great turning point in Japanese history. During the centuries from 1200 to 1500, the Island Empire sprang forward independently in government, war, architecture, literature, and religion.

The Church of the East also reached its peak, especially during the supremacy of the Chinese Mongolian rulers when Christian teachers enjoyed not only tolerance and freedom of movement, but even the favor of the emperors. It had ministered in Asia to many more nations and peoples than had the papacy. During these same centuries the Reformation arose to check ecclesiastical tyranny in the West. But now the Church of the East faced its greatest temptations and trials. Prosperity at length undermined it. Reliance upon inner inspiration and upon ceremonies gradually came to be substituted for the Sacred Scriptures. Although looseness of doctrine did not particularly manifest itself, the spirit of urgency and definiteness declined. Simplicity of living ceased to be a characteristic of the people so long devoted to their task. The structure of the faith, generally speaking, remained; but the early spirit of devotion had disappeared. Such was its condition when the fierceness of Mohammedan fanaticism under Tamerlane overwhelmed it in central Asia.

How Tamerlane wreaked his cruelty on all nations from Russia to China has already been related. When the devastating storm had passed, there could be found only a few hundred thousand members of the glorious Church of the East which once counted the faithful by millions. It will be told later what marvelous means God had in reserve to compensate this loss.

Japan's Struggle With the Jesuits

The third turning point in the history of Japan is the arrival of the Jesuit missionaries in the middle of the sixteenth century, which was followed by the rapid progress of their propaganda, the bloody persecution of their converts, and the final expulsion. The restoration of peace and political unity at the beginning of the seventeenth century was followed by the extermination of Catholic propaganda and foreign intercourse.[25]

How did the entrance of Jesuit power into Japan and the Philippines influence these countries as far as Christianity is concerned? William E. Griffis, authoritative writer upon Japan, says:

> Christianity, in the sixteenth century, came to Japan only in its papal or Roman Catholic form. While in it was infused much of the power and spirit of Loyola and Xavier, yet the impartial critic must confess that this form was military, oppressive and political. Nevertheless, though it was impure and saturated with the false principles, the vices and the embodied superstitions of corrupt southern Europe, yet, such as it was, Portuguese Christianity confronted the worst condition of affairs, morally, intellectually and materially which Japan has known in historic times. . . . In the presence of soldierlike Buddhist priests, who had made war their calling, it would have been better if the Christian missionaries had avoided their bad example, and followed only in the footsteps of the Prince of Peace; but they did not. On the contrary, they brought with them the spirit of the Inquisition then in full blast in Spain and Portugal, and the machinery with which they had been familiar for the reclamation of native and Dutch "heretics." Xavier, while at Goa, had even invoked the secular arm to set up the Inquisition in India, and doubtless he and his followers would have put up this infernal enginery in Japan if they could have done so. They had stamped and crushed out "heresy" in their own country, by a system of hellish tortures which in its horrible details is almost indescribable.[26]

The same writer attests concerning the work of the Jesuits in

---

[25] Anesaki, *History of the Japanese Religions,* pages 13, 14.
[26] Griffis, *The Religions of Japan,* pages 346-348.

Japan: "Whole districts were ordered to become Christians. The bonzes [Buddhist priests] were exiled or killed, and fire and sword as well as preaching were employed as a mean of conversion."[27]

No history of Japan would be complete without the record of the century-long work of the Jesuits in that country, their methods, and above all, the disastrous effect they produced upon the nation with respect to Christianity. It was the dread of the uprisings caused by the characteristic cruel work of this organization which produced the final decision of the rulers to shut the doors of the nation to Christianity.[28]

It is greatly to the credit of the Japanese people that they manifested such patience with a religious movement which they linked with foreign aggression. They believed that the safety of the realm was at stake. When at last they put up the signboards all over Japan, "Christians to the sea," it was because their conception of the gospel was from an organization bearing the name of Christ but so opposed to progress as to lead Sansom to write:

> Those were the days when Leonardo da Vinci had laid the foundations of the experimental method and therefore of modern scientific inquiry; Copernicus had taught a new theory of the universe; Harvey had lighted on the circulation of the blood; and Gilbert had commenced the study of electricity. But since these discoveries were unpalatable to the Inquisition, which burned Bruno at the stake and imprisoned Galileo, it is unlikely that the Japanese gained any inkling of them from the missionaries.[29]

Japan now took the resolution to shut herself off from the rest of the world. For nearly two centuries no foreigner was allowed to approach her shores. She knew nothing of the outside world, which in turn knew practically nothing of her until Commodore Perry of the United States Navy anchored his fleet in Uraga harbor. That was the time when mothers hushed their fretful children with the question, "Do you think the Mongols are coming?" The immediate result of the negotiations between the American representative and the agent of the Japanese government was the opening of the ports to foreign commerce in 1859. After that, Japan sent to England to organize her navy; to Germany tò organize her army; and to America to organize

[27] Griffis, *The Religions of Japan*, page 348.
[28] Sansom, *Japan*, pages 413-442.
[29] *Ibid.*, page 445.

her system of education. Had Nippon been favored early with the light of the great Protestant Reformation, and had she continued with it as it moved on to liberty and the Bible, there might now be a different story to tell.

The Subjection of the Philippines

There is evidence that before the Spaniards brought the Philippine Islands under their dominion, education was, comparatively speaking, on a high level. As the Philippines had had no contact with the civilization of the West except through Christianity, the only conclusion that can be drawn is that the splendid state of education at the time of the Spanish conquest (1569), was due to the Church of the East.

What, however, was the condition of things after the Islands were taken over by the Spaniards? We quote from Blair and Robertson:

> If, as is credibly asserted, the knowledge of reading and writing was more generally diffused in the Philippines than among the common people of Europe, we have the singular result that the islands contained relatively more people who could read, and less reading matter of any but purely religious interests, than any other community in the world.[30]

The same authors add that it was a singular fact that in all the lists there is no translation of the parts of the Bible.[31]

The rise, growth, and retreat of the Church of the East has been recounted that it might be an inspiration for the Remnant Church today.

---

[30] Blair and Robertson, *The Philippine Islands,* vol. 1, p. 80.
[31] *Ibid.,* vol. 1, p. 79, note 132.

CHAPTER XXIV

The Remnant Church Succeeds the Church in the Wilderness

Who is this that cometh up from the wilderness, leaning upon her beloved?[1]

IT WAS a glorious hour when the church came up out of the wilderness. She had done her work well; she had been faithful to her task. She emerged from the wilderness condition to lay the treasures of her hard-fought battles at the feet of the church of the last period, that era which the Redeemer called "the times of the Gentiles."[2] The contest had been long. It had not been a Thirty Years' War, or a Hundred Years' War, but a 1260-year struggle. It had been cruel for the Church in the Wilderness. Though she never had peace *from* battle, she always had peace *in* battle. The torture chamber, galley chains, burning at the stake, hard labor, and a plebeian status had been forced upon her. Yet, as victor, what had she won for humanity? Had she not won liberty, enlightenment, and the right to worship God according to the dictates of conscience?

The tendency of modern writers is to reflect upon the erroneous idea, assiduously built up by the interested parties, that the papacy is the connecting link between the church of the apostles and the Christianity of the present time. Even among Protestants and nonreligious people there is much false reasoning. The following quotation will exemplify this. Says a modern writer: "Protestantism must never forget that its faith was communicated through Catholicism. The Roman Church remains the only link during many centuries between the modern world and the early Christian enthusiasts."[3]

This book has sought to make it clear that the Church in the Wilderness, of the 1260-year period, is the connecting link between the apostolic church and our time. To her, we are indebted for the learning and the treasures of truth preserved throughout the Dark Ages. As to the transmission of the pure text of the Holy Bible, credit should

---

[1] Song of Solomon 8:5.
[2] Luke 21:24.
[3] *Protestant Digest,* April-May, 1941, page 62.

not be given to the papacy, which has placed tradition above the Bible, but to the faithful churches who adhered through years of darkness and superstition to the original apostolic writings and their uncorrupted translations. This volume, in some small measure, pays tribute to these unsung heroes of the past of the true Christian church.

The Wilderness Period Ends

"The vision is yet for an appointed time," said the prophet.[4] God works by fixed times. He allots to each period of history the prescribed task. The stars in the heavens are commissioned to mark off the years designated by the appointed prophecy. He who guides the heavens, guards the sacred oracles. The origin, growth, and spread of the true church in Great Britain, Europe, Africa, and Asia have been followed. When the 1260-year prophecy expired, God's church laid aside her wilderness life and prophesied "again before many peoples, and nations, and tongues."[5] It was impossible to hold back, or to miss the "appointed time."

When the marvelous chains of prophecy were given to the prophet Daniel, the angel Gabriel distinctly singled out the close of the 1260-year time period as the hour set for the unsealing of the divine predictions. "But thou, O Daniel," he said, "shut up the words, and seal the book, even to the time of the end: many shall run to and fro, and knowledge shall be increased."[6]

What could be meant by that expression, "the time of the end"? Note, it was not *the end of time.* Evidently, the phrase was intended to describe a comparatively short final stretch of years between the close of the 1260-year prophecy and the end of the world. At "the time of the end" the church would be unfolding to a listening world the meaning of the symbols which had passed before the captive prophet. This in itself would indicate that the church had emerged from the wilderness. Daniel had seen a lion, a bear, a leopard, and a beast with ten horns. These were succeeded by a little horn that would wear out the saints of the Most High and would continue 1260 years. Other chains of symbols were made to pass before him. All these, the angel said, represented successions of kingdoms, and stu-

---

[4] Habbakuk 2:3.
[5] Revelation 10:11.
[6] Daniel 12:4.

pendous events affecting the history of the church. "The time of the end" thus signalizes the hour when no further time prophecies would begin, when all prophetic chains would be understood, when the seals were to be broken and the church would teach no longer in terms of symbols, but with the burning lessons and warnings contained in the foretelling and fulfilling of the events.

Jesus, the prophet Daniel, and the apostle John laid great stress on the tribulation running through the 1260-year period. Jesus said: "For then shall be great tribulation, such as was not since the beginning of the world to this time, no, nor ever shall be. And except those days should be shortened, there should no flesh be saved: but for the elect's sake those days shall be shortened."[7] Note, Christ repeatedly mentioned "those days." The fact that the imperious horn of Daniel 7:25 would be forced to terminate the oppression of the saints at the end of the 1260 years, foreshadowed, at their close, a respite of tribulation for the oppressed. The Redeemer Himself distinctly predicted this close. This accounts for the statement of the revelator that the end of the tribulation would be marked by a deadly wound delivered to the oppressor.[8]

Before considering what is meant by "those days" in the foregoing scripture, the length of "those days" should be determined. The apostle John wrote: "The Holy City shall they tread underfoot forty and two months. And I will give power unto My two witnesses, and they shall prophesy a thousand two hundred and threescore days."[9] Counting, as the Bible indicates, a month to be thirty days, forty-two times thirty equals 1260.

What is meant in Matthew 24 by Christ's expression, "great tribulation"? There have been three periods of tribulation for the Christian church: the first, reaching into the fall of Jerusalem, during which time the Jews persecuted the Christians; the second, reaching to A. D. 325, during which period the pagans greatly afflicted the church; and the third, the 1260-year period (mentioned directly seven times in the Scriptures) when the politico-ecclesiastical power persecuted the Church in the Wilderness. A careful consideration of the many angles of the Saviour's prophecy in Matthew 24 will definitely show that by

---

[7] Matthew 24:21, 22.
[8] Revelation 13:3.
[9] Revelation 11:2, 3.

the expressions "those days" and "great tribulation," He meant the 1260-year period. In Daniel 11 :31-35, prophesying of the same "great tribulation," the prophet begins it from the time "the abomination that maketh desolate" is set up, or the papacy was given independent dominion (verse 31), and terminates it with "the time of the end" (verse 35). When the prophet previously (Daniel 7 :25) dealt with this same treading underfoot of the saints, he began the 1260-year period with the plucking up of the third of three horns which were to be plucked up. The date of this event was evidently a. d. 538.[10]

During the Dark Ages, therefore, one would not find the true church favored by princes and kings, but constantly pursued by wolves in sheep's clothing. During those 1260 years the Church in the Wilderness did not ally herself with governments to form a state church, neither was she clothed with the robes of an imperial hierarchy. Otherwise, she could not have been singled out by the Redeemer to suffer a tribulation so deep and long that the church could not have endured it unless the days were shortened.

The unutterable sufferings during the years of the "great tribulation" increased as the papacy secured additional power over the ten kingdoms. By the time of the famous Lateran Council held in Rome in 1215, more nations were forced into the armies of the persecutor. In the days of Claude of Turin (c. a. d. 800) and his leadership in the Church in the Wilderness, this church was fairly strong. Passing on to the tenth and eleventh centuries, one can plainly see the growing voice of dissent and the extensive increase of New Testament believers throughout Europe. All these bodies have been falsely and persistently accused of Manichaeism. It was the splendid work of the Albigenses, however, which aroused the alarm of the papacy and led to the Lateran Council of 1215. This same year will be remembered as the date when the Magna Charta, the first step toward constitutional government, was written by the barons of England. The growth of Bible preaching had evidently been influencing political thinking.

From 1215 on, the increasing severity of papal persecutions is seen. This is followed by the spread of the Church in the Wilderness in all lands. Again the blood of the martyrs became the seed of the church. Two examples of this may be cited. The Waldenses, and the churches

---

[10]See the author's discussion in Chapter x, entitled, "How the Church Was Driven Into the Wilderness."

who believed as they did, though bearing other names, spread all over Europe. Mosheim has already been quoted to prove that, prior to the age of Luther, there lay concealed in almost every country of the Continent, especially in Bohemia, Moravia, Switzerland, and Germany, many peoples in whose minds the principles maintained by the Waldenses, the Wycliffites, and the Hussites were deeply planted. Also in former chapters there has been traced the spread of the true church throughout Syria, Persia, India, central Asia, China, and Japan.

Important Dates in Church History

Several chains of prophecy were given which run more or less parallel to the 1260-year period. Four dates stand out prominently in the latter part of the 1260-year period. In a special sense the movement mirrored in these events brought the Church in the Wilderness out from her unrecognized leadership into the foreground. These dates were: 1453, when Constantinople was conquered by the Turks; 1483, when Martin Luther was born; 1492, when Columbus discovered America; and 1491, when Ignatius Loyola was born. A consideration of the new era ushered in by each one of these events throws light upon the steps of the church as she comes forth from the wilderness.

Forty years before Columbus discovered the New World, Europe discovered the Ancient World. The locating of the Western Hemisphere was such a revolutionary event that it is easy to overlook the great discovery in 1453. The treasures disclosed to wondering humanity by the finding of America meet their counterpart in the literary wealth thrown upon Europe by the fall of Constantinople, capital of the Eastern Roman Empire. Until that time, the Greek manuscripts containing the knowledge possessed by a brilliant antiquity were confined to the Eastern Roman Empire, often called the Greek Empire. The fall of Constantinople before the armies of the Moslem Turks opened to Western Europe the empire's libraries with their thousands of manuscripts. The nations west of Constantinople awoke from the sleep of centuries. For nearly a thousand years the ecclesiastical power of Rome had eliminated the study of Greek language and literature. "Knowledge of the Greek language died out in Western Europe," says one whose pro-Roman leanings are well known.[11] Italy, France, Germany, and England were stunned by the sudden revela-

---

[11] Westcott and Hort, *The New Testament in the Original Greek*, vol. 2, p. 142.

tions in history, science, literature, and philosophy which came to them. Immediately they appropriated their newly found treasures. Scholars were as much intent upon manuscript hunting as Columbus was upon continent hunting.

The greatest treasure accruing to the world by the fall of Constantinople was the recovery of multiplied manuscripts of the Greek New Testament. The vast majority of these manuscripts were the Received Text. Having had only the Latin Bible of Rome, called the Vulgate, the western world in general lacked the exact words written by the apostles of the revelations of Jesus.

At this moment appeared the astounding scholar of the age. In erudition Erasmus of Holland has never been surpassed, in the opinion of many. He brought his gigantic intellect to bear upon the realm of classical literature. He was ever on the wing, ransacking libraries and every nook and corner where ancient manuscripts might be found. He divided all Greek New Testament manuscripts into two classes: those which followed the Received Text, edited by Lucian; and those which followed the Vaticanus manuscript, the pride of the Vatican library. He specified the positive grounds on which he rejected the Vaticanus while receiving the other.[12] And when he brought forth his edition of the Greek New Testament, a new day dawned. This was the edition which all the Protestant churches of that period used. It became the text for Luther's Bible in German and for Tyndale's translation in English. Tyndale, an accomplished scholar in seven languages, had been a student of Erasmus' Greek edition.

Luther and the Reformation

The next epochal date is 1483, the year of Luther's birth. The name of Luther is almost synonymous with that of the Reformation. As a monk in his cloister cell, his spiritual struggles with God were so powerful that the waves of evangelical feelings which later swept over Europe were, to a certain extent, but the expressions of Luther's own experience. The Reformation made vocal the longings of the people for a new heart, a heart like Christ's, in place of their sinful heart. At first, even for some time, Luther had no thought or desire to break with the Church of Rome. However, the ever-growing power of gospel truth was exalting the Bible above the church. The papacy refused to

---

[12]Nolan, *The Integrity of the Greek Vulgate*, pages 413, 414.

surrender its claim that the church was above the Bible. The people were weary with the swarms of monks and nuns who were propagating a vast round of processions, genuflections, prayer beads, amulets, images on the walls of the churches, glorification of relics, and much ado about purgatory—all of these resembling the minutiae of the Pharisees which Jesus came to abolish.

The break came in 1517 when Luther challenged the papacy by nailing his ninety-five theses to the church door at Wittenberg. Apparently the majority of citizens throughout Europe were members of the Church of Rome; but actually a vast spiritual work had been done in the hearts of the masses before this time. Thomas Armitage shows that in 1310, two hundred years before Luther's theses, the Bohemian brethren constituted one fourth of the population of Bohemia, and that they were in touch with the Waldenses who abounded in Austria, Lombardy, Bohemia, north Germany, Thuringia, Brandenburg, and Moravia.[13] Erasmus pointed out how strictly Bohemian Waldenses kept the seventh-day Sabbath.

The Reformation was a mighty movement, much like the departure of the children of Israel from the land of Egypt. It rejected the supremacy of the pope, and tore practically all of northern Europe away from the papacy. At first there was in it no abolition of the union of church and state; nevertheless, it did not use the state for the widespread, cruel persecutions which darkened the history of Rome. It was a movement struggling toward the light. It abolished the vast gulf which separated the clergy from the people. It acknowledged the Bible as the supreme and only authority in doctrine. It rejected purgatory, worship of saints and images, and took its stand against the orders of monks and nuns. It rejected the celibacy of the clergy. Unquestionably, it was a movement of God; and although it did not attain to the complete purity of doctrine and separation from worldliness as did the early evangelical bodies which fought the prolonged battle through the Dark Ages, to a great extent it restored primitive Christianity to northern Europe which later would pass on these great benefits to the Americas. William Muir says:

> It is a serious error to think of the Reformation era, glorious and fruitful as it was, as if it were the golden age of the church, or as if everything

---

[13]Armitage, *A History of the Baptists*, page 318.

was perfect even when it was at its best. The best is yet to be; the best for which all ages have done their work.[14]

The Reformers in general took a wrong attitude on the Ten Commandments. They respected them as a code of teaching, but not as a law of binding obligation. Most all the Reformers could be quoted, but only one statement will be given, from the English Reformer Tyndale: "As for the Saboth, a great matter, we be lords over the Saboth; and may yet change it into the Monday, or any other day, as we see need; or may make every tenth day holy day only, if we see a cause why."[15]

From the teachings of the leading evangelical Reformers it can be seen that they received from the papacy the conviction that down through the ages Sunday never had any standing whatsoever, because the Roman Catholic Church always took the attitude that Sunday was simply a festival day like Christmas or any other holiday. The papacy did not recognize the obligatory observance of the Sabbath of the fourth commandment. Therefore, during the 1260 years, whenever the fourth commandment had its proper place, it was always the work of Sabbathkeepers of the Church in the Wilderness. We have seen the crises brought on by the powerful antagonism of the papacy to the Sabbath of the fourth commandment.

The Background of the Day of Worship

It was a great moment in the agelong struggle between the Bible and tradition when, in 489 the Roman emperor in his zeal for hierarchical doctrine, closed the notable college established by the Assyrian Church at Edessa. This act resulted in the erection of a barrier between the evangelical East and the papal West. The Church of the East promptly left Edessa, which was just within the border of the Roman dominion, and moved the institution to Nisibis, a few hundred miles within the Persian Empire. Here, near the Tigris River, a great university was established, which for a thousand years not only confirmed the Persian Christians in the Judean type of teachings as against the papal type, but also spread Greek culture and Roman civilization to the nations of the Orient. Nine years later (A. D. 498) the Assyrian Church, in council assembled, renounced all connection with

---

[14] Muir, *The Arrested Reformation,* page 9.
[15] Tyndale, *An Answer to Sir Thomas More's Dialogue,* b. 1, ch. 25, p. 97.

the church of the Roman Empire. Many writers point out the Semitic nature of the nations in the midst of which this new college was placed. This settled once and forever that the teachings of Semitic Abraham and his descendants, not the state religion of the West in its pagan philosophy, would color the churches of Asia. Thus, the graduates of Nisibis as they stood like prophets before the sovereigns of China and Japan would preach the Sabbath of the fourth commandment.

It was attested by the early church historians, Socrates and Sozomen, already cited, as well as by other authorities, that at this time all the churches of the world, except Rome and Alexandria, sanctified with divine services the worship of the Sabbath of the Decalogue. Wherever Sunday was also observed, it was with memorial resurrection services. The papal church, yes, even the Reformers, did not recognize Sunday as a continuation of, or a substitute for, the Sabbath. Sunday was in no way considered a divine commandment, only a church ordinance.

The Civilization of the Church of the East

It has been noted how in the ninth century the civilizing education system of the Church of the East dominated the golden age of the mighty Arabian Empire—so much so that it permeated the literature of China and Japan in the east, and paved the way for the founding of universities in Europe.

When the papal armies made a temporary conquest of the city of Constantinople in 1204, many writers make plain the contrast between the high culture and civilization of the nations in which were located Eastern and Asiatic Christianity as compared to the barbarous conditions of the papal nations of Europe. Thus, Arthur P. Stanley writes:

> There can be no doubt that the civilization of the Eastern Church was far higher than that of the Western. No one can read the account of the capture of Constantinople by the crusaders of the thirteenth century, without perceiving that it is the occupation of a refined and civilized capital by a horde of comparative barbarians. The arrival of the Greek scholars in Europe in the fifteenth century was the signal for the most progressive step that Western theology has ever made.[16]

---

[16] Stanley, *History of the Eastern Church*, page 26.

Adeney testifies to the same contrast when commenting upon the conversion of the Russian church in the eleventh century by Eastern Christianity:

> Commerce followed the gospel. Art and culture came in its train. A Christian civilization now began to spread slowly through Russia. The consequence was that in the course of the next century this country, which we are now accustomed to think of as the most backward of European nations, became more advanced than Germany or even France. She took a foremost place in the early part of the Middle Ages. Byzantine culture was now at its height and incomparably superior to the rude condition of the Western nations.[17]

In the middle of this same century, the thirteenth, occurred the devastating conquest of nearly all Asia by the Mongols. They also overran Russia, Poland, Bohemia, and Austria-Hungary, but were stopped on the eastern border of Germany. France, Germany, and England were saved when the grandson of the first Mongolian conqueror refused to pursue the conquest farther west. While the Mongolian armies spread in their path the devastations of war, their victorious march threw doors open through which were revealed to the eyes of an astonished Europe not only the splendid civilization of Asia, but also the widespread activities of the Church of the East. Consideration of these factors discloses the attachments of this church to the Sabbath of the fourth commandment.

Consideration of the great voyages which sent Columbus to the west and Vasco da Gama to the east in the early years of the sixteenth century, reveals more than the commercial motives of these expeditions. Commenting on the splendor and civilization of the Orient in connection with the voyages of the Polos, especially of Marco Polo, the latter part of the thirteenth century, Edward M. Hulme writes:

> The contributions of the Polos to geographical knowledge completely eclipsed those of all other previous travelers. They included the first extensive and reliable account of the riches and the splendors of Indo-China, the Indian archipelago, and China; and they included, too, the first actual information about Japan. So picturesque was the account, so attractive the story, so marvelous were the facts disclosed, that thousands read it with unabated interest for generations afterwards. Columbus tells us that he found it an absorbing narrative. It aroused in many a breast the desire to follow in the steps of the men whose journeyings it recounted.[18]

---

[17] Adeney, *The Greek and Eastern Churches*, page 363.
[18] Hulme, *Renaissance and Reformation*, page 178.

The religious motives in undertaking the voyages of discovery were the deepest. Now unrolls the history of how the Jesuits invaded and cruelly oppressed Abyssinia in Africa, persecuted the Church of the East in India, and plotted for dominion in China and Japan. The famous Jesuit, Francis Xavier, exploring the church problems of the Orient, called in 1545 for the establishment of the cruel and bloody Inquisition, which was set up in Goa, India, in 1560. Adeney indicates why this horrible engine was considered necessary: "In a letter written towards the end of the year 1545, Xavier begged the king of Portugal to establish the Inquisition in order to check 'the Jewish wickedness' that was spreading through his Eastern dominions."[19] The "Jewish wickedness" which the Jesuits undertook to fight in the Church of the East meant, among other things, the observance of the seventh day as the Sabbath. War on the Sabbath is precisely what the Jesuits made in Abyssinia, which for centuries kept the seventh day of the week as the Sabbath.

The Mongolian conquest did not injure the Church of the East. On the contrary, a number of the Mongolian princes and a larger number of Mongolian queens were members of this church. It was rather the fierce opposition of the fanatical Mohammedan conqueror, Tamerlane, a century later which brought great grief to the Assyrian Church. Nevertheless, in spite of that and in spite of the horrible work of the Jesuits, the Church of the East was strong enough in 1643 to send a director from its home base in Persia to daughter communities in southwestern India. Let it be remembered that at this very time Europe was in the convulsions of the dreadful Thirty Years' War. This was a fierce unsuccessful effort of the Jesuits to destroy Protestantism on the Continent. From the days of Luther until 1648, when the famous Peace of Westphalia terminated the Thirty Year's War, Protestantism could not say that it had gained a secure place under the sun. During this same period and prior to the Reformation there were strong movements in Russia, Bohemia, France, England, and Germany, seeking freedom to observe unmolested the seventh day as the Sabbath. Yet intolerance reigned in Asia and Europe. But it is gratifying to note that in the last period of the Thirty Years' War, for the first time in the history of the world, a government granted religious freedom.

---

[19]Adeney, *The Greek and Eastern Churches,* pages 527, 528.

This was the case of Roger Williams in Rhode Island when he made a practical application of the great teaching of Christ which called for the separation of church and state. The spread of religious freedom was bound to be followed by a latter-day message on the binding claims of the fourth commandment.

Other Shortcomings of the Reformation

Other unfortunate deficiencies of the Reformation might be mentioned, such as the union of church and state. Prophecy seemed to indicate, however, that full return to primitive Christianity of the Bible would not come until the church emerged from its subordinate position, or when the Church in the Wilderness became the Remnant Church.

The following words from William Muir indicate the lack of stability manifested by many believers in the Reformation prior to the days of John Wesley. He writes: "In England the masses, who were never really evangelized until John Wesley's time, changed sides as the monarchs changed and were usually ready to shout with the biggest crowd."[20] What was there unusual in the message of John Wesley? It was the emphasis placed by Methodism on redemption through the blood of Christ.[21] The Scriptures teach that Christ is the one and only divine sacrifice and that salvation comes through the sufficiency of His death on the cross as our substitute and surety. The substitutionary death of Christ as a divine sacrifice was not clearly emphasized by the early Reformers.

The later Moravian movement, which swept through eastern Europe and later established its missions in North America, was strong through its exaltation of the Pauline, not the papal, attitude toward Christ's substitutionary death. It is stated that when Zinzendorf in 1722 founded Herrnhut on his estates, he preached the doctrine of salvation through the blood of Christ.[22] Now, sad to relate, many Protestants following in the steps of Rome, belittle the blood atonement and ignore the substitutionary death.

Only when the church emerged from the wilderness to become the Remnant Church was complete apostolic truth to be restored. The

---

[20] Muir, *The Arrested Reformation,* page 10.
[21] Emory, *The Works of the Reverend John Wesley,* vol. 5, p. 688.
[22] Sessler, *Communal Pietism Among Early Armenian Moravians,* page 8.

church would preach again with power not only the substitutionary death of Christ, but also the sacredness of the Ten Commandments, which were to be magnified by the death of Christ—especially the fourth, sanctifying the seventh day. Can we not say that in "the time of the end" the Sabbath would become a test? Thus, it is written by the revelator, "The dragon was wroth with the woman, and went to make war with the remnant of her seed, which keep the commandments of God, and have the testimony of Jesus Christ."[23]

The End of the Great Tribulation

The last of the four prominent dates under consideration is 1491, when Ignatius Loyola, founder of the Jesuits, was born. When it seemed as if the Church of Rome were ruined and crushed by the Reformation, the order of the Jesuits was formed, the most powerful and cruel of all the orders within the papacy. It undertook first of all to capture colleges and universities, then to climb to power in the state. It succeeded in dominating certain nations and in persecuting with unspeakable cruelty that Protestantism which it was invented to destroy. As Thomas B. Macaulay writes of Jesuitic cruelty:

> If Protestantism, or the semblance of Protestantism, showed itself in any quarter, it was instantly met, not by petty, teasing persecution, but by persecution of that sort which bows down and crushes all but a very few select spirits. Whoever was suspected of heresy, whatever his rank, his learning, or his reputation, knew that he must purge himself to the satisfaction of a severe and vigilant tribunal, or die by fire. Heretical books were sought out and destroyed with similar rigor.[24]

The Saviour made a clear distinction between the end of the days and the end of the tribulation in the days. He said, "In those days, after that tribulation." The days, as previously discussed, ended in 1798; but by 1772 every country in the world, even those which are called Catholic, arose in horror and demanded that the pope abolish the order of the Jesuits. Finally a pontiff was found who made a show of disbanding them, and they made a show of getting out of sight. As one present-day writer says:

> Proof of the subversive influence exercised by the Jesuits, in both spiritual and civil affairs, throughout the four hundred years of their exist-

---

[23] Revelation 12:17.
[24] Macaulay, *Critical, Historical, and Miscellaneous Essays and Poems,* vol. 5, pp. 482, 483. See also his essay, "Von Ranke."

ence, is plentifully evident by the number of times they have been disbanded by the Catholic Church itself, by the Catholic people and by liberal and progressive governments in Catholic and non-Catholic countries. They have been expelled, at one time or another (many times over in some countries) from practically every country in the world—except the United States.[25]

Thus the 1260 years ended in 1798, but the great tribulation can be considered to have ended in 1772. The date 1798 is worthy of fuller consideration.

The Accomplishment of the Indigation

"And some of them of understanding shall fall, to try them, and to purge, and to make them white, even to the time of the end: because it is yet for a time appointed. And the king shall do according to his will; and he shall exalt himself, and magnify himself above every god, and shall speak marvelous things against the God of gods, and shall prosper till the indignation be accomplished."[26]

Here a persecution against the saints is foretold which would last until "the time of the end." It has previously been shown that "the time of the end" would begin when the 1260-year period ended, or in 1798. In the above verses is predicted the appearance upon the scene of world action of a willful king who would wreak God's indignation upon the persecutor of His people. Since the persecutor was the papacy, one must look elsewhere than the medieval hierarchy to locate the willful king destined to put an end to the 1260-year period and to inflict a deadly wound upon the destroyer. What power was swinging into strength, seized with a religious antagonism to the papacy, about 1798? What other nation could fulfill these specifications better than France, the oldest daughter of the church, driven to atheism. Astonished humanity suddenly beheld break forth in France a revolution, the like of which the world had never previously seen. It engulfed the ecclesiastical tyranny of the papacy.

Napoleon, the product and the consummation of the French Revolution, was in Egypt when, on February 10, 1798, General Berthier took the pope prisoner, abolished the college of cardinals, and proclaimed on Capitoline Hill what had been absent from Rome for 1260

---

[25]Lehmann, "What Is Wrong With the Jesuits?" *Protestant Digest*, vol. 4, no. 1, Aug.-Sept., 1941.
[26]Daniel 11:35, 36.

years—religious liberty! This act struck down the head of the system which had pursued the elect flock. But in the wreaking of God's indignation as indicated in the scriptures above, the "deadly wound" embraced more than this. A quotation from Lord Bryce will help show how the French Revolution, the willful king or kingdom, through Napoleon demolished the political regime of the papacy.

It was his mission—a mission more beneficent in its result than in its means—to break up in Germany and Italy the abominable system of petty states, to reawaken the spirit of the people, to sweep away the relics of an effete feudalism, and leave the ground clear for the growth of newer and better forms of political life. . . . New kingdoms were erected, electorates created and extinguished, the lesser princes mediatized, the free cities occupied by troops and bestowed on some neighboring potentate. More than any other change, *the secularization of the dominions of the prince-bishops and abbots* proclaimed the fall of the old constitution, whose principals had *required the existence of a spiritual alongside of the temporal aristocracy.*[27]

Inquiry Into the Prophecies

"But thou, O Daniel," said the angel, "shut up the words, and seal the book, even to the time of the end: many shall run to and fro, and knowledge shall be increased." The Hebrew for the expression "run to and fro," in its deepest sense, means "to study diligently and minutely," or "to travel through." The German Bible, as well as the French, translates this phrase thus: "Many shall search thoroughly and knowledge shall be increased." What caused so great an increase in Bible searching that it became a study on prophetic prediction? When the delivering of the "deadly wound" to the gigantic ecclesiastical dictatorship had lifted the ban on Bible study and the termination of the wilderness condition of the true church had been so strikingly fulfilled, the question "What next?" was in the hearts of God's people. This led to a sweeping wave of inquiry into the great chains of prophecy.

At this very date a vast increase in the publication of Bibles began. Bible societies, one after another, appeared. The British and Foreign Bible Society was organized March 7, 1804. The American Bible Society came into existence May 8, 1816. Copies of the Holy Scriptures poured from printing presses by the hundreds of thousands, and

---

[27] James Bryce, *The Holy Roman Empire,* pages 295, 296.

have been sent out literally by carloads and shiploads. This made possible the fulfillment of the prediction that men everywhere would run to and fro through Holy Writ. In particular there was intense interest to learn how much prophecy remained yet unfulfilled.

The 1260-year period was fulfilled. But there was left another remarkable prophetic chain which extended to 1844, or forty-six years beyond the termination of the 1260 years. This was the 2300-year-day chain in Daniel 8:14, challenging special attention because it was, as the reading of the chapter shows, the subject of celestial discussion between Michael (Christ) and Gabriel.

Many pages might be written concerning the Bible writers and preachers who now appeared prominently before the public, convinced by this 2300-year prophecy that they were living in the time of the end. However, mention will be made briefly of Manuel Lacunza, Edward Irving, Joseph Wolff, and William Miller.

Lacunza at the opening of the nineteenth century was a Jesuit of a monastery in South America. Becoming a convert to Protestantism, he diligently studied the Bible, giving special attention to the field of prophecy. He became so aroused over the 2300-year period as indicating that the promised return of Christ was not far distant that he attempted to write a book upon the subject. This being known, it aroused religious antagonism, and he was driven out of Chile. He continued his work in Europe, experiencing the same persecution. Remarkable to relate, while the Continent was still in the death struggle of ecclesiastical tyranny, he completed his volume entitled, *La Venida del Mesías en Gloria y Majestad (The Coming of Christ in Glory and Majesty)*, writing under the name of Juan Josafat Ben-Ezra.[28]

Approximately the same time Edward Irving began his astonishing labors along the same line in England and Scotland. He too, after his call from Scotland in 1812 to become the leading preacher in London, applied himself unceasingly to the study of prophecy. Concentrating especially upon the 2300-year time period of Daniel 8:14, he arrived at practically the same conclusion as did Lacunza. Tremendous crowds attended his lectures not only in London, but throughout the large cities of Great Britain. Auditoriums were not large enough

---

[28]Lacunza, *La Venida del Mesías en Gloria y Majestad;* see Urzua, *Las Doctrinas de P. Manuel Lacunza.*

to accommodate those who sought to hear him.[29] His fame reached the ears of Lacunza, who sent him a copy of his own book. Irving was astonished to see how God had separately led a Scotch Presbyterian and a converted South American Jesuit to recognize the commanding value of this prophecy and to conclude from it that the time of the end had come.

Another remarkable preacher of prophecy was Ezra Ben-Ezra who, after his conversion from Judaism, took the name of Joseph Wolff. Of him D. T. Taylor writes:

> Joseph Wolffe, D. D., according to his Journals, between the years 1821 and 1845, proclaimed the Lord's speedy advent in Palestine, Egypt, on the shores of the Red Sea, Mesopotamia, the Crimea, Persia, Georgia, throughout the Ottoman Empire, in Greece, Arabia, Turkistan, Bokhara, Affghanistan, Cashmere, Hindostan, Thibet, in Holland, Scotland and Ireland, at Constantinople, Jerusalem, St. Helena, also on shipboard in the Mediterranean, and at New York City, to all denominations. He declares he has preached among Jews, Turks, Mohammedans, Parsees, Hindoos, Chaldeans, Yeseedes, Syrians, Sabeans, to pachas, sheiks, shahs, the kings of Organtsh and Bokhara, the queen of Greece, etc., and of his extraordinary labors, the *Investigator* says: "No individual has, perhaps, given greater publicity to the doctrine of the second coming of the Lord Jesus Christ, than has this well-known missionary to the world. Wherever he goes, he proclaims the approaching advent of the Messiah in glory." [30]

The converted South American Jesuit, the Scotch Presbyterian, and the converted son of a rabbi were followed in the study and preaching of the same pivotal prophecy by William Miller who was an American farmer, a veteran of the War of 1812, and a converted infidel. Later he was ordained a Baptist preacher, and he stirred to their foundations the churches of America during the years 1828-1844. He has never yet been surpassed in giving to the world an original and generally correct analysis of the prophetic time periods. With respect to his claim that the world would come to an end in 1844, this was a mistaken interpretation of the event, but the accurate and substantial verification of the date still stands. Later and clearer light upon Daniel 8:14 revealed that Christ was speaking to Gabriel of the cleansing of the sanctuary, an Old Testament expression applying to the

---

[29] Oliphant, *The Life of Edward Irving*, 6th ed., pages 80, 82, 84, 405, 406.
[30] Taylor, *The Voice of the Church on the Coming and Kingdom of the Redeemer*, pages 342, 344.

Day of Atonement, which in reality is the antitype of the day of judgment.[31]

The World's Unparalleled Progress After 1798

When the 1260-year period ended in 1798, when religious freedom had at last dawned upon the race, centuries of progress were crowded into a few short years. Up to 1798 there were no railroads, no steamboats, no telegraph, no electric lights, no reapers, automobiles, movies, airplanes, or radios. In fact, up until that time man still had about the same level of material progress as when Noah came out of the ark.

When religious freedom was granted, all this changed. The mind was free; no one was compelled to believe. As Shakespeare wrote: "And this our life, exempt from public haunt, finds tongues in trees, books in the running brooks, sermons in stones, and good in everything." The mind must be free to learn from nature, books, the Bible, or society; to believe according to the dictates of conscience. When this freedom exists, material civilization increases. May all the gains made by the Church in the Wilderness be preserved! God forbid that civil or religious despotism should regain the ascendancy, reverse all that has been gained since 1798, and send us back to the Dark Ages!

The French Revolution, following upon the American Revolution, delivered to the papacy a wound as it were unto death. For 1260 years Rome had entrenched itself almost invincibly behind two theories: one, the union of church and state; the other, the divine right of kings. It can be easily seen that if monarchs believed that they ruled by divine right, they would favor and exalt the head of that church who would perform the consecration service at their coronation. That period was called the Dark Ages. It took centuries of blood and suffering to open the eyes of men to the colossal evils inherent in these two theories of government. Edgar Quinet, Protestant historian of the French Revolution, believed that up to that event the history of France was not worth writing. When in February, 1798, religious liberty was proclaimed by the French army in Rome and the pope was taken prisoner to France, the cardinals, as they drew their cloaks over their heads and abandoned the city, exclaimed, "This is the end of religion!"

Nevertheless, the prophet predicted, "His deadly wound was healed: and all the world wondered after the beast." Here was a de-

---

[31] See Leviticus 16.

mand for eternal vigilance, lest defeated tyranny would regain its lost ground. "Democracy is character," exclaimed an American statesman. As prosperity increased, character declined. The fathers won freedom and happiness through blood and suffering. The children turned back in their hearts to the vices and luxuries of the Old World. The Oxford Movement arose in 1833, and rapidly growing in strength and gathering these worldly desires of the next generation into an organized society, began the glorification of the Dark Ages and the belittling of modern freedoms, as well as of those who won them. The papacy in its leading publications gives credit to Dr. J. H. Newman, of Oxford University, who later became Cardinal Newman, and the Oxford Movement for the present world-wide Catholic revival. Of him *The Catholic Encyclopedia* writes: "No finer triumph of talent in the service of conscience has been put on record. From that day the Catholic religion may date its re-entrance into the national literature." [32]

Why was it that in 1833 England believed that the Reformation was the work of God, but fifty years later it believed that the Reformation had been a rebellion, as was pointed out by the historian Froude, who was at Oxford during those years of the movement; and that whereas in 1833 the pope was looked upon as antichrist, in 1883 he was considered the successor of the apostles? The deadly wound to tyranny was being healed and those who inflicted it were being vilified. All the arts of tricky reasoning and of corrupting the records of history reappeared in the Oxford Movement. Its leaders, many of them Jesuits in disguise, began to build up a case for Romanism. This movement, assisted by gold and by disguised agents from the Continent, spread through the Church of England. It then entered the Protestant theological schools of America. Now is being witnessed the de-Protestantization of the English-speaking world. The pope has now been made king. The "deadly wound" is reaching complete healing.

The Approaching Age

In "the time of the end" stupendous and unprecedented are the scenes through which the Remnant Church must pass. The Remnant Church will occupy a position such as was never before occupied by God's people. Her message will embrace all the messages of the past

---

[32] *The Catholic Encyclopedia*, art. "Newman, John Henry."

and bring them to final consummation. She will fix her eyes upon the soon return of Christ as the next event in this stupendous program. Of her amid the vast scenes of Christ's return, the revelator writes: "Here are they that keep the commandments of God, and the faith of Jesus."[33] While those who walk in the broad way are losing their awareness of things eternal, God's final church will be alert to things not seen. She will endure, like Moses, by seeing Him who is invisible. She will take time to follow after holiness. These believers will behold the momentous events leading up to, and constituting, the battle of Armageddon. Of the steps preparatory to this catastrophe the revelator says: "The nations were angry, and Thy wrath is come, and the time of the dead, that they should be judged, and that Thou shouldest give reward unto Thy servants the prophets, and to the saints, and them that fear Thy name, small and great; and shouldest destroy them which destroy the earth."[34]

Paganism is symbolized in the book of Revelation by the great red dragon. The war which paganism made upon the early church was bitter; and the long, cruel persecutions carried on by the beast, that medieval union of church and state which succeeded to the power of paganism in the European nations, was still more bitter. But the church of the last days must endure the wrath and persecutions of the image to the beast, which is the final colossal union of church and state, or the healing of the deadly wound of the beast.[35] These terms are used because God uses them. And so offensive to the Eternal is the stand of the image to the beast, into whose vast apostasy flow all the deceptions of the dragon and the beast, that God proclaims to mankind in advance a special warning along this line: "If any man worship the beast and his image, and receive his mark in his forehead, or in his hand, the same shall drink of the wine of the wrath of God, which is poured out without mixture into the cup of His indignation." "I looked, and behold a white cloud, and upon the cloud One sat like unto the Son of man, having on His head a golden crown, and in His hand a sharp sickle."[36] This message proclaimed by the Remnant Church will take away blindness from those who are willing to see.

---

[33] Revelation 14:12.
[34] Revelation 11:18.
[35] Revelation 13.
[36] Revelation 14:9, 10, 14.

THE REMNANT CHURCH   399

The most dreadful language ever used in the Scriptures is that which foretells the visitation of the seven last plagues, the last divine indignation, the untempered wrath of God: "I saw another sign in heaven, great and marvelous, seven angels having the seven last plagues; for in them is filled up the wrath of God."[37] That the seven last plagues are leveled against the beast and his image is plainly indicated. The long pent-up indignation of Jehovah in His wrath against hypocrisy finally bursts forth. The Bible says that "the kings of the earth, and the great men, and the rich men, and the chief captains, and the mighty men, and every bondman, and every freeman, hid themselves in the dens and in the rocks of the mountains," asking the mountains and rocks to fall on them and to hide them, "for the great day of His wrath is come; and who shall be able to stand?"[38]

When this is over, the revelator beholds that "the heaven departed as a scroll when it is rolled together; and every mountain and island were moved out of their places."[39] From now on there will be no dull moments among the children of men. How solemn and how unprecedented are the scenes through which the last church passes, preparing and perfecting a character which will be acceptable to the Lord Jesus Christ when He returns!

The events of earth are now being agitated by the breath of the approaching age. The world that now is, is passing; the arrival of the world to come is imminent. The principalities and powers of darkness are making a last effort to gain possession of souls. There is still power in prayer to resist the increasing darkness. Remember the pleading of the apostle Peter: "Seeing then that all these things shall be dissolved, what manner of persons ought ye to be in all holy conversation and godliness, looking for and hasting unto the coming of the day of God."[40]

May that day, so vividly described in the following words, find all who read these pages ready:

> Amid the reeling of the earth, the flash of lightning, and the roar of thunder, the voice of the Son of God calls forth the sleeping saints. He looks upon the graves of the righteous, then raising His hands to heaven He

---

[37] Revelation 15:1.
[38] Revelation 6:15-17.
[39] Revelation 6:14.
[40] 2 Peter 3:11, 12.

cries, "Awake, awake, awake, ye that sleep in the dust, and arise!" Throughout the length and breadth of the earth, the dead shall hear that voice; and they that hear shall live. And the whole earth shall ring with the tread of the exceeding great army of every nation, kindred, tongue, and people. From the prison house of death they come, clothed with immortal glory, crying, "O death, where is thy sting? O grave, where is thy victory?" And the living righteous and the risen saints unite their voices in a long, glad shout of victory.[41]

This consummation will truly be Truth Triumphant.

"Here are they that keep the commandments of God, and the faith of Jesus."[42]

---

[41] White, *The Great Controversy Between Christ and Satan,* page 644.
[42] Revelation 14:12.

Bibliography

Original Sources

ABUL FARAJ, GREGORY. *Chronography* (translated from the Syriac by Sir E. A. Wallis Budge), 2 vols., University Press, Oxford, 1932.

D'ACHERY, J. L. *Spicilegium,* 13 vols., ed. of 1677; 3 vols., ed. of 1723, Parisiis, apud Montalant.

ADAMNAN. *Life of Columba* (translated by Wentworth Huyshe), George Routledge & Sons, London, 1922.

ALANUS DE INSULIS. *Contra Haereticos,* in Migne, *Patrologia Latina,* vol. 210.

Annals of Roger de Hoveden, The (translated by H. T. Riley), 2 vols., London, 1853.

Annals of the Kingdom of Ireland by the Four Masters From Earliest Period to 1616 (edited by John O. Donovan), 7 vols., Dublin, 1851.

Ante-Nicene Fathers (English translation), Roberts and Donaldson, editors, 10 vols., Charles Scribner's Sons, New York, 1899.

APOLLINARIS SIDONIUS. *Epistolae,* in Migne, *Patrologia Latina,* vol. 58.

ARNOBIUS. *Against the Heathen,* in *Ante-Nicene Fathers,* vol. 6.

ATHANASIUS. *Select Works and Letters* (English translation), in *Nicene and Post-Nicene Fathers,* 2d Series, vol. 4.

BAR HEBRAEUS, GREGORY. *Chronicon Ecclesiasticum,* 3 vols., Abbeloos and Lamy, Paris, 1877.

BARONIO, CAESARE. *Annales Ecclesiastici,* 12 vols., Coloniae Agrippianae Sumptibus Ioannis Gymnici et Antonii Hierati, 1609.

BEDE, VENERABLE. *Ecclesiastical History of England* (translated by Henry Bohn), London, 1847.

BERNARD OF CLAIRVAUX. *Works* (translated by S. T. Eales), 4 vols., 1896.

BONACURSUS. *Contra Haereticos,* in d'Achery, *Spicilegium,* vol. 1.

Chronicles and Memorials of Great Britain and Ireland During the Middle Ages, 99 vols., Rerum Britannicarum Medii aevi Scriptores, London, 1858-1911.

DAMIANUS, PETRUS. *Opuscula,* in Migne, *Patrologia Latina,* vol. 452.

Der Blutige Schau-Platz, Oder Martyrer Spiegel der Taufs Gesinnten, Bruderschaft Publishing House, Ephrata, Pa., 1749.

DU CANGE, C. DU FRESNE. *Glossarium Mediae et Infimae Latinitatis,* 7 vols., ed. of Henschel, Paris, 1840-50; 10 vols., ed. of Fayre, 1883-87.

EBRARDUS BETHUENSIS. *Liber Antihaeresis Maxima Bibliotheca,* vol. 25.

ECBERTUS. *Contra Haereticos,* in Migne, *Patrologia Latina,* vol. 195.

EUSEBIUS. *Ecclesiastical History* (English translation), in *Nicene and Post-Nicene Fathers,* 2d Series, vol. 1.

EUSEBIUS OF CAESAREA. *Life of Constantine,* in *Nicene and Post-Nicene Fathers,* 2d Series, vol. 1.

GREGORY I, POPE. *Epistles* (English translation), in *Nicene and Post-Nicene Fathers,* 2d Series, vol. 13.

GRETZER, J. *Opera Omnia,* 17 vols., Sumptibus J. C. Peez et F. Boder, 1734-41.

——. *Proloquia a Ebrardus Bethuensis,* in *Maxima Bibliotheca,* vol. 24.

GUI, BERNARD. *Manuel d' Inquisiteur,* Traduit par G. Mollat, Paris, 1926.

HADDON, A. W., AND STUBBS, W. *Councils and Ecclesiastical Documents Relating to Great Britain and Ireland,* 4 vols., Oxford, 1869-78.

HUMBERTUS, S. R. E. CARDINALIS. *Adversus Graecorum Columnias,* in Migne, *Patrologia Latina,* vol. 134.

26

JEROME. *Against Helvidius,* in *Nicene and Post-Nicene Fathers,* 2d Series, vol. 6.

JEROME. *Against Jovinian,* in *Nicene and Post-Nicene Fathers,* 2d Series, vol. 6.

JEROME. *Against Vigilantius,* in *Nicene and Post-Nicene Fathers,* 2d Series, vol. 6.

JEROME. *Select Works and Letters,* in *Nicene and Post-Nicene Fathers,* 2d Series, vol. 6.

JONAS, ABBAS ELNONENSIS. *Vita Columbani,* in Migne, *Patrologia Latina,* vol. 87.

LABBE ET GABR., PHILIP COSSARTII. *Sacrosanta Concilia ad Regiam Editionem Exacta, Quae Nunc Quarta Parte Prodit Auctior,* 16 vols., Lutetise Parisiorum, 1671.

LUCAS TUDENSIS. *De Altera Vita Fideique Controversiis Adverus Albigensium,* in *Maxima Bibliotheca,* vol. 25.

MAIGNE D'ARNIS, W. H. *Lexicon Manuale ad Scriptores Mediae et Infimae Latinitatis,* Migne, Paris, 1866.

MANSI, J. D. *Sacrorum Conciliorum Nova et Amplissima Collectio,* 31 vols., Florence and Venice, 1759-98. Reprint, Martin, J. B., and Petit, L. Paris, 1901 (in progress).

Maxima Bibliotheca Veterum Patrum, 27 vols., apud Anissonios, Lugdunum, France, 1677.

MICHAEL THE SYRIAN. *Chronique de Michel le Syrien, Partiarche Jacobite d'Antioche (1166-99)* (translated and edited by J. B. Chabot), 4 vols. and Index, Ernest Leroux, Paris, 1924.

MIGNE, J. P. *Patrologia Cursus Completus . . . in Qua Prodeunt Patres Doctores Scriptoresque Eclesia Latina,* Series graeca, 161 vols. in 166 Do., Paris, 1857-66. Series latina, 221 vols., Paris, 1844-55. Index, 4 vols., 1862-64.

Nicene and Post-Nicene Fathers (edited by Philip Schaff and Henry Wace), 14 vols., The Christian Literature Co., New York. English translation, 2d Series, Oxford and London, 1890.

Nicene and Post-Nicene Fathers (English translation), Philip Schaff, editor, 1st Series, 14 vols., The Christian Literature Co., Buffalo, 1886.

ORIGENES. *Opera Omnia,* in Migne, *Patrologia Graeca,* vols. 11-17.

PETRI, VALLIS CERNAE. *Historia Albigensium,* in Migne, *Patrologia Latina,* vol. 213.

PETRUS CLUNIACENSIS. *Tractatus Contra Petrobrussianos,* in Migne, *Patrologia Latina,* vol. 189.

PETRUS DE PILCHDORFFIUS. *Contra Haeresin Waldensium Tractatus,* in *Maxima Bibliotheca,* vol. 25.

———. *Contra Pauperes de Lugduno,* in *Maxima Bibliotheca,* vol. 25.

Recognitions of Clement, in *Ante-Nicene Fathers,* vol. 8.

Rheims New Testament, translated 1582 into English from the Latin Vulgate, 1834.

SACCHO, REINERIUS. *Contra Waldenses,* in *Maxima Bibliotheca,* vol. 25.

Seven Oecumenical Councils, in *Nicene and Post-Nicene Fathers,* 2d Series, vol. 14.

SOCRATES. *Ecclesiastical History,* in *Nicene and Post-Nicene Fathers,* 2d Series, vol. 2.

SOZOMEN. *Ecclesiastical History,* in *Nicene and Post-Nicene Fathers,* 2d Series, vol. 2.

SULPITIUS SEVERUS. *Sacred History,* in *Nicene and Post-Nicene Fathers,* 2d Series, vol. 11.

TERTULLIAN. *An Answer to the Jews,* in *Ante-Nicene Fathers,* vol. 3.

———. *The Chaplet or De Corona,* in *Ante-Nicene Fathers,* vol. 3.

———. *Apology,* in *Ante-Nicene Fathers,* vol. 3.

THEODORET. *Ecclesiastical History,* in *Nicene and Post-Nicene Fathers,* 2d Series, vol. 3.

VICTORINUS. *On the Creation of the World* (English translation), in *Ante-Nicene Fathers,* vol. 7.

Books

ABUDACNUS, JOSEPHUS. *Historia Jacobitarum*, Lugdunum Batavorum, J. Hasebroek, 1740. Notes by J. Nicholai.

ADAMNAN. *Life of St. Columba* (translated by Wentworth Huyshe), E. P. Dutton and Sons, New York, 1922.

ADAMS, GEORGE BURTON. *Civilization During the Middle Ages*, rev. ed., Charles Scribner's Sons, New York, 1914.

ADENEY, WALTER F. *The Greek and Eastern Churches*, T. & T. Clark, Edinburgh, 1908.

Allgemeine Deutche Biographie, 56 vols., Lilliencron and Wegele, Leipsig, 1875.

ALLIX, PETER. *Remarks Upon the Ecclesiastical History of the Ancient Church of the Albigenses*, Richard Chiswell, London, 1692.

———. *The Ancient Churches of Piedmont*, Richard Chiswell, London, 1690.

ANESAKI, MASAHARU. *Religious Life of the Japanese Peoples*, reprint from vol. 2, Tokyo, 1938.

———. *History of the Japanese Religions*, Kegan Paul, Trench, Trübner and Co., London, 1930.

ARMITAGE, THOMAS. *A History of the Baptists*, Bryan Taylor and Company, New York, 1890.

ARNAUD, HENRI. *The Glorious Recovery by the Vaudois*, John Murray, London, 1827.

AYER, JOSEPH CULLEN. *A Source Book for Ancient Church History*, Charles Scribner's Sons, New York, 1926.

BADGER, G. P. *The Nestorians and Their Rituals*, 2 vols., London, 1852.

BARNETT, T. RATCLIFFE. *Margaret of Scotland: Queen and Saint*, Oliver and Boyd, London, 1926.

BEAL, SAMUEL. *Buddhists' Records of the Western World*, 2 vols., Trübner & Co., London, 1884.

BEATTIE, WILLIAM. *The Waldenses*, George Virtue, London, 1838.

BELLESHEIM, ALPHONS. *History of the Catholic Church of Scotland*, 4 vols., William Blackwood and Sons, London, 1887.

BENEDICT, DAVID. *A General History of the Baptist Denomination*, 2 vols., Lincoln and Edmonds, Boston, 1813.

BENTLEY, JOHN. *Historical View of Hindu Astronomy*, Smith, Elder and Co., London, 1825.

BETHAM, SIR WILLIAM. *Irish Antiquarian Researches*, W. Curry, Jr., and Co., Dublin, 1827.

BEUZART, P. *Les Heresies*, Librairie Ancienne, Paris, 1912.

BIDEZ, JOSEPH, AND CUMONT, FRANZ. *Les Mages Hellenisés*, 2 vols., Paris, 1938.

BIGG, CHARLES. *The Origins of Christianity*, Clarendon Press, Oxford, 1909.

BINGHAM, JOSEPH. *The Antiquities of the Christian Church*, 2 vols., Henry G. Bohn, London, 1850.

BISPHAM, CLARENCE WYATT. *Columban—Saint, Monk, Missionary*, E. S. Gorham, New York, 1903.

BLACKSTONE, SIR WILLIAM. *Commentaries on the Laws of England*, Harper & Brothers, New York, 1854.

BLAIR, ADAM. *History of the Waldenses*, 2 vols., Adam & Charles Black, Edinburgh, 1833.

BLAIR, E. H., AND ROBERTSON, J. A. *The Philippine Islands (1493-1803)*, 55 vols., The A. H. Clark Co., Cleveland, Ohio, 1903.

BOMPIANI, SOPHIA V. *A Short History of the Italian Waldenses*, Hodder and Stoughton, 1897.

BOSSUET, JACQUES BENIGNE. *Variations of the Protestant Churches*, D. and J. Sadlier, New York, 1845.

BOSWELL, JAMES. *The Life of Samuel Johnson,* 5 vols., George Routledge and Sons, London, 1885.

BOWER, ARCHIBALD. *The History of the Popes,* 3 vols., L. Johnson, Philadelphia, 1844-47.

BRADLEY, HENRY. *The Goths,* London, 1888; and G. P. Putnam's Sons, New York, 1891.

BRYCE, JAMES. *The Holy Roman Empire,* Montgomery Ward and Company, Chicago, 1886.

BUCHANAN, CLAUDIUS. *Christian Researches in Asia,* G. Sydney, London, 1812.

BUCKLEY, THEODORE ALOIS. *Canons and Decrees of the Council of Trent,* George Routledge and Co., London, 1851.

BUDGE, SIR E. A. WALLIS. *The Monks of Kublai Khan, Emperor of China,* Religious Tract Society, London, 1928.

BULL, GEORGE BISHOP. *Defence of the Nicene Faith (Defensio Fidei Nicaenae),* 2 vols., John Henry Parker, Oxford, 1851.

Bulletin of John Ryland's Library, 19 vols., University Press, Manchester, 1925, 1926.

BUND, J. W. WILLIS. *The Celtic Church of Wales,* D. Nutt, London, 1897.

BUNSEN, ERNEST DE. *The Angel-Messiah of Buddhists, Essenes, and Christians,* Longmans, Green & Co., London, 1880.

BURGON, JOHN WILLIAM. *The Revision Revised,* John Murray, London, 1883.

BURGON, JOHN WILLIAM, AND MILLER, EDWARD. *The Traditional Text of the Holy Gospels,* George Bell and Sons, London, 1896.

BURKITT, F. CRAWFORD. *Early Eastern Christianity,* John Murray, London, 1904.

BUTLER, ALBAN. *Lives of the Saints,* Edinburgh, 1799, and London, 1815, 1854.

BUTLER, HOWARD CROSBY. *Early Churches in Syria,* C. Dolman, Holland, 1929.

CABLE, MILDRED, AND FRENCH, FRANCESCA. *Through Jade Gate and Central Asia,* Constable & Co., Ltd., London, 1927.

CADMAN, S. PARKES. *The Three Religious Leaders of Oxford,* The Macmillan Company, New York, 1916.

CAESARIUS OF HEISTERBACH. *The Dialogue of Miracles,* 2 vols., George Routledge and Sons, London, 1929.

Cambridge Medieval History, The (planned by J. B. Bury), 8 vols., The Macmillan Company, New York, 1936.

CANAVAN, J. E. *The Mystery of the Incarnation,* Catholic Truth Society, Dublin, 1928.

CATHCART, WILLIAM. *The Ancient British and Irish Churches,* Baptist Tract and Book Society, London, 1894.

Catholic Encyclopedia, The, 14 vols., Robert Appleton Co., New York, 1907.

CHEETHAM, S. *A History of the Christian Church,* The Macmillan Company, London, 1898.

CHURCH, R. W. *The Beginning of the Middle Ages,* Charles Scribner's Sons, New York, 1890 (1882, 1887).

CLARKE, ADAM. *The Succession of Sacred Literature,* 2 vols., T. T. and J. Tegg, London, 1830.

———. *The Holy Bible With a Commentary and Critical Notes,* 6 vols., Phillips and Hunt, New York, 1814.

COATES, C. R. *The Red Theology in the Far East,* Thynne and Jarvis, London.

COBERN, CAMDEN M. *The New Archaeological Discoveries,* 6th ed., Funk & Wagnalls Company, New York, 1917.

COULING, MRS. C. E. *The Luminous Religion,* 1924. Reprint from the *Chinese Recorder,* April and May, 1924.

COX, ROBERT. *The Literature of the Sabbath Question,* 2 vols., Maclachlan and Stewart, Edinburgh, 1865.

CROLY, GEORGE. *The Apocalypse of St. John*, C. & J. Rivington, London, 1827.
CUBBERLEY, ELLWOOD, P. *The History of Education*, Houghton Mifflin Company, Boston and New York, 1920.
CUMONT, FRANZ. *The Mysteries of Mithra*, Opencourt Publishing Company, Chicago, 1903.
D'ACHERY, J. L. *Spicilegium*, 13 vols., ed. of 1677; 3 vols., ed. of 1723, Paris.
DARMESTETER, JAMES. *Parsi-ism: Its Place in History*, "Voice of India" Printing Press, Bombay, 1887.
D'AUBIGNE, J. H. MERLE. *History of the Reformation*, 5 vols., Oliver & Boyd, Edinburgh, 1853.
DELLON, M. GABRIEL. *Account of the Inquisition at Goa*, Baldwin, Cradock & Sons, Boston, 1815.
DESANCTIS, LUIGI. *Popery, Puseyism, and Jesuitism*, D. Catt, London, 1905.
DEVINNE, DANIEL. *History of the Irish Primitive Church*, Francis Hart and Co., New York, 1870.
DOLLINGER, IGNAZ VON. *Beitrage zur Sektengeschichte des Mittelalters*, 2 vols., C. H. Becksche Verlagsbuchhandlung, Munich, 1890.
D'ORSEY, J. D. *Portuguese Discoveries, Dependencies, and Missions in Asia and Africa*, W. H. Allen and Co., London, 1893.
DOWDEN, JOHN. *The Celtic Church in Scotland*, Society for Promoting Christian Knowledge, London, 1894.
DOWLING, JOHN. *The History of Romanism*, Edward Walker, New York, 1846.
DRAPER, JOHN WILLIAM. *History of the Intellectual Development of Europe*, 5th ed., Harper & Brothers, New York, 1875.
DUCHESNE, L. *Early History of the Christian Church*, 3 vols., John Murray, London, 1923.

EALES, S. J. *The Works of St. Bernard* (translated from the Latin), 4 vols., J. Hodges, London, 1889.
EBRARD, A. *Bonifatius, der Zerstörer des Columbanischen Kirchentums auf dem Festlande*, C. Bertelsmann, Gütersloh, 1882.
EDERSHEIM, ALFRED. *The Life and Times of Jesus the Messiah*, 2 vols., E. R. Herrick and Company, New York, 1886.
EDGAR, SAMUEL. *The Variations of Popery*, S. W. Benedict, New York, 1850.
ELLIOTT, E. B. *Horae Apocalypticae*, 4 vols., Seeleys, London, 1862.
EMORY, JOHN. *The Works of the Reverend John Wesley*, 5 vols., B. Waugh and T. Mason, New York, 1832.
Encyclopedia Britannica, 25 vols., 9th ed., 1888; 29 vols., 11th ed., 1910; 24 vols., 14th ed., 1929.
ETHERIDGE, J. W. *The Syrian Churches*, Longmans, Green and Company, London, 1846.
EYMERICUS. *Directorum Haereticorum*, c. 1358.

FABER, GEORGE STANLEY. *An Inquiry Into the History and Theology of the Ancient Vallenses and Albigenses*, Seeley and Burnside, London, 1838.
FARRAR, FREDERIC WILLIAM. *History of Interpretation*, The Macmillan Company, London, 1886.
FAVYN, ANDRE. *Histoire de Navarre*, Espagne, et Ailleurs, Paris, 1612.
FINN, JAMES. *The Jews in China*, B. Wertheim, London, 1843.
FISHER, EDWARD. *Tracts on the Sabbath*, 1635.
FISHER, GEORGE PARK. *History of the Christian Church*, Charles Scribner's Sons, New York, 1907.
———. *History of Christian Doctrines*, Charles Scribner's Sons, New York, 1902.

FITZPATRICK, BENEDICT. *Ireland and the Foundations of Europe*, Funk & Wagnalls Company, New York, 1927.

――――. *Ireland and the Making of Britain*, 4th ed., Funk & Wagnalls Company, New York, 1921.

FLICK, A. C. *The Rise of the Medieval Church*, G. P. Putnam's Sons, New York and London, 1909.

FLUEGEL, MAURICE. *The Zend-Avesta and Eastern Religions*, H. Fluegel & Co., Baltimore, 1898.

FOAKES-JACKSON, F. J. *The History of the Christian Church*, Richard R. Smith, New York, 1930.

FORTESCUE, ADRIAN. *The Lesser Eastern Churches*, Catholic Truth Soc., London, 1913.

FROUDE, JAMES ANTHONY. *The Council of Trent*, Charles Scribner's Sons, New York, 1896.

FULKE, WILLIAM. *A Defense of the Sincere and True Translations of the Holy Scripture*, University Press, Cambridge, 1843.

GEDDES, MICHAEL. *The Church History of Malabar*, S. Smith and B. Walford, London, 1694.

――――. *The Church History of Ethiopia*, Richard Chiswell, London, 1696.

――――. *Miscellaneous Tracts*, B. Barker, London, 1730.

GEIKIE, J. CUNNINGHAM. *Hours With the Bible*, 10 vols., Hartford, 1912.

GENEBRARD, GILBERT. *Sacred Chronology*.

GIBBON, EDWARD. *The History of the Decline and Fall of the Roman Empire*, 6 vols., Harper & Brothers, New York, 1845.

GIBBONS, JAMES CARDINAL. *The Faith of Our Fathers*, 63d ed. (1905), 76th ed., John Murphy Company, Baltimore.

GILLY, WILLIAM STEPHEN. *Vigilantius and His Times*, Seeley, Burnside, and Seeley, London, 1844.

――――. *Waldensian Researches*, C. J. G. and F. Rivington, London, 1831.

GODDARD, DWIGHT. *Was Jesus Influenced by Buddha?* Thetford, Vt., 1927.

GORDON, MRS. E. A. *"World Healers,"* or *The Lotus Gospel and Its Bodhisattvas Compared With Early Christianity*, Eugene L. Morice, London, 1912.

――――. *Asian Chronology*, Maruzen & Co., Ltd., Tokyo, 1921.

GRANT, ASAHEL. *The Nestorians, or the Lost Tribes*. Harper & Brothers, New York, 1841.

GREEN, JOHN RICHARD. *A Short History of the English People*, 4 vols., Donohue Henneberry and Company, Chicago.

GREEN, SAMUEL G. *A Handbook of Church History*, Religious Tract Society, London, 1904.

GRIFFIS, WILLIAM ELLIOT. *The Religions of Japan*, Charles Scribner's Sons, New York, 1904.

HARLEZ, CHARLES DE. *Le Yih-King: A French Translation of the Confucian Classic on Change*, Bruxelles, 1889.

HASTINGS, JAMES. *Encyclopedia of Religion and Ethics*, 12 vols., Charles Scribner's Sons, New York, 1924.

HEALY, JOHN. *Insula Sanctorum et Doctorum*, Sealy, Bryers & Walker, Dublin, London, 1902.

HEDIN, SVEN. *Central Asia and Tibet*, 2 vols., London and New York, 1903.

HEFELE, CHARLES JOSEPH. *History of the Christian Councils*, 5 vols., T. & T. Clark, Edinburgh, 1872.

HEFELE, KARL JOSEPH VON. *Conciliengeschicte*, 9 vols., Freiburg im Breisgau, Herder, 1877-79.

HENDERSON, EBENEZER. *The Vaudois*, J. Snow, London, 1845.

HERGENROETHER, JOSEPH A. G. *Photius,* 3 vols., G. J. Manz, Regensburg, 1867-69.

HERRMANN, A. *Atlas of China,* Harvard University Press, Cambridge, 1935.

HETHERINGTON, W. M. *History of the Church of Scotland,* 2 vols., 7th ed., John Johnstone, Edinburgh and London, 1848.

HEYLYN, PETER. *Historical and Miscellaneous Tracts,* part 2, *The History of the Sabbath,* London, 1681.

HILL, DAVID JAYNE. *History of Diplomacy in the International Development of Europe,* 3 vols., Longmans, Green and Co., London, 1914-24. (New York, 1905-14.)

Historians' History of the World, The (edited by Henry Smith Williams), 25 vols., 1907.

Historical Papers on Seventh Day Baptists, American Sabbath Tract Society, Plainfield, N. J., 1915.

HODGKIN, THOMAS. *Italy and Her Invaders,* 8 vols., 2d ed., Clarendon Press, Oxford, 1880-99.

HOLTZMANN, H. J. *Kanon und Tradition,* Ludwigsburg, 1859.

HOPKINS, EDWARD WASHBURN. *History of Religions,* The Macmillan Company, New York, 1918.

HORNE, THOMAS HARTWELL. *Introduction to the Critical Study and Knowledge of the Holy Scriptures,* 2 vols., Robert Carter & Bros., New York, 1872.

HORT, FENTON JOHN ANTHONY, AND WESTCOTT, BROOKE FOSS. *The New Testament in the Original Greek,* 2 vols., Harper & Brothers, New York, 1882.

HOWELLS, GEORGE. *The Soul of India,* J. Clarke and Co., London, 1913.

HOWORTH, H. H. *History of the Mongols,* 3 vols. in 4, Longmans, Green and Company, London, 1876-88.

HUC, M. L'ABBE, EVARISTE REGIS. *Christianity in China, Tartary, and Thibet,* 3 vols., Longmans, Brown, Green, Longmans, and Roberts, London, 1857.

HULME, EDWARD MASLIN. *A History of the British People,* The Century Company, New York, 1924.

———. *Renaissance and Reformation.*

HUMBOLDT, ALEXANDER VON. *Cosmos: A Sketch of a Physical Description of the Universe,* 2 vols., Harper & Brothers, New York, 1850.

HUNTER, WILLIAM WILSON. *A Brief History of the Indian People,* Clarendon Press, Oxford, 1903.

———. *The Indian Empire,* Trübner and Co., London, 1886.

HYDE, DOUGLAS. *A Literary History of Ireland,* T. Fisher Unwin, London, 1901.

INNES, A. TAYLOR. *Church and State,* 2d ed., T. & T. Clark, Edinburgh.

International Encyclopedia, The New, 23 vols., 2d ed., Dodd, Mead and Company, New York, 1916.

JACKSON, A. V. WILLIAMS. *Persia, Past and Present,* The Macmillan Company, New York, 1906.

JACOBUS, MELANCTHON WILLIAMS. *Roman Catholic and Protestant Bibles Compared,* Charles Scribner's Sons, New York, 1908.

JAMIESON, JOHN. *Historical Account of the Ancient Culdees of Iona,* Thomas D. Morison, London, 1890.

JONES, WILLIAM. *The History of the Christian Church,* 2 vols., Hargette and Savill, London, 1826.

JOSEPHUS, FLAVIUS. *Works,* 3 vols., A. L. Burt Company, New York.

KAYE, G. R. *A Guide to the Old Observatories,* Superintendent Government Printing, Calcutta, 1920.

KAYE, J. W. *Christianity in India,* reviewed in *Dublin University Magazine,* vol. 54, 1859.

KEAY, F. E. *A History of the Syrian Church in India,* S. P. C. K., Madras, 1938.

KILLEN, W. D. *Ecclesiastical History of Ireland*, 2 vols., The Macmillan Company, London, 1875.
———. *The Old Catholic Church*, T. & T. Clark, Edinburgh, 1871.
KIRCHER, D'ATHANESE. *La Chine* (translated by F. S. Dalquie), A. Amsterdam, 1670.
KOMROFF, MANUEL. *The Travels of Marco Polo*, Garden City Publishing Co., New York, 1926.
KURTZ, PROFESSOR. *Church History*, 3 vols., Funk & Wagnalls Company, New York, 1889.

LABOURT, J. *Le Christianisme dans l'Empire Perse*, V. Lecoffre, Paris, 1904.
LACOUPERIE, TERRIEN DE. *Western Origin of Early Chinese Civilisation*, Asher and Co., London, 1894.
LACUNZA, MANUEL [JUAN JOSAFAT BEN-EZRA]. *La Venida del Mesias en Gloria y Majestad*, Santiago, Imprenta, reprint, 1914.
LAMY. *The History of Socinianism*, W. Roberts, London, 1729.
LANE, C. A. *Illustrated Notes on English Church History*, 2 vols., E. and J. B. Young Company, New York, 1898-1900.
LANG, ANDREW. *A History of Scotland*, 2 vols., William Blackwood & Sons, Edinburgh, 1900.
LATOURETTE, KENNETH SCOTT. *The Thousand Years of Uncertainty*, Harper & Brothers, New York, 1938.
LEA, HENRY CHARLES. *Inquisition of the Middle Ages*, 3 vols., Harper & Brothers, New York, 1888.
LECOY DE LA MARCHE. *Anecdotes*, Librairie Renouard, Paris, 1877.
LÉGER, JEAN. *Historie Generale des Eglises Vaudoises*, Carpentier, Leyden, 1669.
LE NAIN DE TILLEMONT. *Memoires*, 16 vols., 1723.
LE STRANGE, G. *Mesopotamia and Persia Under the Mongols in the Fourteenth Century*, London, 1903.
———. *The Lands of the Eastern Caliphate*, Cambridge, 1905.
———. *Bagdad During the Abbasid Caliphate*, Oxford, 1900; and reprint, 1924.
LEWIS, A. H. *A Critical History of Sabbath and Sunday*, American Sabbath Tract Society, Alfred Center, New York, 1886.
———. *Seventh Day Baptists in Europe and America.*
LIMBORCH, PHILIPPUS. *The History of the Inquisition*, 2 vols., J. Gray, London, 1731.
LINGARD, JOHN. *The Antiquities of the Anglo-Saxon Church*, 2 vols., Keating, Brown and Keating, London, 1806.
LI UNG BING. *Outlines of Chinese History* (edited by J. Whiteside of Soochow, China), Shanghai, 1914.
LLOYD, ARTHUR. *The Creed of Half Japan*, E. P. Dutton & Co., New York, 1912.
LUCHAIRE, ACHILLE. *Innocent III; Les Albigeois*, Hachette et Cie, Paris, 1907.
LUKE, H. C. *Mosul and Its Minorities*, M. Hopkinson and Co., Ltd., London, 1925.
LUTHER, MARTIN. *Table Talk*, W. Bogue, London, 1848.

McCABE, JAMES D., JR. *Cross and Crown*, National Publishing Co., New York, 1873.
MACAULAY, THOMAS BABINGTON. *Critical, Historical, and Miscellaneous Essays and Poems*, Gould and Lincoln, Boston, 1860.
MACKINTOSH, SIR JAMES. *History of England*, in Lardner's *Cabinet Encyclopedia*, vols. 76-85, London, 1850.
M'CLATCHIE, CANON THOMAS. *A Translation of the Confucian Classic of Change*, Shanghai, 1826.
———. *Notes and Queries on China and Japan* (edited by N. B. Dennys), 4 vols., Hong Kong, 1867.
M'CLATCHIE, I. "The Chinese in the Plain of Shinar," *Journal of Royal Asiatic Society*, vol. 16, American Presbyterian Mission Press.

MACLAUCHLAN, THOMAS. *Early Scottish Church,* T. & T. Clark, Edinburgh, 1865.

M'CLINTOCK, JOHN, AND STRONG, JAMES. *Cyclopedia of Biblical, Theological, and Ecclesiastical Literature,* 12 vols., Harper & Brothers, New York, 1894.

MAITLAND, S. R. *Facts and Documents Illustrative of the History, Doctrine, and Rites of the Ancient Albigenses and Waldenses,* C. J. C. Rivington, London, 1833.

MAJOR, RICHARD HENRY. *India in the Fifteenth Century,* London, 1857.

MALCOLM, COL. SIR JOHN. *History of Persia,* 2 vols., John Murray, London, 1815.

MALMESBURY, WILLIAM OF. *De Gestis Pontificorum Anglorum Rolls,* H. G. Bohn, London, 1847.

MATTHEW OF WESTMINSTER. *The Flowers of History,* 2 vols., H. G. Bohn, London, 1853.

MEISSNER, JOHN L. *The Celtic Church in England,* Martin Hopkinson, London, 1929.

MELIA, PIRES. *The Waldenses,* James Toovey, London, 1870.

MENZIES, LUCY. *Saint Columba of Iona,* J. M. Dent and Sons, London, 1920.

MEZERAY, FRANCOIS EUDES DE. *Abregé Chronologique de L'Histoire de France,* A. Wolfgang, Amsterdam, 1682.

MICHELET, JULES. *History of France* (translated by G. H. Smith), vol. 1, London, 1834-44.

MIEROW, CHARLES C. *Chronicle of the Two Cities,* Columbia University Press, New York, 1928.

MILMAN, HENRY HART. *The History of Christianity,* 3 vols., John Murray, London, 1867.

———. *History of Latin Christianity,* 6 vols., John Murray, London, 1867.

MILNER, JOSEPH. *History of the Church of Christ,* 5 vols., L. Hansard & Sons, London, 1827.

MINGANA, ALPHONSE. "Early Spread of Christianity," *Bulletin of John Ryland's Library,* vols. 9, 10, University Press, Manchester, 1925, 1926.

MOBERG, A. *The Book of the Himyarites,* Lund, Sweden, and Oxford University Press, 1924.

MOFFAT, JAMES C. *History of the Catholic Church in Scotland,* Presbyterian Board of Publication, Philadelphia, 1882.

MONASTIER, ANTOINE. *A History of the Vaudois Church,* Religious Tract Society, London, 1848.

MONIER-WILLIAMS, SIR MONIER. *Indian Wisdom,* W. H. Allen & Co., London, 1875.

MONTALEMBERT, COUNT DE. *Monks of the West,* 7 vols., W. Blackwood and Sons, Edinburgh and London, 1867.

MONTGOMERY, JAMES A. *The History of Yaballaha III,* Columbia University Press, New York, 1927.

MOORE, THOMAS. *Irish Melodies,* Longmans, Brown, Green, and Longmans, London, 1849.

MOORE, T. V. *The Culdee Church,* Presbyterian Committee of Publications, Richmond, Va., 1868.

MORLAND, SIR SAMUEL. *The History of the Evangelical Churches of the Valleys of the Piedmont,* Henry Hills, London, 1658.

MORNAY, PHILLIP (DU PLESSIS). *The Mysterie of Iniquitie* (translated into English by Samson Lennard), London, 1612.

MOSHEIM, JOHN L. VON. *Commentaries,* 2 vols., S. Converse, New York, 1856.

———. *Institutes of Ecclesiastical History,* 4 books in 1 volume, Robert Carter & Brothers, New York, 1881.

MOULTON, W. F. *The History of the English Bible,* Cassell, Petter, and Galpin, London.

MUIR, WILLIAM. *The Arrested Reformation,* Morgan and Scott, London, 1912.

MUSTON, ALEXIS. *The Israel of the Alps,* 2 vols., Bladen & Sons, London, 1875.

NEALE, JOHN MASON. *A History of the Holy Eastern Church,* 2 vols., London, 1850.

———. *The Patriarchate of Antioch,* Rivingtons, London, 1873.

NEANDER, AUGUSTUS. *General History of the Christian Religion and Church*, 6 vols., Geo. Bell and Sons, London, 1871.

NEWELL, E. J. *St. Patrick, His Life and Teaching*, 2d ed., rev., E. S. Gorham, New York, 1907.

NEWMAN, ALBERT HENRY. *A Manual of Church History*, 2 vols., The American Baptist Publishing Society, Philadelphia, 1933.

NEWMAN, JOHN HENRY. *The Arians of the Fourth Century*, J. G. and F. Rivington, London, 1833.

NEWTON, THOMAS. *Dissertation on the Prophecies*, James Martin, Philadelphia, 1813.

NOLAN, FREDERICK. *The Integrity of the Greek Vulgate*, F. C. and J. Rivington, London, 1815.

O'KELLY, COL. CHARLES. *Macariae Excidium or The Destruction of Cyprus*, Dublin for Irish Archaeological Society, 1850.

O'LEARY, DELACY. *The Syriac Church and Fathers*, Society for Promoting Christian Knowledge, London, 1909.

OLIPHANT, MRS. *The Life of Edward Irving*, 6th ed., Hurst and Blackett, London, 1862.

O'NEILL, JOHN. *Night of the Gods*, B. Quaritch, London, 1893-97.

PALLAVICINI, SFORZA. *Histoire du Concile de Trente*, 3 vols., Imprimerie, Catholique de Migne, Montrouge, 1844.

PARKER, E. H. *A Thousand Years of the Tartars*, Kelly and Walsh, Shanghai, 1895.

PELHISSE, WILLIAM. *Chronicon*, c. 1268.

PERKINS, JUSTIN. *A Residence of Eight Years in Persia*, Allen, Morrill, and Wardwell, Andover, 1843.

PERRIN, J. P. *History of the Ancient Christians*, Griffith and Simon, Philadelphia, 1847.

PERRIN, JEAN PAUL. *Luther's Forerunners*, N. Newbery, London, 1624.

PEYRAN, JEAN. *An Historical Defense of Waldenses*, C. and J. Rivington, London, 1826.

POTT, F. L. HAWKS. *A Sketch of Chinese History*, 2d ed., Kelly and Walsh, Ltd., Shanghai, 1908.

PRENTICE, WILLIAM KELLY. Taken from *Publication of an American Archaeological Expedition to Syria*, 1904, 1905, 1909.

PRESBYTERIAN BOARD OF PUBLICATION. *The Waldenses*, Philadelphia, 1853.

PRESSENSE, E. DE. *The Early Years of Christianity*, Hodder & Stoughton, London, 1869.

PRIDEAUX, HUMPHREY, *The Old and New Testament Connected*, 2 vols., Harper & Brothers, New York, 1871.

PURCHAS, SAMUEL. *His Pilgrimes*, 20 vols., James MacLebose and Sons, Glasgow, 1905.

PUTNAM, GEORGE HAVEN. *The Censorship of the Church of Rome*, 2 vols., G. P. Putnam's Sons, New York, 1907.

QUATREMERE, E. *Notices des Manuscrits*, Institut de France, Academie des Inscriptions.

RAE, GEORGE MILNE. *The Syrian Church in India*, William Blackwood & Sons, London, 1892.

RAWLINSON, GEORGE. *The Seven Great Monarchies of the Ancient Eastern World*, 3 vols., Lovell, Cornell and Co., New York, 1875.

Realencyclopadie für Protestantische Theologie und Kirche (edited by J. J. Herzog), 24 vols., D. A. Hauck, Leipzig, 1896.

REICHELT, KARL LUDVIG. *Truth and Tradition in Chinese Buddhism*, The Commercial Press, Shanghai, 1928.

RENAN, ERNEST. *Histoire General et Systéme Comparé des Langues Semitiques*, 1863.

RIDGEWAY, SIR WILLIAM. *The Early Age of Greece,* 2 vols., University Press, Cambridge, 1931.

ROBINSON, JAMES HARVEY. *An Introduction to the History of Western Europe,* Ginn & Company, Boston and New York, 1903.

ROBINSON, ROBERT. *Ecclesiastical Researches,* Francis Hodson, Cambridge, England, 1792.

ROCKHILL, WILLIAM WOODVILLE. *The Journey of William of Rubruck,* 2d Series, vol. 4, Hakluyt Society, 1900.

ROSS, ALEXANDER. *Religions in the World,* 3d ed., London, 1658.

———. *Les Religions du Monde* (translated by Thomas LaGrue), Amsterdam, 1666.

RUFFINI, FRANCESCO. *Religious Liberty,* G. P. Putnam's Sons, New York, 1912.

SAEKI, P. Y. *The Nestorian Monument in China,* Society for Promoting Christian Knowledge, London, 1916, 1928.

SANSOM, G. B. *Japan,* Cresset Press, London, 1932.

SCHAFF-HERZOG. *The New Encyclopedia of Religious Knowledge,* 12 vols. and Index, Funk & Wagnalls Company, New York and London, 1910.

SCHAFF, PHILIP. *History of the Christian Church,* 7 vols., G. P. Putnam's Sons, New York, 1883, 1893, 1927.

SCHMIDT, C. *Histoire et Doctrine de la Secte de Catheres ou Albigeois,* 2 vols., J. Cherbuliez, Paris, 1849.

SCHURER, EMIL. *A History of the Jewish People in the Time of Christ,* 5 vols., Charles Scribner's Sons, New York, 1898.

SCRIVENER, FREDERICK HENRY AMBROSE. *Introduction to the Criticism of the New Testament,* 2 vols., George Bell and Sons, London, 1894.

SERGEANT, LEWIS. *The Franks,* 1898.

SESSLER, JOHN JACOB. *Communal Pietism Among Early Armenian Moravians,* Henry Holt and Co., New York, 1933.

SETH, M. J. *History of the Armenians in India,* Central Press, Calcutta, 1895.

SEWELL, ROBERT. *A Forgotten Empire, Vijayanagar,* S. Sonnenschein and Co., London, 1900.

SHOTWELL, JAMES T., AND LOOMIS, LOUISE ROPES. *The See of Peter,* Columbia University Press, New York, 1927.

SISMONDI, J. C. L. DE. *History of Crusades Against Albigenses,* Wightman & Cramp, London, 1826.

SKENE, WILLIAM F. *Celtic Scotland,* David Douglas, Edinburgh, 1877.

SKRINE AND ROSS. *The Heart of Asia,* Methune and Co., London, 1899.

SMITH, JOHN. *The Life of Columba,* Mundell and Sons, Edinburgh, 1798.

SMITH, VINCENT A. *The Oxford History of India,* 2d ed., Clarendon Press, Oxford, 1921.

———. *Early History of India,* Clarendon Press, Oxford, 1904.

SMITH, WILLIAM, AND WACE, HENRY. *A Dictionary of Christian Biography,* 4 vols., John Murray, London, 1877.

SOAMES, HENRY. *The Anglo-Saxon Church,* London, 1835.

SOOTHILL, W. E. *China and the West,* Oxford University Press, London, 1925.

STANLEY, ARTHUR PENRHYN. *History of the Eastern Church,* new ed., John Murray, London, 1884.

STEWART, JOHN. *Nestorian Missionary Enterprises,* T. & T. Clark, Edinburgh, 1928.

STILLINGFLEET, EDWARD. *The Antiquities of the British Churches,* 2 vols., University Press, Oxford, 1842.

STOKES, GEORGE T. *Ireland and the Celtic Church,* Hodder and Stoughton, London, 1886.

STOKES, WHITELY [editor and translator of *The Tripartite Life of Patrick*]. *Chronicles and Memorials of Great Britain and Ireland*, vol. 89, pts. 1, 2, 1887.

SULLIVAN, SIR EDWARD. *The Book of Kells*, 3d ed., The Studio, Ltd., London, 1923.

SWETE, HENRY BARCLAY. *Introduction to the Old Testament in Greek*, University Press, Cambridge, 1914.

SYKES, ELLA C. *Persia and Its Peoples*, The Macmillan Company, New York, 1910.

SYKES, P. M. *A History of Persia*, 2 vols., The Macmillan Company, London, 1915.

TAYLOR, DANIEL T. *The Voice of the Church on the Coming and Kingdom of the Redeemer*, rev. ed., H. S. Hastings, Boston, 1855.

TAYLOR, W. C. *History of Ireland*, 2 vols., Harper & Brothers, New York, 1854.

TEMPLE, SIR RICHARD CARNAC. *The Itinerary of Ludovico di Varthema of Bologna From 1502 to 1508*, The Argonaut Press, London, 1928.

TERRY, BENJAMIN. *A History of England*, Scott, Foresman and Co., Chicago, 1902.

THATCHER, OLIVER, AND SCHWILL, FERDINAND. *Europe in the Middle Ages*, Charles Scribner's Sons, New York, 1897.

THOMPSON, R. W. *The Papacy and the Civil Power*, Harper & Brothers, New York, 1876.

THORNDIKE, LYNN. *History of Medieval Europe*, rev. ed., Houghton Mifflin Co., Boston, 1928.

THOYRAS, RAPIN DE. *History of England*, 2 vols., John Harrison, London, 1784.

TILLEMONT, SEBASTIEN LE NAIN DE. *Memoires Pour Servir a l'Histoire Ecclesiastique des Six Premiers Siecles*, 16 vols., 1732.

TODD, JAMES HENTHORN. *St. Patrick, Apostle to Ireland*, Hodges, Smith and Company, Dublin, 1864.

Two members of the New Testament Company [Charles J. Ellicott and Edwin Palmer]. *On the Revisers and the Greek Text*.

TYMMS, WILLIAM ROBERT. *The Art of Illuminating as Practiced in Europe From Earliest Times*, Day and Son, London, 1860.

TYNDALE, WILLIAM. *An Answer to Sir Thomas More's Dialogue*, Cambridge, 1850.

UNDERWOOD, A. C. *Shintoism*, Epworth Press, London, 1934.

URZUA, MIGUEL R. *Lás Doctrinas de P. Manuel Lacunza*, Soc. Imprenta y Litografia Universo Santiago de Chile, 1917.

USSHER, JAMES ARCHBISHOP. *Gravissimae Quaestionis de Christianarum Ecclesiarum Successione* (see vol. 2 of the Latin editions of his works), C. R. Elrington, Dublin, 1847.

———. *The Whole Works*, 17 vols., Dublin, 1864.

———. *Discourse on the Religion Anciently Professed by the Irish and British*, John Jones, Dublin, 1815.

VAMBERY, ARMINIUS. *History of Bokhara*, H. S. King and Company, London, 1873.

VOLTAIRE. *Additions to Ancient and Modern History*, E. R. DuMont, 1901.

WALKER, WILLISTON. *A History of the Christian Church*, Charles Scribner's Sons, New York, 1918.

WALL, CHARLES WILLIAM. *Ancient Orthography of the Jews*, 4 vols., Whittaker and Company, London, 1840.

WALSH, WALTER. *The Secret History of the Oxford Movement*, Chas. J. Thynne, London, 1898.

———. *The Jesuits in England*, George Routledge & Sons, London, 1903.

WARNER, H. J. *The Albigensian Heresy*, 2 vols., Society for Promoting Christian Knowledge, London, 1922.

WESTCOTT, BROOKE FOSS, AND HORT, FENTON JOHN ANTHONY. *The New Testament in the Original Greek,* 2 vols., The Macmillan Company, New York, 1929, 1925.

WHISHAW, BERNHARD, AND ELLEN M. *Arabic Spain,* Smith Elder & Company, London, 1912.

WHITE, ELLEN G. *The Great Controversy Between Christ and Satan,* Pacific Press Publishing Assn., Mountain View, California, 1888, 1907, 1911.

WHITE, FRANCIS. BISHOP OF ELI. *A Treatise on the Sabbath Day,* in Edward Fisher, *Tracts on the Sabbath,* 1635.

WIGRAM, W. A. *Introduction to the History of the Assyrian Church,* Society for Promoting Christian Knowledge, London, 1910.

WIGRAM, W. A. AND WIGRAM, EDGAR T. A. *The Cradle of Mankind,* 2d ed., A. and C. Black, London, Ltd., 1922.

WILKINSON, BENJAMIN G. *Our Authorized Bible Vindicated,* Washington, D. C., 1930.

WILLIAMS, HUGH. *Christianity in Early Britain,* Clarendon Press, Oxford, 1912.

WILLIAMS, S. W. *The Middle Kingdom,* Charles Scribner's Sons, New York, 1899.

WILTSCH, JOHANN. *Geography and Statistics of the Church,* 2 vols., T. Bosworth, London, 1868.

WISHARD, JOHN G. *Twenty Years in Persia,* Fleming H. Revell, New York, 1908.

WISHART, A. W. *A Short History of Monks and Monasticism,* Albert Brandt, Trenton, 1908.

WYLIE, ALEXANDER. *Chinese Researches,* Chinese Repository, Shanghai, 1897.

WYLIE, J. A. *The History of Protestantism,* 3 vols., Cassell, Petter & Galpin, London.

YEATES, THOMAS. *East Indian Church History,* 1921. (Republished by Mrs. E. A. Gordon under the title, *Asian Christology and the Mahayana,* Maruzen and Co., Tokyo, 1921.

YOHANNAN, ABRAHAM. *The Death of a Nation,* G. P. Putnam's Sons, New York, 1916.

YULE, H., AND CORDIER, H. *Cathay and the Way Thither,* 4 vols., Hakluyt Society, London, 1913, 1916.

YULE, SIR HENRY. *Travels of Marco Polo,* 2 vols., John Murray, London, 1903, 1921.

ZIMMER, HEINRICH. *The Irish Element in Medieval Culture,* G. P. Putnam's Sons, New York, 1891.

Magazines

Century Magazine, vol. 66, N. S. 44.

Dublin University Magazine.

Journal of the Royal Geographical Society, 50 vols., 1867.

Journal of the Royal Asiatic Society.

The Nation, vol. 95, no. 2464.

Protestant Digest, April-May, 1941; August-September, 1941.

Quarterly Review.

The United States Catholic Magazine, vol. 4, 1845.

Index

(415)

Index of Authorities

We'd love to have you download our catalog of titles we publish at:

www.TEACHServices.com

or write or email us your thoughts, reactions, or criticism about this or any other book we publish at:

TEACH Services, Inc.
254 Donovan Road
Brushton, NY 12916

info@TEACHServices.com

or you may call us at:

518/358-3494